The Smile of the Human Bomb

THE SMILE OF THE HUMAN BOMB

New Perspectives on Suicide Terrorism

GIDEON ARAN

TRANSLATED BY JEFFREY GREEN

CORNELL UNIVERSITY PRESS
ITHACA AND LONDON

First published 2018 by Cornell University Press

Printed in the United States of America

Library of Congress Cataloging-in-Publication Data

Names: Aran, Gideon, author. | Green, Yaacov Jeffrey, translator.
Title: The smile of the human bomb : new perspectives on suicide
    terrorism / Gideon Aran ; translated by Jeffrey Green.
Description: Ithaca : Cornell University Press, 2018. | Includes
    bibliographical references and index.
Identifiers: LCCN 2018005817 (print) | LCCN 2018007686 (ebook) |
    ISBN 9781501724763 (pdf) | ISBN 9781501724770 (epub/mobi) |
    ISBN 9781501724756 | ISBN 9781501724756 (cloth : alk. paper)
Subjects: LCSH: Suicide bombers—Israel. | Suicide bombings—Israel. |
    Terrorists—Suicidal behavior—Israel. | Palestinian Arabs—Suicidal
    behavior—Israel. | Victims of terrorism—Israel. | Al-Aqsa Intifada,
    2000–
Classification: LCC HV6433.I75 (ebook) | LCC HV6433.I75 A735 2018
    (print) | DDC 363.325095694—dc23
LC record available at https://lccn.loc.gov/2018005817

CONTENTS

PREFACE: ANNA AND 'ABED

Macabre Intimacy

Anna was fifty-four, a pleasant woman, nice-looking and honest. She enjoyed reading novels and poetry, was well-informed about world culture, and was liberal and dovish in her outlook. She had studied humanities at the Hebrew University in Jerusalem, was active in organizing art events, and translated films from English to Hebrew professionally. She was a friendly person but had met with disappointment in her efforts to form a permanent conjugal relationship. She lived modestly, in slight sadness.

On June 11, 2003, Anna was returning home from a visit to her elderly parents. She boarded the no. 14 bus at the Central Station, on her way home to her tiny apartment in southern Jerusalem. Her friends knew that, despite her limited means, she usually treated herself to a taxi ride home. Apparently though, because of the heavy traffic, this time she was forced to ride the crowded public bus, which slowly crossed the commercial center of the city. At the second stop, on the edge of the public produce market, a young Palestinian man stood in the long line, pushed onto the crowded bus, and, after a while, at exactly 5:30 p.m., blew himself up with a charge of dynamite, intensified with nails and steel balls. The explosion took place in the main street of the city, close to a busy intersection and, along with the suicide terrorist, seventeen Israeli passengers were killed, and more than a hundred people were injured. Anna's charred and battered body, when it was extricated from the fire and fragments of steel, was hard to identify, and her death was announced to her relatives only a day later.

Anna was a close family friend of ours. To this day a book of poetry by Yehuda Amichai that belonged to her stands in our bookcase. Anna greatly admired his work and was personally acquainted with him. After her funeral, my wife helped clear out her apartment and took the book to remember her by. For us those beautiful love poems will always be connected to the traumatic attack. Suicide terrorism has preoccupied me since then. The shock passed, and after it came pain and anger. In time they, too, subsided. Only the mystery remained, and it is still unsettling: Who killed her? Why? What did they have to do with each other? Again and again my thoughts return to that bus on that horrible afternoon, concentrating on the aisle near the rear door at 5:29.

Immediately after the attack, Hamas took responsibility for it. On its home page the organization published information about the human bomb: 'Abed al-Mu'ati Shabana, who acted in the service of the Izz ad-Din al-Qassam Brigades. He was defined as a *shahid* who had volunteered and was sent on his mission of revenge to deal a decisive blow against the Jews. Afterward his mother was interviewed. She expressed joy and pride for his deed. The next day we all viewed the video that was released by the organization for television broadcast, containing his last will and testament, recorded before he went out on his assignment. Still photographs of him were also released, showing him posing in firing position with an assault rifle and wearing a green bandanna, with Arabic words on it meaning, "There is no God but Allah." Somewhat later a photomontage was added to the collection, showing the *living* human bomb at the arena of the attack, as it were, while the rescue teams were still removing the bodies of the Israeli victims from the ruins of the bus.

Figure 1. 'Abed al-Mu'ati Shabana, from the West Bank. A human bomb, bus no. 14, Jerusalem, seventeen dead, June 11, 2003. Dispatched by Izz ad-Din al-Qassam. Image published on the Hamas website on the morning after the attack, attached to the *shahid*'s last will and testament. (Photo: https://www.alqassam. net/arabic/)

A few years after the attack, I tried to obtain more information about the man who had killed Anna. Below are some of the facts I elicited from investigations conducted by the security forces, which were once classified; from Hamas publications; from the Palestinian press; from the minutes of the trial of his handlers; and from interviews with those involved in the event and its aftermath.[1]

'Abed was eighteen, of dark complexion, solidly built, and with a serious gaze. He was a student from Hebron at the local branch of the Palestine Polytechnic University and grew up in the Tel-Rumeida neighborhood, which is adjacent to the activist Jewish settlement there—among the most extreme national-religious settlers. He was a fairly talented soccer player on the team that contended for the championship of the local league. Several suicide terrorists were recruited both from his soccer team and from its rival, the team of the Jihad Mosque.[2] Researchers have taken note of this fact to demonstrate the importance of social networks in recruiting suicide terrorists.[3]

In an interview with a Palestinian researcher his mother added: "I did not expect my calm son to do what he did. I thought he was going to bring homework exercises in order to prepare himself for the secondary school (Tawjihi) tests. He insisted that I pray and ask God to make him succeed in his coming exam. I was surprised how he was able to carry out this operation. I don't remember that he ever entered Jerusalem. He was used to staying at home."[4] She spoke also of his love of sports.

It might be possible to gain an approximation of his state of mind as he executed the attack from the testimony of a Palestinian with almost the same profile, who was caught somewhat earlier, just as he was about to commit an act of suicide terrorism in rather similar circumstances. He said, "The feeling is that you are floating in the air, flying . . ."[5]

'Abed's three handlers, who were later arrested and put on trial, provided the dynamite vest and guidance. Before he set out on his mission, they bought him a *kippah* (skullcap) and *tzizit* (ritual fringes) in a Jerusalem shopping center, to enable him to disguise himself as an ultra-Orthodox (Haredi) Jew and meld into the mass of Israelis. He did not even arouse the suspicion of the security guard on duty at the bus stop.

Bitter fate made Anna meet 'Abed. The explosion literally joined them together: their blood was mingled, their bodily tissues and clothing were interchanged, and their limbs were fused together. Some observers maintained that their souls rose to heaven together in a blazing fury. The task of separating the fragments of 'Abed's body from the shattered limbs of his victims was so complex that it was hard to determine the final number of victims with certainty. There was a disturbing postmortem intimacy between the attacker and his victims.

Most likely something of the macabre proximity that was created between Anna and 'Abed in the immediate aftermath of the attack was also shared by them in the final moments before the explosion. Exactly what happened in the interval between 'Abed's boarding of the bus and his pressing the switch that also killed Anna? Only a few inches separated them. In the heavy crowding, did their garments brush against each other? Maybe he even put out a hand instinctively for a moment to help her keep her balance, as sometimes happens when a bus pulls out into the street, or else they might have been thrown against each other by a sudden stop.

Sometimes the crazy thought sneaks into my feverish mind that, just before the explosion, with a sharp and sudden movement, 'Abed placed his arms around Anna, encircled her slender body, and hugged it tightly as he shouted, "Allahu Akbar." After all, this isn't entirely unlikely, and things like this have happened. I remember the later testimony of a young Israeli who was miraculously saved in a similar suicide attack by Hamas, less than a year before the horrible encounter between Anna and 'Abed (the 361 bus from Acre to Safed, August 2002). Eyel, who was then twenty, was wounded severely in the attack and left blind and deaf. He cannot forget: "I was sitting next to [the one who later proved to be] the human bomb. When the bus stopped [near Mount Miron], I got up and walked toward the door. There were two people between us. When the driver opened the door, I heard him shout something [maybe "Allahu Akbar"]. I looked behind me and saw him standing and hugging one of the passengers, and then there was an explosion."[6] We will return to the attacker's embrace of his victim throughout the book.

Anna and 'Abed almost certainly stood face to face. The police investigators determined that the explosive charge was belted to 'Abed's stomach and chest, and it is known that suicide terrorists face in the direction of their victims and approach them, to increase the murderous effect of the explosion. Perhaps their gazes met. Yes, their gazes. After all, those were days of gazes. In the rising tide of suicide terrorism that summer, everyone suspected everyone, examined everyone very closely, and feared lest the person beside them was planning to kill them, despite his innocent appearance.[7]

Several minutes had passed from the time 'Abed was swallowed up in the crowd of passengers, and for a while nothing happened. A community formed in the bus: at every stop the mutual trust among the veteran passengers was suspended, and they carefully inspected the new arrivals on board. Fear and suspicion increased, and for a short time they dissipated, until the next stage of insecurity. Perhaps Anna surveyed 'Abed's appearance, and when she detected no suspicious signs, she relaxed slightly and trusted him. Would he betray her and her fellows on the bus, among whom a covenant of reserved confidence had been formed? Perhaps 'Abed noticed that Anna was alert and concentrating her gaze on his face, and he felt pressured and was impelled to shout, "Allahu Akbar" (now she certainly knew an explosion was imminent) and activate the charge. And perhaps, only perhaps, he smiled at her. It could have been a mocking smile, the mockery of someone who knows everything about someone else's fate, and it might have been an embarrassed smile, the embarrassment of someone apologizing for violating trust.

A severely injured survivor of the Dolphinarium suicide attack reported that he clearly remembers the human bomb's smile (Tel Aviv, June 2001, twenty-one casualties).[8] Once an Israeli Border Police officer attacked a man who was approaching him and killed him because something in his behavior aroused his suspicion. Indeed, an explosive charge was found on the man's body. In his testimony, the suspicious killer said, "He came toward me, put his hand in his pocket, and smiled. I immediately realized he was a suicide terrorist."[9]

From the moment the human bomb with a false identity reaches his chosen target and mingles with the crowd in his target, until he finds the appropriate situation for blowing himself up, thereby revealing his true identity, some time passes, from a few seconds to long minutes, even hours. In that time it is likely that a sort of solidarity develops, or some interaction—usually unspoken—between him and his surroundings. This suspended and fictitious coexistence is probably laden with feelings and thoughts of each of the passengers about his fellows: fears, shame, hopes, various sorts of fantasies.

Suicide attacks differ from each other by, among other things, the length of time between the arrival of the human bomb at his target—the crowded market or the busy restaurant—and the explosion. In retrospect it is relatively easy to estimate the time between the human bomb's boarding of the bus until his activation of the charge going by the number of stops that he shared with the other passengers. Israel Security Agency (ISA) investigators categorize terror attacks in buses by the length of the trip with the ticking bomb. Among local counterterrorism experts, the Jerusalem record is held by Jara, the suicide terrorist of the 19 bus (January 2004), who boarded it at a shopping mall on the southern edge of the city and exploded himself as it entered the center of the city, near the prime minister's house.[10] In this respect, Anna's terror attack was near the recorded average.

Members of the Israeli rescue forces who removed the bodies of the victims from Anna's bus and its surroundings told me that 'Abed's head was thrown far from the scene and remained intact (as frequently occurs to the head of human bombs). They could not help being fascinated by his frozen and petrifying gaze. They tried to decipher his expression and tended to think it projected lofty contempt. In response, one of the Jewish workers stuck his tongue out at the severed head.

The thought of the exchange of gazes, before and after death, reminded me of the legend of the Medusa, a Greek myth that my mother told me when I was a child. In brief: Athena transformed Medusa's beautiful hair into serpents and made her face so terrible to behold that gazing directly at her would turn unwary onlookers to stone. Later Perseus was sent to kill her and bring back her head. He was provided with a mirrored shield and was warned that if he looked directly at her, he would die. He accomplished the impossible mission of beheading the monster while looking at Medusa's reflection from his shield, thus avoiding her lethal gaze. Thereafter he used her severed head—still terrifying—to put his enemies to death.

The Medusa's gaze has been widely discussed in the humanities as a representation of horror, and it has become synonymous with dread and cruel death.[11] This mythological gaze is described as terror incarnate.[12] Let us briefly consider three motives in the image of Medusa. First, she has a deceitful element. Her deadliness is hidden behind beauty and charm. She has a cunning double identity, since nobody expects her to kill. Similarly, Palestinian suicide terrorists pass as Israelis until they disclose their true selves by detonating the explosives concealed under their stereotypically Jewish attire. Second, the look of Medusa, so famous for its mesmerizing attraction, is not just terror-inspiring but conveys the state of being terrorized as well. This is precisely the way it was ingeniously depicted by the master artists Caravaggio (1596) and Rubens (1618), who portrayed Medusa's face as terribly startled and shocked. The killer knows he is doomed to be killed very soon. Medusa, as an archetype of the human bomb, is terrified no less than terrifying, both aggressor and victim. Medusa's look implies and causes death, but it also gazes upon death. Similarly, whereas the Israeli victims of suicide terrorism have seen death without knowing it, the suicide terrorist has seen death with acute awareness.

Third, Perseus did not look directly at Medusa but at her reflection, and she looked at his reflection looking at her reflection. Thus, a closed system of mirror images was created, a loop in which images mirror each other ad infinitum. Who, then, is the viewer and who is being viewed? Who is the subject and who is the object: Medusa or Perseus, the aggressor or the victim, the human bomb or his targets?[13] The Middle Eastern cycle of bloodshed has the same dynamic. Anna and 'Abed, the regional victim and aggressor, are hopelessly caught in each other's lethal embrace. Neither has existence and meaning without the close and mutual relationship with the other. The tragic dialectic and morbid interaction between the Palestinian suicide terrorist and the Israelis he attacks hint at a solution to the mystery concentrated at the site of the explosion.[14]

Lacuna in Suicide Terrorism Studies

In recent decades the phenomenon of suicide terrorism has become extremely prominent throughout the world, and it has influenced our lives by sowing grief, fear, and disorientation. To this day suicide terrorism has significant influence on our minds, our habits, our policies, and our economies. Almost everyone has been exposed to suicide terrorism, either directly or through the media and politics. It has cast a shadow of dread and perplexity on our lives.[15] Against this background, quite naturally a vast publication industry has developed, producing books and articles on terrorism in general and on suicide terrorism, which is regarded as the most severe challenge to understand and combat. The first wave of publications—which was both urgent and, to a degree, panic-stricken—has died down. Now the time has come to take a retrospective look and reopen the discussion. A significant portion of the literature on suicide terrorism is either journalistic[16] or fictional,[17] and it is possible, with caution, to glean vital information and stimulating insight from it. Other publications are more pragmatic, with no theoretical pretensions: intelligence surveys and political analyses that lead to proposals for preventing suicide terrorism, combating it, and dealing with its consequences.[18] Along with many studies with operational potential, representing the interface between universities, governments, and defense establishments, there are also examples of humanistic and philosophical discussions, mainly of the polemical and moralistic variety.[19] Similarly, scholarly essays about suicide terrorism have appeared, some of which are ambitious, brilliant, and thought-provoking, though they are basically speculative and not necessarily based on reliable research.[20] The more scientific literature about suicide terrorism naturally belongs to the fields of political science, international relations, and strategic studies, in addition to psychology and, to a lesser degree, analysis of the social and cultural aspects of suicide terrorism. Meanwhile, there have been only the first stirrings of anthropological and sociological interest in terrorism.[21] It still lacks, on the one hand, a soft analysis, close to the field, of the ethnographic type, and, on the other side, an integral theoretical framework. Most books and articles on terrorism are based on secondary or official sources, largely reports issued by counterterrorism agencies; on the more or less authorized pronouncements of the leaders and representatives of terrorism; and on (Western) media reports.[22] All of these sources tend to be tendentious and distorted. Most of the publications that appeared in academic journals, especially in the social sciences, deal with particular aspects of suicide terrorism—analysis from the psychopathological,[23] economic,[24] criminological[25] angles, as well as organizational studies,[26] or communication studies[27]—and there is an impressive repertoire of prominent studies that offer a comprehensive view of the phenomenon.[28]

Regarding the perpetrators of suicide terrorism—the human bombs themselves and the organization for whom they acted—I have found an abundance of material, as well as on their political, social, and cultural context. I have also found interesting material about the target community of suicide terrorism: the individuals, groups and institutions who are directly or indirectly injured.[29] However, I have not found anything about the link between the two.[30] In reality, of course, there can be no suicide terrorism without victims and no victims of suicide terrorism without an attacker. What is violence, if not a relationship between attacker and victim? Yet the study of terrorism and suicide terrorism tends to discuss each side separately, as if it were independent of the other. Suicide terrorism is inherently the outcome of the close contact between the two. Nevertheless, the literature virtually ignores the critical situation in which the attacker and the victim meet.[31] Furthermore, the tendency of academic study to focus *either* on the precipitants of suicide terrorism *or* on its consequences has never been challenged. On the one hand, the literature looks at what preceded and ostensibly led to the attack (i.e., the human bomb's psychological and social profile, his/her motivations and the organization's ideology, his/her recruitment and indoctrination, the structure of the terrorist cell, the socioeconomic conditions that give rise to suicide terrorism, the policies and military actions that elicit it, and the culture that embraces suicide terrorism and praises the human bomb). On the other hand, the literature has examined what happens after the attack and as a result of it (i.e., state responses to terrorism including counterterrorist measures, reorganization of the targeted group, the rehabilitation of the injured, post-traumatic stress syndrome, the media processing of the event, the ensuing public discourse on terrorism, and the formation of collective memory in both opposing communities). Academic studies do not connect these two bodies of knowledge. There are experts in pre- and post-terrorism, but none in what happens in between. The study of suicide terrorism turns away from the thing itself. In other words, studies of suicide terrorism deal with everything except the arena in which the attack takes place.[32] However, that arena is in fact the heart of the phenomenon, and there, too, as I claim, are hidden the keys to understanding it. I was drawn to the arena, the site of the explosion at the time of the explosion, and its immediate surroundings, and this book focuses on it.

ZAKA

I tried to reach the arena of suicide terrorism indirectly, by analyzing the testimonies of failed suicide terrorists or survivors of suicide terrorism.

The results, however, were disappointing. Interviews with jailed would-be human bombs elicited quite standard laconic confessions or the rote recitation of well-rehearsed slogans, both of which have been extensively documented. Recorded interviews, clearly constrained by the censorship exercised by the leadership of the terrorist organizations or by its agents in prison, yielded little more than mere propaganda, or trivial—often miserable—life stories, without nuance or personal reflection. Thus, for example, many of the Palestinian prisoners who intended to commit suicide attacks strongly insisted that they regretted "not becoming martyrs." It is difficult to determine how sincere they were in declaring vehemently that they would rather have died, for these are clearly formulaic declarations, part of their effort to cloak themselves in heroism, no matter what may have been the circumstances of their failure to accomplish their missions and of their arrest.

The same holds true for interviews with the human bomb's relatives and acquaintances. The familiar statements by the mothers and fathers of Palestinian suicide terrorists—that they are pleased to have had the privilege of being the parents of a *shahid*—are of dubious credibility, though they are interesting in themselves as evidence of the mood of the community and the social pressure exerted at that time. Only a few family members dared to reveal, in secret, something of their deep sorrow for the loss, and sometimes anger, at those who sent their sons to their deaths. My attempts to obtain insight into the essence of suicide terrorism from other informants, especially by talking with survivors of attacks, also produced only a limited repertoire of clichés.

I might also have stood in the center of the city at rush hour and waited for a suicide attack. But this strategy would have entailed endless, boring hours of expectation, with virtually no chance of success. Of course, if, against all probability, I did manage to be close to a suicide terrorist attack, I would not survive to report about it. The danger of physical or mental suffering as well as statistical logic, and perhaps ethical reservations as well, make direct (participant) observation of suicide terrorism practically impossible. These obstacles can be partially overcome only through sophisticated methods of simulation, reconstruction, and proximation.[33] The arena at the moment of explosion will probably forever remain enigmatic and necessarily elude the investigator. The scholar's only recourse is a systematic study of the scene during the minutes immediately after the attack and the following hours. Such study will at least provide a foundation for conjectures. But how can this be accomplished? A curiously practical way of getting as close as possible to a suicide terrorism act, both in space and in time, is offered by ZAKA.

Anyone who has viewed footage of a suicide attack in Israel will have seen peculiar-looking bearded men busily working at the center of the gruesome site. At first their fluorescent safety vests are marked "medic," but when they have finished evacuating the wounded and begin dealing with the dead, they turn the vests inside out. Now they display the Hebrew acronym "ZAKA," which stands for Disaster Victim Identification. ZAKA is an organization of ultra-Orthodox (Haredi) Jewish volunteers that has gained a monopoly on dealing with the bodies of victims of terrorism in Israel. It operates a network of a few hundred well-trained and well-equipped personnel throughout the country. These men can arrive at any terrorism site rapidly, offer first aid, and then turn to their central task—caring for the bodies in keeping with traditional Jewish respect for the dead. At the site of the attack they evacuate the corpses, collect severed limbs and organs, assign them to their bodies, mark the pieces, and pack them up. They search out and scrape up small pieces of flesh and tissue and soak up every drop of blood they can. Their purpose is both to identify the bodies and to ensure that all are buried in accordance with Orthodox Jewish law. For the last several years, as Palestinian terrorism has waned, ZAKA has turned its attention and resources to other forms of unnatural death, as well as to rescue projects. While most of its time and energy is now devoted to automobile accidents, suicides, and other routine tragedies, work at the sites of suicide terrorism remains its quintessential task and most exciting experience. Recently some volunteers secretly admitted to me that they miss the glory days of the intifada, the finest hour, so to speak, of the human bombs and those who deal with their bodies.

Although terrorism has become a global phenomenon, ZAKA, with its specialty of caring for the bodies of the dead killed in terrorist acts, is unique. While extensively covered by the Israeli and world media, it has been the subject of little systematic research.[34] ZAKA's work falls under the rubric of emergency services such as first aid and firefighting, and it bears some similarity to the work of the explosives experts and intelligence agents who hasten to the site immediately following an attack. ZAKA can also be likened to agencies that deal with the less tangible and immediate consequences of terrorism attacks, such as social workers, psychologists, counterterrorism personnel, and even clergy. ZAKA is one more kind of "terrorism specialist."[35] Such interventionist elements—the organizations that play a role in the aftermath of terrorist acts—must be included in any study of the phenomenon. They constitute an inseparable part of the scene of terrorism and have an important influence on its effects. A young Palestinian man brandishes an assault rifle in one hand and holds a Koran in the other. He is photographed against the background of the golden Dome of the Rock. This is the iconic image of the Middle Eastern suicide terrorist. A bearded Jewish man, wearing a skullcap, leans over a body lying in a pool of blood amid vegetable stands that have been overturned. He holds a plastic bag in one hand and pincers in the other. This is the parallel and complementary icon of the Middle Eastern suicide terrorist. In collective memory and especially in the visual archives of both parties to the Middle East conflict, alongside the human bomb, the ZAKA volunteer stands out. Both in the Palestinian mythography, which glorifies the spectacle of suicide terrorism, and in Israeli mythography, which has not succeeded in repressing the trauma of suicide terrorism, we find images of ultra-Orthodox men gathering severed limbs, continually rekindling the nightmarish imagination of the people of the region.

These two figures are champions of hostile tribes, priests of gruesome death who bring the macabre to center stage after it has been thrust to the hidden margins. Two breeds of fundamentalists try to impose their political agenda, mythical-historical precedents, and cultic norms from their holy books, and to bring the regional, ethno-national conflict down to a deeper, religious level. This is the bloody project both of the Hamas suicide terrorists and of the men of ZAKA, defined as holy work by the societies that sent them.

A brief warning against a possible misreading of my argument is in order here. No ethical conclusions may be drawn from emphasizing the closeness between the attacker and his victim, from pointing out the interdependence of the Palestinian who commits the violence and the Israelis who deal with the bodies he has murdered. Clearly, by the central place I give to ZAKA in this book on suicide terrorism, and, furthermore, by juxtaposing the ZAKA volunteers with the suicide terrorists, while pointing out the similarities between them and the reciprocity, even tacit cooperation, between them, I do not wish to imply that human bombs and

ZAKA volunteers are morally equivalent. Nor do I wish to in any way minimize the responsibility and the ghastly murderous brutality of the former or to disparage the compassionate work of the latter. On the contrary, viewing the two as macabre twins would be wholly intolerable—and pointless—without recognizing the moral abyss that separates them.[36] Nevertheless, suicide terrorism does bring the Palestinian terrorist and the Haredi ZAKA volunteer together in a Gordian knot. It turns out that they are alike in some ways, and there is a two-way relationship between them. I address their common ground and mutuality at length elsewhere.[37] Suffice it to say here that their reciprocal association is not limited to mutual disdain and hatred. The human bomb and the member of ZAKA are prominent figures in their communities, objects of admiration and emulation. Not only is there a similarity between a suicide terrorist and a member of ZAKA, there is also a mutual awareness and relationship. Each of them appears as the dominant counterpart in the consciousness of the other and fills a complementary role in the other's repertoire of images. They are even fascinated by each other. In many of the suicide terrorists' testaments, they express clear awareness of what they expect to happen to their bodies after the explosion, and in some cases they refer explicitly to the way ZAKA will deal with their body parts. In the videotape recorded just before he set out on his mission, a Hamas human bomb cheerfully addressed his parents, promising they would be joyful and proud when "thousands of pieces of [his] body's flesh disperse and are smeared on sidewalks and treetops, to be scraped up and gathered in plastic bags by pious Jews."[38] On the other side of the barrier, the ZAKA volunteers carry photographs of the human bombs whose bodies they have treated in their wallets. They also speak about them a lot and say that they even dream about them. In addition to representing the target of terrorism in the Middle East, ZAKA plays an active role at the scene of the terrorism attack itself. Although it responds ex post facto to the explosion, nevertheless it has significant input in defining the nature, status, and imprint of the attack. With much caution, it could be said that ZAKA is a partner in the Middle East's cycle of violence.

During the al-Aqsa Intifada (2000–5), I joined the ranks of ZAKA unofficially to become a participant-observer in the suicide terrorism scene. I formed connections with the volunteers, I was included in their radio calls, and I rode in their ambulances. In that way I arrived at the arena of terrorism while it was still bleeding and smoking. In the course of my extensive field study of suicide terrorism, ZAKA proved to be not only an ingenious and indispensable medium by which I could investigate the arena from close range in real time, but also an organic part of the arena that played an active role in the regional suicide terrorism scene. ZAKA was at the same time a useful methodological tool and a fruitful heuristic medium. Not only did my membership in ZAKA make firsthand observation of the scene possible, but ZAKA volunteers proved to be clever, sensitive and original observers of the scene, providing authentic testimony and intelligent commentary about suicide terrorism.

By means of ZAKA I was able to penetrate the arena of suicide terrorism immediately after the explosion. My findings there provided the key for understanding the human bomb and those who dispatched him before the explosion. I will present one example here of this retrospective understanding, which I admit is somewhat tentative. According to the testimony of some of those who dealt with the mutilated bodies of suicide terrorists, their sexual organs were wrapped in rags and rolls of toilet paper.[39] Just as with Muhammad Atta, the leader of the September 11 terrorists, it is clear that the thoughts of the Palestinians sent on a suicide mission by Hamas were focused on that part of their body. In conversations with ZAKA volunteers this phenomenon was frequently discussed, and, as expected, it was also the subject of jokes. They could not help connecting it with the information they had about the Palestinians' beliefs in the promised union with seventy-two virgins after their death as *shahids*. Perhaps this is an indication of the prominence, ingenuousness, and concreteness of the suicide terrorists' conceptions of the paradise they would enter after the explosion. The information and explanation offered by ZAKA shed light on factors that had been in shadow at the scene of suicide terrorism, and it gave a voice to the silent participants in discourse on suicide terrorism. As a witness and interpreter and especially as a vital protagonist in the arena, ZAKA maintained a dialogue with the human bomb. Central insights offered in this book draw on the unique encounter between the believing Muslim suicide terrorist—or his mutilated body—and the believing Jew who recovers his body parts, which are scattered and mingled with the limbs of his Israeli victims. The dialogue between ZAKA and the suicide terrorist is virtually wordless, and it is not necessarily synchronized. Often the answer comes before the question, and sometimes the exchange is mediated, asymmetrical, involuntary, or unintended. Yet this subtle dialogue between the two sides is often particularly revealing.

Here is an example of the conversation between them, which begins before the terrorist crosses the border and nears his target and continues when the ZAKA volunteer places his body parts in numbered plastic bags. ZAKA volunteers confided to me that they found tattoos on the body parts of human bombs, bearing messages about their mission. In one case, confirmed by police pathology reports, the skin of a human bomb bore an image of a man waving a Palestinian flag, with a saintly halo over his head and an explosive belt around his waist. In this image, the human bomb prophesied his fate, and perhaps dictated it, sentencing himself to his death.[40] It reminds one of Franz Kafka's story "The Penal Colony," where a person's death sentence is inscribed on his naked body by the needles of a rotating machine until he bleeds to death. By means of his tattoo, the human bomb communicates with those who would handle his body after the attack. The body of the Palestinian terrorist conveys a replica of his mute but violent conversation with Israeli society. Here the dead terrorist finally speaks, after being forced to remain silent while still alive. And the ZAKA volunteers respond to him—literally. They sometimes actually speak to the pieces of the terrorist's body, on the site and afterward. Their speech goes beyond curses. Some of them imagine that they can see a response in the expression on the terrorist's severed head. While ZAKA plays a major role in the book, at times even seeming to occupy the entire stage and dominate the logic of my argumentation, the reader should be aware that ZAKA is merely a vehicle to better understand the principal, closely related phenomenon: suicide terrorism. ZAKA is a fascinating topic in itself and deserves a book of its own.[41] Suicide terrorism is the center of gravity of the present book, while ZAKA is just a mirror, a peculiar essential reflection of and about the main topic.

Objectives, Subject Matter, and Approach

This book concerns suicide terrorism in general, and Palestinian suicide terrorism in Israel during the intifada in particular. It describes and analyzes suicide terrorism from an anthropological-sociological perspective based on extensive field research focusing on the site of the act of suicide terrorism in real time. A main source of the book's findings is participant observation with the religious death specialists who deal with the casualties of the terrorist attack.

The main contention of this book—the manifestations and implications of which are examined in all of its chapters—is that suicide terrorism is exceptional in that it breaks down the fundamental distinction between aggressor and victim.

This book does not pretend to offer an exclusive approach to suicide terrorism as an alternative to the existing literature, but rather to enrich the study of suicide terrorism by presenting the phenomenon from a point of view that, to date, was not sufficiently emphasized and clarified. Indeed, it has been largely ignored. I do so by bringing parameters into the discussion that were not developed in the past as well as hitherto unavailable empirical observations. My research project can be seen as a proposal for reopening discussion of suicide terrorism and as a program for further research.

Anyone consulting this book in search of a definitive answer to the urgent question of how to deal with suicide terrorism will be disappointed. This research has no practical consequences that can be translated into recommendations for counterterrorism measures. I made no effort to reach operational or political conclusions, aiming instead to trace the characteristics of this dreadful phenomenon and to explain it from a purely academic point of view.

To cope with those involved in suicide terrorism we must not regard them as either beasts or supermen, for then they are dehumanized. Underlying both contrasting depictions is relegation of suicide terrorism to beyond the pale. It is pushed outside the bounds of civilization. However, suicide terrorism, regardless of how terrible, is integral to our culture and nature—the domain of reason of one kind or another. This act should be returned to the realm where, even if still not fully known, it is in principle knowable. In calling for the return of suicide terrorism to within the bounds of the anthropological and therefore the explicable world, it is not my intention to minimize in the slightest the import and gravity of this mass murder or to trivialize it. To treat it as something beyond the horizon of social behavior is to exempt us from the—basically moral—obligation to account for suicide terrorism, and thus it deprives us of the possibility of combating it. In other words, the human bomb should be humanized and thus rationalized.

The book is to be read more as a series of propositions than as a web of conclusions. It offers a set of theses, some of which are well grounded, and some will require further investigation to refine and confirm them. Ethnographical passages are embedded in the chapters of the book, and these imply elements of a theoretical model, which, for the moment, is preliminary and tentative. The claims of this book draw inspiration and validity from my fieldwork concentrated on the arena of suicide terrorism. Specifically, the research took place in Israel, mainly in Jerusalem, in 2003–7. The material presented here was first collected at the very time of the attacks, which gives more credibility to the description and analysis. The final processing and writing took place nearly ten years later, at a time when terrorism in general and suicide terrorism in particular had moved beyond the local horizon, though there is no guarantee that terror will not return and take over our lives again. For the moment, though, what had been daily reality has become a fading memory, and the searing wound has become a scar. The element of dread and alarm that accompanied the ethnographic documentation at that time has died down. The book is marked by a certain distance from the phenomenon. Thus it has both the authenticity of real time and also the perspective of passing time, making possible a balanced view. This book is both up-to-date and a retrospective study of suicide terrorism. It examines the findings derived from fieldwork and the processing of primary materials in the light of secondary literature and arguments that have appeared in the last seven years (such as master's theses and doctoral dissertations written on both sides of the Israeli-Palestinian divide but not yet published).

More than a decade has passed since the wave of suicide attacks discussed in the book, and almost a decade has passed since the wave of publications on the subject. Hence this book is able to exploit the historical perspective for the purpose of comprehensive and deep discussion. Similarly, it can profit from the lessons of an integrative and critical survey of the literature that has accumulated in the meanwhile and evaluate the subject in that light. Regrettably, suicide terrorism has not disappeared. Therefore the book has lost nothing of its relevance. On the contrary, suicide terrorism has become more widespread and lethal, although it has changed its location and some of its typical traits. The book can provide a starting point for the development of a renewed discussion of suicide terrorism, presenting a specific case with an analytical model as a basis for a fresh comparative and theoretical examination of the phenomenon that continues to threaten the world.

There is a shortage in research on suicide terrorism dealing with its "softer" aspects addressed in the following chapters. The majority of suicide terrorism (and terrorism) studies are based on secondary and mostly official sources such as press reports and government and military pronouncements, formal and tendentious statements on the part of terrorist organizations, collected statistical data, and structured interviews. This book is based on qualitative research and primary data: mainly field observations at the scene of suicide terrorism and in-depth interviews with various agents involved in the scene. It also uses rare authentic materials and privileged information (formerly classified).

In this book I am not concerned with the strategic logic of suicide terrorism but rather with its anthropological logic, that is, its social and cultural dimension. This is partly a micro-sociological and micro-anthropological study of suicide terrorism.[42] It is based on interpretive analysis and focuses on social interaction and agency in face-to-face situations. Indeed, this research of suicide bombing concentrates on the arena of explosion and its immediate environment. It is a study of a situation—the setting, the actual circumstances, and the very act itself of suicide terrorism.

Themes, Line of Reasoning, and Conventions Challenged

History has introduced us to graver instances of mass murder than those that characterize suicide terrorism, including in living memory.[43] History also offers many well-known examples of individuals who gave up their lives for collective goals, including model heroes in the Western tradition.[44] Thus, what makes suicide terrorism in general and its Palestinian version in particular so shocking? And what is new about it? First, it is the very combination of the two familiar components, the bond of suicide and massacre that makes suicide terrorism unique. Second is the spectacle—extravagant and enticing. The impact of the spectacle is magnified by turning into a media event.[45] There is another immanent characteristic to this phenomenon—its inscrutability. Perhaps suicide terrorism was intended from the start to be unintelligible, at least in the sense that each new strategy employed by the actors in the arena aims to completely upset the stable order of possibilities the opposing strategy has created, to impose a new set of priorities, to render the rational irrational. Suicide terrorism is an assault on our ability to give a coherent account of the things we witness and experience. It combines fear, on which all terrorism is built, with incomprehension. The essential unintelligible quality of suicide terrorism is at the root of its horrific impact, making it so effectively subversive.

Suicide terrorism contains a palpable demonstration of impossible, confusing, and disconcerting connections, between the living and the dead, the Jew and the Arab, the comrade and the enemy, as well as a confusing mingling of body parts. As elaborated throughout the book's chapters, most disturbing is the mixture of aggressor and victim that makes suicide terrorism extraordinary.

Mass murder and self-murder. Much has already been written about both of these phenomena, but little has been written about them in combination, which is the unique characteristic of suicide terrorism. This book emphasizes murder and suicide as simultaneous phenomena, amalgamated and interdependent. Studies usually examine suicide terrorism either from the angle of the massacre or from the angle of the voluntary autodestruction of the perpetrator, but as long as the connection between the two is not discussed, the main point has been missed.

It has been argued that "people go around killing people in movies all the time, but the reason they make all those movies is that for 99.9 percent of the audience it's impossible to do. And if it's that hard to kill someone else, someone you have every reason to want to destroy, imagine how hard it is to succeed in killing yourself."[46] In the spirit of this provocative but not unreasonable statement, it can be assumed that since each of these two acts is challenging in itself, then their combination will double or square the challenge. But I claim that the opposite is the case. To kill while committing suicide is something essentially different from the sum of the two components of the act, something that may not necessarily be more difficult to do or explain than the doing or explaining of its two parts. Indeed, it may be that the two contribute to each other and enable each other. If someone combines the killing of others with suicide, then the murder will sanction the suicide, and the suicide will sanction the murder. This is because making a murderous attack on others conditional on self-destruction and committing both simultaneously blurs the distinction between the attacker and the victim. Thus, although he is a murderer, he demands a moral status for himself, as it were, and implicitly claims to have ethical superiority over his victims. This logic is fundamental to suicide terrorism, one component of the explanation of this horrifying and enigmatic phenomenon.

The present book brings the victim into the equation of suicide terrorism, along with the perpetrator. The victim is not merely a marginal, passive object. Rather, he is an integral part of the scene, playing an important role in the dynamic of suicide terrorism, and therefore he must be given a major place in explaining the phenomenon. In the following chapters I emphasize the close and multidimensional connection between the attacker and his victim. They are similar to each other, preoccupied with each other, identify with one another, collaborate, and each of them can take on the other's identity. The connection between attacker and victim is a crucial definer of suicide terrorism, distinguishing it and explaining its great influence on us. The connection between attacker and victim is a central theme of this book, running through it like a scarlet thread. The chapters of the book present various expressions of this connection and discuss its consequences.

The vast majority of books on suicide terrorism begin by presenting the contemporary phenomenon as a link in a rich historical chain going back to antiquity and the Middle Ages. This book sees contemporary suicide bombing as an unprecedented novelty, since in all the analogous cases the binary distinction between the aggressor and his victim was maintained. Breaking down this culturally fundamental dichotomy makes suicide terrorism subversive, not only a physical and strategic challenge, but one that threatens our sense of order, truth, and justice as well.

Here is another example of an argument that demonstrates the interesting aspects of suicide terrorism, which are inferred from the particular relations between attacker and victim that typify it. Let us return to the point of departure, which was that killing and the use of physical aggression in general are not simple matters. According to one claim, "violence poses a quandary, for to initiate violence is to invite it in turn, so one would think that people do everything possible to avoid it."[47] However, we have already stated that this is not always the case. Here we present other possible ways of making the use of violence easier and more likely. One can name two very familiar situations in which the use of violence does not incur the danger of a violent reaction. One is that in which there is extreme asymmetry between the great power of the aggressor and the weakness of the victim. In this situation, the total annihilation of the other side is possible, thus either neutralizing his ability to respond or creating paralyzing deterrence. Another situation is one in which the attacker hides in such a way that he cannot imagine he will be located in order to take revenge. For example, he can disappear within the multitude, remain anonymous, as in mass race riots, and then there is no address for the counterviolence (of the police, of vigilantes, or the like). The attacker can also disappear by destroying himself. Not only does he attack the other and make him a victim, but he also attacks himself and also becomes a victim. This situation characterizes suicide terrorism.

In regrettably common cases, no one remains alive to retaliate against the attacker, to avenge the blood of his victim. In the previously unfamiliar case of suicide terrorism, no one remains to retaliate against, to take revenge. The attacker immediately made himself a victim, making a counterattack against him impossible. In suicide terrorism, the survivors, members of the victim's group who were not injured, are denied the sole privilege left to them, to punish the attacker for his aggression.

As in the case of the target group that is entirely obliterated, so, too, the attacker who departs from the world nullifies the option of revenge, the slight satisfaction that had been available to the victims, and hence he nullifies the possibility of reestablishing the balance that was violated by his aggression.

Suicide terrorism has a particularly powerful effect because it turns the attacker into a victim too, and as a result, he deprives the objects of aggression of the possibility of attaining justice and restoring order to the world. This makes suicide terrorism subversive, maybe even crueler than other types of terrorism. Dr. Goldstein, the Jewish settler who murdered dozens of Palestinians in Hebron (1994), did not commit an act of suicide terrorism. Those who survived his violence overpowered and killed him, taking revenge and punishing him. The Haredi Jews who take care of the bodies of the victims of suicide terrorism are eager to find the attacker, but he has destroyed himself. Not even a whole body is in their possession, against which they can vent their anger, frustration, and hatred, which they can curse, kick, direct physical and verbal violence against. It is hard to respond with violence to an attacker of whom only a few torn pieces of flesh and some shattered bones remain. What is left to those who view themselves as representatives of the victims is to try to find the attacker's severed head at all cost.

Organization of the Book and Intended Audience

This preface is followed by nine chapters, each one divided into subsections whose titles indicate their content. Chapter 1 offers a general background for dealing with suicide terrorism. It is intended mainly for those who are not experts in the study of terrorism and may not be aware of the problematics involved in defining the phenomenon and the questions raised by the effort to characterize it. Readers who are familiar with the professional literature will find here a reorganization and critical reading of existing knowledge, an alternative conceptualization, and emphasis on unfamiliar aspects of the subject. The introductory notes sharpen the distinction between suicide terrorism and similar forms of violence, which are commonly viewed as suicide terrorism, and this is done in order to clarify the most basic essence of the phenomenon, that which makes it historically unique and particular from the sociological and psychological perspective. Evidently this implies rejection of the common claim that suicide terrorism has precedents in the past. Suicide terrorism is presented here as a distinct type of violence rather than just one more variant of terrorism.

Now we can enter the thick of the particular case of Palestinian suicide terrorism. The next three chapters present exclusive primary materials on the phenomenon, bringing up to date, expanding on, and critically refining conclusions reached by others. Chapter 2 presents abundant and varied details about the figure of the suicide terrorist. The result is a surprising profile full of paradoxes. Chapter 3 address questions that were not previously raised about suicide terrorists, and for this purpose it makes use of disciplines and analogies that do not appear in the literature. Chapter 4 details the operative side of suicide terrorism. It presents the dynamics of the attacks of suicide terrorism in Israel, from beginning to end, including its background and consequences, by following the career of the entrepreneurs of suicide terrorism. The source of the information presented here is mainly the protocols of ISA interrogations and the decisions of military courts.

Chapter 5 deals with one specific trait of suicide terrorism that the literature tends to ignore or at most restrict to a merely technical matter, although it is an integral part of the phenomenon and in spite of its fascinating consequences. The issue discussed here is the pre-explosion phase of the suicide attack—the crossing of the border and getting to the target site in disguise, and the mingling of the still-living human bomb with his soon-to-be victims. I propose the concept of "passing" and apply the extensively researched implications of this phenomenon to enrich the study of suicide terrorism.

Chapter 6 relates to some more overlooked aspects of suicide terrorism and focuses on their bearing on the Middle East conflict. In this chapter I study the relations between the attacker and his victims in terms previously unexplored, shedding new light on charged Israeli-Palestinian relations. Suicide terrorism subtly reflects mutual attraction between the two protagonists in the bitter armed conflict. On the one hand, this chapter clarifies the place of suicide terrorism in the Middle East, and on the other, understanding of the Middle East increases sensitivity to the complexity of suicide terrorism.

Chapter 7 observes suicide terrorism through the prism of classical anthropology. Beyond the tactical and strategic dimension of suicide terrorism is revealed its ritual dimension, which betrays a latent similarity and denied collaboration between the two conflicted sides. Analysis of the logic directing the symbolic patterns of social behavior involved in suicide terrorism leads to better understanding of this phenomenon. In this chapter I discuss suicide terrorism in terms of sacrifice and the dialectical relationship between the victimizer and the victim. I offer fresh analysis of suicide terrorism that has far-reaching political and ethical implications.

Chapter 8 covers the methodological aspects of this study. I present my research methods, the source of my findings, and the basis for my conclusions. This is an account of the techniques used in this study and their problematic nature, as well as a presentation of the metalogic of the thinking behind the study. Chapter 9 is a comparative and theoretical addition that takes an opportunity to fill a vital gap by commenting on the place of Palestinian suicide terrorism, researched as a case study, in the context of other cases in the world, a survey of the development of suicide terrorism since the conclusion of this research, and an evaluation of its present state. It also proposes an analytical model that can serve for future research into suicide terrorism. In the end I consider the question of the universal applicability of the paradigm that emerges from this book. To what degree is it possible to apply the insights from my research into the Israeli-Palestinian case to cases in other cultures and historical circumstances, such as Iraq or Belgium?

The afterword of the book focuses on the moral logic of suicide terrorism. The analysis is based on comparison of two vicious and devious attacks on the humanist foundations of our culture—one that took place seventy-five years ago and another that happened in our own time.

The discussion in the various chapters touches on subjects that could arouse curiosity and be of significance to those whose field of interest is not necessarily terrorism. Naturally the book is primarily addressed to individuals in the social sciences and humanities, students and scholars of political science, international relations, strategic studies, sociology, anthropology, history, and psychology who specialize in aspects of terrorism, armed conflict, and political violence in general. The book is additionally intended for people interested in the Middle East, in Palestine and Israel, those concerned with religion, religious radicalism, orthodoxy and fundamentalism, and scholars of contemporary Islam and Judaism. It also deals with boundaries, rituals, cults, the body, and death. Finally, I hope that the book will reach a general, not necessarily academic, readership, made up of individuals who seek better knowledge of a central phenomenon that disturbs the world we live in.

Personal Note

Beyond Anna's heartbreaking story, other events helped create the almost physical closeness between me and suicide terrorism. On July 31, 2002, an explosive charge blew up the central cafeteria at the Hebrew University campus on Mount Scopus, right next to the table where I regularly eat lunch. I happened to be on vacation on that day. Nine people were killed, including staff members, students, and lecturers, some of whom I knew very well. There have been four more suicide attacks on buses to the university campus and the nearby neighborhood, in which twenty-two people were killed.[48] In three other instances children of acquaintances were killed or wounded, and a father and daughter who were close relatives of a colleague whose office is next to mine in the Sociology Department were killed. Just living in Jerusalem during the al-Aqsa Intifada, especially as the son of an elderly mother and the father of young children, made Palestinian suicide terrorism a palpable and perpetually horrifying experience. In addition to the intellectual challenge posed by fieldwork at the arena of suicide terrorism, it was no simple matter ethically and emotionally, even viscerally—literally, in the sense of the stomach's ability to digest horrifying impressions, sights, smells, and sounds without vomiting. Later I realized that it was also no simple matter to write about these things. I have made an effort to spare the readers, which required great caution. In particular, I had to avoid the trap of the pornography of death and the kitschy treatment of disastrous misfortune, and I also had to avoid trivializing death or taking too detached and mechanical an attitude toward human tragedy. Determined clinging to professional codes was insufficient. Spiritual strength was needed, if not from me, then from my colleagues and family, who supported and watched over me. A bit of humor also did no harm, though this might sound paradoxical in the circumstances of Middle Eastern suicide terrorism. Sometimes the arena itself inspired ironic chuckles and a philosophical perspective. See, for example, the following paragraph, based on my field notes.

In 2005 I participated-observed a ZAKA squad tending to the body of a Jewish victim of a brutal Palestinian attack. After security personnel left the arena, past midnight, the six of us were alone in the desert, in the dark, squatting over a disfigured body with flashlights. The Haredi ZAKA volunteer who led the operation suddenly put his hand to my ear and, with a broad smile, produced a ten-shekel coin. No doubt this amateur sleight of hand was a way for him to defuse the tension we felt and was meant to display "role distance," proving self-control. However, it was also an exegetical statement about the status of this surreal situation. The deliberate, utter mutilation of the body left even the experienced ZAKA volunteers in a state of disbelief. Later, the pious rabbi-cum-magician confirmed that his act was also a reaction to the absurdity of terrorism in the Middle East.

Acknowledgments

First, I wish to thank again those whom I have already thanked personally but cannot thank publicly. These are Palestinian activists in resistance organizations and those associated with them, as well as Israelis from the security forces, past and present, whose identity I may not reveal for clear reasons that involve protecting their status and honor, and sometimes also their safety. Their contribution was invaluable, and without their good-will, courage, and intelligence, this study could not have been completed.

Below is a list of contributors to this work who may be mentioned by name, and I am pleased to do so. These are expert colleagues from the academy or authentic representatives of the field of research, who invested more than a little time and effort in my work and generously provided vital information and thoughtful insights. Fortunately for me, they also showed interest in the subject. They hosted me among them, conversed with me at length, provided documents, and directed me to sources. They corroborated, corrected, or refuted information in my possession and expressed their opinion about the conjectures I raised before them, not always agreeing with my conclusions: Hanni Abu-Assad, Eitan Alimi, Scott Appleby, Bassam Banat, Barak Ben-Zur, Anat Berko, Yoram Bilu, Alon Burstein, Ofer Dekel, Avi Dichter, David Enoch, Amir Eshel, Gil Eyal, Claude Fischer, Huneida Ghanem, Carmi Gilon, Yehuda Goodman, Zali Gurevitch, Ron Hassner, Meir Hatina, David Heyd, Bruce Hoffman, Mark Juergensmeyer, Aziz Khaidar, Badi Khasisi, Nabil Khatav, Avi Kimhin, Adam Klin-Oron, Hilel Kohen, Ziv Koren, Betty Lahat, Zevik Levy, Meir Litvak, Dano Mentakovitch, Gil Merom, Yehuda Meshi-Zahav, Ebrahim Moosa, Raya Morag, Assaf Mughadam, Bentzi Oeiring, Reuven Paz, Ami Pedahzur, Simon Pery, Martin Rieserbrodt, Maya Rosenfeld, Yakov Rudja, Shimon Schapira, Danny Schwartz, Ori Schwartz, Avraham Sela, Aedel Shadid, Ronni Shaked, Wahel Shamasna, Sy Spilerman, Ali Taha, Dror Walk, Amin al-Warda, Haim Watzman, Haim Weingarten, Yisrael Yuval, Ozer Zilberschlag, Shmuel Zoltek, and three anonymous reviewers.

Two days after submission of the manuscript to the Press, my former student and colleague Michael Feige was assassinated in a terrorist attack in Tel Aviv (August 6, 2016). He read several chapters, and his thoughtful comments are highly valued.

Special credit goes to Jeffrey Green for translating large portions of the text in good spirit and with much skill, erudition, and humane concern.

I would like to express my gratitude and appreciation also to my editor Roger Haydon, and Ange Romeo-Hall, Marie Flaherty-Jones, and

Bethany Wasik at Cornell University Press for their sympathetic and professional support.

Finally, I am indebted to the foundations and academic institutions that trusted and generously supported me in the phases of research and writing: Israel Science Foundation (ISF); Scholion Center for Interdisciplinary Studies, Hebrew University; Schein and Eshkol Program, Sociology Department, Hebrew University; Research and Development, Hebrew University; Minerva Center, Tel Aviv University; Kroc Institute, University of Notre Dame; Sir Zelman Cowen Universities Fund, Sydney University.

The book is dedicated to Avshalom, Ruth, David, Dan, Uri, Tal.

GLOSSARY

Fatah Founded as the Palestinian National Liberation Movement. Political party (the largest and leading faction of the Palestine Liberation Organization, or PLO) and armed resistance movement.

Green Line Internationally recognized border between the State of Israel and its neighbors, including the occupied Palestinian territories. (The ceasefire line from 1948 to 1967.)

Halakha Body of Jewish religious laws derived from the scriptural (biblical) Torah and the oral Torah (Talmudic and later rabbinic ruling). Set of commandments binding Orthodox religious Jews.

Hamas Palestinian Islamist (Sunni) radical resistance organization ruling the Gaza Strip and active in the West Bank. Izz ad-Din al-Qassam Brigades is its military wing.

Haredim Ultra-Orthodox Jews.

Hezbollah   Party of Allah. Radical Islamist (Shiite) political and military organization based in (southern) Lebanon. Active in armed opposition to Israel.

human bomb   Synonymous and interchangeable with "suicide terrorist."

IDF   Israel Defense Forces.

intifada   Comes from the Arabic term meaning "to shake off, get rid of," referring to a Palestinian uprising against Israeli occupation. The first intifada (1987–93) was a popular, aggressive, but not predominantly lethal resistance to Israeli military rule of the West Bank. The second (al-Aqsa) intifada (2000–5) was an intensified armed resistance involving massive terrorist measures.

ISA   Israel (internal) Security Agency. Known also as Shin Bet or Shabak.

Palestinian Islamic Jihad (PIJ)   Radical paramilitary organization based in the Gaza Strip, competing with Hamas in militant opposition to Israel.

shahid (plural, *shuhada*)   "Witness" in Arabic. A Muslim martyr.

West Bank (of the Jordan River)   The eastern part of the historical land of Israel/Palestine. The territories bordering with Israel and occupied by Israel since 1967, populated by 2.5 million Palestinians and about 350,000 Jewish settlers. Sometimes referred to as "the territories."

ZAKA   Israeli organization of ultra-Orthodox Jewish volunteers devoted to caring for the victims of terrorist attacks.

Note: In several instances throughout the book, male gender–specific language is used only for reasons of brevity.

THE SMILE OF THE HUMAN BOMB

1

SUICIDE TERRORISM REVISITED

Introductory Notes

When It All Began?

Many influential studies mistakenly date the inception of suicide terrorism to 1983.[1] They refer to the explosion that took place on October 23 at the US Marine Corps barracks of the multinational force in Beirut (241 dead), which was followed a few minutes later by an explosion in the barracks of French paratroopers (58 dead), both carried out by Hezbollah, as the first shocking appearance of this violent phenomenon. Less than two weeks later, a human bomb sent by Hezbollah exploded the IDF headquarters in Tyre, Lebanon (sixty dead). The latter event is known as the second Tyre disaster because near that place, a year earlier, shortly after the IDF invasion of Lebanon, the building that housed the Israeli military government in southern Lebanon blew up (91 dead). The Israeli defense establishment explained the event as the result of a gas leak. But this implausible explanation and rumors that contradicted it raised the need for an official commission, which was indeed established to investigate the event. The conclusion, though somewhat hesitant, stated that it was a regrettable

accident due to negligent logistics. Over time there were increased indications that it was a terrorist attack, but Israel maintained its original claim
in a desperate effort to preserve its sullied honor.

There was another reason for the difficulty in admitting the alternative explanation: at that time the experts—and even more so the public at
large—had no idea what suicide terrorism was and did not even entertain
the hypothesis that such a thing was possible.[2] Today it is clear that the
first Tyre disaster, in November 1982, almost a year before the official
birthday of suicide terrorism, was when it came into being.[3]

The following findings show that the first Tyre disaster was the initial
instance of suicide terrorism: (1) three reliable, independent sources saw a
loaded Peugeot speed toward the building, break through the gates, stop
next to the wall, and explode; (2) the serial number of the motor proved
that the automobile was not in use by the Israelis; (3) in the wreckage of
the car a severed leg was found that did not belong to any of the bodies
of the soldiers who were killed in the explosion. Later more information
trickled in, indicating that the attack had indeed been suicide terrorism.
The human bomb who drove the car, whose name was Ahmad Qesir, was
declared a *shahid* by Hezbollah. A symbolic funeral was held for him, and
later a monument was erected in his memory in his native village near
Baalbek. Israeli intelligence learned that the agent who dispatched him
was the Hezbollah operations chief, Imad Mughniyah.[4] And, as if there
were not enough indications that this was not an accident but rather a
terrorist attack, the first anniversary of the event was celebrated by the Islamic resistance movement in southern Lebanon by means of yet another
act of suicide terrorism, which sought to repeat the spectacular murderousness of the first one. This time it was not difficult to identify it as such,
and it was listed as the fourth suicide attack in the notorious heritage of
Hezbollah, which called the first attack the "Haibar Operation." The organization described the terrorist as someone "whose blood heralded the
dawn of Islamic martyrdom in our time."

Notwithstanding the above discussion about the first appearance of
suicide terrorism, many scholars date it centuries earlier. Most of the
publications about suicide terrorism begin by claiming that there is nothing new about the phenomenon, and that its present manifestations are
merely an extension of a tradition that began in antiquity, traversed the
Middle Ages, and reached the modern age.[5]

Two cases regularly star in the all too often repeated list of historical precedents. The first is the Sicarii, who were active in Judaea/Palestine in the second half of the first century AD. They were the most extreme regional opponents of the Roman Empire, which oppressed the ancient Jews, thwarting their national aspirations for political autonomy and rejecting their demand to hold religious rites in their temple in Jerusalem without the imposition of pagan elements. By assassinating representatives of the foreign military regime, especially Jewish notables of the moderate, allegedly nonpatriotic camp, the Sicarii provoked increased political and religious oppression at the hand of the Romans and inner conflicts among the factions in Judaea. Thus they triggered futile revolt against the Roman legions and civil war. The result was catastrophic: devastation and exile, recorded in traumatic Jewish memory as the destruction of the Second Temple.[6]

The second case is the Assassins (*Khashashin*) from the Nizari sect of the Ismaili Shiites, who murdered Sunni Muslim rulers and notables, especially representatives of the Turkish Seljuk Empire, as well as European crusaders, in regions of what is now Syria and Iran, from the end of the eleventh to the end of the thirteenth century. Their mission was to rid Islam of the infidels and heretics who deviated from orthodoxy. They gathered in isolated garrison communities in the mountains, a kind of federation of small city-states (the best known among them was the Alamut fortress), and from there they would make sorties to the urban administrative centers where they established secret cells and were assisted by collaborators among the ruling establishment. In the end they were defeated by Arab and Mongol armies.[7]

These classic cases have a common denominator reminiscent of several central characteristics of suicide terrorism. First of all, they are striking examples of religious zealotry.[8] They are marked by an esoteric theology that entailed a messianic doctrine, and they also possessed cultic characteristics expressed in a very demanding ritual system. The Sicarii, who believed that after the catastrophe, complete redemption was assured, were trying to bring on the end-time. They acted in the vicinity of the temple, during pilgrimages, and on the Sabbath, and their targets were chosen from the priesthood. The Assassins' act of killing had a sacramental quality, and their project was driven by millenarian impulse and a promise of imminent paradise. They also committed their murders on festival days and in and around palaces. Both cases were a mixture of a secret religious order and a violent, subversive band. They were surrounded by a romantic aura of heroic mystery, which was nourished by uncertainty regarding the historical details. Both cases have been a focus of fierce controversy. To this day, opinions in the respective local cultures are polarized. Some (usually among the militants) see them as models for imitation, while the more moderate (usually the majority) regard them as bizarre, not to say outrageous and revolting, criminals.

Another important feature found in the two historical cases is highly relevant to suicide terrorism—the aggressor acted with cunning and a degree of treachery. He disguised himself and deceivingly mingled with his target group, until he attained intimate closeness with his intended victim, which was when, very efficiently, he committed the deed. Josephus, who is in fact almost the sole historiographical source regarding the Sicarii,[9] states that they used to behave like ordinary citizens in the narrow alleys of the markets of Jerusalem, while hiding a short dagger (*sica*) under the folds of their cloaks. The sources on the Assassins, which are also biased, tell how they penetrated into the deepest recesses of their intended victims' strongholds in the guise of servants and janitors or, ironically, as bodyguards. In time, after they had acquired the full trust of the rulers, at the proper moment, when the man in power was defenseless, they would draw their daggers and strike. According to one tradition, the Assassins were contemptuous of killing at a distance or indirectly, as by shooting an arrow or by poison, and they used to remain at the scene of the murder until they were discovered by the followers of their victims, who killed them on the spot. Later folklore that developed around this medieval tradition makes an interesting claim: that the Assassins' challenge was not only operational—how to approach the target—but also psychological—how to overcome the inhibitions deriving from the sympathy that might develop between the attacker and his victim after they had spent time in each other's company.

These historical cases can be defined by a term used by contemporary researchers: a "zero range" violent attack. Zero range is also a necessary but insufficient condition for the definition of suicide terrorism. Some researchers call such historical cases "high-risk" violent attacks, or by another term: "no-escape" violent attack. Suicide terrorism also fits the latter definitions, but they are not exhaustive.

There are several other, more recent, historical analogies of zero-range or no-escape terrorism. These ostensible precedents, like the earlier classical examples, are spectacular. First was the socialist Narodnaya Volya, which was active in Russia at the end of the nineteenth century. Its activities climaxed in the assassination of Czar Alexander II. Its members were usually caught because of the short range of their guns and flaws in their explosives, and they were sentenced to death.[10] Second were Japanese kamikaze pilots in World War II, who crashed their planes into US ships and sank them.[11] Finally, there were the young Iranian *basiji*, the so-called Key Boys, who, exposed and enthusiastic, raced into Iraqi minefields in the Shatt al-Arab War of 1980–88. Hoping that, after their death, the gates of paradise would be open for them, they cleared the way for elite troops to advance and attack without obstacles.[12]

Actually none of the above examples from the distant and recent past are instances of suicide terrorism in the sense that this book focuses on it. Some are political assassinations, with a personal, defined, and eminent target, as with the Sicarii, the Assassins, and the Narodnaya Volya. Others are not acts of violence against citizens in the rear, but against soldiers at the front in a declared war, which is the case of the kamikaze, who were actually soldiers, or perhaps a unique variant of airborne guerrillas. As for the Shiite Key Boys, they, too, were not actually citizens, and their aggression was only indirect and not aimed at citizens.

Even if the cases mentioned above partake of terrorism, it is face-to-face terrorism and, as a result, high-risk terrorism, and sometimes even no-escape terrorism. However, there is still no reason to accept the prevalent tendency to use concepts such as close-range, very dangerous terrorism as a synonym for *suicide* terrorism. For none of the previous cases necessitates the death of the attacker, though they all usually do entail a high probability of the attacker's being killed in action. The distinction between extremely risky terrorism and suicide terrorism is often overlooked. Thus most known historical instances of terrorism are wrongly taken to be suicide terrorism.[13]

During the intifada, the counterterrorism agencies in Israel drew a distinction between suicide terrorism and what they called "sacrificial attacks." At that time they noted that the profile of the suicide terrorist was different from that of the sacrificial attacker. Among other things, the latter were of a far more autonomous, assertive, and active personality type than the former. The erroneous tendency to identify terrorism at point-blank range, high-risk terrorism, and terrorism with no escape as suicide terrorism is taken ad absurdum in the frequently heard argument that, in fact, "it is difficult to think of terrorist movements that have not engaged in suicide missions."[14] Some scholars even maintain that anyone who chooses to commit a terrorist attack against a well-defended target, especially if he knows in advance that the target collective will try him and sentence him to death, is in fact a suicide terrorist. In contrast to these claims, I argue that suicide terrorism is significantly different from other kinds of terrorism. It is a unique, contemporary, and unprecedented phenomenon.

Most of the cases discussed above resemble suicide terrorism in their enormous deadly effect, which is based on the attacker's ability to choose and switch his target in real time, to get extremely close to the target, and to control the timing of the attack, on the one hand, and in their freedom from the need to maximize the attacker's chances of coming out alive, on the other hand. (Incidentally, this kind of terrorism also has conspicuous disadvantages.)[15] The similarity between suicide terrorism and the examples to which it is compared brings out the features that distinguish them, which might otherwise escape our attention. Seeing suicide terrorism as sui generis, and emphasis on the difference between it and rather similar types of terrorism, opens up questions that have not been discussed heretofore, such as that of the connection between the attacker and his or her victim.

Vive la Petite Différence

Unlike the comparable cases mentioned above, suicide terrorism has five unique characteristics:[16]

> First, the death of the attacker has an intrinsic importance, and must not be conceived only as a tactical necessity, an operative means, but as an objective, having a value in and of itself.
> Second, the attacker's death is certain, and is acknowledged as such from the outset.
> Third, the attacker's death is caused by himself and is of his own free will. The attacker must be the agent of his own death—he must

actively kill himself rather than being killed by the other side in reaction or by his dispatchers.

Fourth, the attacker dies simultaneously with his victims after being
with them in the same place for some time.

Fifth, there must be a principled (and accounted for) mutual dependence between the attacker's and the victims' death.

Only in the case of suicide terrorism is the death of the terrorist assured
and decreed in advance; it is known to himself, to his handlers, and, in a
vague and peculiar sense, perhaps to his potential victims as well. In all
the kinds of terrorism mentioned above, it was likely that the operation
would end with the death of the terrorist, but, at least hypothetically, that
might not happen. Both in the case of the Assassins and the Key Boys,
even if the chance that the attacker might survive was infinitesimal, it was
still a possibility.

There is an essential and critical difference between a possibility esti-
mated in advance to be very small and a probability of absolute zero. It
is the difference between open-endedness, though the uncertainty is negligible, and an ending that is hermetically sealed, the difference between a
future with some degree of mystery and doubt, and a future predictable in
all its most minute details. This is also the difference between a modicum
of hope, perhaps illusory, and the absence of any optimism, giving up life
without a struggle, indeed, making an active initiative to part with it. This
is why the suicide terrorist is naturally linked with a culture of death. Decisive empirical evidence of the suicide terrorist's certainty of death is the
holding of a funeral with rites of bereavement *before* the attack is actually
launched. Furthermore, the recording of a testament as the ceremonial
initiation of the mission, which assures the terrorist's desired death, is a
substantial element in suicide terrorism.

In terms of the prospect theory,[17] in all the analogous types of terrorism mentioned above the attacker's death is a matter of probability, which
might be very high, whereas the death of the suicide terrorist is a certainty.
From the psychological and sociological point of view, the difference between 99.9 percent and 100 percent is a quantum leap. Probability and
certainty are entirely different frames of mind, and, with the transition
from one to the other, an essential change occurs in the definition of the
situation.

Two notorious instances of terrorism in the Middle East are the murder of the Egyptian president Anwar Sadat in 1981 by Khalid Islambouli, and the murder of the Israeli prime minister Yitzhak Rabin by Yigal Amir in 1995. These were high-risk, zero-range terrorist attacks, but by no means were they acts of suicide terrorism, and not because, in both cases, the murderer survived the attack. The latter outcome was a matter of luck (and the failure of the VIP's bodyguards to act quickly enough to prevent the attack). Had the Muslim Islambouli or the Jewish Amir been killed in action, their death would not have made their attack suicidal.

In some terrorist attacks, the perpetrator's death is regarded as a failure; in others, the death of the perpetrator is accepted as an operational necessity; and there are attacks that seek the perpetrator's death and glorify it. Sometimes it is possible to carry out the murderous mission without causing the terrorist's death, meaning that it is not essential to the mission, but, nevertheless, the person who plans to kill also aspires to die. In contrast to the implications of analogous historical cases, and to the three alternative definitions (zero-range, high-risk, no-escape), in suicide terrorism, the attacker's death is not just a means but also an end with intrinsic value. In suicide terrorism, the attacker's death is a sanctified principle conveying an ethical message. His death gives him a moral advantage over his victims and the sanction to kill them.

The unique notion of mandatory death in suicide terrorism is thrown into relief by contrasting it with moral dilemmas characteristic of regular armies in modern nation-states. It is acknowledged that commanding officers may legitimately send soldiers—for example, elite commando units manned by volunteers—on missions entailing dubious chances of survival, but they do not arrogate to themselves the right to send soldiers to certain death, known in advance, even if success in the mission is of paramount importance.[18] In the spirit of this argument, it is difficult to imagine liberal democratic governments recognized in the international community that would dispatch suicide terrorists.

In suicide terrorism the death of the terrorist is just as important as the death of his target group. It is the crux of the matter. The death of the attacker along with his victims is so vital that in the rare cases when the terrorist remains alive, the mission can be called a partial failure. Willingness to die is not enough. The test is actual death. A rather strange illustration of this is found in the case of a Palestinian suicide terrorist who blew himself up in the midst of a group of Jews. There were a number of casualties among them, yet he, unexpectedly, was gravely wounded but saved by Israeli physicians. When he regained consciousness, in great disappointment of staying alive, he insisted on regarding himself as a dead person.

Even when the terrorist dies, if his death is not bound up immediately and physically with the death of his victims, and, more important, if his death is not caused as a direct result of his action but as an indirect consequence—that is, as the result of other people's reactions to his deed—it cannot be defined unreservedly as suicide terrorism. This view reflects the understanding of the suicide terrorist, at least in the Palestinian case, that he should take his own life, retaining sole control and absolute responsibility for his death, and neither entrust nor abandon his fate to his enemies.

Technical examination of several incidents of suicide terrorism in Israel as well as incidents mainly in countries where counterterrorism measures are ineffective, such as Iraq, shows that it would have been possible to employ ordinary means of terrorism, such as planting a disguised booby trap at the site, with the same degree of effectiveness, that is, killing the same number of people. Nevertheless, the method of terrorism that entails the death of the attacker along with his victims was preferred because of its symbolic value. It is also argued that the terrorist's interest in his own death projects to his enemies that no deterrent will be effective, and this fills them with paralyzing fear.

Suicide terrorism is distinguished by agency reserved solely to the suicide terrorist. In his death, the Palestinian suicide terrorist enjoys the privilege of agency, of which he is usually deprived in life, either because of his subordinate social status or because he is subject to a regime of military occupation. Activating the explosive charge attached to the terrorist's body by the terrorist himself is the ultimate proof of the killer's voluntary choice of death, of his mastery of his own fate, of his self-sufficiency and excellence. The ideal suicide terrorist, particularly in the Middle East, emphasizes his free will by his insistence, and that of the organization behind him, on not activating the explosive from a distance. Self-activation does have tactical advantages as well, because it makes possible an explosion in a time and place that promise maximal slaughter. However, activation from a distance by the suicide terrorist's handlers (for example, sending an electronic signal by a lookout's cell phone) can make certain that the explosion will take place. It has happened that suicide terrorists approached the target and withdrew without blowing themselves up, sometimes because of a technical slipup or because they were discovered and neutralized, but also because they were struck by fear or remorse at the last minute. Following several such cases, during the intifada persistent rumors spread in the region implying that the Palestinians were in doubt as to whether self-activation of the suicide terrorist's explosives was preferable to activation from a distance. The Israeli security services regarded self-activation as testimony to the cowardice of the minders and handlers and their desire to avoid moral and legal responsibility. The Palestinian organizations, in contrast, emphasized their preference for self-activation as an expression of the human bomb's autonomy, heroism, and admirable values.

The question of agency takes on an acute dimension against the background of reports heard on both sides of the Israeli-Palestinian conflict regarding suicide terrorists that the mission had been imposed on them directly or indirectly. The folklore of regional terrorism tells of the drivers of car bombs who were sent to their target with their hands shackled to the wheel.[19] The latter are no more suicide terrorists than are the Shiites in southern Lebanon who drove trucks in the areas of confrontation with the IDF without even knowing they were going to explode, according to the plan of those who sent them, who maintained radio contact in order to activate the explosive device concealed in the baggage compartment.[20] There are many stories, some of them confirmed, about Palestinian terrorists who were accused of collaboration with Israeli intelligence and given the alternative of public execution or accepting a suicide mission, which would be a form of atonement and rehabilitation. There is rich documentation of numerous variations on the same theme regarding female Palestinian suicide terrorists who were involved in an illicit erotic relationship (premarital or extramarital), and suicide terrorism was offered to them as an honorable way of escaping a life of shame and ostracism in their puritanical, patriarchal society.[21] The definition of the cases described here as suicide terrorism must be qualified.

Practically speaking, it would be possible to attach a timer to the explosives on the terrorist's body to prevent any last minute doubts and turning him into a ticking bomb in the literal sense of the term. However, in all recorded cases of suicide terrorism, the human bomb was both the weapon and its operator. ISA reports of a number of intercepted telephone conversations between Palestinian suicide terrorists and their handlers at the last moments before the explosion show that sometimes negotiations ensued between the terrorist, who was stricken by panic in the target area, and representatives of the terrorist organization, who exerted heavy pressure—including threats and vain promises—to prevent him from reneging.

The following distinction also appears to be tactical or technical, but in fact it entails another expression of the issue of agency, which is of essential importance in suicide terrorism. Like the previous one, this distinction is also made explicitly by the suicide terrorist and his handlers. This is the distinction between an act of terrorism committed by firing an automatic weapon (or throwing grenades) and one that is carried out by blowing up an explosive charge. All of these are zero-range, no-escape lethal attacks. In either spraying the target group with bullets or exploding a charge attached to the terrorist's body, it is difficult to imagine that the terrorist would survive. In the first instance, he would be killed by the adversary's security forces or by armed citizens who happened to be present, or by blunt instruments like pieces of furniture that might be available. One way or another, the initiative would be with the party that was attacked, a somewhat delayed reaction, though it might be a matter of less than a minute. Several potential suicide terrorists preferred to blow themselves up, although it meant forgoing a small chance of escaping alive.[22] They adopted the value hierarchy of the Palestinian resistance movement, according to which in suicide terrorism worthy of its name the terrorist plays an active role in killing himself as well. This normative perspective is unmistakable in the differential subsidization of various kinds of terrorism. Islamic charity funds (as well as Saddam Hussein, when he was the ruler of Iraq) offered financial rewards to the families of "martyrs" who fell in the Middle Eastern struggle. The family of a suicide terrorist would receive $25,000, whereas those killed in any other action initiated against the Israeli occupation would receive only $10,000.[23]

Al-Amaliyat al-Istish'hadiya

The *shahada* (literally, "testimony" in Arabic) is the Islamic credo, comprising a declaration of the uniqueness of Allah ("There is no God except Allah") and the Prophet's divine mission ("and Muhammad is his

Prophet"). Repetition of this sentence and its recitation out loud is one of the pillars of Islam—the five basic commandments required of the believer. The testimony is repeated both in the call to prayer and in the prayer itself, several times a day, as well as on special occasions such as the conversion ceremony, coming of age, and the deathbed. The *shahada* is the believer's verbal testimony to the greatness of God or to the strength of his belief in God. The believer can also bear witness to this in action. Giving one's life to protect the honor of Islam and one's faith, as well as protecting the interests of believers, is also *shahada*. Just as martyrdom (derived from the Greek word for "witness") is the Christian believer's death in testimony to his belief, so too *istishhad* is the Muslim believer's death in testimony to his God and his faith. The Muslim parallel to the Christian martyr is the *shahid* (plural, *shuhada*). The *shahid* must be distinguished from the *istishhadi* (plural, *istishhadiyn*), who is an active martyr, that is, a believer who seeks to die for Islam. Hence, suicide terrorists are called *istishhadiyn*. In Arabic, *amaliyat istish'hadiya* refers to the action by which a person becomes a *shahid*, that is, the way by which he bears witness to his God and his faith. In the Palestinian vernacular used in the West Bank and the Gaza Strip, *al-amaliyat al-istish'hadiya* is the idiom for what in the West is termed a suicide terrorism operation.

A religious conception lay behind the preference for Palestinian suicide terrorism as expressed in the financial reward, making a distinction between two types of death for the honor of Islam. Scholars of suicide terrorism, including that of the Palestinians, usually ignored a tradition according to which there were two levels of martyrdom, called by different names, with different status in this world, and especially in the world to come. A *shahid* is a Muslim who is killed in connection with his religion or because of it. Usually this is a passive death, inflicted by opposition to Islam. Hence, any Palestinian killed by IDF gunfire, even if by mistake, is a shahid. In contrast, the title "*istishhadi*" is reserved for those who incur mortal danger voluntarily on behalf of Islam.

This distinction of *istishhad* is rooted in classical Islam, but in the past generation it has become sharper, with a shift of emphasis from Arab Muslim victimhood to heroic activism. "*Istishhad*" is a grammatical construction based on the verb "*shahada*." This semantic move transfers emphasis from martyrdom to the active pursuit of martyrdom, an innovative development of an old concept. This creative interpretation—both linguistic and ideological—of a familiar motive has led purists and apologists to declare that it is incorrect, non-Islamic. Every *istishhadi* is automatically a *shahid,* but not every *shahid* is an *istishhadi.* Above and beyond the *shahada* is the *istishhad,* which refers to the vanguard who sacrifice themselves intentionally. *Istishhadiyn* are active seekers of martyrdom, giving the suicide terrorist and his family a place close to the throne of the Prophet in paradise. The first Palestinian suicide terrorist, Taher Tamam, a twenty-four-year-old resident of Nablus, a student at An-Najah University, who blew himself up next to a bus at a refreshment stand in the Jordan Valley (April 1995), is known as "Amir Istishhadi-yun" (prince of the martyrs). Though there were no Israeli casualties, he was guaranteed eternal life with all the pleasures of paradise. Following the first cluster of suicide terrorist attacks, the spiritual leader of Hamas, Ahmad Yassin, decreed that every suicide terrorist who received a blessing from an authorized sheikh would be regarded as an *istishhadi* (March 1995).[24]

In one of the murderous attacks in the early part of the al-Aqsa Intifada, Palestinian terrorists stole a car and drove it rapidly into the busy downtown area of an outlying Israeli city. There they fired in every direction and killed and wounded customers in the shopping center, until they were stopped and killed by policemen and armed guards.[25] In Israel this incident was not classified as suicide terrorism, while among the Palestinians a dispute arose as to whether to define the attackers as suicide terrorists and to reward the perpetrators accordingly. Those who maintained there was no difference between the cases were a minority. Some Palestinian terrorists who were going to be sent out for an attack by gunfire prepared for their mission as though they were suicide terrorists, including recording a testament in advance, but following their death certain authorities in the territories decreed that they were only second-order martyrs, that is to say, *shahids* and not *istishhadiyn,* because they did not carry explosive charges on their bodies.[26]

A somewhat parallel disagreement arose in Israel regarding the Jewish settler Dr. Baruch Goldstein, who opened fire massively on Arabs praying in the area reserved for Muslims in the Cave of the Patriarchs in Hebron (1994). The Jewish terrorist was killed by some of the survivors remaining in the mosque. They fell on him with fists and beat him to death with fire extinguishers when he stopped shooting for a moment, apparently to change magazines. After the slaughter, the question arose as to whether the Orthodox Jewish zealot could be called a suicide terrorist. This question, which was discussed heatedly by politicians, journalists, and intellectuals, also had echoes in the academy among scholars of terrorism, in the wake of another case of Jewish terrorism, when an IDF soldier who was AWOL opened fire on bus passengers in the heart of an Israeli Arab town, killing four and wounding a dozen more before a local mob beat him to death.[27]

Propagandists of the Palestinian terrorist organizations tended to praise certain perpetrators as being alone responsible for activating the explosive charge, so that it would be possible to represent them as suicide terrorists, although some signs indicated that the definition might not fit them. In many cases of Palestinian terrorism the degree of the terrorist's agency and consequently his definition as a suicide terrorist remained doubtful after the explosion, and in a certain sense it was hard to define the responsibility for his action even during the terrorist attack, from its first stages to its very last ones. In a significant portion of the incidents listed as Palestinian suicide terrorism in Israel, heavy pressure was exerted on the individual chosen to carry out the mission. This pressure was social and psychological, subtle and indirect, or coarse and direct in the form of shaming and threat. The pressure was exerted not only in the home base, in the West Bank and Gaza—during the stages of conscription and training and in the stage of mental, religious, and operational preparation—but also after the border crossing, in the enemy territory of Israel, as the terrorist approached the target. The suicide terrorist was usually accompanied by handlers appointed by the organization to help him with transportation, get through checkpoints, find his way in unfamiliar areas, and identify the target. The Israeli security agencies were convinced that the purpose of the close escorting was not only logistical; it was also meant to ensure that the terrorist would not abandon his intention to blow himself up in the midst of the target group. The handlers learned from experience that the place and time when the terrorist was left alone to go on by himself were critical. When a terrorist was sent from a relatively distant place, and he had to face operational difficulties as well as isolation and fear, he was liable to crack. Sometimes the terrorist was left alone only a few minutes and a few dozen meters away from the target. The ISA learned to analyze the success or failure of attacks in terms of the escorts' and supervisors' distance from the target. In the attack on the Sbarro pizzeria in Jerusalem in August 2001, which left twenty people dead, the woman who escorted the suicide terrorist came so close that she herself was wounded in the explosion.[28] At least one incident is known (May 2002, Rishon LeZion) in which the suicide terrorist got cold feet precisely at the point where the explosion was planned, and his handler had to come and encourage or force him to finish the task.

Far Fewer Suicide Terrorism Cases Than Generally Thought

Underlining the attacker's control over his own death, as well as the simultaneity of the attacker's and victims' death, sharpens and narrows the definition of suicide terrorism. Applying this double criterion significantly restricts the range of acts that can be included in the category of suicide terrorism.[29] Several phenomena that are conventionally taken to be prime examples of suicide terrorism do not, according to our understanding, deserve that title.

It is within this context that I view a form of terrorist attack that has become popular in recent years, mainly in Iraq and Syria: car bombs. These are seen and recorded almost automatically as suicide terrorism, although in some of them this is not the case. Occasionally the driver manages to park the vehicle near the target and escape before the explosion is triggered from a distance or with a timer,[30] and sometimes the driver is spotted and killed by the defense forces of the target community and not by the explosion.

Two of the organizations that are regarded as the epitome of suicide terrorism—Hezbollah in Lebanon and the Liberation Tigers of Tamil Eelam (LTTE) in Sri Lanka—are discussed below to illustrate the need to qualify prevalent estimates of the scale of suicide terrorism. Indeed, in another essay I pointed out the necessity of qualifying the inclusion of these movements in the category of suicide terrorism, because to certain degree they are not terrorist organizations.[31] Hezbollah is essentially a guerrilla movement, a militia that fights against military forces, mainly the IDF. As for the LTTE, a significant part of its operations were aimed at specific prominent officials, such as generals, party leaders, presidential candidates, the president, and even a world leader, the prime minister of

India, Rajiv Gandhi. Hence a large part of their actions should be classi-fied as political assassinations.

Let us dwell further on the case of LTTE, regarded as a suicide ter-rorism movement par excellence. Among other things, the astronomical number of five hundred human bombs is attributed to the Tamil Tigers.[32] To this are added exaggerated reports that have the Tamil Tigers boast-ing about cyanide pills worn around their necks. True, the LTTE did de-velop a mystique of death, and there were many instances of suicide. Some members of the organization, imprisoned by the Sinhalese, even starved themselves to death.[33] But suicide was not an organic, necessary, and cen-tral part of Tamil terrorism. A considerable number of the organization's operations, which are listed as acts of suicide terrorism, were shooting or grenade attacks from which the attacker could flee or which left at least some possibility of flight, even if it often failed. Hence, these were zero-range attacks with very high risk, but not acts of suicide terrorism. When they were able to carry out a mission, survive, and escape, they preferred to do so. Many cases of Tamil Tiger suicide were neither simultaneous with the killing of members of the target community nor dependent on it. Instead, they were meant to prevent the attacker's capture.

Against the background of Hezbollah and the LTTE, the Palestinian national-religious movements Hamas and the Islamic Jihad stand out be-cause most of the attacks classified as suicide terrorism during the intifada were exactly that. This is yet another reason to concentrate on Palestinian suicide terrorism.

The reductionist definition presented here changes the statistics. The number of instances that can be included in a global list of suicide ter-rorist attacks fitting my definition comes to about half of what is claimed in the literature.[34] Suicide terrorism is the most murderous, the most dramatic, and the most famous kind. It is also the hardest to prevent. However, it is the least common of all types of terrorism. Other typi-cal aspects of suicide terrorism make it a more complex and intriguing phenomenon than it might seem. For example, it is a form of armed violence in which the attacker places himself within the target group, and the face-to-face situation between him and his victims is usually not restricted to a fraction of a second. Rather it may be prolonged for sev-eral seconds, minutes, or even longer. This situation makes it possible for the two sides to be aware of one another, at least superficially. Even if no words are exchanged, most likely glances are exchanged, and maybe even fragments of impressions of each other are formed. At least a minimal communication is created between them. The suicide terrorist, for his part, can develop a kind of attitude toward his potential victims in general and a specific relationship—negative or positive—toward individuals among them, so that he might chose to get close to some of them and not to others and thus to determine their fate.[35] In the area of the suicide terrorist's target, an illusion of community develops, even a kind of elementary and momentary intimacy between the attacker and his victims, which is based on the suicide terrorist's disguise. There is an aspect of secrecy, deception, and treachery in the nature of suicide terrorism, which I discuss in other chapters.

The Human Bomb's Subversive Project

At the very inception of suicide terrorism, in the mid-1980s, in southern Lebanon, the leaders of Hezbollah were alert to its effect, not only the bloodshed it caused, but also the total confusion on the Israeli side. Sheikh Salah a-Din Arqa said that suicide terrorism "caused an upheaval among the Jews, making them lose their way." ISA agents described the effect of suicide terrorism when it first began in a similar way, as "breaking all the vessels," which in modern Hebrew means the breaking of all the rules of the game, causing absolute disorder.[36]

The root of the anarchic nature of suicide terrorism lies in the subtle parallelism and macabre proximity between the attacker and his victim. Between Anna and 'Abed there existed, in an uncanny way, a degree of intimacy.

Terrorism in general breaks down customary barriers and nullifies fundamental oppositions. It blurs the boundaries of the human body and binds one body to another.[37] Furthermore, terrorism is a hybrid phenomenon straddling the line separating the front from the rear, the military from the civilian, war from peace.[38] Suicide terrorism in particular breaks down all of these barriers and nullifies all of these oppositions in extreme fashion, even breaking down further binary formulas and more elementary dichotomies. The effectiveness of suicide terrorism derives not only from its extreme lethality, but also from its dual nature and inner tensions that confound the coordinates of the target collective's self-definition and threaten the foundations of its social order. Disorientation, insecurity, paralysis—these are not just by-products of suicide terrorism. They are its central objectives. It is commonly argued that coercion is the paramount objective of suicide bombing.[39] I argue that the suicide terrorist is no less subversive than coercive.

First, the suicide terrorist deconstructs the distinction between Palestinian and Israeli because he is a hybrid creature disguised as the polar opposite of what he really is. A male suicide terrorist can also disguise himself as a woman and thus challenge differences in gender. He evidently confounds the essential distinction between life and death, being a curious mix of a living-dead and dead-living. Typically he is already dead in life and also living after his death. To these we may add briefly the simultaneous embodiment of the operator of a weapon and the weapon itself, the violent person and the instrument of his violence, the man and the machine, and the living human flesh with organic limbs and the metal, plastic, and synthetic parts.

Theoretically it is possible to implant an explosive charge *within* the terrorist's body—beneath his skin or in one of his digestive organs—by means of surgical intervention. With respect to biotechnology, this is not impossible.[40] Operationally it could certainly improve the terrorist's chances of reaching his target without arousing suspicion. The result would be a perfect suicide terrorist, the epitome of a human bomb. He would activate the explosive—his own body—by means of an electronic device connected to a thin wire that would dangle out of a stitched and scabbed wound in his flesh. I do not know of the actual existence of any extreme case like this.[41] However, according to published reports, the idea has been discussed in inner forums of suicide terrorism organizations throughout the world, has been presented as a possible scenario in the situational evaluations of counterterrorism establishments in the West, and was even discussed by airline companies as a threat that could require changes in the security checks of passengers.[42] Suicide terrorists who are very thin are likely to be discovered, because the explosive charge strapped to their bodies bulges out, especially in the Middle Eastern summer, which rules out disguising the explosives under a heavy coat.[43] On a Palestinian poster hung on the walls during the intifada, a freedom fighter is shown opening his mouth to swallow a hand grenade, and, on another poster, a female suicide terrorist pretends to be pregnant, while the explosive charge is hidden in her belly. The explosion is giving birth, as it were.

That is what took place in March 2002 when the Palestinian female suicide terrorist Andaleeb Takatkah set out on a mission in the Mahane Yehuda open produce market in Jerusalem. She bound the explosive charge to her chest and stomach, pretending to be pregnant. A widespread rumor in the West Bank has it that she was indeed pregnant as a result of extramarital relationship with a local Tanzim operative. After pushing into the crowd among the stalls, she blew herself up. Six people were killed with her, and dozens wounded. A few days later Agi Mish'ol, an acclaimed Israeli poet, wrote a poem entitled "Shahida" ("Woman Martyr").[44]

> You are only twenty
> and your first pregnancy is an exploding bomb.
> Under your broad skirt you are pregnant with dynamite
> and metal shavings. This is how you walk in the market,
> ticking among the people, you, Andaleeb Takatkah.
>
> Someone changed the workings in your head
> and launched you toward the city;
> . . . you chose a bakery.
> And there you pulled the trigger inside yourself,
> and together with the Sabbath loaves,
> sesame and poppy seed,
> you flung yourself into the sky.
>
> Together with Rebecca Fink you flew up
> with Yelena Konreeb from the Caucasus
> and Nissim Cohen from Afghanistan
> and Suhila Houshy from Iran[45]
> and two Chinese you swept along
> to death.[46]

In an interview, Mish'ol said she was drawn at first to the sound of the terrorist's name, Takatkah, which seemed like an onomatopoeia for the ticking of a bomb.[47] Literary critics pointed out the theme of disguise—the sign of a new life that hides death. Also mentioned were, first, the identification of the human body with the murderous mechanism, as expressed in the image of the martyr as a warhead, in which, before it is launched, the time and place of the explosion are set. Second, the maelstrom of death into which the attacker and her victims were swept—all marginal in their respective communities.

A terrorist who carries the bomb in a pack on his back or a suitcase in his hand is also regarded as a suicide terrorist. But he occupies a slightly lower level of prestige than the one who straps the charge onto his body—usually his chest and stomach—with tape or a belt. The latter appears as a global image of the suicide terrorist, embodying the mythic expressions of suicide terrorism, especially among the Palestinians. Children in refugee camps in the West Bank, who dressed up as suicide terrorists in carnivalesque political processions, never carried their fake explosive charges in their hands or on their backs, but wore distinctive vests on their bodies. This is also true of the posters that glorify suicide terrorists in Palestinian cities and villages. The explosive belt, as distinct from the bomb in a bag, makes it very difficult to separate the man from the bomb, and thus practically impossible to slip out of the mission. The explosive belt creates a fullness of form, body-like, and it testifies to fullness of awareness, that is, unconditional identification with the murderous mission. The explosive belt makes preparations more complicated and expensive, but the organizations that dispatch the terrorists regarded it as preferable operationally, especially since it testified to a higher degree of dedication on the part of the terrorists themselves. Therefore it was also preferable on ideological grounds. An important activist in suicide terror expressed reservations about explosive belts—mainly because they necessitate the use of relatively small charges, which cause limited slaughter compared to a backpack or suitcase—but he added that he gave in to the exigencies of the tradition that had already been formed in the organization.[48] In current Palestinian culture the explosive belt became a sanctified ritual accoutrement. In parallel, a kind of intimacy developed between the body of the terrorist and his means of murder, as expressed sometimes in the stage of preparation for the mission, when the appointed suicide terrorist did not receive a finished belt at the last moment but took part in acquiring and assembling it. Of the approximately two hundred Palestinian suicide attacks, about 20 percent were executed by means of explosive vests, 20 percent were committed with car bombs, and another 14 percent employed backpacks or suitcases carried by the terrorists.[49] There is some similarity between the human bomb and a bionic man, half born of woman and half robot, a man with artificial limbs or eyes, with synthetic blood, and his power and abilities are unlimited. Some people compare the suicide terrorist to a cyborg, a creature that is no longer futuristic and imaginary, but part of the existing technological reality that functions in military contexts as a human-machine weapon system, and also in civilian contexts as a self-regulating organism that combines natural and artificial together in one unit.[50] The suicide terrorist blurs the boundary between conventional and unconventional warfare. Islamic suicide terrorists, somewhat like versions of Dr. Strangelove, ride on a bomb and think in terms of Judgment Day. Erasing the boundary between man and killing machine leads to behavior peculiar to the suicide terrorist. For example, the suicide terrorist's handlers instruct him to spread his arms out to the sides at the moment of the explosion so that his flesh will not diminish the impact of the explosion and block the flying pieces of metal that are mixed with the explosives, thus maximizing the murderous effect. Of course the direction in which the suicide terrorist turns is important for the results of the attack, because the explosive charge is attached to the front of his body. Hence, those in the target group whom he chooses to look at—thus creating eye contact, which always has a degree of mutuality and perhaps even a spark of humanity—are the ones chosen to be his certain victims.

The suicide terrorist is not a marionette on a string, operated by others. He is a subject with consciousness who imposes his violence on his surroundings and on the other within him. Similarly, the suicide terrorist does not kill only other subjects, but while doing so he also kills himself, as if he were also the other. He is the object of his own violence. In suicide terrorism there is a kind of confrontation between oneself and oneself.[51] The suicide terrorist is both the subject and the object of his murderous act, and thus he also blurs the boundary between subject and object. Furthermore, the subject and the object share the same fate. In other words, the subject becomes part of the object.

In the short time before the explosion and in the short time after it, the suicide terrorist cannot be located. Before the explosion, while he is a living person among the living, he has mingled indistinguishably with those who soon will be killed by him, and after the explosion, when he is a dead man among the dead, his body and theirs are mingled. There is close contact in both the antemortem and the postmortem situations, a mixture and exchange between the human bomb and his target group. As a result, important distinctions break down, those that make the suicide terrorist not only murderous but also destructive of the other's assurance in his personal judgment and agency, striking at his selfhood, and in fact impairing his very otherness. The suicide terrorist acts against the other and thus emphasizes his otherness, but at the same time he blurs and blunts it.

The human bomb undermines the self-confidence of the others and erodes their identity by neutralizing their ability to distinguish between friend and foe, like fighter pilots and tank commanders immersed in the chaos of battle, who urgently need this basic classification in order to function. This is also the distinction between us and them, which is so crucial in situations of existential confrontation between groups, especially when their collective identity requires sharpening and their solidarity demands reinforcement. Both in the stage when he passes as an Israeli on his way to the scene of the carnage and while penetrating it, and also in the stage when he is lying dead and mutilated among dead and mangled Israelis, the suicide terrorist makes it very difficult for the Jews to separate themselves from him and in general to distinguish themselves from all Gentiles, and, more specifically and crucially, from Palestinian Arabs.

The challenge to the distinction between attacker and victim undermines the foundations of human society. In any instance of suicide the attacker and victim are bound to and identified with one another. Certainly suicide is an aggressive act, since the attacker is the victim of his aggression. But in suicide terrorism the essential connection between aggressor and victim becomes unique and more complex in several senses. First, of course, while striking at himself, the suicide terrorist also strikes at other victims. Thus he becomes *another* victim of aggression with many victims, sharing their fate, one of them. Second, according to the suicide terrorist's conception of himself and the conception of the community from which he comes and in whose name he acts, he was a victim of aggression even before he himself became an aggressor. The Palestinian suicide terrorist is regarded as a victim of the Israeli occupation, and perhaps of his fate as an Arab and a refugee in general, before he is his own victim. This victimhood brought him to aggression. His aggression only expresses and perpetuates his victimhood. Thus, the suicide terrorist's aggression is often presented as fundamentally defensive. The suicide terrorist's double victimhood is seen by many as a justification for his aggression, as a response to the claim that his terrorist act is immoral. The suicide terrorist as a victim is a quid pro quo for his Israeli victims both as aggressors and also as fellow victims. Now the suicide terrorist no longer stands before the Israelis as an attacker before his victims, but as a victim before aggressors, and as a victim alongside the victims. At the scene, latent competition develops between the Israelis and the representative of the Palestinians: Which one is more of a victim than the other? Behind suicide terrorism, which is known as a particularly violent act, lurks the obsession of victimhood. Third, all of the suicide terrorist's victims, including himself, are sacrificial. Viewing the victim as a sacrifice enables us to see more sharply that which distinguishes suicide terrorism from ordinary suicide.

Suicide, Altruistic Suicide, and Protest Suicide

Suicide terrorism's uniqueness is not rooted solely in its operational advantages or its strategic rationale. The added instrumental value of suicide terrorism is not sufficient to explain the phenomenon. The explanation must be sought in its expressive dimension, which brings us to the matter of the suicide intrinsic to this form of terrorism. However, the effort to understand suicide terrorism as a specific kind of suicide is only partially relevant and not particularly productive. This includes what Durkheim called altruistic suicide, which became a remarkably popular analytical tool adopted by researchers into suicide terrorism, and was inappropriately applied to describe and explain the phenomenon.[52] The difference in principle between suicide terrorism and ordinary suicide of various kinds requires us to overcome the temptation to use the huge theoretical, clinical, and statistical data that has accrued regarding suicide to advance understanding of suicide terrorism. First, empirically, the relation between suicide terrorism and suicide is inverse. Where frequency of suicide terrorism is high, the frequency of suicide is relatively low—and this has been verified not only in the Palestinian Arab case. More so, suicide terrorism developed in the Islamic Middle East where cultural and social sanctions against suicide are exceptionally severe. Indeed, the initiators and perpetrators of suicide terrorism found it particularly hard to overcome the taboo against suicide. Moreover, no correlation has been found between suicide terrorists and personal, social, or circumstantial characteristics known to be connected to suicidal tendencies. The human bombs were rather normal both in their mental constitution and in their biographical and demographic traits. It is noteworthy that critiques of suicide terrorism within Palestinian society as well as on the Israeli side have accused the terrorist organizations of exploiting the personal distress of individuals to manipulate them into becoming suicide terrorists and thus solving their personal mental or social problems. In response, spokesmen for the terrorist organizations repeatedly stated that whenever any of the volunteers indicated they were seeking an honorable way to commit suicide, they were immediately rejected. In reality, several cases are known, especially among women, in which their suicidal tendencies were manipulated to serve the project of religious-national terrorism.[53] After all, suicide—even altruistic suicide—is an individual act (which usually offers a solution to personal distress or expresses a personal position), whereas suicide terrorism is first of all a collective act, conceived, planned, and executed by and for a community or organization. As distinguished from any other type of suicide—altruistic suicide included—suicide terrorism is an integral component of a group coproduction, the culmination of a series of collaborative acts by other people. Suicide terrorism is at one and the same time an individual project par excellence and a project that is mobilized by an institution and tightly controlled by that institution. Furthermore, suicide terrorism is performed publicly, in the center of the communal stage, while suicide is generally committed privately.

Indeed, there is an exception to this rule: protest suicide, which has been compared to suicide terrorism.[54] The arena of suicide terrorism is the market, the main street, or the shrine. Certainly suicide terrorism contains a demonstrative political element, and it can be seen as protest. However, historically, protest suicide completely lacks the element of murder directed at others, though it does possess a high degree of provocation and also aggression, which the perpetrator directs against himself. On the contrary, in instances of suicide as political protest—of which the most prominent were that of the student Jan Palach, who protested against the Soviet invasion of Czechoslovakia (Prague 1969), and the

Buddhist monk Thích Quảng Đức, who protested against the persecution of religion during the Vietnam War (Saigon 1963)—there is a decidedly antiviolent element.

Romantic and Exotic Parallels

In March 2015 the world was startled by the mysterious Germanwings plane crash, caused by a copilot who locked himself into the cockpit alone and caused his own death along with the deaths of more than 150 passengers and crew members. The press described this event as "suicide turned into an act of mass murder."[55] The question arose, though, about the connection between the copilot's death and that of the innocent passengers, and the possibility of an act of terrorism was considered, showing lines of similarity between this case and both rampage shooters and other self-destructive shooters (e.g., Columbine) as well as suicide terrorism, claiming that all these cases derived from the psychopathological condition of the perpetrator (who might have suffered from anxiety or bipolar disorder).[56] As explained below, I do not accept this thesis, but it does contain an insight consistent with the argumentation in the present book. The various types of suicidal murderers usually see themselves as victims. Sometimes they see their own victims as directly responsible for their frustrating situation, and sometimes as only indirectly connected, because they represent the factors responsible for the killer's frustration.

I suggest examining the limited analogy between suicide terrorism and another worrisome type of incident, known to us from the past as well as from present-day reality, a human phenomenon to which a great deal of attention and research has been devoted. What can we learn about suicide terrorism from a survey of tragic events that are too often reported in the mass communications media: murder suicide? There are over six hundred such cases a year in the United States alone, with roughly 1,500 casualties. Comparison between suicide terrorism and murder suicide shows some evident similarities and few differences, and will enrich our insight into suicide terrorism.

But first we have to exclude from our examination two types of suicide following a murder because they are absolutely irrelevant to suicide terrorism. One is murder-suicide committed by mentally unstable persons (such as those involved in school shootings). By and large, suicide terrorists are not insane. The attempt to pathologize the suicide terrorist and present his extraordinarily gruesome act in terms of personality disorder amounts to explaining away suicide terrorism and rests on false evidence or no evidence at all. Another type of murder-suicide irrelevant to our current discussion is that in which the murder is incidental to the suicide, that is, the murder is a collateral outcome of the suicide, like driving a car with passengers off a bridge. Contrary to popular opinion, in the large majority of suicide terrorism cases, the suicidal component of the combined act is by no means the primary motive. Valid scientific research shows that suicide terrorists should not be diagnosed as suicidal. Also, statistical data pertaining to US murder-suicide cases convincingly disproves the hypothesis that people with a suicide potentiality nature are prone to murder. Only 5 percent of murders are followed by suicide. And just 1 percent of suicide cases involve murder.

Now, there are two other types of murder-suicide that seem pertinent to my argument. The first is quite telling: a suicide after murder as a form of self-punishment due to a sense of guilt. Through killing himself the murderer seeks repentance. This is interesting though only partly applicable.

On the one hand, the suicide-murderer gives society a certain feeling of satisfaction. He has understood that he deserves severe punishment for his crime, and therefore he takes the initiative and punishes himself by his own hand. Thus he has spared society the need of trying and executing him. Symmetry has been created, and order has been restored to the world, without any need for society to intervene. Justice, as it were, has been done, but society has been deprived of the right, not to say the pleasure, of taking vengeance. Society wants to retain the prerogative of punishing, and denial of this prerogative causes frustration. ZAKA volunteers repeatedly testified to distress and anger because it was impossible to exact retribution from the human bomb for his horrible actions in the name of his victims and of Israelis in general. The human bomb avoided punishment by his enemies, thus increasing their pain.

On the other hand, in several places in this book where the connection between murder and suicide is emphasized, it is suggested that suicide imparts an ethical quality to murder. It diminishes the murderer's responsibility and expunges his guilt. It can even give him moral superiority. Especially in Islamic suicide terrorism, it is something of an act of penitence, following which redemption is promised. The delights of paradise in store for the human bomb are a sign that, in God's eyes, suicide terrorism is a good path to atonement and salvation.

The last type of murder-suicide to be mentioned is analogous to suicide terrorism in a peculiar way that carries heuristic exploratory value. Its stereotypical representative is the humiliated spouse or lover who is betrayed or deserted by his/her partner thus frustrating the latter's desire to remain in the impossible partnership despite everything. By killing the compromising, even objecting, partner and then killing himself, he imposes his will on the other and finally fulfills the wish he failed to fulfill while the two were alive—maintaining the bond—albeit a posthumous one. This way, the frustrated partner guarantees equality (i.e., justice), resemblance, proximity, affinity, as it were, for himself. This is the ultimate revenge, along with lethally enforced intimacy, forever.

Not infrequently these cases (sometimes bordering on crimes of passion—another genre that deserves our attention) are pathetic and tinted with romantic or erotic flavor, though romanticism and eroticism— it should be admitted—are hardly appropriate terms in this context of deadly violence. To push the argument a little further, this kind of murder-suicide is an ironic variant of the case of a joint suicide in the form of killing the other with consent and then killing oneself. In both cases, contrasts notwithstanding, only the simultaneous death of the two sides enables realization of something that was impossible to achieve while the two were alive—union, eternal bond. In the cliché Romeo and Juliet type it was voluntary and mutual, while in the jealous lover type it was violently enforced.

The ZAKA volunteers compared the situation at the arena of suicide terrorism, when the shattered body of the Israeli victim is inextricably attached to the shattered body of the Palestinian attacker, to another kind of event that they encounter as experts in various arenas of unnatural death not connected to the Middle East conflict: the case of a father who commits suicide while hugging his small child in his arms by leaping from the roof of a tall building. In most cases the father is divorced and unable to cope with separation from his family.

Another lesson can be learned about the motive of suicide in suicide terrorism, and about the complex relation between this motive and that of murder in suicide terrorism, from comparison to another somewhat

similar instance. Presentation of the following case will help us understand that suicide terrorism is not merely suicide committed by means of
murder, but also not exactly murder by means of suicide. The following
case of a highly structured act of mass murder by means of suicide can
change its character and become its opposite: highly structured suicide
by means of mass murder. In the end the distinction between suicide and
mass murder is blurred, and they blend. Against this background it is
easier to understand the case of suicide terrorism, in which suicide and
murder are a single bundle, in which neither is the goal or the means, that
is, neither of the two is an instrument for the other.

A perceptive article invites us to learn about an unfamiliar and enthralling phenomenon, suggesting, with anthropological imagination, its
resemblance to suicide terrorism.[57] The phenomenon is called "juramentado," and it takes place among the tribes of the Muslim minority in the
southern Philippines, the Moros, who are distinguished by their violent
culture, in which there is a tendency to slip easily into murder, especially
in response to an insult to honor, and also in bitter rebellion against the
rule of the Catholic majority. According to limited ethnographic material,[58] during the three hundred years of Spanish colonization, a tradition
developed among them of a kind of private jihad, combining orthodox
Islam with indigenous customs: men equip themselves with weapons that
are deadly only at zero range, sneak into population centers of the hated
infidels, and there, in surprise and fury, they attack random targets, not
ceasing their mass murder until members of the target population respond
and eliminate them. The perpetrators are not recruited for the mission
by authorities. Rather they volunteer on their own initiative, but they do
not embark on their enterprise without asking permission of their parents
and authorization from the leaders of the community. From the moment
they take it upon themselves, this voluntary project becomes obligatory.
No longer personal, it is now collective. From this moment the personal
motives of the terrorist become irrelevant, and even if he had personal reasons for which he wished to die, they become largely trivial with respect
to his mission. The public commitment is made by means of a formal oath
(in Spanish, *juramentado* means "one who swears an oath"). This is not
the only detail reminiscent of the Palestinian case. See also the complex
system of rituals that precedes going out on the attack, making it a holy
mission in the name of the entire community: ceremonial arming with the

local dagger, prayer, shaving (and plucking the eyebrows), ritual purification through immersion of the entire body, and careful wrapping of the
penis in a specific manner.[59] This is done to increase the magic potency of
the suicidal murderer and augment his courage and resolution. Most of
these ritual elements are taken from the traditional treatment of corpses
before burial. They relate to the warrior as if he were already dead, because his death is certain, known in advance, and desired, and they will be
unable to recover his body for burial.

The juramentado can be seen as *istishhadi* in the style of the islands of
Southeast Asia. It is not an attack whose perpetrators accept high risk, but
an attack whose perpetrators actively guarantee their own death and hope
for it, to become martyrs. It has two particular variants that deserve elaboration in order to sharpen our understanding of suicide terrorism. Both
variants make a contemptible death into a praiseworthy one. Some people
volunteer for the mission of terrorism against the background of a severe
religious transgression that they have committed, and which is punishable
by death. They would rather be killed in an attack on the enemy than
be executed. And some volunteer for the terrorism mission against the
background of some crisis that makes life repulsive for them. They would
rather be killed in an attack on the enemy than commit suicide.[60] This is
a kind of murder in the service of their religion and their tribe, for the
purpose of committing suicide. Among the Moros in the Philippines, as
among other pious Muslims, suicide is taboo, punishable by damnation.
By contrast, someone who chooses the venerated alternative of jihad can
guarantee a place for himself in paradise with his death. The suicide here
reverses the means of jihad with its end: instead of dying in order to kill,
he kills in order to die. Binding up suicide with terrorism against the heretics stands it on its head, turning it from the most negative action to the
most positive one. In the ethnography of the Moros it is said of the men of
the juramentado that they want just as much to slaughter the Christians as
to be slaughtered by them, but they wish to slaughter as many Christians
as possible.[61] For its part, the community is indifferent to the motivation
of the jihadist, whether it be altruistic or egocentric. The oath before going
out on the suicide mission, in its Philippine variant, also makes the self-
centered act into one that sanctifies the name of Allah and brings honor to
the believers. Suicide and murder are bound together, mingled, and they
become identical with each other in one organic act.

The prescribed procedures that the suicide-murderer must undergo before leaving on his holy mission are a ritual preparation both for the role of the attacker and that of the victim, the slaughterer and the slaughtered, the sacrificer and the sacrificed. The ritual quality extends through the stages of the operation. According to certain accounts, at least until the end of the nineteenth century, sometimes, when the enemy had nearly overcome him and was about to bayonet him, the suicide-murderer would grasp the bayonet and thrust it toward himself, thus plunging it deeper into his own body and bringing his enemy closer to him, so as he died he could kill his killer with his own hands. The author of the article calls this "terminal fusion." In other chapters I describe a similar phenomenon that characterizes the Palestinian suicide terrorism in Israel as the "lethal embrace," which the human bomb shares with his victims.

Accidental Monsters, Unlikely Heroes (A)

Confession

Walid Daka, a Palestinian from Baka al-Garbia, was sentenced to life imprisonment for participation in a cell of the Popular Front, which kidnapped and murdered a Jew. As a veteran prisoner in the Security Wing in Israeli jail, he served as a father figure for young Palestinian prisoners, including suicide terrorists who had failed in their missions. After gaining their trust, he recorded some of his conversations with them on the subject of the suicide terrorism in which they had been involved. In these dialogues the suicide terrorists relate their motivations and the circumstances of their recruitment in a surprisingly offhand manner and tone. The main impression their words make is by what is absent in them: there is no particular patriotic engagement or religious faith, neither emotionality nor determination, no anger, hatred, or aggression. Here is a section from the authentic testimony of a suicide terrorist, which was spirited out of the prison at the height of the intifada:

> Everyone says there is a reason [why we are willing to go on a suicide mission], but there isn't. I don't know what I was thinking of. The truth is that before that I saw pictures of children who were killed and wounded on television. . . . But to tell you that there was one reason or a few reasons. . . . No. . . . My cousin came to me one day and asked: "What's your opinion about doing an *istishhad* action?" At first I thought my relative was making fun of me. I refused, because I believed he was just asking. But he insisted. I answered that if there was a possibility, I'd go on an action. I had no objection. He asked me what action I would choose, with a gun or an explosion. . . . I said to him, I want an explosion. Because I'm afraid that I would shoot and not hit anyone, and then they would arrest me and beat me and break [my bones]. . . . He said OK. . . . I didn't even have any connection with anyone in the organizations, and I didn't have any relative or friend who had been killed. I asked him when I could do the action, and he said to me, "Tomorrow we'll go and settle things in the city." We made a video clip. . . . He told me it would be in the name of Fatah. . . . On Monday we sat in a restaurant, ate hummus and *ful* with a guy, after that I went with him and put on the explosive vest.[1]

Champions or Losers?

"The jewels in the Palestinian crown." This is what the suicide terrorists were called during the intifada in the West Bank and Gaza Strip. They were also given other hugely honorific titles such as "the Supreme Way to Victory" and "the Greatest of All Sorts of Jihad Fighters in the Cause of Allah and the Nation."[2] In the Palestinian public, the communications media, the speeches of political and spiritual leaders, and, of course, in the declarations of the Palestinian resistance movements, the suicide terrorists were an exalted manifestation of heroism and devotion to Islam and the motherland, leaders in the armed struggle, and defeaters of the Israeli occupiers. They were regarded as the ultimate representatives of patriotism and faith, and stood for awakening, rebellion, and revenge. In textbooks, popular songs, and murals, on Internet sites, and in the activities of university students, they were accorded a particular place of honor. They were a model to be identified with. In the periods of suicide attacks, phalanxes of masked young men led fervid mass parades in Gaza streets, dressed in white from head to foot, with mock-ups of bombs strapped to their chests. Small children in the crowd, dressed in similar costume, cheered them.

Agenda setters on the Israeli side also contributed to glorifying the suicide terrorists. They inadvertently cooperated with Palestinian molders of opinion in making the suicide terrorist a mysterious figure, enthralling and impressive. The Israeli security forces joined with journalists and politicians in Israel to boost the image of the suicide terrorist, either because of apprehension in response to it or to justify the huge efforts invested at the beginning of the intifada in wiping out suicide terrorism—and the failure to do so—and in order to capitalize on success in dealing with it later on. Only a few years after suicide terrorism ceased to be a dominant factor in the Israeli-Palestinian conflict were senior officers of the ISA willing to admit that human bombs actually had the "weight of a feather." For those combating suicide terrorism it took time to understand what those who activated it knew but concealed: that the suicide terrorist was "disposable like a tissue," to quote the expression tossed out in an interview with a veteran, disabused ISA officer, an expression repeated almost verbatim in a frank and blunt conversation with a formerly influential functionary in a Palestinian suicide terrorism organization, who was getting things off his chest.[3]

The respective heroization and vilification of suicide terrorists on the part of both sides in the Middle Eastern conflict mingled with the romanticization that spread among Western scholars and commentators, especially all sorts of "terrorist whisperers," whose ambivalent attitude toward human bombs, with whom their acquaintance was usually only superficial, was full of the confusion that characterizes moral panic, along with a degree of wonder, which they found difficult to conceal, and gullible self-abnegation toward it.[4] The families of the suicide terrorists, like the relatives of the victims, Hamas spokesmen like those of the IDF, as well as experts in institutes of strategic research and the authors of books in the West found themselves supporting each other in the effort to reject the possibility of the banalization of suicide terrorism, and especially to prevent representing the suicide terrorist as an insignificant and pathetic creature. The caliber of the suicide terrorist was viewed as testifying to that of those who dispatched him, in whose name they acted, and to that of those who opposed them and saw themselves as overcoming them. On both sides of the Middle Eastern confrontation, and even overseas, many people had vested interests in suicide terrorism or in countering it or in writing about it, and they therefore wished to emphasis its importance.[5] An Israeli police officer who was responsible for profiling in the antiterrorism department during the intifada admitted to me that it took him several months to realize that he, too, had fallen into the "trap of glorification" of suicide terrorists.

Take, for example, Wafa Idris, a twenty-eight-year-old woman from the al-Amari refugee camp, who blew herself up in Jerusalem (January 2002). The Palestinians presented her as an impeccable suicide terrorist. However, the examination of the police forensic laboratory refuted this boast. Among her remains was found a timer, which caused the explosion at the hour set in advance. The ISA investigation, based on the arrest of her accomplices, produced additional evidence. She had been divorced by her husband after nine years of marriage because she was barren, and she lived in her brother's house, where she was a financial burden and suffered from humiliation and abuse. As a result, she also lapsed into periods of depression. She joined the ranks of the Palestinian Red Crescent, where she found a friend who knew about her difficult situation and volunteered her for a Fatah suicide mission. At first she refused, but after being strongly pressured she agreed to deliver an explosive charge, supposedly to an emissary of the organization in Jerusalem. Disguised in a nurse's uniform, she crossed the border in an ambulance and met the designated man, but for reasons that remain unclear, she did not transfer the package to him. Then she was stuck with an explosive charge, apparently fully aware that the time remaining until it exploded was running out. Her handler, Abu Talal, tried to convince her by telephone to place the charge near a gathering of Israelis and quickly run away, to save her life. But this time as well she refused. In the end she moved away from the crowd in a busy commercial center, entered a shoe store, stood behind a concrete pillar, and exploded there.[6] Only one other person died with her. The Palestinian resistance movements and the communications media in the territories and in Israel described her as a suicide terrorist and never retracted that version of the story. In the history of the Arab-Israeli conflict, she is listed as the first female suicide terrorist, and thus she appears both in the Palestinian pantheon and in reports of the ISA. The true story is less appropriate for both sides. While Israelis contribute to the trend

of mystifying suicide terrorism and according it potency, they also bestial-
ize the suicide terrorist by presenting him as a bloodthirsty unscrupulous
fiend. The following passage comes from the testimony of a senior plastic
surgeon in the hospital at my university, founder and chief of Israel National Skin Bank:

> I was asked to supply skin for a Palestinian woman from Gaza who was hos-
> pitalized in Beersheva after her family burned her because she was suspected
> of having an affair. We supplied all the needed homograft for her treatment.
> She was successfully treated and discharged to return to Gaza. She was in-
> vited for regular follow-up visits to the outpatient clinic. In one of her bi-
> weekly visits she was caught at a border crossing wearing a suicide belt. Her
> mission was to explode herself in the outpatient clinic of the hospital where
> they saved her life. Her family promised her that if she did that, they would
> [posthumously] forgive her.[7]

Two opposite tendencies are notable in the Israeli attitude to suicide
terrorism. On the one hand, they aggrandize the human bombs. On the
other hand, they belittle them, so as to deny their importance. This is done
by discrediting the motivations of the suicide terrorist, and by depicting
him as a robot and a victim. One tactic for deflating the image of the
suicide terrorist is to reveal the circumstances of his recruitment, which
shows suicide terrorism as something less pure and idealistic than it pretends to be, and the suicide terrorist is portrayed as a person whose moral
failings and social vulnerability are exploited by the organizations that
manipulate him into setting out on a suicide mission as an alternative to a
worse and shameful end. The second tactic is to show the suicide terrorist
as someone passively set into action, with no independent sense of judgment or freedom of choice, because he was drugged or brainwashed. Thus
he has become an automaton, with no consciousness or will of his own.

Palestinian propaganda rejects the possibility that human bombs lack
agency, or that they are flawed. We know of a number of suicide terrorists who were driven to action against the background of a certain
mental deficiency or the accusation that they or a member of their family
were collaborators with Israel. However, spokesmen of the movements
consistently deny this. Ibrahim Hamed, one of the heads of the military
wing of Hamas in the West Bank, who was responsible for the suicide
terrorist attacks on Café Moment, Café Hillel, the Sheffield Club, and

others, and who was captured in May 2006 and condemned to fifty-four life sentences, related that in the area under his command there was an enthusiastic young man who volunteered to be a human bomb, but when it turned out that he was the son of a collaborator who wanted to atone for his father's crimes, he was rejected because "there has to be a pure motivation."[8]

The Palestinian idealization of the human bomb and the Israeli demonization of the human bomb reinforce each other. "The engineer," Yehiya Ayash, the patron saint of Palestinian suicide terrorism, was chosen as "Man of the Year" by the Israeli state radio station. Together, the Palestinians and the Israelis create the image of the suicide terrorist as dedicated and potent. Against this background it is surprising to find that the spiritual leader of Hamas, Sheikh Ahmad Yassin, after extravagant praise of suicide terrorism, did not even remember the name of a single human bomb, nor could he relate their places of residence, their age, or their families.[9]

Though it is customarily thought that the desire for fame is an important motivation for enlisting suicide terrorists, and the status of the human bomb does in fact improve, it turns out that just as the suicide terrorist had no name in his life before committing his attack, he also has no name after his death. In informal surveys that I made on the streets of East Jerusalem and the West Bank a short time after the intifada, Palestinians found it difficult to remember details about the identity of any suicide terrorist, with the exception of isolated interviewees who remembered only the name of a suicide terrorist who was a relative or from their village. As the years passed, memory faded. Familiarity with the Palestinian suicide terrorists was short, local, collective, and anonymous.[10] Elsewhere I term it "short-term sainthood."[11] While the phenomenon of suicide terrorism was engraved in the consciousness, the individual terrorist was forgotten. In contrast, the interviewees were very familiar with the names and identities of the heroes of the intifada who were not suicide terrorists, chief among them being the "engineers," those who were killed by Israel, the shahids, as well as the living ones, either wanted or imprisoned.

The Palestinian suicide terrorist is a godforsaken saint. In the gallery of superheroes in the Palestinian national struggle, suicide terrorists are not represented. It is difficult to make a saint out of a human bomb. First, they have no body to glow at night and no grave that pilgrims can visit, where they can pray, and to which they can attribute miracles. Second, in their lifetimes they were not composed of the right materials for sanctification. Neither in their personalities nor in their biographies was there any potential that could be exploited in a manner to arouse veneration. A splendid death was not always capable of redeeming a pallid and shameful life. Furthermore, for glorification, let alone sanctification, agents with an interest and means are needed. Saints do not emerge on their own. To create a saint and afterward to maintain his sanctity over time, people and organizations are needed as sponsors of sainthood.[12] The suicide terrorists had no sponsors. The natural candidate for the position were the families and organizations, but the suicide terrorists' relatives were poor and lacking in status, while the entrepreneurs of suicide terrorism turned to tasks that appeared to be more urgent.

Information about the personal and social characteristics of suicide terrorists, which are revealed by unmediated contact with people close to them, by unofficial testimony, and by authentic documents, is surprising. Sometimes, however, relatives and acquaintances will admit that the truth is not usually told about the suicide terrorist because of respect for the dead and family honor.

An example is the case of sixteen-year-old Amar al-Far, who came from a particularly deprived family in the Askar refugee camp and was sent by the Popular Front to blow himself up in the Carmel Market in Tel Aviv (September 2004, three dead). It was whispered that he had a conflicted gender identity and wished to undergo a sex-change operation.[13] Even those that denied it secretly admitted that Palestinian public opinion found it difficult to glorify the name of someone who, when alive, had been the object of mockery in his community, and his recruiters exploited this to force him into suicide terrorism.

Contrary to expectations, the mourning ceremonies for suicide terrorists are relatively low-key, and their commemoration is limited in time and place. A suicide terrorist could conceivably receive two funeral ceremonies: the first immediately after the explosion, when a mourning tent would be erected in the parents' courtyard, a ceremony not observed in the ordinary way, mainly because there would be no body to bury; and a second funeral, the actual burial, which could only take place in extraordinary instances, if the Israelis removed the remains of the suicide terrorist's body from their secret temporary cemetery and returned them to the

Palestinians. On one of these rare occasions (May 2014), the remains of a prominent suicide terrorist, Muhammad al-Masri, who was dispatched by Hamas to blow himself up at the Sbarro pizzeria in Jerusalem, were returned along with the bodies of Imad and Adel Awadala, activists of the military wing of Hamas, who were killed as wanted men in an armed confrontation with the IDF. These two ceremonies, held simultaneously, merit comparison. Al-Masri was buried in an honorable but modest way in Aqaba, near Jenin. While a volley of shots was fired in his honor, Hamas made no effort to make the ceremony more than basically a family and village event. The bodies of other suicide terrorists were returned at the same time. They were delivered directly to their families and buried in their hometown in an entirely private ceremony.[14] By contrast, the Awadala brothers were buried in the Palestinian capital of Ramallah, under the aegis of the Palestinian Authority, in an impressive ceremony with the participation of thousands, organized by Hamas. This demonstration of the movement's power included the display of weapons, dozens of posters, hundreds of green flags, speeches by leaders at the entrance to the main mosque, and the rhythmic chanting of "Destroy Israel"—emphasizing the gap between the funerals.

In Palestinian society, where there is inflation of the idea of martyrdom,[15] the commemoration of shahids follows distinct models. Lacking tombs and monuments, they have turned the Internet into a prominent site of commemoration. There the late suicide terrorists also have a considerable presence, as they do at events such as football matches. Unlike other heroes of the intifada, however, no book has been written about a suicide terrorist. The graffiti that glorified their names on city streets have long since faded, erased by sun and rain, and the posters honoring them that were hung on the walls in the streets of villages and refugee camps have peeled off and fallen. In a short while the pictures of new shahids were pasted over them. To become an icon was the sole privilege of the various "engineers," leaders of the movements, officers of the resistance, and even women fighters.[16] The suicide terrorists were given room only in portraits at the entrance to their neighborhoods,[17] on the walls of their parents' businesses,[18] and mainly in the center of the family room, cared for by their mothers.

We can learn a bit about the status of suicide terrorists in Palestinian society from the situation of those among them who were apprehended and imprisoned in Israel. While most of them were freed in various prisoner exchanges, not a single one was given a high place on the list of prisoners whose release was demanded by Fatah or Hamas, and the Palestinian public did not protest. In the stubborn and prolonged negotiations between the resistance organizations and Israel, represented by the ISA, a surprising tacit agreement emerged regarding the release of suicide terrorists. *Neither side* saw them as a threat. In Israel it was known that even if they returned to the circle of violence, they would not pose a significant challenge.

Observation of Palestinian security prisoners in Israeli jails also reveals the low status of suicide terrorists. All the positions of internal influence over the prisoners and their outward representation are filled by former Fatah and Hamas fighters and commanders, and not a single suicide terrorist occupies a position of any power or privilege. Perhaps their low status in prisons does not derive from their being suicide terrorists so much as from their failure and capture, indicating that they are not worthy of admiration because of operational failure, cowardice, and lack of resolution. They might also be suspected by their colleagues. In any event, it appears that the suicide terrorists are somewhat outcasts in prison, held in contempt and silenced. Both regarding the management of prison life and in political matters, the dispatchers of suicide terrorists are among the leaders of the prisoners, whereas the suicide terrorists themselves are always subordinate to them. Furthermore, after their release, not a single suicide terrorist made his way to a key position in the organizations, unlike other released prisoners, who translated their years of prison into capital that gave them a leg up over their competitors for leadership. They were regarded as partners with the leaders of the national struggle, a new elite in Palestinian society, whereas the suicide terrorists barely received attention, aside from a modest monthly stipend. While in prison and after their release, only their families communicated with them.

In the resistance organizations and in Palestinian public life, along with a degree of esteem and admiration for the suicide terrorist, there were also reservations about him, even among those who generally supported terrorism. There are various reasons for the mediocre status of the suicide terrorist, even for implicit contempt for him. First, there were critical voices among the Palestinians that belittled the strategic value of suicide terrorism, especially in light of the bad public relations abroad that it caused, thinking that its gains were outweighed by the damage it inflicted on the national struggle. Second, voices were raised against suicide terrorism for religious reasons, mainly in light of the sanctions against suicide in Islam. Various circles among the faithful were not convinced by the identification of suicide terrorism with legitimate martyrdom. Criticism of a third kind relates to the identity of the human bombs and the circumstances of their mobilization, and it is based on information about specific cases. Those who are familiar with the social and personal weakness of some of the human bombs, and who are aware that their conscription involved exploitative manipulation of their weaknesses, find it hard to join in the proud chorus of praise. Indeed, suicide terrorists often arouse a mixture of pity and disdain.

Criticism of the suicide terrorism organizations related to the weakness of the human bombs, which was usually tacit and concealed, increased after the organizations began to send women, children, only sons, and fathers who supported families. Especially significant among the critics were the parents of suicide terrorists who expressed bitter anger against the pitiless and cowardly handlers, who preferred to send other people's sons rather than their own. These factors, too, eroded the status of human bombs and called attention to the fact that organizational, communal, and especially familial forces did not stand behind them to promote their reputation.

The people who conscripted and dispatched the human bombs treated them with disrespect. Although in their official statements the handlers paid lip service to the terrorists, and one cannot find explicit statements of condescension toward them, this attitude is implicit in private and indirect statements. The entrepreneurs of suicide terrorism tended to describe the social status of the human bombs as lower than it actually was, and they also undervalued their personalities. An imprisoned senior member of a resistance organization described the suicide terrorists as poor and ignorant, contrary to the findings of demographic research about them.[19] At most the attitude toward them was instrumental, manifesting lack of empathy. Several heads of organizations implied that the very sending of people on suicide missions indicates disdain for them. In an entirely businesslike manner a senior Hamas leader, Ibrahim Hamed, stated in his interrogation that when high-quality candidates became available to the organization, he preferred to use them for missions of assistance to suicide terrorism such as gathering intelligence and concealing arms rather than sending them to blow themselves up. He spoke of a certain volunteer whom they tried to dissuade from committing suicide, "to get better use out of him."[20] In handlers' talk about suicide terrorists, and in their behavior toward suicide terrorists, especially in prison, the expected expressions of admiration, given the propaganda of the organizations, did not appear at all. Compared with the gestures of army officers and the heads of espionage agencies in Western democracies, who send their subordinates on extremely dangerous missions, among the handlers of suicide terrorists, expressions of gratitude and giving credit to "brave fighters who gave their souls for the sake of the holy cause" were conspicuously absent. Among handlers there was no trace of self-righteous phrases of humility in relation to their operatives or the assumption of responsibility for their death.

The low status of suicide terrorists in the views of their superiors was demonstrated innumerable times in interviews with them, when they were asked over and over again to answer a question that was expected to embarrass and humiliate them: "Why didn't you go on a suicide mission yourself? Why didn't you send your own children to be human bombs?" The engineers themselves always preferred to continue as wanted men and run the risk of being killed in a confrontation with the Israelis or to give himself up. Without any sign of discomfort, reluctance, or apology, they answered that every person has a role in the struggle—one sends and the other is sent—neither can do without the other, and success in the struggle depends on them both. According to them, the human bombs were a vital link in the chain, but by no means the most important one. The human bombs can be replaced, but not their handlers. In interrogations or interviews with the handlers of suicide terrorists, they try to create a kind of tacit understanding with the Israeli facing them—the solidarity of people who know the ropes—who share a smidgen of contempt for the suicide terrorists. With no feeling of shame, some of them admitted that if their children had volunteered for suicide missions, they would have prevented them.

Contrary to what one might think based on the propaganda of the organizations during the intifada and from reading academic articles about suicide terrorism, the human bomb does not stand at the apex of the hierarchy of Palestinian heroism. It is doubtful whether any place at all is assured for him in the pantheon of mythological figures of the struggle against Israel. Those who head this splendid list are the men who handle the human bombs. In the street surveys I carried out two years after the intifada, specific suicide terrorists were not mentioned at all in the list of heroes of the nation and the land. The attitude toward the human bombs ranges between ignoring them, denying them, and ambivalence about them.

There is dissonance between the status of the suicide terrorist on the declarative Palestinian level, which resonates in Western journalism and research, and sociological indexes of that status.[21] A well-oiled public relations apparatus created a spurious image, which hides a different reality.[22] In fact, the highest place is not given to the human bomb but to those who initiate attacks and longtime activists and who possess a terrorist résumé, seniority in the organization, and macho charisma. The true attitude toward the suicide terrorists was hinted at in moments of sincere openness, free of censorship and the need to pretend. For example, at the beginning of the intifada, when competition began between Hamas and Fatah for prestige and popularity, and Hamas seemed to be the clear victor, because it was widely identified with suicide terrorism, envious representatives of Fatah tried to belittle the achievements of the rival organization by mocking them for using suicide terrorists who were nothing but *kafa* kids ("whipping boys")—schoolboys whom the class bullies pick on because of their physical weakness and marginal social status, hitting them on the nape of their necks whenever they run into them, to humiliate them as much as to hurt them.[23] One senses that the Palestinian organizations are aware, though they deny it, that there is something pathetic about committing suicide terrorism. Even the handlers of the human bombs have more respect for warlike heroism, in which combatants engage with the enemy. There is a sad irony in the fact that the act of suicide terrorism is not regarded as manly, whereas a great number of suicide terrorists were largely motivated by fear that refusal to set out on their mission would make them look effeminate.

Profiling the Palestinian Human Bomb

In the two waves of Palestinian suicide terrorism in Israel, about 154 attacks were carried out (and, according to ISA estimates, about three times as many planned attacks were thwarted at various stages). There were at least twenty-one attacks between 1993 and 1999, and more than 130 attacks in the al-Aqsa Intifada, from 2000 to 2008. About 160 human bombs (according to some estimates, up to two hundred) were responsible for these attacks. Who were these people?

Organizational Affiliation

Although all the human bombs were known to the public as having one organizational identity or another, at least half of them had had no connection to any organization before they set out on their missions (in contrast to the vast majority of the nonsuicidal terrorists who were killed or arrested by the IDF). According to the organizational affiliation of their handlers, 42 percent of the suicide terrorists were identified with Hamas, 29 percent with the Palestinian Islamic Jihad, 24 percent with Fatah, and 4 percent with smaller movements (mostly the Fronts). Sometimes it is difficult to connect a suicide terrorist to a specific movement, either because of cooperation in initiating the attacks (usually Hamas and the Jihad) or because of a dispute over the credit among the movements. Apparently only a single suicide terrorist acted on his own initiative, without coordination or assistance from any movement. Hamas is the primary and leading suicide terrorism organization. The other movements adopted suicide terrorism afterward, in imitation and competition. The number of attacks attributed to the Jihad is impressive, given the relatively small size of the organization. It stood out especially at the end of the intifada, against the background of the tendency toward restraint shown by the larger organizations. Fatah (Tanzim) appears as a suicide terrorism organization only at a later stage of the intifada (2002). Hamas is the senior Palestinian suicide terrorism organization in the selectivity of its human bombs and their homogeneity. The list of Fatah suicide terrorists, and of the Jihad, are more varied with respect to gender, age, and educational level, and are of lesser status according to several criteria valued by Palestinian society, such as maturity. Each of the three organizations had areas of natural specialization in dispatching suicide terrorists. For example, the attacks in Jerusalem were committed by Hamas and Fatah, almost without the intervention of the Jihad, which concentrated on attacks in northern Israel. In contrast, Fatah had almost no involvement in suicide attacks dispatched from the Gaza Strip.

Gender

Four to five percent of suicide terrorists were women. In the first wave of suicide terrorism, until 2000, there were no women at all, and this was mainly because of the monopoly of the Islamic organizations. As years passed, and as a result of Fatah's adoption of suicide terrorism, the circle of conscripts was enlarged, the religious prohibitions were relaxed, and the representation of women grew. In the second wave there were eight (or ten) women versus 155 men. Fatah sent five women suicide terrorists, the Jihad sent two, and Hamas sent one. Thus there was an inverse relation between the part played in suicide terrorism by the religious organizations and the proportion of women who were dispatched. With one exception, the women suicide terrorists were less involved in the labor market and less aware politically than the male suicide terrorists.[24] The average educational level of the female human bombs was slightly higher than that of the men (34% of the women were university students or graduates). One of the women was married, one was a mother, and one was a sixty-four-year-old grandmother. Quite a few women failed and were apprehended by Israel. Among them was a conspicuous presence of divorced or separated women. In contrast, the eight women who completed their mission were relatively more murderous than the men: only one of them blew herself up without killing anyone in the target group. The proportion of female Palestinian suicide terrorists is considerably smaller than in Lebanon (17%), Sri Lanka (25%), and Russia-Chechnya (43%). In recent years, with the spread of suicide terrorism to Africa and Syria-Iraq, the number of women involved rose significantly, despite the dominance of Islamic groups. However, the proportion of women among suicide terrorists everywhere, including among Palestinians, was significantly greater than the proportion of women among terrorists who were not human bombs.

Age

A large majority of suicide terrorists, 81.5 percent, were younger than twenty-five (75% were between seventeen and twenty-four). Fifteen percent were between twenty-five and thirty, and only 3.5 percent were older than thirty. Over the years, the number of those over thirty decreased, and by the end of the intifada there were none. At the same time, the number of minors kept increasing. The mean age of suicide terrorists was 22.3. In the first wave of suicide terrorism the ages of the human bombs ranged between sixteen and fifty-seven, whereas in the second wave they ranged between eighteen and thirty-eight. That is to say, over time the range of ages narrowed and grew younger. Generally speaking, the age of suicide terrorists was parallel to that of soldiers in regular armies and guerrilla fighters but younger than the average for terrorists who were not suicidal. The average age of Hamas suicide terrorists was higher than that of other Palestinian organizations—23.6—and none of them was younger than eighteen. In contrast, the average age of Fatah suicide terrorists was lower, twenty-one, and some were sixteen, or even younger. The suicide terrorists of the Jihad were also relatively young.

Marital Status

Ninety percent of suicide terrorists were unmarried, 8.5 percent were married, and of those who were married, 7.5 percent were parents. These extreme statistics mainly reflect the young age of the suicide terrorists, as well as the conscription policy of the organizations, which preferred to send on suicide missions people without the responsibility of supporting a family. Moreover, unmarried people were free of conflicting loyalties and therefore easier to conscript.

Socioeconomic Status

Sixty percent of suicide terrorists were from the middle class, 30 percent were from the lower class, and 10 percent were from the upper-middle and professional class. The class division among suicide terrorists is similar to that of Palestinian society in general. While the data are not exact, and the criteria for determining socioeconomic status are not uniform, the dominance of the middle class, represented slightly more than in the society at large, is conspicuous. However, the definition of "middle class" relates mainly to the average family income and not necessarily to lifestyle and mentality. While the suicide terrorists of 9/11 came from the middle and upper-middle class of emigrants to the West, the suicide terrorists in Africa, Sri Lanka, and Afghanistan-Pakistan usually come from local lower classes. With two or three exceptions, the Palestinian suicide terrorists did not include any representatives of the local aristocracy or people connected with the higher-echelon administration or intelligentsia.

Employment

The rate of unemployment among suicide terrorists is similar to that in the general Palestinian population (38% in the Gaza Strip, 18% in the West Bank). Among those working, 60 percent are salaried blue-collar workers, while another 30 percent are students at various levels. There does not appear to be a strong correlation between poverty or unemployment and suicide terrorism in a way that could explain the conscription of certain people to be human bombs. Although it is difficult to ignore the fact that most of the societies and regions where suicide terrorism is practiced are relatively poor, the Middle East in general and the Palestinians in particular are not the poorest of populations. The same may be said of the following parameter.

Education

Ten to twenty percent of the suicide terrorists had only elementary or partial primary education, 35 to 50 percent had full or partial secondary education, and 20 to 30 percent had a university education, though in most instances it was only partial. Because there was no agreement among the results of various research projects regarding the variable of education, the results were rounded off, and the range of difference among them was presented. One reason for the difference is inconsistency in defining categories. For example, there was disagreement as to whether to count studies for a diploma as higher education. If we include religious colleges in this category, as well as technical colleges, the number exceeds 35 percent. The data also suffered from imprecision because of the families' tendency to exaggerate the educational achievements of their children. However, even if we take these reservations into account, we still find that the education of the suicide terrorists was higher than the average educational level in Palestinian society. The gap remains somewhat smaller if one compares the education of the suicide terrorists with that of young people of the same age in Palestinian society. The gap is particularly great in that suicide terrorists with only primary education are underrepresented, and those with university education are overrepresented. On the one hand, only the recent generation of Palestinian society has not been satisfied with primary education alone. On the other hand, the representation of suicide terrorists among university students is disproportional because the campuses are strongholds of the resistance movements, and there, far from home and family supervision, while they are subject to peer group pressure and charismatic political and religious figures, it is easier to recruit them.[25] A well-qualified scholar of terrorism argues that the lower the educational achievement of the suicide terrorist, the greater is his determination and enthusiasm to set out on a suicide mission.[26]

The human bombs who acted before 2000 (all from Hamas) had a higher educational level than those of the human bombs of the al-Aqsa Intifada. When the Jihad and Fatah took up suicide terrorism, the average educational level of the human bombs fell, and expansion of the circle of conscripts toward the end of the Intifada brought the educational level to an all-time low. It should also be remembered that the educational level of the suicide terrorists should not be evaluated by the standards of Western education, which in general is superior to Palestinian education in its academic and liberal orientation. Attention should be paid not only to the number of years of study of the suicide terrorists, but also to the content and fields of studies. Thus, among the suicide terrorists who were university students, none of them studied sociology, anthropology, or liberal arts such as philosophy, history, comparative literature, and art. Though some of them studied science—for example, mathematics and physics—they were applied rather than theoretical. Almost all the suicide terrorists majored in Islam or in professional fields such as accounting, law, agriculture, and pharmacy, and mainly in technological fields like computer and electrical engineering. This tendency characterizes not only the suicide terrorists but also their handlers, who were generally better educated. It is possible that the variable of gender and especially religiosity influenced the connection between suicide terrorism and the preference for practical studies. Sunni Arab Islam fundamentalists like those of the radical wing of the Muslim Brothers have a similar academic profile. Compared to the Palestinian suicide terrorists, the Afghani-Pakistani, Syrian-Iraqi, and African terrorists are on a substantially lower educational level.

Religiosity

This dimension is difficult to define and measure, and the data on it are scarce and vague. According to the only (Palestinian) source of data, the vast majority of suicide terrorists were religious, at least according to the testimony of their families. Sixty percent were described as highly religious (25% according to another source), and another 36 percent as moderately religious (75% according to another source), and just 4 percent of the suicide terrorists were religious to a small degree. According to all the sources, there was not even a single suicide terrorist of whom it was said that he was not at all religious. Palestinian society, in particular rural society, is traditional, and very few of its members would define themselves as completely secular. As stated above, three-quarters of the suicide terrorists were dispatched by Islamic organizations.

Civil Status

The proportion of refugees among suicide terrorists is higher than among the general population. Fifty-three percent of the parents of suicide terrorists define themselves and their children, the shahids, as refugees, while in the Palestinian population in the region, 40 percent are regarded as refugees. The formal definition of a refugee is someone born in the territory of the present State of Israel who was forced to move away from there in 1948–67. Their children are also listed as refugees, regardless of where they live. Only 21 to 28 percent of suicide terrorists lived in refugee camps, although there are conditions in the camps that make conscription easier: overcrowding, erosion of the status of the father and of family unity, and so forth. The vast majority of suicide terrorists from the Jihad were refugees, and fewer among those dispatched by Fatah and Hamas. A great proportion came from the West Bank, where refugees are a minority (26%), whereas far fewer suicide terrorists came from Gaza, where the refugees are a large majority (65%).

Region of Origin

According to Palestinian sources, 75 percent of the suicide terrorists were originally residents of the West Bank, and 25 percent were from the Gaza

Strip, whereas according to Israeli sources 81 percent were from the West Bank and only 16 percent were from the Gaza Strip. In the advanced stages of the intifada, the proportion of suicide terrorists from Gaza grew, and in 2005 it reached more than 40 percent. During all the years of suicide terrorism, only four human bombs lived in East Jerusalem, and only two were from abroad (British citizens of Pakistani origin who acted together). Some handlers and suicide terrorists moved from Gaza to the West Bank because of pressure from Israeli security and operational considerations.

Place of Residence

The prevalent notion connecting suicide terrorism to villages and refugee camps is groundless. The largest portion of suicide terrorists, 38 percent, came from cities and towns, and only 32 percent from villages, and about 25 percent from refugee camps. Roughly speaking, the suicide terrorists come from the following places: Nablus and its near vicinity, 27 percent; the Gaza Strip, 25 percent; Jenin and the surrounding area, 15 percent; Hebron and its surroundings, 10 percent; Bethlehem and its surroundings, 9 percent; the Tul Karem region, 6 percent; Kalkiliya and Ramallah, 3.5 percent each; and Jerusalem, 2 percent.

Family Size

Only 20 percent of the suicide terrorists came from families of one to four children, which are regarded as small by Palestinian standards (the average number of children is around six). Forty-four percent of the suicide terrorists came from families with five to nine children, and 36 percent from families with ten or more children. The proportion of suicide terrorists from families with many children is disproportionate to their numbers in the population. There might be intervening variables such as the religiosity of the family, its educational level, and its economic situation. In any event, it is easier to enlist children from large families because they are less strictly supervised, and they are less necessary for supporting the family, which also suits the recruiting criteria of the organizations.

In conclusion, human bombs are basically normal—a statistical rather than a normative concept. Regarding a large part of the variables that characterize suicide terrorists, the average might create a deceptive impression because variance is great. Thus, for example, one may say that a suicide terrorist is likely to be young and unmarried. The Israeli security forces made a selection on the basis of this assumption until, to their surprise, middle-aged and married suicide terrorists, including parents, showed up. The efforts at profiling made by intelligence investigators and academic researchers were exhausting and frustrating. In the case of the Palestinian suicide terrorist, one can speak only of a negative profile: there were, for example, no Christian or intellectual suicide terrorists (although in the history of Palestinian terrorism, the latter two played a central role). The Palestinian suicide terrorist was not necessarily lacking in education (though some were), nor necessarily poor and unemployed (though some were), nor necessarily a criminal (though some were).

Who They Are Not

We turn now from the demographic to the biographical characteristics of the Palestinian suicide terrorists, especially the factors of their lives that may explain their participation in suicide attacks. On the basis of Palestinian research, it is possible to examine two variables that might be connected and partially overlapping: the first is prior affiliation of some kind with one of the resistance organizations or adoption of a clear political position, and the second is a past connection with an event or series of confrontations with Israel that could have been experienced as formative and even traumatic.[27]

Among the 150 to 200 Palestinian suicide terrorists, not a single one, prior to his mission, could be identified as a permanent active member of a specific organization. It is also difficult to find an example of a suicide terrorist who was faithful to a given ideology, and only a few of them had a decidedly political consciousness beyond support in principle for the national struggle and being in favor of relatively activist strategic views. In general they were not known as extreme haters of Israel. Even after their recruitment for the mission under the aegis of one of the organizations, just as they barely received any military training, they also were given no indoctrination, except on a superficial and spotty level. The intensity of the suicide terrorist's politicization was no greater than that of most of the young people in the Gaza Strip and the West Bank, which is to say, they took part in the organizations' mass demonstrations. Even those who tended toward one movement rather than another can be defined at most as passive grassroots adherents who had no specific task or responsibility. In any event, there was not necessarily any correlation between the organization's goals and the motivations of the individual suicide terrorist.

The vast majority of suicide terrorists were identified with one of the Palestinian resistance organizations only after their death or imprisonment. The act of suicide terrorism can be seen as a rite of initiation in the organization, or a confirmation ceremony bestowing full membership in an exclusive secret society. The partial nature of the connection between the suicide terrorist and the suicide terrorism organization is expressed in the uncertainty in claiming credit after the explosion. While organizations cooperated in carrying out a few attacks, there were also attacks for which two organizations vied for the right to boast of their monopoly over the suicide terrorist. Cases are known in which the human bomb transferred his loyalty from one organization to another or received operational backing from one organization after being rejected by another. Darin Abu Aisha contacted Hamas activists several times, asking to be sent out by them on a suicide attack, but she was rejected. In the end she blew herself up in the name of Fatah (Makabim checkpoint, February 2002). Ali Jara, a Palestinian policeman, was sent on a suicide mission by Hamas. After recording his testament, he crossed the border, encountered an Israeli checkpoint, and was forced to go back. During negotiations with his handlers, representatives of Fatah made themselves known to him, and in the end they were the ones who dispatched him (bus 19, December 2004). Both organizations tried to take responsibility for this suicide terrorist.

Commitment to a definite organization is mainly typical of Hamas, whereas Fatah and the Jihad recruited volunteers solely on the basis of tenuous loyalty. The tendency to attribute a suicide terrorist to a specific organization, although on occasion the connection between them was only partial and random, characterized not only the Palestinian groups, who competed among themselves for credit, but it also typified the Israeli side, which found it difficult to grasp that an act of suicide terrorism might not be undertaken by someone with a long-standing commitment to a specific organization, for if the initiative to become a suicide terrorist is personal and spontaneous, this indicates broad popular sentiment, which is even more threatening.

Suicide terrorism, as opposed to a sacrificial attack by means of knives, for example, requires an advanced logistical and operative infrastructure, which only an organization can supply. Thus, as expected, almost all human bombs had organizational sponsorship. However, few of the suicide terrorists had a firm commitment to one of the organizations prior to their acceptance of the suicide mission. Indeed some kind of organizational affiliation was attributed to about half of them, but this affiliation turned out to be only transitory and superficial. In contrast, about 70 percent of the perpetrators of conventional terrorism were more or less solidly connected to organizations.[28]

Suicide terrorists are also different from the ordinary terrorists of the Palestinian organizations in that not a single one of them was ever a prisoner in an Israeli jail.[29] This is a salient fact against the background of Israel's extensive arrest policy in the occupied territories during the intifada: the two hundred suicide terrorists were not included among the tens of thousands of young Palestinians who passed through the revolving doors of Israeli prisons. A quarter of the security prisoners, who were not suicide terrorists, served two or more sentences, but the organizations refrained from using former prisoners as suicide terrorists, to make it harder for the ISA and IDF to discover them on their way to the target. Most of the suicide terrorists had not been involved previously in any action against the occupation, including minor acts of violence, mainly throwing stones, which were so widespread among Palestinian young men. Eighty-five percent of the security prisoners took part in violent actions of that kind against soldiers or Jewish settlers in the early stages of their terrorist socialization, as opposed to only 45 percent of the suicide terrorists.

Just as the suicide terrorists were not distinguished by a personal history of violent action against Israel, generally they were not subject to particular acts of Israeli violence directed against them or their dear ones. According to the testimony of the parents and friends of suicide terrorists, less than half had themselves been exposed to physical injury or a specific humiliating incident on the part of IDF soldiers.[30] Exposure of that kind could encourage the enlistment of a suicide terrorist, and it certainly serves the organizations as justification for suicide terrorism. In the testaments, especially those of women, there is always an emphatic expression of the desire for revenge against injuries to relatives of the suicide terrorist, and 75 percent of the relatives of suicide terrorists state that one of them was the victim of violence or humiliation by soldiers. This fact could explain hatred and anger and be a motivation for counterviolence. However, such experiences characterize most of the Palestinians in the territories, and only a fraction become suicide terrorists.

Seven exceptional cases indicate the nature of Palestinian suicide terrorists, by contrast. The first is that of Hanadi Jaradat, who was sent by the Jihad to blow herself up in Maxim Restaurant in Haifa (October 2003). She was a handsome and successful woman from a respected urban family, a professional, and an extremist in her anti-Israeli attitudes and religiosity. She sought revenge for the killing of her brother and her fiancé by the IDF. She was particularly assertive and possessed excellent operational abilities. The fact that she was an impressive woman but unmarried led people around her to regard her as sexually promiscuous, meaning a woman against whom one can and must exert pressure to send her to her death. The second exceptional case is the pair of suicide terrorists who blew themselves up in Mike's Place, a bar in Tel Aviv (April 2003). They weren't Palestinian at all but Pakistanis with British citizenship, conscripted by Hamas, who came from abroad and were spirited into Israel from the Gaza Strip. The third case is Shaker Habishi, sent by Hamas to blow himself up in the railroad station in Nahariya (September 2001). He was the only suicide terrorist who was a citizen and resident of Israel, a veteran admirer of the Muslim Brothers movement, a man of broad religious education and expert in the writings of Sayyid Qutb. He was also exceptional in his age, forty-eight, and his family status, being married and the father of three. Though he did not have a profile that aroused suspicion, the ISA discovered his intentions ten days before the suicide terror attack (apparently from an informer), but his Palestinian handlers hid him and the Israeli efforts to capture him and prevent the attack were in vain. The fourth exception is Ahab Salim, a student from Ramallah who attacked a hitchhiking station in the military base of Sarafand (September 2003, nine dead). Unlike most of the suicide terrorists, he had a history of terrorism, and because of it he had even been imprisoned in Israel for several months. He had extended and close connections with Hamas, and immediately after his release from prison, he set out on the suicide mission.[31] Aside from him, we know of no other Palestinian who had a significant history of terrorist activity and went on to become a suicide terrorist. Even the perpetrators of ordinary terrorism who take high risks state that they would not consider the possibility of being suicide terrorists themselves. Apparently terrorism and suicide terrorism require different types. The fifth exception is Dia Tawil, twenty years old, who was sent by Hamas and blew himself up at the crossroads of French Hill in Jerusalem (March 2001, no one was killed except him). He stood out against the background of other suicide terrorists not only in that he was a student at Birzeit University, which leads in terrorism but not really in suicide terrorism, but also in that he was a member of a family close to senior members of the organization—a nephew of Jamal Tawil, a prominent Hamas functionary and military commander in the Ramallah region of the West Bank.[32]

To this roster of exceptions we can add Taher Tamam, who blew himself up in the name of Hamas at the Mehula crossroads (April 1993). First of all, he was the first Palestinian suicide terrorist, and one might say that he was before his time, in that he blew himself up a full year before the wave of suicide terrorism that rose up in response to the massacre at the Tomb of the Patriarchs in Hebron. He had no predecessor or model to imitate, nor did he have a routine of structured patterns that he could base himself on. One might surmise that there was a degree of coincidence here, a mutation, if one didn't know that this act of suicide terrorism was committed on the initiative of the heads of the organization in Gaza, including, prominently, Yehiya Ayash, and were it not planned to be in full synchronization with the meeting of the expelled Palestinians in Marj al-Zahor in southern Lebanon, as the organization's spokesmen claimed. Senior Hamas people met with representatives of Hezbollah there, and apparently they adopted the idea of suicide terrorism from them. Taher was not only a pioneer among the suicide terrorists, but he was also the richest of them. His family was respected and influential in the West Bank. His father was a successful industrialist in Nablus, whose sesame mill exported raw materials to large food manufacturers in Israel. He was twenty-two years old, a gifted student at An-Najah University, active in the student cell of the Muslim Brothers, and extreme in his religiosity. He drove a stolen van loaded with gas cylinders between two parked Israeli buses and exploded a charge that was on him while grasping a Koran.

In entire contrast were two child suicide terrorists, who were sent by Fatah and caught at the Hawara checkpoint south of Nablus (March 2004). The first, Abdallah Kur'an, twelve years old, was sent to transfer a heavy satchel to someone on the other side. There was an explosive charge in the satchel, connected to a cell phone, which, when called by someone watching from a distance, was meant to set it off by remote control. The boy apparently did not know what was in the satchel. A week later Husam Abdu Bilal, a fourteen-year-old, was caught when his shirt, which was several sizes too big, barely concealed an explosive charge, from which an electric wire protruded, connected to a switch, grasped in his little hand. Like the other boy, he was from a marginal and poor family of refugees, who was not fully aware of the implications of suicide terrorism. In an interrogation that was carried out immediately, on the spot, he reported that a few hours earlier, people he didn't know suggested that he should blow up Israelis, and he agreed, "because they gave him one hundred shekels (about thirty dollars) and promised him that he could have sex with virgins in paradise."[33]

It also turned out that Husam, who suffered from attention deficit disorder (ADD), had disturbed a lesson in school and been thrown out of class by the teacher. In the parking lot he broke the mirror on the teacher's car in revenge. When his father was told of this, he beat him severely, as did the local policeman. He was weeping openly about his bitter fate, and passersby who heard him howling that he wanted to give his soul up to death sent him to a Fatah activist, who sent him on a suicide mission on the spot.

While the earlier instance represents the start of the first wave of suicide terrorism (1993–2000), the latter represent the end of the second wave (2000–5). The figure of the suicide terrorist as presented in this chapter relates mainly to the second wave, which arose and ebbed with the al-Aqsa Intifada. The first wave was smaller and less significant than the second. In the terms used by counterterrorism agencies, it may be said in general that the forty-three suicide terrorists of the first wave were of "higher quality" than the 161 suicide terrorists of the second wave. The transition from the first to the second wave is indicative of a change in various parameters of suicide terrorism such as variation in the motivation of the suicide terrorists, which became less ideological or vengeful and more economic; the inclusion of women in the circle of suicide terror as accomplices and as human bombs; increase in the number of organizations that employed suicide terrorism; and decrease in the age of suicide terrorists. Similarly there was a decline in the political consciousness of the suicide terrorists and their involvement in the conflict prior to their recruitment. The background of the first wave of suicide terrorism was a popular uprising that swept the candidates for suicide terrorism, like most young people, to take an active part in the confrontation with Israel. Hence some of those suicide terrorists had been arrested previously. In contrast, the suicide terrorists of the second wave did not have a background of violence or arrest. Although suicide terrorism at the time was an integral part of the al-Aqsa Intifada, which was armed, its activists were relatively few, and the would-be suicide terrorists did not come from among their ranks.

In the first wave of suicide terrorism it was difficult to enlist volunteers, because the phenomenon was unknown and not yet backed by an effective recruitment machinery and an enthusiastic subculture. Nevertheless, rigorous selection brought volunteers with relatively pure motivation. In the second wave, public sympathy increased, and the recruitment machinery was improved. Thus the number of suicide terrorists grew several times over, but the social and personal capital they brought with them decreased. The greater the dimensions of suicide terrorism grew, as it was molded in part by institutional patterns and underwent a certain routinization, the more internal criticism arose from Palestinians opposed to suicide terrorism. They fastened on cases of weak suicide terrorists, according to various parameters, and they exposed their exploitation by the organizations. While the systems of recruitment and activation improved, the training of the suicide terrorists became shorter, and their preparation for the mission became superficial and interrupted. As a result, along with the effect of the reservations, which depreciated suicide terrorism, an increasing proportion of the missions failed or were thwarted by Israeli security forces (which, for their part, improved their ability to cope with suicide terrorism). The first wave of suicide terrorism was more spontaneous and expressed feelings of frustration and resentment. It had an element of catharsis. During the second wave of suicide terrorism, which had a strategic rationale and weighed costs against benefits, the quality of the suicide terrorists deteriorated.

One may infer nothing from the ideology and strategy of the resistance organizations about the figure of the suicide terrorist that they glorify. Rather than being committed to the manifesto, quoting from it, and motivated by it, he is prone to expressions of sentiments and moods. Similarly, the suicide terrorist does not believe in any strategic conception, nor does he think in terms of strategy at all, in contrast to the organization. Unlike the suicide terrorism organization that dispatches him, in effect the suicide terrorist is not radical. Senior ISA men who are experienced in counter-terrorism admit that time and resources were wasted in an effort to create the profile of the suicide terrorist. A senior member of a Palestinian resistance movement and a veteran terrorist told me that the ideal suicide terrorist was "someone the ISA wouldn't suspect." From his explanations it became clear that he did not mean someone with a demographic and biographical profile that would make it hard for the Israelis to isolate him from others and locate him, but someone with a personal profile that would make it easy for Fatah and Hamas to persuade him to undertake the mission.

Almost no features of the demography and biography of suicide terrorists distinguish them from the general population, and it would be hard to explain their choice of suicide terrorism by means of these variables. What about the third variable, the distinct personal characteristics of the suicide terrorist? Let us try to answer this question in the light of a critical examination of some of the stereotypes about suicide terrorists, several erroneous images on which people tried in the past to pin explanations of the phenomenon of suicide terrorism.[34] First there was the effort at a pathological explanation, which we have already discussed. Let us emphasize once again that there is no direct or indirect indication that suicide terrorists are insane. While it can be assumed that some of them had particularly unstable personality structures, in no way can they be described as suffering from a psychotic or sociopathic syndrome, or in any event, these are by no means a significant number.

The suicide terrorist does not necessarily have an extremist character. There is no indication of behavior that is customarily called fanatical or militant in his life history prior to the suicide attack. Before they were recruited, the suicide terrorists did not show political or religious radicalism. Their religiosity, for example, did not go beyond the familiar Palestinian norms of prayer or recitation of verses from the Koran. None of those recruited for suicide terrorism had dedicated themselves to a life of devotion and asceticism with fasts, growing a beard, ritual immersions, puritanical abstinence, and the like. Mystical religious experience or ritual rigidity appeared in their lives, if at all, only close to the time of the suicide mission. Nor, before their recruitment, could the suicide terrorists be characterized as holding a nationalist ideology or moral principles. They were apolitical not only with respect to their distance from active political frameworks, something not self-evident in a mobilized society, under occupation, during a time of popular insurrection. They had no solid worldview, nor did they adhere to a coherent system of thought. Their way of life was not subordinate to any discipline nor devoted to any goal. They were neither idealists nor romantics, not deep thinkers, and not imaginative. When they are induced to speak, they prove to be intellectually and emotionally superficial, unoriginal, materialistic, and prosaic.

The vast majority of suicide terrorists had no history of violence toward members of their family or strangers, nor did they have any criminal record. The recruiters made certain that the suicide terrorists had a clean past, whether, as they claimed, for ethical reasons or to make it harder for the ISA to find them. Moreover, the suicide terrorists' way of life before their mission (and their behavior in prison after failed suicide missions) did not hint that they were belligerent, antagonistic, or assertive toward their surroundings. They were neither rebels against their fates nor protesters against injustice done to them or to others. The suicide terrorist was not extroverted or passionate, like someone demonstrating his pain and anger (or joy). They did not even express their frustration because of the occupation and their hatred of Israelis in a particularly blunt or vociferous way.

In the Israeli police force and the IDF a special task force, including psychologists and criminologists, was created to negotiate with people about to commit suicide as well as with criminals and terrorists who held hostages and were threatening to murder them. In the intifada the ISA entertained the possibility that a suicide attack that went awry might evolve into a hostage situation, and the counterterrorist forces would be called on to negotiate with the human bomb to prevent him from blowing himself up with his victims. During the training of this unit, several simulations of such an event were acted out, based on the profile of the suicide terrorist as drawn by investigators of the Israeli defense system. Below is the abstract of a classified internal document describing the traits of a suicide terrorist whom they had to talk to: he had a poor self-image, an external locus of control that tended to project blame on others; he was introverted and suggestible; he might suffer from existential despair, but not clinical depression; he was not someone who had previously been exposed to violence, but sometimes he had fear of abandonment (causing him to give himself over to the embrace of others); he was not exceptional in hatred of Israel or in aggression beyond what was common in Palestinian society.

Analogues

To examine the characteristics of the human bomb, we will compare him to several types that apparently resemble him and about which we have extensive research-based information. The first analogue has already been discussed in the literature on suicide terrorism and was mentioned in the previous chapter: the altruistic suicide who immolates himself as an expression of protest. Clearly this analogy is limited, because it has no evident aspect of murder, but rather it is violence that a person directs solely against himself. Unlike the suicide terrorist, in this case not only the suicide itself but the rhetoric and practice that precede it testify to ultrapolitical and ethical virtuosity. Usually these altruistic suicides were purists who directed demands for higher standards of morality to their surroundings and to themselves. Unlike the protest suicides and suicides in general, with the suicide terrorists there is no hint of any psychological drama and self-torment that preceded the final, fatal stage, and there are no signs of soul-searching before committing the act of murder. Some of the suicide terrorists did have second thoughts, hesitations, and moments of regret, but these derived from fear of death and fear for the fate of their loved ones, not because of doubts about ideas, religion, or ethics that arose from a principled self-examination. Also after the fact, the suicide terrorists who failed and were arrested did not raise questions regarding the justice of suicide terrorism, nor did they even reevaluate its strategic logic.

A second optional analogy of the suicide terrorist is the young man who joins a cult or new religious movement (NRM). In the past generation, rich research literature has accrued about joining groups of this kind and the motivations for it (though the context is usually that of advanced Western society). Can we learn anything from what is known about joining a sect or church in relation to joining the order of suicide terrorism? Is becoming a human bomb anything like becoming a Moonie?[35] Religious conversion entails abandoning one's former faith and way of life and adopting new ones in their place, a deep change in attitude and identity, indeed, a transformation of personality. Perhaps we can grasp the suicide terrorist as an apostate since undertaking a suicide mission is a step with grave consequences, beyond a transition from normality to a life (however brief) of ultimate devotion, requiring huge investment and radical commitment. However, the suicide terrorist does not join a permanent, intense, and total framework that poses challenges to him over time. Rather this is a focused move, one-off and momentary, perhaps superficial and random, from which there is no turning back.

In studies of adhesion to radical religious and political groups, three possibly overlapping categories of motivations are mentioned: pursuit of meaning or salvation, sensation or action seeking, and pursuit of community or fellowship. The first category characterizes spiritual seekers, people with a career of wandering among various solutions to their existential distress. Very often they are immature and confused, and their search for wholeness and happiness may lead them to murder (as with the Charles Manson group, for example) and suicide. In the history of the suicide terrorists there is no tendency toward experimentation and variety in life experience, and in their mind-set there is no tendency toward philosophical contemplation, as elementary as it might be, of themselves or their surroundings.

One might try to examine suicide terrorists in terms of adventurousness. People in search of excitement flee from routine and boredom and sometimes get involved in experimentation with alcohol, drugs, random sex, fast driving, violation of law and order, and even violence and crime. They can also show openness and imagination that lead them to daring action in business, art, or science. All the behavioral correlatives of a wild and creative mentality like this are absent from the record of the suicide terrorists. The analogy suggested here is to a person who seeks varied, novel, complex, and intense experiences, and therefore takes risks, including physical risks. The perpetrator of an act of suicide terrorism appears to correspond to only some of these characteristics, though it is likely that he does feel the thrill of overcoming fear, which is accompanied by the secretion of high levels of adrenaline. Yet, contrary to expectations and to stubborn rumors, there are no signs that suicide terrorists, as they approach their target, are in what is known as a high state.

A third motivational category, the search for a social framework that will embrace the individual and rescue him from his isolation and marginality, characterizes those who join cults, and it certainly does appear to apply to the case of suicide terrorists. Their demographic, biographical, and personality characteristics make them particularly susceptible to the influence of social networks that offer them a warm home. Members of cults and new religious movements are said to be drawn first of all to a framework that offers close and supportive interpersonal relationships, and only then do they undergo the cognitive transformation that conforms to their new social milieu and ratifies it. Also of suicide terrorism it may be said that it is connected more with affiliation than with conversion.

The comparison of suicide terrorism to religious and political groups that, at a certain stage of their development, channel their energy and devotion in a murderous and suicidal direction is apt. Among these were the People's Temple (1978), Branch Davidians (1993), the Solar Temple (1994–97), and Aum Shinrikyo (1995). The similarity between such doomsday cults and suicide terrorism leads us to discuss a third analogy to the suicide terrorist: the type known in political culture as the fanatic. Here I will mention two heroic projects of historians, sociologists, and psychologists who try to make this pejorative term into an analytical one that seeks to be scientific and objective. I refer to two research traditions that were started and flourished in the 1940s and '50s, after the appearance of mass totalitarian social movements, mainly fascism and Nazism, as well as Bolshevism, in awareness of the results of WWII.

The first of these intellectual traditions under whose inspiration it is possible to examine the suicide terrorist is identified with *The True Believer.*[36] This book examines movements that demand surrender of a distinct self to the degree of self-sacrifice. Even if the goals and worldviews of these movements are contradictory, they are interchangeable, so that an individual can transfer his absolute fidelity from one to another. The crusader remains a crusader, no matter what cross he bears on his back. The movement gives the individual a feeling that he would be incomplete and insecure were he not to meld with it. The identity of the true believer is determined by his belonging to the collective that the movement represents. When he is alone, he has no selfhood, and his identification with the collective and the movement is the source of his potency. And the suicide terrorist? Some researchers regard him as the embodiment of the individual who is so deeply identified with the collective that he nullifies himself within it unto death, and others see him as the embodiment of radical individualism, which alone controls his life and death.

The second tradition is identified with the *Authoritarian Personality* and its ilk.[37] It calls attention to the existence of a personality type characterized by belief and blind obedience to an authority higher than the individual, and the administration of that belief through oppression of one's subordinates. This insight relates to phenomena like the 1940s German who venerated the Führer and subjugated his will to the dictator's whims. At the same time he imposed iron discipline on his household, his wife, and children. There is a correlation between this tendency of the individual to radical conformism and self-negation in relation to the charismatic leader, who is identified with the nation or the religion, and the following traits: rigid and stereotypical thinking, compulsiveness and intolerance of vague situations, toughness and aggressiveness. These are a defense mechanism for a type with a weak ego, who tends to project the causes of his anxiety on groups of others in his surroundings whom he defines as inferior and deserving of extermination. This ethnocentricity usually appears as anti-Semitism as well. Although these studies have gained almost canonical status, certain reservations exist regarding their scientific validity. Nevertheless, they can be a fertile source of inspiration in the effort to understand the suicide terrorist and his motivations.

The dominance of Hamas in Palestinian suicide terrorism invites comparison of the suicide terrorist to the religious zealots known since the 1980s as fundamentalists. Thus, the fourth type to which one may compare the suicide terrorist is the member of a movement of religious reaction against modern secularism in its liberal version. Fundamentalism is characterized by literal interpretation of scripture as a platform for political action and the life of the individual, the family, and the community. Opposition to both the political (and national) and religious establishments, social conservatism, and stringency in the observance of religious norms lead to isolation from the surrounding society and later to an effort to take control of its institutions, with expert exploitation of sophisticated means, including the apparatus of democracy, propaganda, and advanced technology, which they appropriate from the culture they criticize. The suicide terrorist may be seen at best as sympathetic to the fundamentalist movement but not as an activist and certainly not as a leader. The fundamentalist movement, for its part, adopted him and held him up as an example.

The fifth and last type to which we will compare the suicide terrorist is the *nonsuicidal* terrorist. The three types of terrorist mentioned below bring out by contrast the uniqueness of suicide terrorism. The first type is the classical terrorist known to us from the history of terrorism preceding the present generation: from the terrorists against the czar in Russia to Lehi (the Stern Gang), IRA, FLN, and the Basque Underground, as well as Baader-Meinhof and the Red Brigades. Most of them were Western or representatives of ideologies whose source was in the West but which they rejected at the same time—such as Marxists and national liberation groups. All of these terrorists had a total and continuous connection with an organized group with the well-developed worldview of a revolutionary vanguard. They can be characterized as having a career and identity as terrorists. A decided expression of this is found in the engaged rhetoric they share. It is permeated by doctrinairism, polemics, and moralism, infected with messianic romanticism and replete with self-conscious pathos. Since they understand the propaganda function of terrorism, they make use of every possible stage—as seen in their proud declarations, their ceremoniousness, and their fluent eloquence in court—to spread their message. In contrast, the suicide terrorist is inarticulate, prosaic, and laconic. In his interrogation and trial, he shows evasiveness and excuses himself with self-abnegation and diminution of responsibility, or he repeats hollow slogans in mechanical fashion.

The second kind of terrorist to be compared to the Palestinian suicide terrorist is the representative of Jewish terrorism, usually religious, that has played an increasing part in Israeli politics and the Middle-East conflict.[38] He appears either as a virtuoso soloist (like Baruch Goldstein and Yigal Amir); or as a lone wolf, usually a misfit (for example, Ami Poper and Jack Tytell); or as a member of a protofascist gang of immature adolescents who have thrown off every restriction of education and family (mainly the Hilltop Youth); or as members of an elite underground, outstanding in ideological, strategic, and operational sophistication, with high standards of education, elevated socioeconomic status, family connections, prominence in their communities, and extensive connections with the political and rabbinical establishment (e.g., the Jewish

Underground in the Territories). Not a single one of these variants applies to the Palestinian suicide terrorist.

Comparison of a suicide terrorist to the third kind of terrorist, the Palestinian, was implicit in several places in this chapter and will appear below. Here I merely add a number of comments on the margins of the comparison. First, let us point to a similarity, which, though it is only partial, still provokes thought, that between the suicide terrorist and the one who appears to be at the opposite end of the spectrum, the Palestinian terrorist whose violence against Jews is expressed with sudden knife attacks or by running them over with a car. The ISA calls these attacks "atmosphere strikes," and of course it is difficult to prevent them, because there are no warning signs. This is spontaneous terrorism, without any ideological commitment and outside of any organizational context: a momentary impulse, a response to an immediate stimulus, or the exploitation of an opportunity. In contrast, suicide terrorism naturally cannot be simply an individual initiative, though it does have elements of atmosphere and a certain randomness. The perpetrators of the types of Palestinian terrorism discussed here usually have the character of petty terrorists, and it is not by chance that in both cases there is a disproportionate representation of divorced women and other marginal or vulnerable types. Moreover, knife-wielding terrorists take an enormous risk, of which they are well aware. Most if not all of them are killed during the attack. But they do not leave testaments. They are "sacrificial attacks," similar but essentially different from suicide attacks, where the death of the attacker is not only certain but also self-administered.

The Palestinian suicide terrorist and the conventional terrorist share several other characteristics, which have not received sufficient attention in the literature. For example, there is the intermediate place that some of them occupy between the realm of national and religious idealism and that of crime and moral transgression. The history of wars for freedom and revolutions is replete with precedents that demonstrate the thin and permeable boundary between these two realms, and the two-way movement between them. Quite a few terrorists began as criminals who enlisted to serve the exalted values of the collective and thus expressed their special abilities and even gained rehabilitation. Similarly, while engaged in devoted service of the collective, quite a few terrorists were drawn into criminal and violent action unconnected to exalted goals. Among other things, Palestinian terrorism also moves in these gray areas. Among the volunteers and recruits for suicide terrorism were petty criminals and especially people who had committed moral transgressions, such as drug addiction. Their death as suicide terrorists was a form of atonement and return to the path of the just. Former sinners are prominent among the saints of all religions and nations.

I conclude the comparison between suicide and nonsuicidal terrorists with the presentation of a positive finding of solid research regarding the relation between them.[39] A control group was formed of Palestinians with profiles identical to those of suicide terrorists with respect to age, education, organizational affiliation, and other demographic traits, but, unlike suicide terrorists, all of them had a background of terrorism against the Israeli occupation during the intifada. When asked whether at any stage in their armed national and religious struggle they considered volunteering for a suicide mission, they all answered categorically no. It seems that the pressure of social networks and a supportive subculture prove to be an insufficient explanation for turning a person into a human bomb. Suicide terrorism and ordinary terrorism are not on the same continuum. Rather they are two essentially different generic types of terrorism.

Psychology and Social Psychology of Human Bombs

Robert Pape, a prominent researcher into suicide terrorism, asserts that the human bombs are "socially integrated and highly capable [and politically conscious] people who could be expected to have a good future."[40] On the basis of critical examination of all that is known to us about suicide terrorists, particularly the Palestinians, this observation demands substantial correction. Even if we rely on sources of information that tend to glorify the suicide terrorists, such as interviews with members of their families, or viewing of their testaments, we are constrained to locate them on the relatively weak end of the social and psychological scale. Examination of those who failed and were arrested supports this impression.

As reported by both junior and senior prison guards, the most typical characteristic of suicide terrorists is lack of any distinctive or prominent feature. Israeli counterterrorism agents defined most human bombs as colorless, and therefore they were unable to identify them in advance, to prevent attacks, except with the aid of an informer. The suicide terrorist is undistinguished in any possible sense. That is why he suits suicide terrorism, an act that requires blending in. In the early stages of his operation the suicide terrorist must not stand out from his Palestinian brethren, and in the later stages he should not attract attention as he walks among the members of his Israeli target group.

We have no information about suicide terrorists, dead or alive, who can be defined as especially talented, sophisticated, or particularly smart. This was also evident in their operational behavior, which points to their limitations—for example, in choosing a target and penetrating it.[41] They are not charismatic, not curious, not eloquent, nor are they introspective or inquisitive. As mentioned earlier, they do not show aggression, anger, or resentment. One may add that they also lack impressive physical presence: they were not outstandingly handsome, tall, or muscular. Those who spent time with them and conversed with them described them as "vulnerable." Many of them had a history of failure. For every successful act of suicide terrorism, three fell flat. A high proportion of suicide terrorists were identified and arrested, which evidently strengthened their public image and self-image as losers. As for the suicide terrorists who succeeded, their death with their victims was the first and last event that made it possible to see them as having the character or record of winners. Take Muhammad al-Masri, one of the most effective and murderous of the suicide terrorists (Sbarro pizzeria, August 2001), who is described even by his accomplice as a loner, bashful, restrained, and subdued. His mother was surprised that he volunteered for the mission, since he was shy, a poor student, and awkward.

Evaluation of the personality of suicide terrorists requires professional psychological tests, which are always subject to methodological limitations. Against the background of speculative publications lacking an empirical basis, the scholarship of Ariel Merari, who conducted a methodical examination of the population of suicide terrorists imprisoned in Israel during the Intifada, is impressively solid.[42] In a controlled study of those whom he defined as would-be suicide terrorists, in which the standard categories of the American Psychological Association (APA) were applied, and the questionnaires and clinical interviews were analyzed, it was found that the suicide terrorist had a typical personality decidedly different from the personality of the control group, contrary to what is maintained in the literature.[43] Indeed, while a quarter of the control group of nonsuicidal terrorists were found to have psychotic tendencies, not a single one of the suicide terrorists was diagnosed as such. Nor was any suicide terrorist found with a history of hospitalization in a psychiatric ward. In contrast, half of the suicide terrorists were diagnosed as having a tendency to mild depression, whereas among the ordinary terrorists almost none were categorized as such.[44] Many of the suicide terrorists showed signs of discomfort, personal distress, and unhappiness.[45] Researchers quote a senior Hamas leader who told his assistants, charged with recruiting suicide terrorists, "Bring me gloomy boys."[46]

Clear findings indicate introversion, lack of self-confidence, and tendency to be ashamed and to blame others. On the basis of clinical psychology it is possible to link the personality type of the suicide terrorist with the following traits: conventionality, conformism, and a tendency to locate, criticize, and punish those who deviate from the values of the group; lack of criticism of the collective authority; cynicism and hostility toward humanitarian values and humanistic ideas; an obsession with the distinction between strong and weak and ruler and ruled; concern with promiscuity; and superstition and attribution of significance to mystical matters.

Almost two-thirds of the group of suicide terrorists who were examined clinically were found to suffer from a syndrome described by psychologists as dependent-avoidant (four times more than among nonsuicidal terrorists). This personality type is connected to particularly low self-confidence and difficulty in forming independent positions, strong desire to conciliate others, acute fear of rejection, avoidance of confrontational situations, and desire to prevent possible conflict. These traits lead to a tendency to obedience and extreme conformity, and they can be interpreted as encouraging altruistic behavior. Such behavior can lead to the sacrifice of one's life for the collective. The following research finding is especially interesting and consequential: the subjects with the weakest characters, who were the most dependent on others, showed a more positive attitude toward suicide terrorism and categorical willingness to volunteer to be suicide terrorists. Those who were the least apprehensive lest their behavior draw criticism, contempt, and humiliation from others expressed reservations about suicide terrorism and hesitation about enlistment as suicide terrorists.

Enormous pressure was exerted on Palestinian youths during the intifada to become suicide terrorists, the spearhead of the armed struggle against the Israeli occupation. The pressure affected them all, but not to the same extent. Only a few succumbed to it. Public opinion in the West Bank and Gaza Strip encouraged suicide terrorism to such a degree that to be a suicide terrorist was recommended not just as a splendid option for enthusiastic, patriotic youth, but as a natural option, almost a default route to take. Hence, what required explanation, excuses, and opposition was the refusal to become a suicide terrorist. The ability to withstand this pressure required not only the individual's mental resources but also his social resources. The research findings presented above support the claim that the key to the riddle of submission to the suicide terrorism machine can be found in the existence of a personality susceptible to the influence of the recruiters of suicide terrorists. Below I add a suggestion to this argumentation, contending that the solution to the mystery of recruitment is to be found in vulnerability, whose source is also in social structures and interpersonal dynamics, supplementing the logic of personal psychology with that of social psychology.

Despite the supportive atmosphere for suicide terrorism, the recruitment of suicide terrorists was no simple matter. It required overcoming the human tendency to preserve physical security and perhaps also overcoming ethical inhibitions. When the individual is alone, he is less able to resist persuasion to change attitudes that contradict his interests and values than when he is in full interaction with a social milieu that provides him with empathy. Between the agents of influence and the individual whose attitudes they wish to mold, important factors may intervene, such as networks of peers or authoritative and charismatic figures. They back him in the direction of either changing his attitudes or resisting change. The individual cries out for the support of his close and significant surroundings. Sometimes he is trapped in a situation of conflicting loyalties to intermediaries with opposing influence, and they vie with one another, and sometimes loyalties change, and the influence changes direction.

It is no coincidence that a considerable number of suicide terrorists are students in the early years of their studies, and they are recruited in the colleges. A young man arrives in unfamiliar surroundings and is subject to anxiety about success in his demanding studies; he is cut off from his village and childhood friends, and is distant from his family. Then he is exposed to the influence of a sophisticated propaganda machine. In his distress he yearns for a warm social group. Naturally he is drawn to join the networks available in an institutional framework such as worshippers in the local mosque and mainly the student organizations, which are none other than local offshoots of Palestinian resistance movements. At the campus he is also exposed to the charms of various sociometric stars such as admired teachers, student leaders, and religious preachers. All of these forces drive him in one direction, without resistance.

The pressure of social networks and charismatic figures is more effective because of the lack of competitors influencing the potential candidate to move in the opposite direction. In addition, the candidate for recruitment as a suicide terrorist comes from the margins of society, he lacks social skills, and he has experienced social failure. He no longer enjoys the support of the social networks to which he belonged in the past, mainly the family network. The recruitment of a suicide terrorist is a story of struggle between his family and the suicide terrorist organizations. In Palestinian society the power of the individual derives to a great degree from the power of his family, and only it can counter the power of the organizations.

It is difficult not to be horrified at the sight of the jubilant mothers of Palestinian human bombs who shout with joy at their sons' funerals, as if they were their weddings. In the West the impression made by the Palestinian organizations has long been effective: that the families of suicide terrorists are proud of the suicidal attacks of their sons and thank God and the nation for privileging them with the honor of contributing their dearest one to the good of the organization's struggle. Against this background it is surprising to discover that the families of candidates for suicide terrorism are a bastion of resistance to the recruitment efforts of the Palestinian suicide terrorism organizations. It may be said that after the death of their sons, the families speak in two voices. On the one hand, the horrible death is already a fact that cannot be altered. They have to be reconciled to it and alleviate the pain by means of the familiar claim that the sacrifice was not for nothing, but for an exalted aim that justifies it. This rhetoric characterizes the first days after the death, when the family is still in shock, and the mourning is stage-managed by the organization, which dictates not only the ceremonies but also the emotions and declarations of the parents.

The family has several good reasons for playing the role assigned to them by the directors of the intifada culture. First, the glory: usually these families are of marginal status, and at least for some time they gain attention and are given various honors. Similarly the family is promised material support—a high one-time grant and a monthly stipend. These are modest families whose homes have been destroyed by the IDF as a punishment and to be a deterrent. Moreover, their livelihood often suffers because the dead son's contribution to their support has been lost. Hence in their recruitment efforts, suicide terrorism organizations emphasize the reward that accrues in addition to fame, specifically the relatively generous financial compensation made to the suicide terrorist's family.

The family's second voice is heard after the early mourning period has passed, usually in private forums. The happiness was superficial and short-lived. The grief and pain are intimate and prolonged. At a certain stage, most of the families allow themselves to express their pain and feel free to speak critically and angrily about the suicide terrorist organizations in general and about the handlers of the suicide terrorists in particular. They mainly accuse them of exploiting the innocence and weaknesses of their sons against their true wishes and those of their parents.

The residents of the Hebron Hills say that with the passage of time after an attack, the economic status of the families of the human bombs did not improve. Many of them complained that they had been forgotten by the suicide terrorist organizations, and rumors circulate on the West Bank that not a few parents of suicide terrorists developed heart disease and other ailments following the loss of their son.

The central status of the traditional Palestinian family has been increasingly undermined by modernization, especially since the Israeli occupation. Only in small villages in remote areas have enclaves remained in which the patriarchy, the family, and the clan continue to play an important role. Contrary to what is generally thought, less than a third of suicide terrorists come from there. The vast majority of suicide terrorists come from cities, towns, and refugee camps: that is, from places where there has been a decline in the function of the family, and the family has become less consequential for the individual's fate. Moreover, the literature presents data about the hometowns of suicide terrorists, but it does not distinguish between their origins and the place where they were recruited, which is no less interesting. According to one estimate, it may be stated that most suicide terrorists were recruited somewhere other than in their hometowns, that is, far from their families. Hence, there is a connection between the enlistment of Palestinian youth as suicide terrorists and the irrelevance of their families, either because of their weakness or because of their distance from them.

Where the traditional family is less effective, the individual is less resistant to pressures to join the ranks of the suicide terrorists, and that is where suicide terrorist organizations concentrate their recruitment efforts. According to this social-psychological logic, the localities that lend themselves to the capture of souls for suicide terrorism are universities and colleges, central mosques, urban streets and squares, and refugee camps. In the case of the latter, erosion of family unity, decline in the father's authority, and the parents' inability to supervise their children have already been documented and researched. For example, it has been found that the UN Relief and Works Agency for Palestine Refugees in the Near East (UNRWA) contributes to this process by giving advanced education to children, who are better educated than their parents, and by providing free food to anyone, thus undermining the mutual dependence between his family and himself for their livelihood. The Palestinian family, which, in 1960–70, made it difficult for the PLO to establish itself in the West Bank, mainly in the traditional villages, became in the 2000s a difficulty with which Fatah and Hamas had to cope in recruiting suicide terrorists.

During the intifada, a cliché was current in the West Bank that "shahids grow in screwed-up families."[47] A significant number of suicide terrorists come from families that are dysfunctional because of divorce, the parents' illness, or the father's unemployment. Most of the suicide terrorists come from very large families, where there is no effective supervision of the young people's comings and goings during school time and in the evening, times that lend themselves to recruitment. No known suicide terrorist came from the political, intellectual, or financial elite, or from the Palestinian gentry.[48] In the few instances when suicide terrorism organizations began to woo members of families that were strong in their public status and control over their children, this was quickly made known to the heads of the family, and they prevented the recruitment. These families exerted their power both against the organizations, so that they wouldn't approach their children, and against their children, so they wouldn't approach the organizations. An urban legend in the territories speaks of a young man whose father, according to signs and rumors, concluded he was about to volunteer as a suicide terrorist, so he shot him in the leg and wounded him, to prevent his death.

According to Palestinian research, in more than 90 percent of cases, not a single member of the family shared the secret of the young men who went out on a suicide mission. In close to 90 percent of the cases, the families were surprised to learn that their son had become a suicide terrorist because they had not picked up on any warning signs. Almost 70 percent learned about the death of their sons from the media, and more than 60 percent did not notice their son's absence on the night before the mission. Most of the family members of suicide terrorists who were interviewed claim that, had they known that their dear ones intended to become suicide terrorists, they would have stopped them on their way to commit the attack. The ISA knew of several cases in which the family placed itself between their son and his recruiters, preventing his dispatch at the price of a direct confrontation with the suicide terrorist organization. Stubborn rumors, which I was unable to confirm, tell of fathers who threaten both their son and his recruiters that he would report them to the IDF, because a child in prison is better than a dead one. The handlers of suicide terrorists did not dare to deal with candidates who were not cut off from their families, or else they sought to isolate them from their families. The recruiters were afraid that their plot would be discovered by the candidates' families no less than they feared it would be found out by Israeli agents. A young man in the West Bank who had become extremely religious during the months preceding his suicide mission hid his ever more frequent prayers from his parents, for fear they might suspect he was going to become a human bomb and thwart him.

Palestinian suicide terrorism organizations were aware of the conflict of interest with the families of candidates for suicide terrorism and even admitted their weakness with regard to the families. In an interview with a handler of suicide terrorists, sincere revelations of empathy with the families emerged, not to mention qualified willingness to justify them. One senior Hamas operative is quoted as saying, "Only a crazy mother would agree to send her son on a suicide mission." This understanding did not prevent him from dispatching suicide terrorists or make him feel remorseful. I have chosen the case of Naal Abu Halil to demonstrate the tendency of the recruiters to home in on youths from weak families or those far away from their families. He was twenty-two, unmarried, and religious, and he lived in the desert town Dura. His family was a marginal branch of a well-known clan. His father gave up on supporting the family and went to one of the Gulf States. His mother remained in poverty, helpless and mixed up, with seven children, the oldest of whom was in prison. Naal went to Bethlehem to work selling vegetables at a stand in the market, and there he was recruited. Similarly, if a father had taken a second wife in addition to the mother, or if he were unemployed, an alcoholic, or a drug addict, a loving mother would find it hard to keep track of her son and prevent his recruitment. The weakness of the family is a condition for recruitment, and recruitment testifies to the weakness of the family.

In some extreme cases senior members of the organizations apologized for the part they played in recruiting young men who were particularly weak with respect to their personal qualifications or if their recruitment dealt a mortal blow to their family. In one case where they were blamed for sending a sixteen-year-old boy, the only child of a widowed or divorced mother, they had to defend themselves against critical public opinion by admitting to "poor judgment." The public backlash did not focus on the bereaved mother's feelings but on the neglect of her future livelihood, which was dependent on her son's work. Elsewhere I maintain that families that were not strong enough to protect their sons from suicide terrorism organizations and prevent them from becoming human bombs also lacked the power to sustain and perpetuate their sons' glory as shahids. Those who were weak in life went to their death and remained weak afterward.

Fiction and Nonfiction

People have been mulling over the relation between fantasy and reality from time immemorial, which makes the question no less fascinating. Do creations of the imagination reflect actual life, and can they provide insights into it? Following my attempt to present a thorough, unbiased social-scientific picture of suicide terrorists, I would like to juxtapose it with an ambitious effort to portray suicide terrorists from an artistic perspective.

The Attack is an award-winning book by Yasmina Khadra (pseudonym of an Algerian retired army officer),[49] made into an acclaimed movie by the Lebanese-French filmmaker Ziad Doueiri.[50] The main protagonist is an Israeli Palestinian physician who symbolizes the full integration of the two peoples. He is modern in his way of life and enlightened and cosmopolitan in his worldview. His career is successful, he lives in a comfortable fancy home, and he is welcomed among elite Jewish Tel Avivians. He loves his beautiful, bright wife, who shares many of his characteristics and appears to stand out, as he does, by living in the heart of the regional conflict without getting involved in difficult questions about its complexities and tensions. As a senior surgeon, he is summoned one day to treat victims of a severe suicide terrorism attack in which about a dozen patrons of a restaurant were killed. He then learns that his wife, who had disappeared earlier, was one of the victims. Later it becomes clear to him, to his astonishment, that she was the human bomb. Against the background of this discovery, which appears to contradict the values that the couple shared, and as a violation of the trust between them, he loses not only his social status but also his confidence in his fellows and his self-assurance. He gives himself over to a quest for the answer to the secret that led his wife to do what she did, and a solution to the dilemma that churned in secret beneath his happy life until it rose to the surface and exploded. He traces his wife's doings over the year before the event, and thus he discovers the world of his Palestinian brethren in the West Bank. In the course of this orientalist odyssey he meets an Islamic imam and candidates for suicide terrorism, and through them he is exposed to the harsh realities that are meant to explain the act of suicide terrorism: a conquered nation, deprived of its land and its honor, fighting a fierce enemy against which it has no chance. Without his knowledge, his wife freed herself of the illusion of neutrality that had characterized their shared life and chose to identify with the side of the oppressed. This is a stirring drama, replete with rather banal statements about the uselessness of violence between nations.

Both the book and the film contain several interesting comments about human situations, especially about intimacy and trust among couples, but there are no insights that can contribute to an understanding of suicide terrorism. This fiction has a universal, rather apolitical, message, but it borders on the absurd with respect to the phenomenon of suicide terrorism in its historical context. There is hardly a detail in the description of

The Attack that conforms to the facts that were systematically assembled during the intifada. Perhaps the fictional heroine resembles a radical left-ist terrorist in Germany of the 1970s, but if we want to learn something about Palestinian human bombs from *The Attack*, it can only be in a negative way. The shahida of Khadra and Doueiri is secular and liberal (the film makes her a Christian), urbane and sophisticated, from the upper middle class, an ambitious professional, involved in her social surroundings, and a citizen of Israel. It may be added that she is also autonomous, reflective, eloquent, of multifaceted identity, and torn between contradictory loyalties. This suicide terrorist has yet to be born.

3

Accidental Monsters, Unlikely Heroes (B)

Leaders and Followers

Naturally the suicide terrorist draws the most attention from the public and in research because of the spectacular drama and human mystery he embodies. However, the story of suicide terrorism goes beyond the figure and action of the terrorist himself. Suicide terrorism is a collective project, behind which stands a complex political, religious, and operational system: the organization and, within it, the cell—a group of people each of whose members is necessary but not sufficient, and there is division of labor and coordination among them. It is no coincidence that we know of no solo suicide terrorist, acting as a lone wolf. The primary reason for this is practical. Unlike terrorism with guns and knives, the suicide terrorist requires means, planning, and administration, which individual spontaneity cannot provide. There is another reason too: the suicide terrorist does not have the personality or social skills to become a terrorist on his own. He is not autonomous or creative, nor does he possess enough initiative.

This is shown, among other things, by his patterns of behavior in the target area. Only rarely did a Palestinian suicide terrorist stray from the simple instructions laid out for him to overcome unexpected obstacles and facilitate the mission.

The Palestinian human bomb participates in a dynamic system that contains the following elements: a demolition expert who constructs and camouflages the explosive charge; purchasers of various items, from the raw materials of explosive charges (chemical fertilizer, nails, cellular phones, containers, and so on. Such items were often purchased in Israel since Palestinian shops where these things are available were under surveillance), to clothing for disguise as an Israeli; people to locate and lease hideout apartments and a team of lookouts to avoid discovery; scouts and informers to find candidates for recruitment and provide information about them; recruiters for suicide terrorists, who persuade them to commit themselves; gatherers of information about targets in Israel; videographers and photographers responsible for preparing the testament; car thieves and document forgers; money men who transfer cash to finance the apartments and the explosive laboratories, the acquisition of materiel, payment to the activists, and compensation to the families; clergymen who provide a sacred canopy for the operation; decision makers on the strategic level who determine the character and timing of the operation; drivers to transport people and explosives from place to place in the West Bank, and drivers with Israeli identity papers (who usually specialize in transporting illegal workers) to cross the border; delivery men who transfer the explosive charge from its hiding place to the point of departure or a drop-off; pathfinders who precede the suicide terrorist and warn about surprise roadblocks and other obstacles on the way; escorts who make sure the suicide terrorist reaches the target without getting lost and without changing his mind and retreating; and all kinds of other assistants such as people with a European look and individuals, mainly women, who smooth the way through the checkpoints—such as Ahlam Tamimi from the Sbarro attack, who is discussed in another chapter, as well as the case of Irena Polichuk, a prostitute who came from Ukraine and lived in Israel with a stolen identity card. Polichuk married a former client, a Palestinian from the West Bank, and sat next to him in the car when he took a pair of suicide terrorists to the pedestrian mall in Rishon LeZion in May 2002.[1]

This group is flexible in composition and structure. It has members who are connected to an organization and active on a permanent basis in other terrorist actions, suicidal and nonsuicidal. Other elements are sleepers, activated only for the purpose of the attack. Yet others are mobilized and utilized only on an ad hoc basis. Most of these elements are compartmentalized and some are not aware of the imminent consequences of the task they are executing.

Many of those who perform the functions mentioned above are regarded as accomplices by the counterterrorism agencies (*siy'anim*), and others are regarded as organizers. Only one of the latter has a complete picture of the suicide mission. He is responsible for initiating the attack and for coordinating all of its components. He possesses determining authority and is usually a dominant personality. He is the human bomb dispatcher, and sometimes he also makes the explosive charge (the "engineer"). The ability to carry out this function demands a professionalism that is particularly rare, and, though it appears to be technical, it also imparts glamour. The image of the engineer derives from his outstanding character reinforced by the mystique that comes from working with sophisticated explosive materials and esoteric knowledge reserved solely for members of a secret and prestigious guild. This charisma is also inherited, passing from one expert to another, the master to the apprentice, the virtuoso to the one who will take his place after he is killed.

Hereafter this key figure will be called the suicide terrorism entrepreneur. An entrepreneur, by definition, is an independent individualist, with ambition and imagination, prepared to take risks, trained in making decisions and in putting people to work, a pioneer in change, who greatly values self-reliance, strives for distinction through excellence, and assumes responsibility. The Palestinian suicide terrorism entrepreneur is not a link in the chain of command or just a part of the organization. He does not always obey the orders of those above him, and he sometimes is in conflict with the senior members of the organization, especially with the political leadership. Often the entrepreneur not only decides on the operational details of the attack on his own, but he also determines its necessity. He is a talented tactician who often becomes a strategist as well.

The suicide terrorism entrepreneur was a popular hero in the Palestinian community during the intifada, and his popularity exceeded that of the heads of the resistance organizations. While the suicide terrorism entrepreneur headed the wanted list of the Israeli defense agencies, his role has been somewhat neglected in the literature, because attention in the West was diverted to the suicide terrorist, on the one hand, and to the representatives of the organizational leadership, on the other.[2] The archetype of the Palestinian suicide terrorism entrepreneur and the first and foremost figure in the mythos of suicide terrorism was the "engineer" Yehiya Ayash. He was born in 1966 in the village of Rafa, near Kalkiliya in the West Bank, and in mid-1995 he moved to the Gaza Strip, where he lived in cellar hideouts and orchards. He was married, the father of a son, and studied engineering at Birzeit University. From the attack on bus no. 5 in Tel Aviv (October 1994) to his elimination by means of an Israeli booby-trapped cell phone (January 1996) he was directly responsible for the death of fifty-four Israelis. The head of the ISA at that time confided to me, "I went to sleep with him every night and got up with him every morning for fifteen months straight."

The Palestinian suicide terrorism entrepreneur is neither doctrinaire nor an apparatchick, but a man of action. Rather than talking about God and country, he talks about honor and revenge. In comparison to the suicide terrorist whom he dispatches, he is older (twenty-seven or twenty-eight at the time of his activity as an entrepreneur, and some were in their mid-thirties). In most cases he is married with children (often his family connections were his Achilles' heel as a man wanted by the ISA). He is also better educated (almost a quarter of them completed university studies, and about another quarter were forced to leave university because of the intifada; Hamas entrepreneurs stood out in their education), and in some cases they had professional expertise and had gone beyond the limits of parochialism and had seen the world (Abdallah Barghouti studied electrical engineering in Korea; Abas Sayid completed university studies in Jordan and then had two years of training in the United States; Ibrahim Hamed completed an MA at Birzeit).

Most of them were terrorists before the advent of suicide terrorism in the arena of the conflict, and before their imprisonment they had been wanted or arrested by Israel or the Palestinian Authority. They were responsible for more than one act of suicide terrorism (and usually more that were prevented). The terrorism entrepreneur expressed his autonomy and daring not only in the action that preceded his imprisonment but also in his statements after being caught, in interrogation and

Figure 2. Abdallah Barghouti, born in 1972, a Palestinian arch-terrorist, head of the
Hamas military arm in the Ramallah region in the West Bank. A major suicide
terrorism entrepreneur, he initiated and launched many suicide attacks in Israel
(Sbarro pizzeria, Moment Café, Ben-Yehuda mall, Sheffield Club, Hebrew University
cafeteria, and more) during the early years of the second intifada. Caught by the IDF
in 2003, he was sentenced to sixty-seven life sentences and imprisoned in an Israeli
high-security jail. (Photo: Ronni Shaked Private Photography Collection)

in interviews with him, when he allowed himself freedom to deviate
from the clichés of his organization.

An ordinary Palestinian terrorist who stood out in his action within
the framework of the organization and demonstrated ambition and leadership abilities could advance in status and become a senior leader of the
terrorist organization and, as such, initiate suicide terrorism. However,
there is no instance of a terrorist who advanced to become a suicide terrorist; consequently there was never a suicide terrorist who had been an
ordinary terrorist in the past. Whereas an ordinary terrorist can develop
and become an arch-terrorist who handles other terrorists, including suicide terrorists, the suicide terrorist will never become an ordinary terrorist
(not only because if he succeeds in his mission, he will die, and if he fails,
he will be dead from a social point of view) because these are two different

personality types, and their career paths are parallel. Unlike the organizational career of the entrepreneur of suicide terrorism, the career of the suicide terrorist is short and includes just one momentary act. He cannot be promoted to higher ranks, and he has neither a past nor a future.

Based on observation of the Palestinian suicide terrorism entrepreneur when he was still active, and then in his interrogation in prison, and on the basis of interviews with him, one gets the impression of the imposing figure of an intelligent and well-spoken man, authoritative and charismatic, sure of himself and self-aware, resourceful and manipulative. In clinical psychological examination he proves to have a stable personality and a strong ego, resistant to pressure and skillful in dealing with conflicts.[3] Thus, the personality of the suicide terrorism entrepreneur seems the opposite of that of the person he sends on a suicide mission. We have seen that the suicide terrorist is the type known in the literature on groups and social movements as the "follower." The one who dispatches him is definitely the type known as the "leader." These two opposite types are complementary.

On the few occasions when Palestinian terrorists were released from Israeli prisons, most of the living suicide terrorists but not a single suicide terrorism entrepreneur were allowed to stay in the areas of the Palestinian Authority. The latter were sent to Gaza, Jordan, or Turkey. The entrepreneurs headed the lists of the prisoners whose release was demanded by the Palestinian organizations, but Israel objected strenuously because it regarded them as dangerous, especially because they did not express remorse, and some of them hinted that they would resume terrorist activity. In the closed sessions of negotiations for release between ISA delegates and representatives of the organizations, the latter did not insist on the liberation of the entrepreneurs and agreed tacitly with Israel's refusal, because they knew very well that these initiators had leadership qualities, and if they were released, they were liable to challenge the existing leaders and take their place.[4]

Suicide terrorism does not depend on the personality of the entrepreneur in itself or on that of the suicide terrorist, but on their encounter. Instead of thinking in terms of each of their profiles separately, I propose to also view them as one, dynamic, asymmetrical unit. The center of gravity of suicide terrorism is neither the suicide terrorist nor even the entrepreneur, but the relationship between them. Two key figures in suicide terrorism—the dispatched and his dispatcher—are a pair, and I suggest applying the logic of couples to them, according to which observers cannot estimate the full meaning of one without the other, and the dominance of one does not make the other superfluous or decrease his vital necessity to the entire unit. The suicide terrorist identifies with the entrepreneur of suicide terrorism and negates himself before him. The dependence and complementarity between the members of the Palestinian suicide terrorism dyad is not exhausted in the operational aspect, but it has deeper consequences. For example, to borrow an insight from the analysis of married couples, one can overcome the frustrations of the other or fulfill his fantasies. We cannot rule out the possibility that the suicide terrorism entrepreneur enjoys the vicarious experience of blowing himself up in the heart of Israel by means of the suicide terrorist whom he recruits and dispatches.

The suicide terrorist is also the entrepreneur's victim. It seems that the entrepreneur himself, despite his declarations, is not reconciled with the fact that he sends other people to their death, while he himself refrains from volunteering. He denies what could be interpreted as his own cowardice and therefore projects it on the suicide terrorist. The very subtle, impalpable contempt that the entrepreneur feels for the suicide terrorist might stem also from his difficulties in coping with the aspects of his own personality that could be viewed as deserving of contempt.

Although the bond between the entrepreneur and the suicide terrorist is vital, it is not necessarily formed face to face. Usually it is mediated, very short, and sometimes it does not even take place physically at all. For fear of divulging secrets if any component of the network should fail, in Palestinian suicide terrorism—perhaps more than in general terrorism—there is insistence of compartmentalization. Special emphasis is placed in particular on separating the links at either end of the chain—the key figures of suicide terrorism. Communication between the entrepreneur and the terrorist is mainly unidirectional and takes place through messengers and the messengers of messengers. The entrepreneur studies the intended suicide terrorist and transmits instructions regarding his mission by means of notes hidden in drops or codes embedded in telephone conversations, and the like. Until quite an advanced stage, the recruit knows nothing about the identity of the entrepreneur. The human bomb who blew himself up at the Park Hotel only met with his handler once. That man, known by the underground appellation "the Sheikh," came to a secret meeting in the hideout apartment with his head wrapped in a kaffiyeh that hid his face. Even his hands were covered with white gloves, to prevent recognition. Only at the end, actually on the evening before the mission, does the connection between them become direct. The two parties gain an impression of each other without intermediaries for the first and last time. This is an encounter of acquaintance and parting. In the relationships of the entrepreneur and the terrorist, this is a single, fleeting episode of strong connection between two men whose bond has neither past nor future, an enchanted charged moment of intimacy that is not characteristic of the suicide terrorism project.

The fateful meeting is marked by tension between two opposite tendencies. On the one hand, detachment and mystery are built into it. Mainly for reasons of security, maximal precautions are made, going so far as keeping the identity of the entrepreneur a secret. Sometimes he does not reveal his name, and his face is also hidden. On the other hand, there is a breaking of barriers here: direct, open speech, confession, and a physical embrace.

The meeting between the entrepreneur and the suicide terrorist takes place in a bubble, out of any context. Not even the time and place are known to the suicide terrorist, and after he has gone on his way he cannot reconstruct them: late at night, in a closed room in an isolated and unfamiliar safe house. The suicide terrorist is taken blindfolded, bleary from lack of sleep, exhausted from fasting, and emotionally on edge. This is a liminal situation, to which anthropologists attribute great significance, mainly in transitions between statuses.[5] After all, this is almost the last moment between life and death. In this liminal situation, typical of rites of passage, the entrepreneur—here in the role of a shaman who links heaven and earth and gives meaning to things—has total authority over the suicide terrorist, in the role of the novice here, deprived of all defenses, the human raw material in the hands of the master craftsman, who can give him any form he likes.[6]

The relations between the entrepreneur and the suicide terrorist are unique. Critics see them as cynical and cowardly relations of abuse and exploitation. Opponents of suicide terrorism, including those among the Palestinians, represent the suicide terrorist as the victim of interests not his own and blame the entrepreneur and the organization behind him. The suicide terrorist is driven to death by social forces that the entrepreneur embodies. Though his status is authoritative and glorious, the entrepreneur is sometimes forced to relate to the issue of his moral responsibility for the life of the suicide terrorist. In a tone in which it is difficult to distinguish apologetic strains, he repeats a standard set of arguments: it is the will of Allah and of the nation. The mission is unpleasant and thankless, but it was imposed on him by forces greater than ourselves. It is not easy to send people to their deaths, but the dictates of the national conscience outweigh scruples, to submit to which would be a luxury we cannot afford. We also take risks. We are wanted men, living on borrowed time, and ultimately, like all our predecessors, we will be imprisoned or eliminated. If it weren't for us, who would perform this difficult task, which demands special abilities? In addition, the entrepreneurs emphasize the suicide terrorist's motivation to volunteer and reject the argument that the latter have no will or power of their own.

Middle Eastern lore, nourished by a mixture of Palestinian rumors and bits of information released by ISA investigators, is laden with episodes that show that the suicide terrorists are rather passive objects of the cruel and utilitarian manipulation of the entrepreneurs. Several examples that I managed to verify in part refer to suicide terrorists who were gripped by fear or remorse, but whose handlers ignored their requests to retreat, urged them on with various excuses and lies, and even forced them into situations where they had no choice. Ibrahim Sarahna, who sent a pair of suicide terrorists to the pedestrian mall of Rishon LeZion, was at the beach in the city with his wife when he got a telephone call asking him to withdraw the suicide terrorists, who were pleading for their lives. After a long argument they returned to the target area, where the female suicide terrorist, Arin Shibat, managed to squeeze into their car only after a physical struggle. A bitter argument broke out in the car, in which the handlers tried to force her to get out again and complete her mission, despite her reluctance, while the other suicide terrorist, the sixteen-year-old Isa Badir, was left outside, weeping. In his bitter despair and confusion he cried, "I'm hungry." In response they threw him a bill and told him "go buy falafel." They then drove back to Bethlehem (where they were later arrested).[7] The suicide terrorist Mahand Tha'er, who was recruited in Tul Karem during the mourning period for his father, was sent to Ramallah, where no explosive charge was found for him, and his mission was changed. When he refused to go on it, he was imprisoned by his handlers. It was claimed that if he were caught, he might inform on his dispatcher, because he had already seen his face (October 2001). According to other stories, the entrepreneurs are stingy and corrupt. They pocket a large part of the suicide terrorism budget instead of passing it on to the terrorist and his family.[8] The ISA claims that some handlers of suicide terrorists regard their operational service as a good source of income. Other stories testify to their coarseness and contempt toward the suicide terrorist. In a telephone conversation intercepted by the ISA, an entrepreneur was heard calling a suicide terrorist, "Ass!"[9]

The Ideal Candidates and Their Recruitment

"As pure as the white sand at the seashore"—this is how a potential suicide terrorist was described by a sheikh, a man with spiritual authority in Hamas in the Balata Refugee Camp. On the basis of his knowledge of the processes for choosing and training suicide terrorists, he insisted that the minimum demand for recruits must be that they "have a good name in society," "honor their parents," "stand out in study of the Koran," be "mature and responsible," and "be at peace with himself and determined in his path."[10] Very few of the actual suicide terrorists, including those who represented Hamas, met these high standards for acceptance. The public relations of the Palestinian suicide terrorism organizations accentuated the demanding criteria according to which the suicide terrorists were chosen. A pamphlet laying out the characteristics of the ideal suicide terrorist was published in the name of Jamal Mansur, a senior Hamas leader in Nablus, shortly before he was eliminated by Israel (July 2001). Most of the suicide terrorist lacked these qualities.

One hundred ninety-six Palestinians died in suicide attacks between 1993 and 2008, and more than five hundred were captured by Israel before they completed their mission. The head of the ISA during the intifada told me that at the time he had a list of another four hundred residents of the West Bank and Gaza who were on what he called "the waiting list."[11] The recruits waiting to be sent on suicide missions were known on the streets of the West Bank as *shuhada al-hayim* (living martyrs). Persistent rumors circulated according to which the candidates for suicide terrorism were given certificates of honor as shahids to-be. Salakh Sheha-deh, a senior Hamas operative, boasted that "four thousand are eager to give up their lives" in suicide missions. Among other things, Israel tried to cope with the multitude of candidates by mass preemptive arrests, so that during the turbulent period of the early 2000s eight thousand Palestinians were arrested and interrogated. At that time, masses of young men roamed around the Palestinian population centers and boasted openly or hinted that they had been recruited for the suicide terrorism project as future human bombs. It is hard to estimate the extent of this phenomenon and especially hard to evaluate the reliability of this self-presentation. But without a doubt it was fashionable and indicative of the public atmosphere in the territories occupied by Israel. The heads of the ISA did not conceal their admiration for the organizations' strong ability to recruit volunteers. They found some consolation in the high proportion of suicide missions that were thwarted: a ratio of three to one between the suicide terrorists who failed and were captured and those who succeeded in their missions.

The significant level of failure in suicide terrorism has not received attention in the research literature. The failures have to be examined against the background of the relative simplicity of suicide terrorism, which is thought of as one of its advantages. The instructions to suicide terrorists are general and elementary. These instructions usually consisted of a basic description of the target (a bus line, for example) and a basic description of the mission ("Try to kill the maximum number of Jews," and "If you're uncovered by the Israelis, blow yourself up with the people who arrest you"). They did not specify the ideal target ("Focus on young males," for example), and no restrictions were imposed ("Avoid killing children," for example). When the woman suicide terrorist Wafa Samir Bas was sent by Fatah to blow herself up at the Erez checkpoint, she asked how she should act if there were Palestinians nearby. The dispatchers instructed her not to take any notice of that (June 2005).

Training of the suicide terrorists was short and superficial, and it was always done on an ad hoc basis. The organizations never had commando brigades of shahids at their disposal—a reservoir of recruited cadres who had already been trained systematically, nurtured, and prepared to leap into action on command.[12] At most, when there was a delay in a mission, the need arose to maintain the intensity of the suicide terrorist's motivation, and for that purpose he was surrounded by supervisors (and sometimes coddled with money to waste). The sloppiness of the preparation of suicide terrorists for their mission is even notable in the religious dimension of suicide terrorism. Ostensibly there ought to have been the sanction of a qualified religious authority, but because of the pressure of the circumstances this was done only in a general and casual way. In cases of complications with ethical implications, all the details were not presented to the sheikh, and they made do with a priori permission granted on condition that they act "according to the law of Islam."[13] Hamas insisted on "spiritual" preparation only in the first ten attacks, which gained mythological status. The Jihad, in some cases, made certain "to strengthen the suicide terrorists' will and accustom them to death" by spending the night in a grave they dug themselves in the Gaza cemetery.[14] The operational training consisted of little more than a few minutes of belting on the explosive charge and instruction on how to press the activation button. As an example of the hasty sloppiness of activating suicide terrorists we will once again offer the case of Naal Abu Halil. Immediately after he was recruited, he was ordered to go to a ravine that leads out of Bethlehem. On the way he met the two handlers, who accompanied him for a few minutes until he approached the border with Israel. The original plan was to commit a double suicide attack, but the second explosive charge never arrived at the launch point. In the field, in the dark, they placed the charge on his body, and to overcome difficulties in belting him, they tore the lining of a sweat suit, which they took out of a plastic bag. After leaving him, he found a cave to spend the night in, and the next morning, at dawn, he entered the Gilo neighborhood in Jerusalem, boarded the no. 20 bus, and blew himself up (November 2002, eleven dead, all of them schoolchildren).

Many failures were caught when they were already in the operational stages of the mission, and a significant number of them were in Israeli territory, on their way to the target, near it, or actually at it. Some of them were seized with fear or remorse and froze or fled, or turned themselves in. Others failed to conceal signs of nervousness and confusion, leading to their discovery in time. Some of them failed to overcome technical problems in activating the charge, and some of them did not manage to react quickly enough to blow themselves up when policemen, soldiers, or citizens fell upon them and caught them. Perhaps if the procedures for recruiting and training them had been more effective, the ratio between successful and failed suicide terrorist attacks would have been reversed.

In rare cases the failed suicide terrorist returned and was sent out on another mission. Muhammad al-Rol was a twenty-two-year-old from Nablus, an advanced student in Islamic religious law at An-Najah University, sent by Hamas to blow himself up on the no. 32 bus in the Gilo neighborhood of Jerusalem, taking nineteen Israelis with him to the grave, all of them elderly or children (June 2002). Before this he had written three testaments, two on the eve of missions that were never carried out. His last mission also got fouled up and was prolonged, and he committed it only after being passed back and forth among several handlers. Most of the failures were caused by a suicide terrorist whose determination was deficient. He always attributed his failure to the will of Allah. In some cases the suicide terrorist retreated at an advanced stage and excused his behavior by claiming a technical failure in activating the charge, difficulty in locating the target, or sensing that he had been identified. In some cases the suicide terrorist tried to evade his obligation even before crossing the border and used childish excuses, as if he only wanted a slight delay until after an upcoming school exam or a visit to a relative who was ill. A suicide terrorist's remorse and retreat usually took place after he had been left alone for a while, mainly when the preparations for the mission encountered logistical or other difficulties—if the explosive charge or transportation were unavailable, for example—and they lasted longer than planned. This is the background for the efforts of the suicide terrorism entrepreneurs to make sure that someone else kept constant, close supervision over the suicide terrorist, and especially to shorten the time between recruiting the suicide terrorist and sending him on his mission as much as possible. To minimize the possibility that someone who had already committed himself to execute a suicide attack might renege, sometimes on the last night they would attach one or two colleagues to him, who would pretend that they, too, were suicide terrorists about to set out on a parallel mission. The heavy pressure exerted by Israeli intelligence agencies also made it necessary to rush the recruitment and training of the suicide terrorist. Senior ISA people and IDF brigade commanders in the West Bank report several cases in which the gap between prevention of an attack because of information received and the suicide terrorist's arrival at the target and the explosion was a matter of just a few minutes. The suicide terrorism entrepreneurs knew that very well, which is why they tended to compress the training stage or forgo it completely, and recruitment was carried out unpredictably, when the opportunity arose. During certain months of the intifada, a norm emerged among the Palestinian suicide terrorism organizations of carrying out the missions after just one night or even on the same day. According to the testimony of family members, more than 60 percent of the suicide terrorists were not absent from home even for a single night before setting out on their mission, and another 20 percent were absent for only one night.[15]

Because of the immediacy of the action, among other factors, several attacks were committed on a local basis without authorization of the organizational leadership. Isa Badir, a seventeen-year-old from Bethlehem, dispatched by Fatah, was recruited near his school and sent from there that very morning straight to Rishon LeZion, so they only had time to link him up with a female accomplice, belt the charge on him, and dye his hair blond (May 2002). Rami Ghanem, from a village near Tul Karem, an accounting student at a local college, transferred his loyalty from the Popular Front to the Jihad because he was suspected of collaboration with Israel, and within a day he went out and blew himself up in a café in Netaniya (March 2003). The charge was stuffed into a small can and attached to his belly with rags. Another suicide terrorist was taken to an open field immediately after his recruitment, fitted with an explosive belt, and sent to Israel in a car that happened to be available, while his only preparation was a few minutes of instruction and examination of the activator of the explosive charge with an electrician's screwdriver.

Usually the suicide terrorist cooperated with the arrangements to hasten his mission, and sometimes he himself pressed his handlers to send him quickly. From the moment he committed himself, he lost patience. Waiting was nerve-racking and aroused doubt in the terrorist himself, that he might be tempted to change his mind. At this stage he became aware that if he did change his mind, he could no longer return to his former life but would be persecuted by the Palestinians, who would mock his cowardice and lack of loyalty, as well as by the Israelis, who would define him as a wanted man and pursue him doggedly. In either case, his life would not be worth living. Similarly, there were suicide terrorists who preferred to go on missions with a partner to make it easier to overcome fear, and together they would reinforce one another. A pair of nineteen-year-old childhood friends from Nablus, Barak Jalima and Samer Nuri, blew themselves up on a mission from Fatah at a distance of two hundred meters and fifty seconds from each other in the central bus station of Tel Aviv (January 2003, twenty-three dead). For their part, the organizations gradually developed the system of pairs, which proved to be particularly effective. First, the murderousness increased, especially if the second suicide terrorist blew himself up shortly after the first one, after people began to provide first aid, the security forces arrived, and curious onlookers gathered. Second, terrorists in pairs supervised each other, and because of mutual embarrassment, there was less of a chance of remorse. The organizations preferred for the two to be strangers to each other and made sure to prepare them for the mission separately, only introducing them to each other at the last moment, for fear that one might weaken the resolve of the other, actually making it easier for them to get cold feet. Compare the double attack at the Beit Lid intersection, which was particularly murderous (January 1995) to the double attack on the pedestrian mall of Rishon LeZion, which failed because of the dynamic of mutual panic (May 2002).

The model of the dual attack came into being by chance, but afterward, in a process of trial and error, it gradually developed on the basis of accumulated local knowledge. The practice of recruiting suicide terrorists and activating them never reached a point of fixed, systematic, and binding consolidation. The pressure of Israeli security agencies imposed decentralization and haste on the organizations, preventing them from working out a doctrine of Palestinian suicide terrorism. At most the organizations acted according to a few rules of thumb, which were developed over the years and passed from cell to cell. For example, an effort was made by the handlers never to leave the recruited suicide terrorist without supervision even for a moment, keeping him busy with pep talks, so he wouldn't change his mind, and at the same time isolating him because, were he to socialize with anyone, something would leak out, or his behavior might betray his identity as a chosen suicide terrorist. There are reports of young men who were recruited and then strutted around town like peacocks, so that everyone around them knew they were about to be sent on a suicide mission.

The process of recruiting suicide terrorists begins with scouting among local supporters of suicide terrorism on the margins of the organizations. Some of them act on their own initiative. While living their ordinary lives, they keep their eyes open and an ear out in their communities, looking for candidates. They are especially attentive to rumors about young men who "are wandering around in the street" and who express themselves in various forums—in cafés or among friends, for example—in a way that seems appropriate. They might curse Israel, speak out strongly against the occupation, or threaten revenge. Sometimes information about young men like this comes from their friends or distant relatives. Some people compare the work of these scouts to that of drug pushers, who sniff around at schoolyard gates for potential users. The moment a youth of this sort is noticed, they close in on him to get him to talk. With various excuses, they start an apparently innocent conversation with him and, indirectly and cautiously, they move forward to the subject of suicide terrorism. Their free dialogue naturally flows in that direction, because suicide terrorism is a hot item. They try to get the youth to speak in favor of the project and test to see how far he is willing to take part in it. If they get the impression that he is a serious candidate, they pass his name on to contacts, usually men in the community who are known to be activists in an organization. They meet the candidate in a concealed place such as a mosque or a nearby ravine, to see how serious he is and whether he has to be persuaded. Sometimes they introduce the candidate to someone senior in the organization in a hiding place, without identifying him. At the same time they make certain to give the candidate a "spiritual envelope"—he's invited to meet with a clergyman, who supplies reasons from the Islamic tradition. Gradually they isolate the candidate and increase the pressure. An explicit proposal on the part of the organization is not voiced until an advanced stage, and they do not go on to the operational stage before ensuring commitment, mainly by recording a testament.

The patterns of recruitment of candidates for suicide terrorism have changed significantly during the decade after the intifada. In the present scene of suicide terrorism in Iraq and Syria, for example, recruitment is transnational, making use of advanced technologies of dissemination, persuasion, and instruction. A connection has been created between recruitment and sophisticated global Internet media. The candidates for suicide terrorism undergo prior radicalization on the Web. Palestinian suicide terrorism was exempt from this requirement. A degree of influence on the recruitment of suicide terrorists for the Palestinian organizations was exerted by the commemorative websites and video testaments that appeared online in Arabic only. The messages there were simple from a visual standpoint and transparent in their psychological manipulations.[16] Below are illustrations of the local, popular, and spontaneous recruitment process of the Palestinian suicide terrorist. Jamal Tawil, a senior Hamas operative in the West Bank, reported in his interrogation: "A young man of about twenty-three, thin, with a mustache, approached me, a resident of Bitunya—I don't remember his name—to ask my advice about something. After we talked about various subjects, he told me that he had a cousin on his father's side, married with a baby, very religious, and she wanted to volunteer for a suicide terrorism action. He asked my opinion. I answered that there were other ways to contribute to Palestinian society. We parted, and then I consulted about the matter with a clergyman (who supported my position)" (April 2002). Hasan Salama, a senior Hamas leader from Gaza, said in his interrogation: "I looked and looked for candidates to be suicide terrorists (in the Hebron region) but I couldn't find any. Somebody told me that at the college in the Ramallah area somebody knew somebody who was leaning toward volunteering for a suicide mission. I met him on Friday, and on Sunday he went out on his mission." We also know of a candidate who had to be evaluated and persuaded, and for that purpose Yehiya Ayash himself was called in. The engineer used all his charisma, but it is not known whether he was identified by the candidate. The meeting lasted only a few minutes, out of town, under a tree.

Social networks intervened in the connection between the candidate and those who recruited him—childhood friends, regular worshippers at the local mosque, the student association, even a soccer team, as was conspicuous in Hebron and Tul Karem. In one instance Israeli security agents burst into a football match to make a preemptive arrest. The networks served to transfer information to their members and to exert group pressure on them. The candidates were usually on the margins of the networks, and a weak link in them. In the internal discourse of the ISA, the system of recruitment of suicide terrorists was referred to ironically as "one friend brings another," as in the joining of exclusive clubs. Veteran intelligence agents raised the question of the differences and similarities between recruiting suicide terrorists and their activation by the suicide terrorism entrepreneurs and the relations between Israeli agents and Palestinian informers.

The suicide terrorist recruiters know how to find candidates in appropriate situations—at prayer on Fridays, at mass rallies, and among those offering condolences in the mourning tent for a shahid in the family's courtyard. There are places represented disproportionately in the list of suicide terrorists, like the Jenin refugee camp, which was controlled by the Jihad organization and where a tradition of martyrdom was established. The ideal location for recruitment was at colleges and universities, where individuals were far from the watchful eye of their families, and where there was a national or religious ideological density. The dominant factors that shaped the local subculture were the student associations, which were bastions of the Palestinian organizations, mainly el-Kutla el-Islamiya, which was connected to Hamas. About half of the suicide terrorists were recruited in institutions of higher education and especially in certain universities and colleges, like the Polytechnic in Hebron, and especially An-Najah in Nablus. This religious institution produced nearly thirty suicide terrorists. The Palestinian press called An-Najah "the womb of shahids." It is interesting to see which institutions have a weak or no correlation with suicide terrorism. The prominent case is the elitist Birzeit University in the West Bank. It has been radical in its anti-Israeli positions, dominated for long periods by the Hamas student association, and was a hotbed of terrorism. Even arch-terrorists emerged from it. Nevertheless, it had practically zero representation among suicide terrorists.[17] The explanation is to be found in several interconnected causes. A significant percentage of the students are Christian, the institution is located among towns with Christian presence,[18] many of the teachers were educated in the United States, the institution has a Western academic orientation, and the tuition is relatively high. Hence the social composition of the student body is middle to upper class. Whereas the perpetrators of suicide terrorism are conspicuous in their absence in the list of students and graduates of the institution, several important suicide terrorism entrepreneurs star in it, headed by Yehiya Ayash and Ibrahim Hamed.

The recruiters of suicide terrorists had several red lines that they were proud of and usually avoided crossing. They mainly tried not to recruit only sons, those whose families' livelihood depended on them, and fathers. In contrast, there were several types of Palestinian youths that suicide terrorism activists homed in on because they had learned from their experience that they were easy to recruit. One type are the bigmouths, who are addressed when they're still "hot" and can be "taken at their word." For example, youths who, during the funeral of a shahid, call for revenge publicly. Then they are taken aside for a talk of clarification and persuasion. Or else there were those who, in a more intimate occasion, told a distant relative that their dream was to die as a shahid. Then they are tested by someone who can make them talk. Also boastful guys, who usually didn't intend at first to volunteer to be suicide terrorists but were gradually swept into a situation where refusal would be interpreted as faintheartedness. In Palestinian youth culture, respect is given to male behavior with honor, and any withdrawal from a declared commitment is regarded as waffling and cowardice, deserving of condemnation and shame. In contrast to social death of that kind stands the glory that recruiters promise in return for acceptance of physical death. ISA investigators report that the suicide terrorists who were caught were usually fearful, but in their interrogation it turned out that they feared what their handlers and the Palestinian public would think about them in light of their failure no less than they feared their fate at the hands of the Israeli enemy.

A second type is someone burdened with a social stigma, who can be leveraged into recruitment by means of the threat to reveal and revile it in the case of refusal. One well-known example are those with homosexual inclinations, who know that if their sexual orientation is made public, they will be subject to absolute contempt and ostracism. Apparently there were cases in which a stigma attributed to a candidate had no basis in reality but was merely a rumor—as when a young man's extravagance arouses suspicion of collaboration—and there were cases in which the recruiters exaggerated or invented the stigma, as when a young woman was seduced into having extramarital sex and then threatened that she would be called a whore in public. About half of the eight female suicide terrorists were variations of this type. Most of the candidates of this type were not only coerced into consent because of the high social price they would have to pay, but were also persuaded by the possibility that their death would atone for their "deviant" behavior.

In addition to these two types, who feared for their good name, there were those whom the recruiters homed in on because they knew they were undergoing a personal crisis, mainly because of childlessness or divorce among the women, and failure in studies among the men. It is assumed the people in distress will be easier to persuade to give up their lives because they feel that they're worthless anyway. In these cases suicide terrorism can be a substitute for suicide, but the kind that will not be regarded as an expression of weakness or a religious transgression, but as a show of the courage that promises religious redemption. The other half of the eight women suicide terrorists were of this kind.

A fourth kind of Palestinian youth that recruiters concentrate on are bashful boys, usually those who lack social skills. A senior activist in one of the suicide terrorism organizations claims that it is well known that this timid and subdued type is also completely nonpolitical and, with respect to public matters, falls somewhere between indifferent and ignorant. It is also known that this type is often religious. He can be found alone, late at night, praying in the local mosque. Suicide terrorist entrepreneurs and their assistants look for him for two reasons: first, it is easy to convince him to become a suicide terrorist because he has almost no ability to resist the representatives of the organization; and second, he is appropriate for suicide terrorism precisely because of his conformist and submissive personal characteristics. When he enters Israeli territory and approaches the target, he must meld into his surroundings and avoid standing out, and in the end he must also avoid confronting it. A senior Tanzim man who was imprisoned for many years said, "The organizations are excellent at choosing the ideal suicide terrorist—they identify those who can't look at someone coming toward them straight in the eye."[19]

Volunteering and Being Volunteered

Not everyone who volunteered to be a suicide terrorist was accepted by the Palestinian organizations. Often the entrepreneurs were reluctant to accept enthusiastic young men who addressed them on their own initiative and asked to be sent on a suicide mission. They underwent various investigations and particularly severe screening. In fact the motivations of the volunteers were seen as suspicious. First, they were apprehensive that collaborators with the ISA might pretend to be interested in suicide terrorism. The organizations also claim that they eliminated those who didn't meet their religious and ethical standards. Hamas, unlike Fatah, apparently rejected several volunteers because of "impure motives." Other volunteers were turned away as inappropriate for different reasons. Darin

Abu-Aisha was rejected by Hamas because of Sheikh Yassin's opposition to dispatching female suicide terrorists, so she was sent by Fatah, which was less choosy (February 2002, Makabim checkpoint).

Tens of thousands attended assemblies in memory of suicide terrorists, but the recruiting of a few hundred suicide terrorists involved difficulties. In a public atmosphere that supports suicide terrorism enthusiastically it is also difficult to distinguish between soliciting and volunteering. Especially in the second wave of suicide terrorism (2000–5), whether or not to call some of the suicide terrorists volunteers is a matter of interpretation, since they were recruited after being found suitable and heavy social pressure was exerted on them. Take a young man of weak character whom recruiters identified and used all sorts of manipulative techniques on after hearing that he had spoken to friends in favor of suicide terrorism. Is he a volunteer or a dupe? According to a senior Fatah member, only a few of those located immediately accepted the recruiters' proposal. Others accepted only after the recruiters invested efforts at persuasion, and many refused despite the pressure. Even among enthusiastic volunteers there were some who changed their minds and withdrew with various excuses. Some were hesitant even as they approached the target.[20]

The organizations try to create the impression that all the suicide terrorists were volunteers. According to a study of would-be suicide terrorists, about half of them were volunteers, and half were pressured into it.[21] However, this conclusion is problematic, since the data is mainly based on research into the suicide terrorists and their handlers while they were in prison. Suicide terrorism entrepreneurs tend to exaggerate the proportion of volunteers, not only to conform with Palestinian propaganda, but also to free themselves of ethical responsibility for recruiting suicide terrorists. The suicide terrorists who failed tend to emphasize the motif of volunteerism to glorify themselves in the eyes of their comrades in prison and Palestinian public opinion. In contrast, in their interrogation, some of the same suicide terrorists reported that pressure was exerted on them to be recruited, but this was in order to decrease their guilt before their trial. Many of the suicide terrorists were what could be called forced volunteers, meaning that they were subject to manipulation of a more or less subtle kind, which hardly allowed them not to volunteer. Of the few who may be called volunteers in the full sense of the word—an exceptional case in several ways—there was Ra'ad Misq. He was twenty-nine, married and father of two, the imam of a mosque, a schoolteacher, and a tutor of the Koran at the college in Hebron, with a master's degree in Islamic studies from An-Najah University. In his youth he was imprisoned in Israel for a year. He volunteered to go on a suicide mission for Hamas in Jerusalem, disguising himself as a Haredi man and blowing up a bus full of people on their way to pray at the Western Wall (August 2003, twenty-three dead). Before setting out on his mission, he recorded a testament lasting almost an hour, during which he was filmed in his office, singing songs, with a rifle in his hands and his little children on his knees.

Here I touch briefly on the motives of the human bomb, that which impels or draws him to suicide attack. I will begin by reviewing several common observations about suicide terrorism, truisms repeated in the research literature. First, a distinction must be drawn between the motives of the suicide terrorist and those of the instigators and the organization behind them.[22] Thus suicide terrorists are not moved by strategic considerations. It must be recalled in this context that they are generally not active members in the organizations, and not particularly political. This implies a distinction between personal and collective motives. Second, a distinction must be made between manifest and declared motives and tacit motives, which are sometimes denied. The attribution of motives is based on examination of the suicide terrorists' testaments, interviews in prison, and the testimony of their families. Hence the suicide terrorist is usually presented as being motivated by ideals and not by the quest for a solution to personal distress. Third, the personal motives of the suicide terrorist must be distinguished from the functions that suicide terrorism fulfills and the achievements of the project in relation to its aims.[23] This is the place to recall the distinction between rational and irrational motivation. This distinction is also reflected in the chronology of commentaries on suicide terrorism. The first generation of observers of suicide terrorism tended to explain it as an expression of insanity, while the prevailing wisdom in the scholarly literature of recent years is that it is in fact a rational act.[24] A slightly different distinction is that between instrumental and symbolic motives. We have emphasized the expressive, cathartic, and ritual aspects of suicide terrorism in other chapters of this book, whereas suicide terrorism is routinely presented as a strategic option, a modus operandi, not an a priori value in and of itself.

The literature is replete with categorizations of suicide terrorists according to their motives. Most of them are variations on the distinction between those whose motives are religious as opposed to those whose motives are political or ethnonational, those whose motives are personal (such as rage or hatred rooted in humiliation), and, finally, those who were manipulated into volunteering as suicide terrorists.[25] However, this categorization is merely analytical, for in fact the motives overlap partially and appear together in various blends. For example, there is no suicide terrorist whose religious motivation is not combined with nationalist motivation, and there is no suicide terrorist whose personal qualities and past were not taken into consideration by the recruiters. Of course there are various types of suicide terrorists for whom one or two motives are dominant, while others are marginal. For most suicide terrorists, the personal motivation is decisive, while collective motives are paid lip service. The suicide terrorist himself usually finds it hard to distinguish among his motivations or to define them precisely. The typical cocktail of patriotic, religious, and personal motivations sounds more like the expression of a mood than of a well-ordered and defensible doctrine.

Academic discussion of the motives of suicide terrorism suffers from two flaws. First, it confuses the motives of the suicide terrorist with the explanations of the phenomenon of suicide terrorism. Note the common accounts of reasons for suicide terrorism in psychological terms (life crisis, deviance, or predisposition), sociological terms (poverty, ignorance, etc.), political terms (the desire to liberate the homeland, and the like), or religious terms (jihad or the desire to enjoy the pleasures of the world to come).[26] The second flaw relates both to the motives of the suicide terrorist and to explanations of the phenomenon of suicide terrorism, and it is more widespread. Most of the reasons given for suicide terrorism in the literature are not unique to it but apply to terrorism in general. One familiar argument in research on suicide terrorism relates it to trauma or to the desire for revenge in response to humiliation, physical injury, or the infringement of the rights or interests of the suicide terrorist or his relatives by agents of the occupation.[27] But trauma and revenge, like hatred and rage, that arise as a result of the humiliating experiences of checkpoints and interrogations are not unique to the background of suicide terrorism but are components of the background of all kinds of terrorism. This is also true of the popular argument regarding the aspiration to liberate the homeland from a foreign yoke as a factor underlying suicide terrorism.[28] Thus matters such as the religious duty of jihad against infidels or the desire to punish Israel and deter it play a role in all the violent actions of Hamas and Fatah, not specifically suicide terrorism.

Below I will focus on three specific motivating factors for suicide terrorism *alone*.[29] All three of the factors to be treated here are present in the recruiters' rhetoric of persuasion and encouragement in conversation with the candidates to become suicide terrorists. The first element is financial reward. Twenty-five thousand dollars was not a trifling sum in the Palestinian territories during the intifada, whether their source was Libya, Iraq, or the West. This sum expressed the organization's responsibility to the suicide terrorist's family, as compensation for the livelihood it lost and to rebuild the house that the IDF would destroy as a deterrent.[30] According to rumors that circulated in the West Bank, the families of suicide terrorists moderated their criticism of the organizations that had sent their sons to their deaths for fear that the material reward would be denied them. In several cases the initiators of suicide terrorism also rewarded the terrorists themselves with cash, to squander and spend on parting gifts to their loved ones.

The second factor is the promise of glory to the suicide terrorist and of raising the status of his family. Repeated broadcasts of photographs of the suicide terrorist in macho poses, with various weapons, or a giant mural portrait of him at the entrance to the neighborhood where he was born were some of the posthumous signs of admiration accorded to the suicide terrorist. He sometimes received honors even before his death, in the short time between his recruitment and setting out on his mission. This was when supervision by the suicide terrorism entrepreneurs was relaxed, despite fear of exposure: the candidate would walk about in the town or refugee camp with the aura of a living shahid. Even if he didn't proclaim it explicitly, the candidate would broadcast signs that he had been chosen to set out on an imminent suicide terrorism mission—such as fine clothing and a fancy haircut. The suicide terrorist's fame as a hero must be seen against the background of his previous marginality and inferior image in his own eyes and in his community. In some cases the image of the chosen one was particularly problematic, so that the suicide mission offered itself as an opportunity to rehabilitate his public status and overcome his inner feeling of guilt. As said above, in most cases the socioeconomic status of the suicide terrorist's family was also low. After their son's death, along with material benefits, his parents and relatives gained social benefits. These families became a new kind of Palestinian aristocracy. There were far more participants and far more honored guests at the shahid's funeral than at his siblings' weddings. Clear knowledge of the rewards for his family helped the potential suicide terrorist overcome his hesitations. Poor villagers in the southern Hebron Hills described the revolution in the status of the suicide terrorist's families with the expression "from the cave to center stage."

The third factor discussed here also is significant only with regard to suicide terrorism. The suicide terrorist is motivated by persuasion that his death won't be so bad. The disparagement of death is of importance only to those who are going to their deaths. In motivating those chosen to be suicide terrorists, the worthlessness and contemptible nature of life in this world are emphasized, compared to the reality of life in the world to come. In contrast to life on earth, which is worth "a fly's wing," two alternatives of life after death are proposed. They are pictured in palpable detail, with their sights, fragrances, and sensations. First are descriptions of the paradise promised to the suicide terrorist: abundance represented by precious stones, rivers flowing with pure water, and especially the satisfaction of sexual desires, represented by seventy-two black-eyed virgins who await the shahid, whose potency will be seven times greater. The motive of male sexuality is conspicuous in creating the attractiveness of suicide terrorism, as is the certainty that in paradise the suicide terrorist will sit on a throne to the right of the Prophet and seventy members of his family will also merit a high place in the first row of those whose sins are forgiven, along with prophets, saints, and shahids. Young Palestinians were bombarded with sermons and videos showing all the miracles of paradise in living color, including the meetings with virgins on their cushioned couches.[31] Photoshop was also harnessed in service of the promise of an eternal life of bliss, blurring the difference between life and death. Scholars of communications found that some of the suicide terrorists' testaments were not broadcast without being retouched: the shahid is not only presented as living, but he also seems particularly tranquil. A calm smile dwells on the face of the living dead, and a deep blue sky is in the background. Here is an example of a popular video clip from the time of the intifada. Twelve minutes of concrete heavenly scenes broadcast over and over (2003):[32]

a young man and a pretty girl stand on either side of a high fence. They desire each other but cannot approach or touch. The young man tries to climb over the fence, but a shot fired by an Israeli sniper puts an end to his efforts and longings. After his death he rises from the grave, full of vitality, and easily leaps over the fence. The lovers are joined together in joy. The fence that separated them is the wall between this world and the world to come, and between the oppressive reality of the occupied territories and the suicide terrorist's longed-for destination—paradise on earth, Tel Aviv.

One of the early attacks, aimed at settlers in the Gaza Strip, failed for technical reasons. A heavy charge composed of explosives recovered from old and stolen land mines failed to catch, and only the fuse and accelerant exploded. There were no Israeli victims, and the suicide terrorist was wounded and sent to an Israeli hospital. When he regained consciousness he didn't believe he had survived the explosion and insisted that he was in paradise. While he maintained this belief, Israeli interrogators began to converse with him ("We questioned a dead man," a senior ISA man told me). He gradually began to doubt the heavenly reality in which he lay, as it were, because "the accursed Jews have no entry in paradise." The interrogators were proud of "entering his dream" and convincing him that, despite everything, he was living in an alternative world, and then he began to spill out all the information he possessed.

The literature on suicide terrorism frequently refers to the marvels of paradise that the suicide terrorist experienced as certain and imminent. However, the research reports do not expatiate on the alternative to paradise, that which awaits him if he does not choose the option of suicide terrorism: torments in the grave and the tortures of Judgment Day. The effectiveness of the pictures of paradise depends on those of hellfire and brimstone that are presented with no less palpable detail. Each draws strength from its opposite. Villagers who listened closely to the sermons of sheikhs from Hamas during the intifada report that they are truly terrifying. Recruits for suicide terrorism in 1994–2000, who were sent to spend a dark night alone in a grave before setting out on their mission, which would end in glorious death, testified about the horrors of abject death awaiting those who shirked the mission. Death in suicide terrorism protects against "real death."

Voices among the Palestinian intelligentsia and its representatives in the West dismiss the importance of this "superstitious, religious-sexual" motivation, claiming that these images of paradise and hell are an invention of Israeli orientalism. It is widely assumed that young people are not concerned with their own mortality and the afterlife. However, solid research proves the opposite.[33]

Terrorists Who Are Afraid of Their Own Shadow

What does the suicide terrorist look like, and how does he feel, from the moment he puts on the explosive charge, records his testimony, crosses the border, approaches his target, and lingers there, until he presses the trigger button? We can only imagine this on the basis of the testimony of survivors, who saw him from up close and had some interaction with him; the testimony of his dispatchers and of some escorts, who were the last to speak with him; and the personal testimony of suicide terrorists who failed and were arrested in Israel. The common denominator in all these descriptions is the conspicuous absence of something that one would expect in them. Close to the time of the explosion, the suicide terrorist shows no signs of being devoured with murderous rage, or with furious hatred. Nor does he show signs that he is full of satisfaction and joy, swept into ecstasy. Most of the evidence contradicts the claims of the suicide terrorist organizations, according to which the human bomb sets out on his mission full of confidence, floating in spiritual exaltation. The recorded testaments also seek to convey this impression. The rhetoric is extremist and fiery, but the facial expression and body language are restrained, not to say frozen and opaque, indeed, somewhat phlegmatic and apathetic. This dissonance indicates that the expressions of joy in preparation for the explosion are dictated and staged.

Very few suicide terrorists reported feeling what the following interviewee felt when he approached the target: "I felt I was soaring, flying up. I parted from everything that was around me, from all the material things, from the world. I wondered, how would paradise be?" Most of the interviewees reported an acute feeling of reality.

An experienced interrogator of would-be suicide terrorists in prison reports that, in response to questions about their feelings before the attack, many of them said, "*Aadi*," which means "normal" or "ordinary" in Arabic.[34] Another viewpoint on the experience of a suicide terrorist in the final stage of his mission can be taken from the reports of Israeli security agents who succeeded in preventing attacks at the last minute, arresting the suicide terrorists, and interrogating them immediately on the spot, before they recovered their wits and were taken into custody. The security agents were surprised to discover a frightened youth, exhausted and confused. They mainly found it hard to understand their great lack of enthusiasm and excitement, charisma and inspiration. The suicide terrorist projected dull ordinariness.

Observation of suicide terrorists elsewhere in the world led to a similar conclusion. On the basis of photographs of suicide terrorists on their way to an attack in Sri Lanka (2002), and on public transportation in London (2005), those who are going to blow themselves up in a short time are described as composed and numb.[35] This finding supports Randall Collins's micro-sociology of violence, which maintains that since killing people in face-to-face situations naturally arouses emotions and fears, the professional killer is chosen on the basis of his excellence in self-control and emotional distance and is trained in "heart management."[36] Collins goes on to claim that such a hit man is similar to another kind of aggressor, who is also said to be expert in confronting his victim: the suicide terrorist. Is this true?

The comparison between the two situations and figures actually brings out the differences between them. First, the hit man is tested not only by his success in killing quickly and neatly, but also in escaping unscathed, whereas the suicide terrorist intends to die voluntarily with his victims. Second, the hit man is chosen carefully and well trained. He has a strong personality, which is not deterred by direct and close confrontation. By contrast, the suicide terrorist is chosen at random and trained superficially, and for various reasons he has a personality that generally avoids face-to-face confrontation. Third, although the hit man is trained to function in conditions of confrontation and pressure, he makes every effort to minimize his proximity to the target and contact with his assigned victim. In contrast, the suicide terrorist, whose operational abilities are slender, actually stays in the target area for quite a long time, visible to the gaze of his designated victims. The hit man emerges from a hiding place, swoops down on his prey, strikes, and runs for his life—a matter of seconds or fractions of a second. In a suicide attack, the killer penetrates the target— a restaurant or a bus—in an apparently relaxed and cautious manner, mingles with his intended victims, looks and behaves like them, and only after choosing the exact time and place to maximize his murderousness does he activate the explosive charge. According to lore current in the West Bank, the ideal suicide terrorist enters the café and orders and drinks a cup of water before setting off the charge.

The hit man's mission is challenging. The suicide terrorist's mission is simpler from a tactical point of view: he has a broad variety of random targets and doesn't have to concentrate on a specific and inaccessible target; he is also free from the complication of escaping. However, his mission is more difficult in other respects, mainly the totally natural fear of certain death. Although Palestinian rhetoric dismisses fear, it has considerable presence in the interviews with would-be suicide terrorists. Merari's systematic research demonstrates and proves this.[37] In contrast to propaganda put out by the organizations, only a third of those interrogated reported positive feelings such as elation following the final decision to undertake a suicide attack. As expected, some of them reported that they had volunteered on their own initiative. Of the nonvolunteers, the vast majority admitted to feelings of fear that made them hesitate. Despite the tendency to retain a heroic and patriotic image before the other prisoners and the organization, as well as in public opinion, two-thirds of those interviewed admitted with surprising candor that on the very day of the mission, they were stricken with distress as a result of fear of death (as well as concern for the fate of their close relatives). As they drew closer to the target, especially after they were left alone without any supervision or support, their level of fear rose. Just before the explosion, even the volunteers were stricken with fear. This was expressed in disturbances in concentration and thoughts about their body, which was going to be shattered, and about their family, who would mourn for them, and also thoughts about the possibility of withdrawing at the last minute and about the excuses they might use that would not damage their public and personal image. Marari quotes a suicide terrorist: "From the minute I put on the explosive belt I thought how frightening it was but the situation was stronger than me. The more I kept going the more I hesitated."[38] In this situation he tried to distract and reinforce himself by repeating verses from the Koran, which he was listening to on earphones.

Naturally, fear is a factor in the failure of many suicide terror missions. The high proportion of suicide terrorists who dropped out is most likely another index of the fear under discussion here. Thirty-six percent of would-be suicide terrorists dropped out at some stage after being recruited. The timing of their dropping out is also significant: 75 percent of them quit on the last day or in the last hours. Though abandoning the mission is usually justified in operational terms—an unexpected checkpoint, a taxi that was delayed—most likely, were it not for their fear, they could have overcome such difficulties. Quite often the excuse is transparent: the desire to pay a debt of some kind to the family or even an attack of hunger. The organizations were aware of the fear factor and the potential for a change of heart. This is the reason why the handlers remained in telephone contact with the suicide terrorist until the last minute, although they knew the ISA might intercept the conversation.

The number of dropouts among Fatah suicide terrorists is double the number who dropped out in Hamas, which was more selective in recruiting, thus guaranteeing a higher level of motivation to overcome fear. The suicide terrorist is not a professional killer with nerves of steel. He was not trained systematically in techniques of self-control. Usually he is neither drugged nor psychotic. Hence, his fear is natural and to be expected.

The suicide terrorist fears to cause his own death as well as the death of others. It has been noted that killing is no simple matter, even if the victim is defined as deserving of death because he is evil or because there are other convincing reasons why killing him is a worthy action. Most people are reluctant to kill, even if they see it as defense, deterrent, or revenge, which can be justified ideologically. While there are social situations that give permission and encouragement to killing, these are defined as exceptional and subject to restriction. Even in such cases—as in war, of course—an effort must be made to overcome the reluctance to kill, for example by creating an intermediate space and estrangement between attacker and victim. A pilot finds it easier to drop a computer-directed bomb from a height of several thousand meters than a sniper who stalks his prey for long minutes and looks at his face with concentration before pulling the trigger. Killing in the circumstances of suicide terrorism is even more difficult. Not only is the suicide terrorist nearly touching his victims, not opposite them, but with them, among them, he is also there for some time, so he can see them, and they can see him. He hears them, smells them, and sometimes even rubs against them. A certain mutual acquaintance is made between them. Even sixty seconds of face-to-face contact makes possible the emergence of some sort of intimacy and community. In the time between two stops of a crowded bus the anonymity and alienation between the aggressor and the person next to him fades: A child? Cute? Looks like your cousin? Or a woman? Delicate? Attractive? The one about to press the button to activate the charge has to close himself off from such thoughts. He has to be able to violate the trust—even if it is a primitive, temporary, conditional trust—that has already been formed between him and his victims, his fellows.

The perpetrator of the mass murder at an African American church in Charleston, South Carolina (June 2015), who appeared to be a shy good guy, the racist Dylann Roof, was present in the crowded church and took part in the prayers for about an hour before he drew his weapon and began to shoot in every direction. During that time, he claimed that he almost reversed his intention of killing those "dogs" (as he called them) because they seemed very nice to him.[39] This is another example of the effect of a direct and prolonged connection between the attacker and his intended victims.

Naal Abu Halil a twenty-two-year-old from the town of Dura, was a suicide terrorist who blew himself up on a bus in Jerusalem (eleven dead, November 2002). I asked his neighbors, who are not members of his family or activists in the Hamas organization that dispatched him, to outline his personality. They said he was particularly bashful, not assertive enough to hold his own selling vegetables in a stall in Bethlehem. Some customers used to take advantage of him, only paying half of what they owed and walking away with the merchandise, and he wasn't able to stop them and force them to pay the full price. I heard about similar weaknesses in the character and behavior of other suicide terrorists in the West Bank. Several Palestinians confirmed the impression of a former Fatah activist: "The organizations homed in on natural candidates for recruitment—the ones who walk next to the walls and are scared of their own shadow."

In the study cited above it was found that the suicide terrorist was not only dependent but also self-effacing, avoiding confrontation by withdrawal or giving in to other people's will, especially conciliatory toward people in power. As I argued, this type of person is easy to recruit. He finds it difficult to resist the entrepreneurs of suicide terrorism. Now I would add that at the next stage, when he undertakes his mission, these characteristics make it easy for him to pass through the border check-points without attracting attention, to blend in with others, his enemies, his victims. In the final stage, these traits are what make it possible for him to press the trigger. Paradoxically, a person who finds it difficult to confront others is capable of killing himself and of killing them because he is dissociated from himself and from them, dissociated from his fears and inhibitions. The suicide terrorist can look closely in the eyes of his victims and violate the human solidarity and the trust that was formed between them, with the aid of the psychological mechanism known as dissociation.

Dissociation is manifest in a variety of situations where the normal integration between people's behavior and their emotions is disrupted, and their conscious connection with their body and emotions is severed. This can be an adaptive response to pressure and fear, a defense against traumatic experience, such as physical proximity to death.[40] Dissociation can appear in various guises. First, there is robotization: the performance of an operation without awareness of its details or the ability to retrace the thoughts and emotions that accompanied it, as when one drives automatically. Second, there is selective and focused imagination: concentration on a single stimulus to the exclusion of irrelevant stimuli, as in waking dreams. Third, there is compartmentalization: applying information about the surroundings only in a specific context, not all the time, in every context. For example, absorption in a task while ignoring various disturbances and indifference to everything around one. We can examine the involvement of the suicide terrorist in the attack in terms of these three criteria. In the final minutes before the explosion, in the bus, he acts like a robot whose body is separated from his consciousness. He is entirely immersed in fantasies about the afterlife that immediately awaits. He can think in two separate and parallel cognitive categories, and thus, for example, he can see the entrepreneur of suicide terrorism as his benefactor (promising him immortality), or he can adopt a life story in which there is no presence of the traumatic factor (such as his own imminent death), in place of his true life story. By means of dissociation, the suicide terrorist can also organize his life in two identity states divided by impenetrable boundaries. With his family and friends, at home and in the university, he is in one world and acts according to its rules. With the dispatcher and his accomplices, in the hideout apartment and the mosque, he is in a different world and acts according to different principles.

While the suicide terrorist is acting with dissociative impetus, all kinds of stimuli that are not in his control—emissaries of reality, so to speak— might burst in, making him connect with himself again, and thus the suicide mission would fail. Such a stimulus might be meeting a person from his village, whom he has known since childhood, or a receiving telephone call from home. Hence, the condition for accomplishing the mission is social isolation and severe prohibition of communication with family members (with the excuse that the phone calls might be intercepted by the ISA).

The suicide terrorist's dissociation in the final chapter of his life is not limited to a short circuit between his body, which functions like an automatic machine, and his thoughts and feelings, such as fear, which are shunted aside, as in the final moments before the explosion. This is a severing of the true self, which continues its daily routine, from the manipulated self, which plans the explosion according to instructions and practical techniques. This split and simultaneous presence and absence, as it were, are apparently intended to avoid arousing the suspicion of family members and others, but in fact it is a condition for continuing the psychic functioning of the suicide terrorist. One suicide terrorist speaks of performing all actions required of him mechanically, while, as he said, he "was wandering far from there in his imagination."[41]

Conduct in two parallel channels that appear to be indifferent to each other is reflected, for example, in those suicide terrorists who, on the night before the attack planned for the following morning, not only recited verses from the Koran but also continued to prepare for their matriculation examinations. The head of the ISA told me that he had positive and detailed information about a suicide terrorist who insisted on going on his mission on a Monday, because on Saturday and Sunday he had committed himself to taking care of family matters, and on the following Tuesday he was going to have a driving test.

In the last stages before the attack, not only is the suicide terrorist's social situation liminal—night, a strange apartment, between life and death—but so, too, is his mental situation. The entrepreneurs of suicide terrorism are masters of creating liminality characterized by sensory deprivation as well: fasting, lack of sleep, isolation. In this situation, the chances of slipping into dissociation and an altered state of consciousness are increased. This produces a tendency to two psychophysiological phenomena, signs of which can be seen in the suicide terrorist. Neither of these is regarded as pathological or abnormal, and they can be extended far longer than a few minutes. First, the suicide terrorist loses his ability to resist and becomes susceptible to autosuggestion and the suggestion of the charismatic figure who seeks to influence him. Herein is the effectiveness of the influence of the instigator of suicide terrorism. Second, the suicide terrorist enters a trance state, in the course of which he might be subject to hallucinations, imagining visions in a most palpable fashion, and he might experience enlightenment or some sort of epiphany. Thus, paradise assumes such total reality that he sees the throne of the Prophet and smells the perfumed flesh of the virgins. Suicide terrorists who failed to blow themselves up because of some technical failure in the very last moments before the explosion had already visualized death and what would follow it.

In clinical research of suicide terrorists imprisoned in Israel, it was found that those who were captured after they had pressed the button to set off a charge that did not explode for technical reasons had a more dependent-avoidant personality type, while those who were caught in earlier stages, because they were frightened or confused, were less dependent and less averse to confrontation.[42]

There is a similarity between the suicide terrorist's connection to his handlers and his connection to his victims. Dissociation enables one to overcome one's reluctance to die as well as to kill. Killing is especially difficult when it involves an interpersonal encounter that is not merely physical or technical but mainly personal, built on communication and the growth of some kind of bond between the attacker and his victim. With no possibility of exchanging words, one of the conditions for forming a connection between attacker and victim, the connection must be visual. Eye contact is the sign of this connection, as weak as it may be, but one that entails commitment. Precisely for this reason, professional killers try to minimize the direct confrontation between themselves and the victim in general, and to avoid eye contact in particular.[43] An executioner—a hangman or a member of a firing squad—covers the victim's eyes. The blindfolding is not for the victim's benefit, but for that of the executioner—to make it easier for him to kill. The victim's eyes are covered less to prevent him from seeing the executioner than to keep the executioner from seeing him, to avoid the possibility of forming a connection between them that would make the execution more demanding. In other killing situations, even in criminal murder, the attacker prefers to surprise his victim from behind, not only so that he won't be able to defend himself, but to avoid eye contact. In suicide terrorism, by contrast, the interpersonal encounter between attacker and victim is at zero range, and it is not limited to the fragment of a second when the explosion occurs. Rather it is prolonged over the time that elapses after entering the target area.

It is in the nature of suicide terrorism that eye contact is made between the attacker and his victim. However, as was previously noted, the Palestinians chosen to be suicide terrorists are those youngsters for whom it is particularly hard to make eye contact. The one who must cope with the probing gazes, which distinguishes the situation in the target group during the moments before the explosion in the bus or the restaurant, is exactly the one who avoids gazing and being gazed at.

The suicide terrorist attack is built on confrontation, to which a person is sent whose personality is dependent and who shuns confrontation. Someone with such a personality is a natural candidate for recruitment because he is truly unable to resist the community and social networks that pressure him to become a suicide terrorist. Paradoxically, after he has been recruited, thanks to personality traits that Palestinian apologetics have called "humble," and the ISA have defined as "weak," he is better able to conceal his future mission from his Palestinian family and friends, and later to blend among Israelis without standing out. In the former two situations, the suicide terrorist closes himself off or effaces himself, and he does the same thing at the target, face to face with those standing or sitting near him, and who will be the object of his aggression in a short time. The person who avoids confrontation with his handlers excuses himself from a confrontation with his victims in the same way. Only someone out of touch with his emotions like the Palestinian suicide terrorist can cut himself off from another person and his emotions, especially if that person is the enemy. Someone lacking the ability to communicate and bond cuts himself off easily. The suicide terrorist, isolated from his surroundings, remains dependent on his handlers. When someone's abilities to form basic solidarity with others are damaged from the start, then, by definition, he won't feel as if he is betraying them. In the first stage the suicide terrorist is impervious to his own fears, and in the second stage he is impervious to the possibility of empathy with the person whom he is about to kill. Were the suicide terrorist not dissociated from himself, he would confront his recruiters and be unable to avoid confrontation with his intended victim, whom he might be reluctant to kill.

We have seen earlier that the attitude of arch-terrorists, including the entrepreneurs of suicide terrorism, toward the suicide terrorist contains a hint of contempt. This contempt might betray a certain understanding that the presumed heroism of suicide terrorists derives from their weakness, from their inability to confront their recruiters, on the one hand, or their victims, on the other. The one who sends the suicide terrorist to kill and be killed is contemptuous of him for agreeing to be sent and for overcoming the inhibitions entailed in carrying out the task. In a culture that makes masculinity central, the suicide terrorist's self-effacement is seen as nonmacho. A "real man" would confront himself, his handlers, and his enemy. Fleeing from confrontation, which, in Palestinian terms, is not manly, is a condition for successful suicide terrorism.

Monitoring, Smiles, and Catharsis

Psychological states usually have behavioral correlatives, and especially when a person is caught in an extreme situation, it affects his facial expression and body language, which are susceptible to observation. Because the appearance and spontaneous movements of the suicide terrorist ought to indicate the stress to which he is subject, counterterrorism agencies try to locate him as he enters the target area, in hopes of stopping him before he sets off the explosives. It is assumed that the suicide terrorist would project his hidden intentions with involuntary signs such as sweating, trembling, stiffening of the limbs, and blinking, in addition to, of course, wearing a garment that is too large and not suitable to the weather, with one hand in his pocket, (supposedly grasping the trigger switch). These traits and others appeared in all the briefings given in Israel during the intifada to policemen, to guards at the doors of restaurants and theaters, drivers of public transportation, and citizens in general. In China, in regions of Muslim separatists, the government announced that it would place cameras at the entrances to railway stations and airports, connected to computer programs enabling them to monitor hundreds of people at the same time and identify those with a suspicious behavioral profile (August 2014). At the height of the wave of suicide terrorism in

Nigeria, manuals were published in the press with tips about the outward appearance of people who look as if "they have no future" and are "keeping a secret."[44] Among the practical suggestions, people were told to keep an eye out for closely shaven men with fresh haircuts, who mumble prayers to themselves, and who smell like drugs. There is no instruction for monitoring suicide terrorists that fails to mention the most outstanding sign: an opaque gaze, indifference to the gestures of people around him, and systematic avoidance of eye contact with them.

The interception of telephone conversations between suicide terrorists and their handlers at the very last stage before the explosion offers another point of view on their mental state at the critical moment. Again, there is no sign of the expected psychological turmoil, but bland anxiety and confusion, overshadowed by laconic and businesslike concern with technicalities, and neutralization of emotions. Some of the interviewees among the would-be suicide terrorists mentioned a vague feeling of pleasure, a kind of floating. This can perhaps be explained as an expression of control[45] or release, the dissolution of fear and the end of the tormenting uncertainty, when the temptation of retraction and retreat is no longer present, and there seems to be no possibility of failure. Persistent rumors claim that the suicide terrorist smiles at the last moment. Rather than a smile of joy, this is the smile of apathy. Some label it a smirk. Perhaps also, as suggested in another chapter, a shy, embarrassed smile.

Article number 25 in the preattack instructions to the 9/11 suicide terrorists, found in the luggage of Muhammad Atta, later widely published and probably inspirational to many other human bombs around the globe, says: "Smile in the face of hardships because you are heading toward eternal paradise." One of the guards at the US Marines barracks in Beirut who saw the human bomb racing toward the building (October 1983) testified later that "the suicide driver was smiling as he passed by him."[46] It is difficult to determine whether there actually were smiles, and, if there were, in how many instances, or whether this is a legend. In the mythology of Middle Eastern suicide terrorism, the suicide terrorist's alleged smile has an important place, prized on both sides of the barrier. On the Israeli side people tell about the thwarting of a suicide terror attack because the terrorist's smile betrayed his intention and made possible his arrest at the last minute. Survivors and security people report of smiles on the terrorists' faces the moment before the explosion.

According to their interpretation, the smile is wicked. Emphasis on the suicide terrorist's smile is meant to demonstrate the evil and heinousness of his act. On the Palestinian side, the smile is presented as an expression of supreme satisfaction upon accomplishing the mission. They claim that that suicide terrorist smiles with delight like the Christian martyrs who sacrificed themselves at the Roman stake—the church altar. Immediate death assures the sweetness of revenge, restoring justice and order, along with fame, the end of frustrations and shame, entry into paradise, which at those moments is envisioned with great concreteness in its full splendor.

Israeli policemen testified that the Hamas suicide terrorist Raad Barghouti, the twenty-six-year-old graduate of an Islamic college who disguised himself as a Haredi Jew, blew himself up with a smile on his face (Jerusalem, September 2001). His family recounts that before setting out on the suicide mission, he had a dream in which he met his cousin who had been killed sometime earlier in an IDF ambush. The holy martyr grasped Raad by the sleeve and led him high up to the heights of paradise, where he pointed exactly at the place reserved for him in the first row next to the Prophet with the other shahids.[47]

Like a Greek tragedy, suicide terrorism is a great drama that takes place in the intervening distance between acceptance of fate and the effort to rebel against it. The climax and goal of tragedy is catharsis, which combines a sad ending, a catastrophe, with satisfaction and spiritual elevation. The tragedy of suicide terrorism also leads to catharsis and ends with it. It is possible to interpret the celebrated smile of the suicide terrorist just before the explosion as an expression of catharsis.

Catharsis is first of all release: freedom from inhibitions or the emancipation of emotions connected to trauma and aggression, the end of fear and a solution to guilt. Second, catharsis is purification, purgation, a process in which a person becomes more virtuous. Third, it is a moment in which the truth is revealed or confirmed. The suicide terrorist's smile symbolizes the three dimensions of the catharsis he accomplishes by means of the attack: at long last, total freedom, moral elevation, and clarification of the crux of matters.

As in ancient Greek tragedy, so too in suicide terrorism the catharsis is not only that of the tragic figure, the suicide terrorist, but also of the audience of the tragedy, the Palestinian community that sent him on his campaign. Together they reach the final moment of the play, the explosion, and the exalted grief. The essence of catharsis is its effect on the witnesses to the play, who identify with what happens on the stage, in the arena of suicide terrorism. The suicide terrorist, his dispatchers, the organization, and the Palestinian public in the West Bank and Gaza join together at the longed-for, unique, holy moment of catharsis, a moment of pain mingled with a feeling of elation and of total, pure truth. They catch their breath, they shed tears of sadness and joy, and it is hard to distinguish between vision and reality.

The cathartic smile of the suicide terrorist—whether imaginary and alleged or real—precedes the explosion by a second, and it is parallel to the catharsis undergone by the suicide terrorist's family and the Palestinian public a few hours later, when the news is heard. Then the post-suicide-terrorism orgy begins, combining shrieks of grief and mourning along with shouts of joy and the candies of a wedding.

The Banality of Suicide Terrorism

At the center of a Greek tragedy stands a hero. There are heroes in the Palestinian national struggle, headed by the engineers of suicide terrorism. In contrast to them, the Palestinian suicide terrorist is an antihero. While he is a momentous protagonist in the human drama, he has none of the characteristics of the classical hero as they appear in folklore, literature, or cinema. He is not particularly strong, handsome, brave, or determined; he is not very intelligent or cunning; and he has no talent or other trait of body or soul to make him impressive or influential. He does not possess complexity or a secret that would make him interesting. Judging by his past, he does not manifest militancy, cruelty, or a killer instinct. He is ordinary, sometimes a bit pathetic, a young man caught in an extraordinary situation, which brought him to the focus of action and attention. The Palestinian suicide terrorist is similar to several variants of the antihero, all of which manifest an element of surprise or dissonance: he is someone who has done an unusual, praiseworthy deed, though it was impossible to predict it; he was thought of as no different from the others all his life, but at one moment, the final one, he was recognized as a virtuoso; he has lived a life without drama but ends it with a gigantic drama; he was ruled by others and the situation around him all his life, and now, suddenly, he can be seen as resourceful and rebellious.

According to one view, the antihero has hidden qualities that are revealed and admired only under particular and challenging circumstances. According to a diverging view, the antihero embodies human weaknesses, and precisely because of them he plays an important role in the plot and can provide a model for identification and be an object of sympathy for certain groups. The political culture of our age, which in general takes an antiheroic direction, which diverts attention from those who try to rise above human weakness to those whose weaknesses direct their lives, tends to attribute centrality to people with a degree of victimhood and to see in their ordinariness, their fragility, and their passivity the personification of truth and justice.

Another way to see the antihero is as someone whose life is led routinely, at random. He has no goal for which he strives with premeditation and determination. Rather he finds himself drifting from one episode to another in a manner he neither intended nor predicted. It is hard to find clear logic in the course of his life, and at every single point in his progress, he could have been elsewhere with the same degree of probability. This is the life story of a typical suicide terrorist: as with most of the stations throughout his biography, the final moments in his life also happened by chance or accident rather than design. Even in his becoming connected with the suicide terrorism project, from his recruitment through the preparations for the attack to the very attack itself, there is a significant degree of haphazardness.

A typical example is the case of Jihad Jarar, a seventeen-year-old boy from Burqin near Jenin, who was sent on a suicide mission in Afula by the Palestinian Islamic Jihad (August 2001). The story began on a vacation day, when he went on a walk with a friend and by chance met a religious man who invited him to pray in the mosque and read a book about the wonders of paradise in store for shahids. Some time afterward, during a condolence visit to a family of shahids, he met an activist in the movement, who drew him into the plot of a suicide terrorist attack. Various events thwarted and delayed departure on the mission, including the dropping out of a fellow suicide terrorist, transportation that became unavailable, and so on. Finally, after the dictated testament was recorded, he was stuffed into a car with another ten passengers and crossed the border.

However, he didn't find an appropriate target and was arrested by suspicious policemen. He tried to explode the charge against them, but it failed because of a technical problem. And so he drifted into an Israeli prison.

The human bomb is "driven to death."[48] Powerful forces—Islam, the Palestinian nation, the community in Gaza and the West Bank, the organizations, friends and neighbors, recruiters and handlers—drive him to be killed in order to kill. Such an argumentation can be read as sociological determinism, which deflects moral responsibility away from the perpetrator of suicide terrorism. This raises an association with the famous thesis of the banality of evil, created by Hannah Arendt, the philosopher of history, in response to the trial of Eichmann, who directed the Nazis' "final solution of the Jewish problem" in World War II.[49] Like many Nazi killers, the figure of the suicide terrorist is banal, and the story of his life up to the time of the attack is also banal. Even the circumstances of his recruitment and dispatching for the attack partake of banality. In both cases, a demystification and de-demonization of the forces that motivate the horror are in order. However, according to the common interpretation of Arendt's thesis, the case of Adolf Eichmann in the Holocaust is not at all comparable to that of the Palestinian human bomb. For the latter did not act as a minor official in a large, complicated, modern, hierarchical bureaucracy. In the case of the Palestinian suicide terrorist, unlike the Nazi case, the anonymous, authoritarian bureaucratic parameter is lacking, nor is there the grinding up of evil into millions of tiny, technical details. Behind the evil there is no ostensibly advanced and enlightened civilization, nor does the evil depend on a political culture of civil obedience and the preservation of law and order on the part of disciplined masses of "decent" citizens.[50]

I agree with the argument of those critics who maintain that Arendt did not refer to the theory of the cog in the machine, which is attributed to her, which transferred the center of gravity to systematic evil, on the one hand, and which implies that no one is immune to such an epidemic of evil, on the other. According to an alternative interpretation of Arendt's thesis, Eichmann was, despite everything, a free agent to a significant degree, and as such he had to stand trial. Although in other contexts Arendt was interested in the crimes of the bureaucracy and ethical aspects of totalitarian structures, in the historical case under discussion, she says explicitly that the question of moral responsibility should not concentrate on the *system* of the party or state. Arendt did not locate the essential element that made mass murder possible in the organizational mechanism. Nor did she locate it in murderous ideology, individual pathology, or some kind of wickedness. Rather she saw it in exceptional *superficiality*, the lack of autonomous and critical reflectiveness.[51] Arendt stated that Eichmann's evil was a "surface phenomenon," and, rather than being radical (penetrating deeply into the roots of things), it was merely extreme.[52] As she said of Eichmann, one may also say of the human bomb that what is banal about him is his sheer thoughtlessness, and especially his inability to oppose the truisms current in the social order in which he lives. An indication of this banality is the tendency to resort to clichés. The differences between Eichmann and the human bomb and between the situation in the concentration camps and that of suicide terrorism are enormous. However, what they have in common is the connection between a horrible deed and a superficial herd mentality.

The explosive charge strapped onto the suicide terrorist's body could be set off from a distance using a telephone, which would exclude the possibility that the human bomb might change his mind and retreat or become confused and fail to set it off. This alternative strategy was discussed by the entrepreneurs of suicide terrorism and probably employed in isolated cases. However, senior members of the organizations and the dispatchers preferred to have the suicide terrorist himself set off the charge. This was not only to maximize the murderous effect, but also to avoid responsibility for the terrorist's death. I have heard the thesis, voiced by Palestinians, that the entrepreneurs were afraid they would be accused of the cowardly murder of members of their nation, and particularly that they wanted to prevent the suicide terrorist's family from seeking blood revenge.[53] The ISA agent who interrogated Palestinian arch-terrorist Barghouti is convinced that he insisted on having the human bomb set off the explosion by himself because of an "ethical position."

There is apparently some truth in the claim of the suicide terrorism entrepreneurs that the human bombs themselves preferred the option of self-immolation. The suicide terrorist insists on being a free and proactive agent, someone who wrests full control from the hands of both the organizations and the Israelis, if not over their lives, at least over their deaths. He deprives the IDF and the ISA of even the role of victimizer. He also denies the Israeli enemy the possibility of punishing him. The suicide terrorist commits a crime and punishes himself with the penalty of death, the most severe of all, and thus he denies the Israelis a privilege that was theirs alone.

Perhaps the Palestinians who refuse to volunteer, as well as the volunteers who withdraw at the last moment, are actually the ones in control of their lives and deaths, superagents in a sense. A suggestion has arisen in the literature to view suicide terrorism as an act of radical conformism and the suicide terrorist as obedient and conformist to the extent of self-denial. In contrast, a suggestion has been made to regard suicide terrorism as an act of self-affirmation and defiance, and the suicide terrorist as autonomous and absolutely liberated. The praise for the human bomb within the Palestinian public included both contradictory positions. It was said that suicide terrorism was the fruit of total identification with the national and religious collective, and at the same time it was said that the suicide was an individual initiative of opposition to the Israeli occupation, a challenge to the human tendency to self-preservation, and a protest against submissive Palestinian behavior.

The suicide terrorist—killed in order to kill, aggressor and victim, living dead—contains several additional inner contradictions, such as being a duped conformist and yet a daring provocateur. The duality in the figure of the suicide terrorist reflects an inner conflict in the Palestinian psyche, an identity dilemma of so many Palestinians. It is no wonder that the human bomb has been adopted as a model by a collective struggling for its freedom and nation building.

The suicide terrorist, replete with contradictions and paradoxes, is what anthropologists call a symbolic type.[54] This hybrid and elusive type usually appears at times of crisis and in ambiguous situations. It disguises itself and appears in various forms, thus outwitting its surroundings. It undergoes mystification, and superpowers are attributed to it. Its behavior can be seen as a charged ritual. The suicide terrorist as a symbolic type embodies the social order and at the same time subverts it.

4

ANATOMY OF A SUICIDE OPERATION

Most Traumatic Suicide Terrorism Campaigns

Of the hundreds of severe Palestinian terrorist attacks in Israel in the past generation, about ten made an especially strong impression, most of them being suicide terrorism. Each of these events had particular characteristics that made it traumatic. Here are some of the events that are deeply etched in Israeli collective memory: the attack on bus no. 5, because it began a wave of attacks, and because it was presented on television almost without censorship (Tel Aviv, October 1994, twenty-two dead, Hamas); the attack on the hitchhiking station at the Beit Lid junction, because it was perpetrated by two human bombs, who acted at an interval of a few minutes from one another, so that the first victims were soldiers—which is exceptional in itself—and then the rescue teams that were summoned (January 1995, twenty-two dead, Islamic Jihad); the attack on the Dolphinarium in Tel Aviv because all the victims were youngsters, new immigrants from the former USSR, in the midst of a dance party (June 2001, twenty-one dead, Hamas); and the attack on Maxim restaurant, because it killed families from three generations during a seaside Sabbath lunch (October 2003, twenty-one dead, Islamic Jihad).

I chose to focus on the following four suicide terrorist attacks from this list mainly because I had access to reliable authentic material about their background. The first is the attack on bus no. 18 in Jerusalem, which stood out because there were two suicide terrorist attacks only a week apart on the same public bus line, at a distance of a few hundred meters from each other, initiated and planned by the same Palestinian activists (late February and early March 1996, twenty-six and nineteen dead respectively, Hamas). The second is the attack on the Sbarro pizzeria, which stood out because it took place at noon at a central intersection in Jerusalem, almost the commercial symbol of the city (August 2001, fifteen dead, Hamas). The third is the attack on the Moment café, because it took place only a few hundred meters from the well-guarded residence of the prime minister, immediately after a demonstration by Peace Now, where they demanded renewal of negotiations with the Palestinians (March 2002, eleven dead, Hamas). The fourth is the attack on the Park Hotel in Netanya, which stands out because it took place during the Passover Seder, the ritual holiday dinner, and it broke the record for the number of victims in a single attack, causing particularly severe Israeli retaliation in Operation Defensive Shield (March 2002, thirty dead, Hamas).

Unlike the human bombs who committed the above attacks, those who recruited, equipped, and dispatched them remained alive and headed the wanted list of Israeli security authorities. After a particularly intense effort, they were captured and tried, and for years they have been the most senior Palestinians imprisoned in Israel. I was privileged to examine the protocols of their ISA interrogations and the deliberations of their military court.[1] On the basis of the integration of these secret documents, I will present, briefly and selectively, the clandestine and violent career of the three Hamas activists who stood behind the attacks. Information about the central projects of these senior figures will be combined to form an anatomy of suicide terrorism.

Hasan Salama

On the streets of the West Bank, people still talk about Hasan Salama, a hero of the resistance movement, who proudly bore the names of and identified with two of his predecessors: Hasan Salama, a Palestinian guerrilla fighter who died in battle in 1948 (a protégé of the mufti of Jerusalem, Haj Amin al-Husseini, a national leader and military commander in the 1930s and 1940s), and his son, Hasan Salama, the head of the Black September terrorist organization who planned the murder of the eleven Israeli athletes at the 1972 Munich Olympics (eliminated by the Mossad in Beirut in 1979). Only Yehiya Ayash, "the Engineer," the mythological father of Palestinian suicide terrorism, the head of the military arm of Hamas; and Muhammad Deif, his legendary heir, who was severely wounded but survived two or more direct hits by the ISA and the IDF, and no one knows whether he is living or dead—only they stood above Hasan Salama as the most dangerous arch-enemies of Israel in the 1990s. His high status came by virtue of his close, hidden ties to the two others and no less so by virtue of his independent initiatives.

Salama was from Khan Yunis in the Gaza Strip, born in 1971. He was thin and a bit short, with a boyish look, restrained and hesitant in speech, and had only a basic education.[2] He was not a man of words, but a man of action, cunning and brave. A senior intelligence agent from a Western allied country who interviewed him stated categorically: "He has no insights." In 1992, at the age of twenty-one, he joined the Shock Forces of Hamas, and in the first year of his activity he concentrated on promoting the goals of the first intifada near where he lived. He began to recruit volunteers, with whom he established a unit of five men who specialized in the investigation and execution of Palestinians suspected of collaboration with Israel. Among other things he commanded an operation involving the kidnapping of a local resident, beating him with pipes and then killing him with axes. After receiving an automatic weapon from his handlers in the organization, he went on to initiate and carry out punitive operations against several other people suspected of collaboration, including a woman. In early 1993 a member of the unit he had recruited was arrested, and Salama was afraid he would divulge details that would enable the ISA to track him down, so he fled to Jordan across the Allenby Bridge. From there he was sent on missions by Hamas, traveling first to Sudan, where he worked in the organization's office for eight months. He then went to Syria, where he received a stipend of two hundred dollars, because he was wanted, and he met with the heads of the organization. There he also underwent ten days of military training, which included riflery and the making of explosive charges. He then joined a group of eighteen wanted men from Hamas who had fled from the occupied territories, and after pressuring the leadership of the organization, they were sent to Iran, where they were given a three-month, systematic course in light arms, machine guns, and anti-tank missiles, the preparation of improvised explosive charges, and intelligence gathering. In his travels, Salama also went to Lebanon, where he made contact with the veteran Palestinian deportees who were living in the Marj al-Zohur temporary tent encampment, and with their assistance he made contact with Hezbollah members. Meanwhile, the Gaza Strip came under the control of the Palestinian Authority, and at the end of 1994 Salama infiltrated back across the Egyptian border. He was arrested in the Gaza Strip by PLO police forces and detained for seven and a half months.

In mid-1995 he made contact with activists of Izz ad-Din al-Qassam, the military arm of Hamas, led by the Engineer, and he gained the confidence of his assistant and successor, Muhammad Deif, becoming his intimate and his emissary on various missions. Among other things, he obtained electric wires, timers, and a meat grinder, and used them to make explosive charges. After the Engineer was killed, it was decided to use these explosive charges to launch immediate revenge attacks on an unprecedented scale. Because of the manhunt for Muhammad Deif, he could only issue general instructions and give free rein to the initiatives of those subordinate to him. After others refused, Salama took upon himself direct control of the implementation of Deif's instructions. For this purpose he made contact with a unit of East Jerusalem residents who had been placed on ice after receiving training a year previously. With their consent, he set up code words with them and received several stolen Israeli identity cards, one of which was to afford him free movement after his picture was inserted in it. Members of a forward unit who specialized in stealing cars were sent to Israel through a hole they made in the fence around the Gaza Strip to prepare logistical infrastructure for the mission. After a coded telephone announcement indicating the location of the gap in the fence, Salama went out to meet them, calling himself Abu Ahmad. He infiltrated into Israel with a team of accomplices, 1,500 Jordanian dinars, a cell phone, names of accessories in Jerusalem and secret means of contacting them, three suitcases, each containing thirteen kilograms of compressed TNT, two pistols, and six hand grenades. The equipment was hidden in a place prepared in advance in the orange orchards around the

Israeli port city of Ashdod. From there Salama headed for the West Bank. In mid-1996 he settled in Hebron, and there he sought out Hamas people whom he had known in the past when they were in the Israeli prison of Ke'tsiot and in the deportee camp in southern Lebanon. With their assistance he tried to locate candidates to be sent as human bombs. His friend Suleiman Kawasme put him up in his house, arranged for sleeping quarters for him in the homes of his relatives, and agreed to locate young men who could be convinced to go out on the mission. Kawasme himself took command of a terrorist unit and received weapons, but he did not manage to find potential human bombs. Salama went to a hiding place, returning from time to time, only to find that there were no candidates. Over two weeks the two men corresponded in secret with letters hidden in the lavatories of a local mosque before Thursday evening prayers, but the project did not move forward.

The ISA attributes Salama's difficulty in recruiting candidates for suicide terrorism to the fact that he came from the Gaza Strip. The people of Hebron, like the other Palestinian residents of the West Bank, regard their brethren from the Gaza Strip as foreigners and feel superior to them. Another explanation for the difficulty is that at the time suicide terrorism had not yet taken hold in Palestinian consciousness. During the failed efforts to locate and enlist suicide terrorists, Salama went to Ramallah to try his luck there. In the local teachers' seminary he met students from Gaza who mediated between him and Muhammad Abu-Warda, the chairman of the Kutla Islamiya, the Hamas student cell. The latter was asked to find volunteers for suicide terrorism, and in response he requested a day to think about it. At the same time Salama renewed contact with the Jerusalem unit and invited its members to a meeting, using the code words set in advance. They agreed to help send a human bomb, and for that purpose they joined Salama in a trip to the weapons cache in the orange groves of Ashdod to transfer explosives to the Jerusalem area. The explosives were hidden again in the courtyard of a local mosque, and Salama slept nearby in his vehicle. From there the unit transferred him to a hiding place in an apartment in Abu Dis, on the outskirts of Jerusalem. His accomplices rented it for three hundred dinars, which he had given them, and, following his instructions, they also bought 150 ball bearings, to increase the deadliness of the explosive charges. From then on the apartment served as the command post for planned missions.

Following Salama's instructions, the Jerusalem unit set out to locate targets for attacks, places "where there are a lot of Jews." Contact with Muhammad Deif was made through a Gazan intermediary, who used to come to the al-Aqsa mosque for Friday prayers. After Suleiman Kawasme called from Hebron and reported that he had failed to locate candidates, Salama met with Abu Warda at a mosque in Ramallah, and the latter told him he had found two candidates: his cousin Majdi and Majdi's friend Ibrahim Sarahna, two young men from the village of al-Fawar. Salama gave him four hundred shekels for his expenses and ordered him to bring them to the same mosque for a meeting. The next day, right after Friday prayers, Salama met with the two volunteers, took them to a friend's apartment in Ramallah, and from there to a meeting place in the local hospital, from which the accomplices drove all of them, as well as the explosive charges, to the hiding place in the rented apartment in Abu Dis.

On February 24, 1996, Salama began to assemble the explosive charges in the safe house: each one with twelve kilograms of TNT with another half kilogram of nails of various sizes and steel ball bearings. These materials were poured into plastic bags and connected to batteries with wires and a switch. The original suitcases were liable to arouse suspicion because of their size, so the accomplices were sent to buy appropriate knapsacks. Each of the two volunteers was given a knapsack with instructions for activating the charge. They were told to arm the charges before reaching the target and then to explode them at the appropriate time. Salama departed for an apartment in Ramallah and left the human bombs with his accomplices, who planned to go into action the following day. On February 25, at dawn, according to Salama's detailed instructions, the suicide terrorist, Majdi Abu Warda, accompanied by two members of the Jerusalem unit, left for Jerusalem in a private car owned by one of them. In busy Jaffa Road, near the Central Post Office, they dropped off the human bomb carrying the explosive charge in his knapsack. They instructed him to board bus no. 18, provided him with a ticket they had bought in advance to restrict interaction between him and the driver and reduce the chance that he would arouse suspicion. The suicide terrorist boarded the bus, which drove off, and a few minutes later, at exactly 6:45, the explosion took place. Along with the Palestinian terrorist, twenty-six Israelis were killed.

That morning, at about the same time, the second human bomb, Ibrahim Sarahna, left the safe house in the direction of Ashkelon with the third Jerusalem accomplice. The human bomb was dropped off at an intersection at the entrance to the southern coastal city, and he acted according to instructions he had received from Salama the day before. He walked to a nearby hitchhiking station, where he stood close to Israelis who were already there. He waited for a while for others to join them and blew himself up at 7:30. In addition to the suicide terrorist, one Israeli woman was killed.

Three days later Salama met once more with Abu Warda and asked him to provide another volunteer for the next suicide attack. That very day Abu Warda located a young man named Raad Sharnubi, who told him, the following day, that he was willing to go out on a mission for Hamas. The Jerusalem unit was told to come promptly and transfer the suicide terrorist and his explosive charge to the safe house in Abu Dis, while Salama remained in the apartment in Ramallah with his partner, Muhi al-Din al-Sharif. In the presence of the suicide terrorist, Salama constructed an explosive charge exactly like the first two. Then he instructed him about the technical and operational aspects of the mission, and the two left together to wait for the accomplices near the hospital. According to Salama's instructions, the human bomb and his accomplices spent the night in the safe house, and the next day, on March 3, 1996, at dawn, they left for Jerusalem and the chosen target: again bus no. 18, which left the Pat neighborhood, and again to set the charge off on Jaffa Road, after several stops. The explosion took place at 6:20, killing the Palestinian terrorist and, along with him, sixteen Israelis.

Then Salama, with his partner, Muhi al-Din al-Sharif, went to a safe house in the town of Dura in the southern Hebron Hills. A senior Hamas member from the Bethlehem area went there with orders from the leadership to stop suicide attacks and instead concentrate on kidnapping an IDF soldier. The plan was for one unit, headed by el-Sharif, to kidnap the Israeli, and the second unit led by Salama was to wait in the safe house in Abu Dis, from which the hostage would be transferred to another apartment in the Hebron area, where a video camera had been prepared to document and publicize the kidnapping. From there they were supposed to move to a cave that had been located on the edge of the desert for prolonged concealment. Hamas transferred four thousand dinars to them, with which, along with forged identity papers, they bought a white Volkswagen Passat. One of the members of the unit, who spoke fluent Hebrew, sat next to the driver, and he was given the task of holding a casual conversation with the intended hostage, to gain his confidence. After the soldier entered the car, on a given signal (the driver would clear his throat and turn off the radio), the man sitting in the back was to strike the soldier with an iron rod that was hidden in the car. The unit was equipped with everything needed for disguise—two skullcaps and a Hebrew newspaper—and ropes and tape for the kidnapping. They also broke the rear door handles to prevent the hostage from fleeing. The action was delayed again and again because of logistical difficulties, mainly failure to find safe houses, and because some of the accomplices pulled out. On May 11, 1996, the kidnappers drove to the Beit Shemesh area but failed to find a soldier they could kidnap. Later, near Ben Gurion Airport, they saw soldiers, but because they were in a group, they had to renounce their intention. On the way back to Jerusalem, frustrated, they were presented with an opportunity: a lone soldier, without a gun, was hitchhiking in the direction of Ma'ale Adumim. After inducing him to enter the car, they struck him but did not manage to knock him out. He struggled with his kidnappers and finally managed to crawl out through the window, while the unit quickly fled. Two days later Salama heard about the failure on the radio. He then turned on his cell phone and received the code word confirming the failure.

After another failed kidnapping attempt, Salama drove toward the Ali Beq mosque in Hebron, armed with a pistol, grenades, and a submachine gun hidden in his car in a sack full of wheat. On the way he was stopped by the IDF at a surprise roadblock. Afraid he would be identified, Salama leaped from the car and began to flee, ignoring the soldiers' calls to surrender. He drew his pistol and tried to shoot, but the soldiers fired first. Though he was wounded, and his pistol had fallen, he managed to disappear in the alleys of the Casbah of Hebron. Shortly afterward he reported to the local hospital, where he tried to pass himself off as someone else, but in the end he was arrested (May 17, 1996). Hasan Salama was sentenced to forty-six successive life sentences.

In prison, where he was kept in solitary confinement for years, Salama wrote a memoir, which was spirited out and read by Hamas sympathizers.[3] His writing confirms what he said during the interrogations and his trial, adding a few details and a certain personal touch. Here are some of his comments regarding the dispatching of the human bombs Abu-Warda and Sarahna (bus no. 18 in Jerusalem and the hitchhiking station in Ashkelon). First, Salama sent the human bombs to a barbershop and asked his aide to be sure that one of them had a Western-style haircut and the other had his hair cut short like a soldier's. New civilian clothes were bought for the first terrorist, and the other was provided with a military uniform his size.

Second, Salama met with the two alone in a room, made sure the atmosphere was relaxed, and, before explaining the nature of the mission to them, he asked them personal questions and took note of their character, motivation, and degree of commitment. He emphasized the importance of maintaining secrecy and asked them to avoid arousing the suspicion of their families by offering convincing reasons for their absence. At the end of the meeting, he told them they could regard themselves as members of the Izz ad-Din al-Qassam Brigades. Third, a day before the operation, at dawn, after prayers, the two were asked to write their testaments by hand for their families, and then they were filmed by video, together and separately, reading declarations dictated by the Hamas movement. Not until the night before the operation were the two suicide terrorists taught how to operate the explosive charges that had been placed in backpacks and camouflaged. They were shown how to open the safety pin that served as a safety before entering the vicinity of the target and how to push the button to set off the charge. Then each of them was given a small sum.

Fourth, the night before the attack, Salama left the safe house, leaving the terrorists with only their escorts. From then until they set out, they fasted and prayed. Salama described his short stay with them while they were preparing to go to their death as a unique experience. At that stage he took care of their needs and was proud that he could serve them. He even cooked for them. According to him, they were happy. Just before they parted, he asked them to include his name in the list of those who would receive God's mercy by virtue of their holy death, and he sent warm greetings to Yehiya Ayash, which they were to deliver to him when they arrived in paradise. When they parted, they insisted on knowing his name and function in the organization, but he refused to tell them.

Abdallah Barghouti

Abdallah Jamal Barghouti, another prominent figure in Palestinian suicide terrorism, was arrested in March 2003, tried, and sentenced in November to sixty-seven consecutive life sentences for the sixty-six Israelis whose death he was directly responsible for (along with about five hundred injured). Since then he has been the most important security prisoner, kept in isolation for seven years and transferred every few months from prison to prison. His name is never included on the lists of prisoners who, although they have "blood on their hands," are liberated in exchange agreements. In the Palestinian consciousness he is a model of courage.

Barghouti was born in Kuwait in 1972 and studied electronic engineering in Korea. When he arrived in the West Bank in 1991, he settled in the village of Beit Rima, in the Ramallah district. After becoming one of the heads of the Izz ad-Din al-Qassam Brigades, the military arm of Hamas in the territories, he was known to be a leader in suicide attacks during the al-Aqsa Intifada of the early 2000s. He was called by the honorific name of "the Engineer," after the mythological "Engineer," Yehiya Ayash, born in 1966, and instigated the killing of about a hundred Israelis, mainly by means of suicide terrorism, which he planned and directed. Barghouti was involved in initiating ordinary terrorism, making weapons in a laboratory, training in terrorism, and military training in the field. He planned the kidnapping of soldiers, sheltering of wanted men, fundraising for the campaign against Israeli occupation ($117,000), sale of stolen weapons, communications between the leadership of the organization and its activists, and more. He possessed several identity papers of other people, in which his picture was inserted.

Barghouti has a moon face and plump body, is the father of a son and two daughters, reads the daily newspaper, speaks Hebrew, and has taken a course at the Open University. In interviews with him he repeatedly emphasizes that if he could, he would resume deadly terrorist attacks against Israelis. He proclaimed that if the occupation continued, his six-year-old daughter, who was studying ballet, would have to move on "to other things." On Israeli television he explained in a serious, quiet way how to make an explosive vest ("It's the length of about two hands . . . the bolts must be clumped together . . ."). When he speaks about his opposition to

Israel, there is a conspicuous difference between the radical meaning of his actions and words and his rather nonchalant way of speaking, lacking any dramatic gestures or bombast.[4]

Barghouti's interrogation by the ISA, his testimony to the police, and his military trial are summarized in a dense, detailed forty-three-page report. Following are the relevant passages from this authentic, formerly classified document.

In July 2001, near Nablus, Barghouti met with Iman Halawa, a senior activist in the military arm of Hamas, who delivered to his "disposal" a man willing to serve as a human bomb. Then Barghouti addressed another activist, Muhammad Douglas, from whom he asked for someone capable of "inserting" the suicide terrorist in Israel. With the intermediary of another activist, Ahlam Tamimi was found, a twenty-year-old woman, a student at Birzeit University and a part-time journalist who was in contact with Hamas people on campus. Later she was arrested, tried, and sentenced to sixteen life sentences but released in the Shalit exchange in October 2011. An ISA agent who interrogated Tamimi reported both her beauty and her extremism, stating that she was exceptional in her anti-Israeli position. He connected this to the fact that she came from Jordan.[5] Barghouti reported on the recruits to the upper echelons, and they instructed him to prepare a "small charge" that would be suitable for an "ordinary attack," so he could test the people and see whether they were worthy.

Barghouti sent Tamimi on a reconnaissance trip to Jerusalem, which she knew well (July 27, 2001). Together with her nephew she scouted out a crowded supermarket in the center of the city. In the evening she reported to her handlers that she had found an ideal target for an attack. The details were conveyed to Barghouti, and he prepared an explosive charge, which he placed into a beer can, and which was then transferred to Tamimi through a series of intermediaries. That very day she went to Jerusalem with the explosives in her pocketbook, went into the supermarket, and placed the can among the others on display on the shelves. Before leaving she activated the timer. At 1:10 p.m. the charge exploded, wounding several people and causing heavy damage. In her interrogation Tamimi stated that she passed herself off as a customer on her mission, and for that reason she took a shopping cart. However, she made certain to choose a cart that was not chained to the others, enabling her to boast to the ISA agents, in a tone full of resentment, "You didn't even make five shekels off me." In his interrogations, Barghouti insisted that he had never met Tamimi.

Soon after, Barghouti addressed Halawa and asked to have a large explosive charge sent to him, and to find a candidate for suicide terrorism. He received explosives packed in plastic bottles, which he stuffed into an acoustic guitar that another activist had bought for him (in an interview in prison, he said that he strummed the guitar before turning it into a bomb). He added two plastic bags full of explosives and a handful of screws to the charge and closed the sound hole with glass, so its contents would not be visible. He put the guitar in a black case, from which an electric wire trailed, for activating the charge from outside.

The human bomb that was found was Muhammad al-Masri, a twenty-two-year-old from the village of Aqaba, near Jenin. His family owns a restaurant and agricultural lands. Following instructions, he went to Ramallah, where he was given a place to sleep. The next morning he was taught how to set off the explosives. At the same time Tamimi went to Jerusalem to locate another target. When she returned, she reported that although the city was full of security forces, it would be possible to set out from Ramallah.

On August 9, 2001, after getting a haircut and putting on an elegant white shirt, Masri met Tamimi, his guide. When they entered Jerusalem, he carried the guitar on his back, to avoid arousing suspicion, and for her part she took off her jacket to show herself in a fashionable, low-cut, sleeveless Israeli T-shirt. The two partners reached a central intersection in Jerusalem, where Jaffa Road crosses King George Street, and Tamimi explained to Masri that he must set off the charge in the center of the crowded pedestrian crosswalk. Then she left him and went to the Old City, on her way to Ramallah. For some reason Masri decided not to follow her instructions. At 2:55 he entered the Sbarro restaurant, which was full of customers, and after a short delay and an exchange of a few words, he exploded the charge. Nineteen people were killed, including two families and seven children. Another 127 people were wounded, and severe damage was caused to buildings, stores, and vehicles. In later interviews with her, Tamimi said that on their way together to the target she and Masri did not exchange a word, but she noticed a "strange" expression in his eyes. When they neared the target, he suddenly asked her whether she was sure enough religious Jews were present there. Based on her impressions from earlier reconnaissance, she said there were. This answer satisfied him. Everyone involved in this attack was recognized as a hero of the Palestinian struggle.[6] The ISA agents responsible for investigating the Sbarro attack searched Tamimi's house, where they found newspaper clippings describing the two attacks in which she had been involved.

After this attack, Barghouti was arrested by the security forces of the Palestinian Authority. After his release, Barghouti began teaching young men (with their faces masked) how to make explosives. With their help he prepared three powerful and sophisticated explosive charges, one in the body of a computer, one in a black briefcase, and the third in a belt. At the same time he worked on developing a poison made from potatoes, planning to add it to the explosives and the metal fragments. Barghouti said that the idea of dipping the metal fragments in poison occurred to him when he read a book by the head of the ISA,[7] which told how a small charge of that kind killed five people. He asked for technical information and manufacturing instructions from Hamas abroad, but after he found out that the poison had no effect, he stopped trying to use it.

On December 1, 2001, in the evening, two human bombs were sent out on a combined mission in central Jerusalem. They were equipped with explosives and instructions sent from Barghouti. One was Osama Bahar, a religious young man of twenty-five from Abu Dis, a town adjacent to East Jerusalem, who was close to Hamas. He exploded the charge in the computer housing at 11:35 p.m. in Zion Square. A few minutes later, about a hundred meters from there, Nabil Abu Halabia blew up the charge in the belt. Halabia, twenty-four, was a plasterer, trained in martial arts, and a friend of Bahar's, who had recommended him for the mission. Immediately afterward the charge in the black briefcase was set off from a distance. It had been placed in a blue Opel Kadett with Israeli license plates, which had been conveyed to the terrorists the day before and was parked in a nearby alley. A total of ten Israelis were killed, most of them young people enjoying a night on the town, and 191 were injured.

At that time a Hamas commander named Ibrahim Hamed, known in the organization as "Sheikh," was placed above Barghouti. Hamed had lost his father at the age of three, and when he was six his brother, a fighter in Fatah, had been killed in an IDF bombing raid in southern

Lebanon. At the start of his activity with Hamas, in 1999, he was arrested by the security police of the Palestinian Authority after his involvement in the interrogation of a suspected collaborator with Israel, following the elimination of senior members of the movement. When he was released from prison in Jericho in 2001, where he was together with senior Hamas people, he understood that he, too, was slated to be eliminated by the ISA, so he began "to act like a wanted man"—keeping a distance from his family, hiding in the mountains, sleeping in a different place every night. He was Barghouti's direct superior, maintaining communications with him via intermediaries, and he took over responsibility for suicide terrorism in the Ramallah area, although he was careful never to meet the human bombs he dispatched. Thus, when he heard there were two volunteers, he had a meeting with Salah Talkahma, another senior Hamas person, his friend dating back to his time studying at Birzeit and being in prison in Jericho. The Sheikh tried to persuade them not to commit suicide, because as residents of Jerusalem, they could be utilized for purposes like gathering intelligence, but the two insisted on committing a double suicide attack in central Jerusalem, at a location they knew well from earlier scouting trips. The handlers chose to send each of them separately, in order to get credit for two attacks. The day before the planned attacks they were to transfer the candidates, via the Siluwan unit, to Barghouti, so they could be equipped with charges and given instructions, and then the accomplice unit would dispatch them. The Sheikh received tens of thousands of dollars to finance his activity and for living expenses. He believed there was no need for any restrictions on suicide terrorism actions against Israelis, because as long as they were occupiers, none of them were innocent, including children ("Israel also kills children, and then it announces that a regrettable accident happened," he said).

A complaint against Barghouti reached the Sheikh, claiming he was "undisciplined" and tended to act on his own. The Sheikh then sent Barghouti a reprimand, demanding that he "behave well." Similarly, the Sheikh ordered Barghouti to prepare more charges, which he did, conveying them to activists in the Ramallah area, camouflaged as cartons of juice or stones. While the Hamas activists of higher rank, mainly the Sheikh, were waiting to receive the charges from Barghouti, via an intermediary (Ahmad Araman) they turned to Wahel Kasm (Abu Sa'ad) and asked him to pick the location for the next attack. The latter scouted around Jerusalem along with two accomplices and reported via Barghouti that they had found an ideal target: Café Moment.

The mission was directed by Hamas headquarters in the Ramallah area with the help of the accomplices in Jerusalem (the Siluwan unit), whose members had Israeli identification papers. On Saturday night, March 9, 2002, at 8:00 p.m., the Sheikh met the activist Araman, who brought with him a candidate for suicide terrorism, Fuad Hourani, twenty-two years old, resident in the al-Arub refugee camp near Bethlehem, the son of an officer in the Palestinian Authority, religious, a Hamas sympathizer, and a student at the teachers' seminary in Ramallah. Hourani and Araman went into an isolated room, where Hourani was fitted with an explosive vest. From a collection point at a mosque in a northern neighborhood of Jerusalem, they took a taxi in the direction of the target. They met Abu Sa'ad, who led the human bomb to a place near Café Moment, pointed in the direction of the target, and cleared out. At 10:30 p.m., when the café was crowded with young people enjoying themselves, the human bomb walked past the guard without any difficulty, reached the interior, and blew up the charge. Eleven people were killed, sixty-five were injured, and severe damage was caused. The identity and personal facts about the suicide terrorist were not made known to Barghouti until two days after the attack, when he was asked to prepare the video cassette of Hourani's testament for publication, and only then was its content made known to him. Immediately afterward the Sheikh asked Barghouti, by means of an intermediary, to make another explosive vest, "identical to the earlier one."

Barghouti used to pour the explosives into shampoo bottles, which he placed in leatherette pouches sewn into a belt. He would wrap the electric trigger switch in wire. To set off the charge, the human bomb had to free the switch from the wire. Barghouti agreed with his interrogators that this arrangement made it awkward "to activate it quickly if needed."

On May 7, 2002, Araman met with a candidate for suicide terrorism whom he had met a month earlier, Muhammad Mu'amar, twenty-eight, of Jordanian origin, a resident of the refugee camp in Nablus. They drove from Nablus with several stops in villages in Samaria, until they reached Beit Anan, where they stopped for a short time so Mu'amar could put on the explosive vest. They then continued to the village of Beit Iksa near

Jerusalem. Abu Sa'ad and another activist took over leading the human bomb. That night they reached the garage area of the city of Rishon LeZion, not far from Tel Aviv, where they came to the basement billiard hall, the Sheffield Club, which had been chosen by the activists. At 10:50 the human bomb entered the hall and set off the charge, killing sixteen and wounding thirty-nine.

During the next two months Barghouti made more charges that were used in the following attacks: the explosion of a gas tanker truck triggered from a distance by means of a cell phone when the truck entered a gas depot (Glilot, severe damage, no casualties); explosion of a charge placed on the railway tracks and activated from a distance by means of a cell phone (Lod, four people injured). Barghouti made the charges in a "laboratory." To do so he chose to buy an apartment (he received $60,000 for this purpose) rather than renting one, "because landlords usually ask a lot of questions about their tenants." He met once a week with his emissaries. When a meeting was not possible, because of pressure from the IDF, they passed coded messages to each other by means of a dead drop—an empty cola can that was placed next to a column in front of the eye hospital. In July Barghouti made a charge that was placed in an attaché case and given to the Siluwan unit in Jerusalem, which was commanded by the Ramallah branch of Hamas. The attaché case was thrown over the fence of the Hebrew University campus on Mount Scopus in Jerusalem and picked up the next day by an activist (Muhammad Uda), who knew the campus well because he had worked there as a painter and was able to enter using an old pass. On July 28, 2002, the attaché case was placed on a table in the central cafeteria, which was crowded with students and faculty members who had come for lunch. A newspaper was put on it to give the impression of an innocent object that had been left for a moment. They tried to set off the explosion with a cell phone but failed. The activist went back to take the attaché case to repair it and returned the next day. The second attempt also failed because of a flaw in the electric circuit. The attaché case was not exploded until July 31, 2002, at 1:00 p.m., leaving nine dead and eighty-one wounded.[8] Barghouti claims that he did not regard the target chosen for this attack as a good one, and he expressed anger on the matter to those responsible. It was then decided not to direct subsequent suicide attacks against educational institutions but to concentrate on places of shopping and entertainment.

Barghouti was asked to prepare two more explosive belts, both of which he passed on via intermediaries to the activist Muhammad Sharitah, twenty-five years old, a resident of Yata, near Hebron, and a member of the Hamas student movement at Birzeit University. Meanwhile Sharitah had heard about a volunteer for suicide terrorism with the appellation Omar. He was Ayad Radad, a twenty-three-year-old who had come to the occupied territories from Jordan in 2000. The meeting set for the two did not take place because of logistical difficulties, so Omar was placed under Barghouti's command by means of intermediaries. Omar spoke about his cousin, Rafah Muqdi, who also wanted to be a suicide terrorist, and the two wanted to commit the act together. It was planned that they would break into a catering hall in the town of Or Yehuda, south of Tel Aviv, open fire with Uzi submachine guns, and then activate the explosives on their body. On a scouting trip it was discovered that the place was protected by guards, so the operation was canceled.

The handlers met with Omar in the safe house in Ramallah, where they let him spend the night, and he was taught how to operate the charge (September 17, 2002). Two days later the human bomb was driven to Tel Aviv by the activist Ashraf Za'ir (a clothing merchant with Israeli identity documents), and there they parted. The guide did not give Omar specific instructions but told him "to kill as many Israelis as possible." Omar boarded bus no. 4, and when he reached Allenby Street, a very busy area, he set off the explosive, killing six, most of them old people, and wounding eighty-four.

Then it was decided to send the cousin, Muqdi, to carry out another suicide attack, and a target was located in Tel Aviv. The chosen human bomb was asked to prepare himself for action in the near future, but he postponed his departure several times with various excuses ("Not until I've seen my sister, who is about to return from a visit to the United States"). On October 11, 2002, he was transferred from his village to an apartment in a-Ram, near Jerusalem, where they placed an explosive belt on him and instructed him in activating it. On that day he was driven to Tel Aviv. At about 8:15 p.m. they let him out at the promenade along the seaside, without specific instructions. He walked here and there, hesitant and fearful, until he started to enter the Yotvata restaurant. The guard was suspicious and blocked his entry. Then he tried to flee, but he was arrested a short distance away. In another interrogation Barghouti denied responsibility for this attempted attack.

After his arrest, the ISA found that Barghouti left equipment and weapons behind in the bathroom of his apartment, including eight or nine shampoo bottles full of TNT, intended for use in the explosive belts of future human bombs.

Abas al-Sayid

Abas al-Sayid, an intifada activist and key political and military leader of Hamas in the northern part of the West Bank, was captured by the IDF, tried, and sentenced to thirty-five life sentences for the thirty-five Israelis whose murder he was found directly responsible for.[9]

Al-Sayid, born in 1966, lived in the city of Tul Karem in central Samaria. He is married and the father of two, tall, handsome, dandyish, articulate, and charming. He studied engineering for five years at Yarmouk University in Jordan and was trained in the operation of medical equipment in the United States (1991–92). He worked in maintenance at the government hospital near where he lived. In November 2000 he joined Hamas and quickly became the movement's spokesman in the region (including appearances on Palestinian television). He organized demonstrations and protests (mainly around the funerals of shahids), and he was the contact man with the Hamas leadership in Damascus, including telephone conversations with the chairman, Khaled Mashal. He also transferred funds for political and military activities: $10,000 a month or more was transferred from the United States to his private account in the Tul Karem branch of the Arab Bank. Along with his visible work, he was an underground commander. He acquired and distributed weapons and terrorism equipment, improved the deadly potential of the explosive charges, and laid the foundations for a cell including six permanent accomplices who served as bodyguards and drivers, transferred messages and arms, recruited volunteers, and organized and accompanied attacks. As early as 1993 he was arrested and imprisoned for eleven months, and then, in 1994, he was sentenced to a year and a half in prison but freed after nine months. According to him, this molded his character and radicalized his attitudes.

During the intifada al-Sayid planned and led three suicide attacks. In the first he sent the human bomb Ahmad Alyan, a twenty-three-year-old bachelor, a muezzin in a mosque, who distributed his inheritance in his will, to a central intersection in the Israeli coastal city of Netanya, where he blew himself up next to a bus, leaving three dead (March 2001). In the second, he sent the human bomb Muhammad Maramash, a twenty-one-year-old bachelor who regularly attended prayers in the old mosque in Tul Karem, to blow himself up in a shopping mall in Netanya, killing five (May 2001). In the final months of 2001 he began to plan the third action, which took place at the end of what is called "Black March" (2002), during which twenty-three Palestinian suicide attacks took place, killing 135 Israelis.

The original plan was to dispatch two human bombs, and in fact two candidates were recruited. The first was Nadal Qalaq, a resident of a refugee camp and a student of religion, the classmate of one of the directors of the cell, who found him after prayers at the mosque and took him for a discreet conversation in which he suggested that he should go on a suicide mission. Qalaq asked for some time to think it over, and when they met again, he said, "Inshallah." His reason for volunteering was that he "wanted to be a shahid in the presence of God, and also to defend his personal honor." After it was apparently published in the student newspaper that he had volunteered, he began to act as if he figured in the Israeli list of wanted men, meaning that he moved from hideout to hideout, with the assistance of local supporters of the movement. He was given a few hundred shekels in pocket money. After a central activist informed him that he had been chosen for a particularly large attack, whose details would be given to him a day in advance, all connections with him were severed until the end of March. Then he was summoned to take part in the attack, but he avoided it by claiming he was sick. Later he was arrested by the IDF, tried, and sentenced to eight years in prison (April 2002). The second volunteer was Uda Abed al-Basat, a twenty-four-year-old unmarried man from Kalkiliya, who used to spend time in Israel as an illegal worker, taking odd jobs and engaging in theft. He was recruited after he was seen praying seriously in the mosque in Tul Karem. Before committing himself to the mission, he asked for a chance to wrap up his affairs with his father and his fiancée, and also to observe *istihara*, the special prayer in which the believer asks God for advice and guidance to choose the good and right path when he is perplexed at a crossroads of fateful decisions. Following al-Sayid's instructions, his needs were provided for, and he was asked to write a will, but the messenger who bore it was killed in an IDF ambush, and the action was postponed (August 2001).

Al-Sayid went underground. He cut himself off from his home and family, lived in caves and in country dwellings and on the edges of cities. He remained in contact with his commanders only through messengers and intermediaries. Following his instructions, an activist was sent to the explosives laboratory in Nablus to bring two explosive vests to him from there. They were hidden temporarily in the women's bathroom in the new mosque in Tul Karem. From there they were brought, wrapped in a blanket, to an apartment that had been rented for the operation. They were examined and found to be in working order. On orders that al-Sayid sent with a woman intermediary other actions were taken at the same time. An activist in the cell was sent to look for a driver to take the human bomb to the border and beyond. Several candidates refused, until a villager from the area was found, a man of forty-eight, married to four wives and the father of thirteen children. In return he received 1,000 Jordanian dinars. Another activist went to Israel to buy a car with Israeli license plates. He did so with a document stolen in Israel two years previously. He returned with a Renault that he had bought for 6,500 shekels. Also, for fifty shekels a day, a video camera was rented from a local photography studio. Two days before the operation, a car in the Israeli city of Rishon LeZion was broken into, and a woman's identity card was stolen. It was sent to a forgery laboratory in Nablus, and several of the details were changed.

The designated human bomb was transferred that day to an apartment in an isolated building that belonged to the grandfather of one of the activists in the cell, and two other activists stayed with him there. That night al-Sayid arrived, speaking by himself with Uda for about two hours. Then they went out to take still photographs and a video of the testament. Al-Sayid wrote it, and Uda read it word for word in front of the camera, holding a Koran in one hand and an M16 assault rifle in the other. On the wall in the background were hung pictures of five shahids, and above them was a quotation from the Koran about the pleasures of paradise promised to martyrs. Then they shaved his beard and mustache, his hair was cut short, he washed thoroughly, and then his face (which, as the activists pointed out, was rather fair) was made up like a woman's, and he received the identity card of an Israeli woman. He was given a cell phone that had never previously been used, to decrease the danger that calls would be intercepted by Israel. At this time a still photograph of the driver who escorted him was also taken, in case he were killed during the operation, and then he would be treated as a shahid by the movement (immediately after he returned safely, the photograph was destroyed).

After Uda put on bell-bottom blue jeans decorated with sequins, al-Sayid himself placed the explosive vest on him (not before the driver tried it on). The vest was made of blue cloth, sewn as a blouse that covered the shoulders, chest, and upper back. In front many pockets were sewn, into which a charge of ten kilograms of nitroglycerin was placed, in containers that resembled smoke grenades. Small ball bearings were placed in every pocket, as well as iron wire, which were cut into many pieces half a centimeter long. Thus a blast effect at a radius of a few meters was obtained, along with the effect of deadly shrapnel at a longer radius. The source of the current was a bundle of nine-volt batteries, and the trigger was a plastic on-off switch. At an earlier stage of his activity, al-Sayid had asked a pharmacist, a relative and protégé, who had been recruited for Hamas while studying in Jordan, to obtain deadly poison that could be inserted in the charge and increase its murderous effect ("to kill as many as a thousand people"). Nerve gas and chlorine were considered, and ultimately al-Sayid received four kilograms of cyanide. For some reason it was decided not to put the cyanide in Uda's charge, and it was saved for a future attack.

Only after this was Uda given a short briefing about activating the charge by pressing the switch, which would be placed in his pocket, and it was agreed that if he was arrested by the Israelis, he would immediately set off the charge when they were close to him. He and his escort were also told that since they knew urban areas in Israel well, they could choose the target for the explosion themselves. All that night and the following morning the chosen human bomb remained silent, interrupted from time to time with short prayers. At noon the activists parted from Uda with a handshake. They asked him to give a warm greeting to their people in paradise. They added that soon they would all meet there, as shahids, inshallah.

Around 2:00 p.m. Uda and his driver left, disguised as a couple. As soon as they left, the apartment where they had been was cleaned and tidied, to avoid leaving any identifying traces. The pair drove from Tul Karem to the Israeli border in the driver's Peugeot, and there they transferred into an "Israeli" car that was waiting for them. They drove south to Herzliya, failed to find an appropriate target there, and continued on to Tel Aviv. After a frustrating time of circling in the streets there, they decided to return to Netanya. Uda told the driver where to go, explaining that he knew the place very well, because he used to steal cars there. After no less than five hours of driving around large Israeli population centers, they came to the entrance of the Park Hotel. There the driver dropped off Uda and drove back to the border. In his testimony he stated that the suicide terrorist's face showed no signs of fear.

The attack was timed for the eve of Passover, the most important Jewish holiday, when almost all Israelis are gathered for the traditional Seder meal. In the hotel dining room almost 250 guests were seated, most of them elderly, and their families. The tables were set and laden with matzoth, wine, and other festive foods. Just before it was time to begin the traditional reading of the Haggadah, at around 7:30 p.m., Uda entered the lobby wearing a long straight wig, fashionable yellow glasses, a three-quarter-length coat with a speckled lapel, and high-heeled shoes or boots. He looked to the guests and waiters as though he were seeking his relatives. In retrospect witnesses said that there was something "strange" about his appearance. They especially mentioned his gaze when it crossed theirs. All that time his hand was in his coat pocket. Then he went into a private room, walked up to the people at the table, and pressed the button. The rescue teams found shattered bodies and severed limbs on the site, floating on water, which had been sprayed by the automatic sprinkler system and had turned red with a mixture of wine and blood. Those who were alive, with no arms and legs, were in shock, screaming with pain, calling for help. Thirty Israelis were killed in the attack, and another 160 people were wounded, some of them severely (March 2002).

The escort who had driven away had not gotten very far when he heard the explosion. He returned to the border village, exchanged cars again, and announced by telephone that the operation had succeeded. Then he went home. The activists in the Tul Karem region, headed by al-Sayid, listened to reports about the event on Israeli radio all that night. The Hamas leadership on the West Bank quickly took responsibility for the attack by means of an official announcement issued from Nablus. The next day posters were circulated with a picture of Uda, the shahid, wearing the explosive belt, and his testament was broadcast on Hezbollah's al-Manar television station in Lebanon.

Al-Sayid's subordinates summoned the residents of the area on loudspeakers to take part in a street procession in memory of Uda, the martyr. In his home a mourning tent was erected, and his mother and father were congratulated and expressed pride in their son. Al-Sayid paid to serve coffee to the hundreds of condolence visitors. On the Israeli side the attack on the Park Hotel was the straw that broke the camel's back. The government decided to launch a comprehensive military operation, called Defensive Shield, which would concentrate on the Jenin district (March 29–May 10, 2002). IDF forces surrounded the city at an unprecedented level, searched it thoroughly, and killed or captured a large number of members of the Palestinian organizations. During the operation civilians who were not involved were also harmed, and the destruction was considerable. Since then the terrorism infrastructure on the West Bank has not recovered.

Al-Sayid knew that the ISA regarded him as one of the most wanted men. Immediately after the attack he fled and hid, commanding his cell only by messengers. But toward the end of the extensive Israeli retaliation operation he was located in a building (May 8, 2002). Without returning fire he came out with his hands up and turned himself in. Israeli intelligence had detailed information about his activities in the past as well as his plans for the future, including another suicide attack that he had initiated. For that reason he was defined as a "ticking bomb," and his interrogation was given high priority, including permission to apply "moderate physical pressure." He was interrogated more than twenty times over a month, with the participation of many investigators, some of them senior. One focus of the interrogation was the effort to locate the third explosive belt before it was used in another attack (the interrogation led to its hiding place in an eighteen-liter paint can, which had been hidden in the ground in one of the activists' yard). At first al-Sayid denied that he was involved in Hamas military operations against Israel and presented himself as only a political activist. Gradually he began to cooperate. He was broken mainly after proof was shown to him that other activists had been arrested and revealed information, including the places where weapons had been hidden. At a certain stage he admitted involvement in suicide terrorism and spoke enthusiastically about the attack on the Park Hotel. Afterward the atmosphere of contacts with him changed. He asked for and received a Koran in his cell, and he held conversations about the "philosophy of Islam" with his interrogators. He claimed before the Israeli judicial authorities that he had been kept in isolation, tortured severely, and humiliated. His interrogators described him as intelligent, well educated, open, tough, close to his wife and children, and also arrogant, self-important, and tricky. Over time, all the members of his terrorist cell were killed or captured. He is the leader of the Hamas prisoners in Israeli prisons, and he is revered among the Palestinians. Last year a special program was broadcast on Palestinian television to celebrate his forty-seventh birthday. Meanwhile, Uda, the suicide terrorist, has been forgotten.

Paradise Now

The human bomb wears an explosive vest on his chest, stuck to his skin, so that he cannot remove or deactivate it. He is disguised as a groom and hides the charge under his fancy outfit. It is a hot summer day, and he is dripping with sweat. Fear and confusion add to his physical distress. Thus he finds himself trapped in a small toilet cubicle. At another time, while still strapped to the sensitive explosive charge, he is leaning over the motor of a car, trying to fix it. He also has a romance with a local beauty, while the vest is still attached to his body. These are some of the tragicomic scenes in *Paradise Now*, winner of the Golden Globe competition.[10] Some of the situations in this movie are hilarious, utterly improbable, and quite outrageous, but nevertheless it is on target and insightful.[11]

The movie is sometimes offensive, but it is more convincing and instructive than other fictional representations of suicide terrorism. The power of the movie lies in its successful penetration through the curtain of self-righteousness and glorification that typifies the apologists of Palestinian suicide terrorism, and through the curtain of bombast and didactics that typifies suicide terrorism pundits. *Paradise Now* gives the human bomb a true face and personality. The humanization of the human bomb presents a reality that is not epic, romantic, or sympathetic, showing him as snubbed, miserable, fragile, and ridiculous.

The film describes forty-eight hours in the life of Said and Khaled, two young men from a refugee camp in the suburbs of Nablus, from the moment they become aware that they have been chosen to go out on a suicide terrorism mission in Tel Aviv to the explosion. Meanwhile, we learn about their preparations: parting from their families, eating a rich meal, recording the will, shaving their beards, putting on the explosive vest and the disguise, being driven to the fence, and crossing over into Israel. An IDF patrol foils their plan, and they have to go back to where they came from. Along the way they start feeling fearful and hesitant about the wisdom and justice of their action, especially after they hear arguments against it, and they have some time to think things over. One of them reneges, and the other goes out once again on his last trip, in a psychological state that seems automatic.

The depiction of the suicide terrorists and their mission is free of any idealization, pathos, or simplistic propaganda. Said and Khaled are marginal figures, acting out of alienation, even boredom, rather than conviction or despair. They remain indifferent as they set out on the mission, and it is hard for them to formulate a clear message that they wish to convey by means of their extreme action, into which they are drawn almost absentmindedly. They show no signs of radical nationalism or religious fervor, and they never belonged to any organizational framework. They are also not boiling with hatred, trying with all their might to take vengeance against Israel. They do not strive for redemption for themselves or for their people. They are not macho, not charismatic, not assertive, and not enthusiastic. Thus they are extremely different from the senior member of the movement who dispatches them. Their volunteering for the project seems rather accidental, and their commitment is built up gradually and without their noticing. The mental, doctrinaire, and operative preparation seems rather casual. In the end, the result is partial failure for technical reasons and lack of method and resolution.

Although the film won prizes and was a box-office success, it disappointed many involved in the regional conflict. One point of criticism common to both sides was the humaneness of the figures portrayed in the film. The Palestinian side wanted them to be superhuman, the embodiment of believers and great patriots, and the Israeli side wanted them to be seen as subhuman beasts full of hatred and evil. In reality the suicide terrorist is neither one nor the other.

At times the movie is unpersuasive, as, for example, when it includes a Jewish accomplice in the Palestinian suicide terrorism mission, who supposedly is in it for the money, although he is aware of the gravity of his betrayal; or when the human bomb chooses a bus as a target, and all of the passengers just happen to be elite IDF soldiers. But the film regains our trust by means of humor. There is authenticity in the moments of satire.[12] *Paradise Now* lies on the border between documentary and feature film. It moves back and forth from reality to fantasy, and in fact when it slips into fantasy, it is more precise in depicting Palestinian suicide terrorism.

5

PASSING

An Overlooked Aspect of Suicide Terrorism

Twenty Minutes

The Palestinians called her "the Iris of the Carmel." She was Hanadi Jaradat, the woman who committed the suicide attack for the Islamic Jihad at Maxim's restaurant (October 2003). Most likely revenge was primary among her motivations. Both her brother and her fiancé had been killed by the IDF several months earlier because of their active membership in the Islamic terrorist movement in the West Bank. Jaradat was then twenty-nine years old, an attorney, from a respected family in Jenin. Her profile was different from that of most of the human bombs at that time who were men, much younger, less well educated, and nonprofessional. During the last few months of her life, she had become ultrareligious.

Jaradat crossed the border on Saturday morning and entered Israel without a permit, despite the closure. She arranged in advance by telephone to meet with an Israeli Arab taxi driver who specialized in transporting workers illegally present in Israel, asking him to drive her to the hospital to visit her aged father. After getting in the taxi she removed her *jilbab* (women's long robe) and scarf, and remained with her head bare, dressed in modern Western clothing. On the way she said she was hungry and asked the driver to stop at the restaurant. At noon, while the place was full of people, they entered a Mediterranean fish restaurant, jointly owned by Jewish and Arab partners. The guard at the entrance did not suspect them at all. After the driver left, she stood in the center of the dining room and blew herself up. Twenty-one Israelis were killed with her.

The Israeli press reported that Jaradat ate in the restaurant before blowing herself up. That sounded so fantastic to me that I found it hard to believe. However, it was fully corroborated by a close reading of the ISA reports, which were based on interrogation of the driver, who was arrested, and from the protocol of the hearing in the Supreme Court, which deliberated on the driver's appeal, after he had been found guilty of being an accomplice to mass murder. I also interviewed the owners of the restaurant, who were present at the attack and injured. Indeed, the human bomb did order a meal. Furthermore, she called the waiter back, said he had made a mistake, and demanded a different dish. After eating, she delayed even longer, went to the restroom, and, according to the cash register, paid for her meal. In total she stayed at the scene of the attack, in immediate proximity with her future victims, for more than twenty minutes. Under the circumstances, this is a long and fraught period of time, complex and demanding. Security officers defined this suicide bombing as the height of chutzpah.

We have before us an extreme case of deception and assimilation mixed with not a little defiance. What temerity and provocation Jaradat displayed. Can it be chalked up to acting talent and self-control—superb operational skill? Her conduct on site and the experience connected with it are baffling. Did it occur to her that her plan could be discovered, that she might be arrested before blowing herself up? Did she listen to the conversations of the guests around her? Did she look straight at her intended victims? Did she choose which ones to concentrate on? Did she notice the children among them? Was she reminded of her young nieces and nephews? Did she enjoy the meal (she left some food on her plate)? Maybe she took pleasure in her achievements up to that moment, from her penetration without being stopped and her control of the orchestration to the thought of what would happen in a short time, and perhaps also what awaited her afterward, after the explosion. She probably derived some intrinsic pleasure related to the circumstances themselves and not only to her objectives.

Possibly she got satisfaction from stretching the situation more and more, pleasure from delaying the end, the frightening and redemptive climax. Perhaps first of all she was gripped by dread of her imminent end, hesitant and considering regret and retreat, or also full of excitement because she was, if only for a moment, somebody entirely different, enjoying herself, part of a community that was quite pleased with its lot, Israeli. Twenty minutes of fear, but also of total freedom. Even loosening her long hair, which was always tightly gathered, wrapped and covered—this is freedom that cannot be ignored. Only when she rose from her chair and pressed the button, did she remind herself and reveal to the other who she really was. Perhaps another fraction of a second passed before the explosion, before she was once again entirely a Palestinian human bomb.

It might be assumed that the suicide terrorist would be interested in making the time in which he is at the target among his intended victims as short as possible. This would reduce the chance that he might be discovered and his plan foiled, and he would also be spared moments of tension and anxiety. Nevertheless one sometimes gets the impression that the suicide terrorist tries to prolong that time as much as possible, and not just to delay his death, but actually to defy nature and increase the challenge. Palestinians connected to suicide terrorism and Israeli counterterrorist experts agree that there could be further explanations. They entertain the possibility that being successful at deceiving the enemy is itself an intoxicating experience to which one becomes addicted for a while. Human bombs might extend the opportunity to enjoy their own fame, as it were, and take pleasure in knowing that the mission is being accomplished as planned, and in displaying self-control and heroism, so they might delay the end for a short moment of self-deception and deception of their future victim. Moreover, they might draw satisfaction from fooling the Israelis, expressing contempt for and mockery of those they are about to kill. The suicide terrorist who exchanges a few words with the human target, whom the terrorist alone knows is about to die, and asks about the menu, is toying with him, like the woman terrorist who complained about her meal to the waiter. After her arrest, Ahlam Tamimi, who escorted and supervised the human bomb al-Masri, was proud that, on an earlier scouting trip in the area of the planned attack, she made sure to remove the coin from the supermarket cart she was using for terrorism, to make sure she wouldn't give even a single shekel to the Zionist enemy.

Blue-Eyed Human Bomb

The Palestinian organizations that employed suicide terrorism chose to send the perpetrators on missions in Israel disguised to fit their conception of a stereotypical Israeli, according to the nature of the operation and of the individual human bomb. Usually the human bomb appeared as an IDF soldier on reserve duty (dressed in khaki fatigues); or as a trendy teenager or university student (dressed in jeans and sneakers, with a fashionable hairdo and sunglasses); or as an Orthodox Jew (with ritual fringes dangling from his waist) of either the more pious and traditional type (mainly for attacks in Jerusalem) or the more modern and nationalist type (mainly in attacks against Israeli targets in the West Bank). The Palestinian accomplices who were sent to stores in Israel to buy typical items of clothing were aware of the subtle nuances of Jewish religiosity, such as the distinction between a knitted *kippah*, in settler style, and a black cloth *kippah* typical of *haredim*. Naturally most versions of Israeliness used by the human bombs were oriental (*mizrahi*), belonging to the large sector of Jews whose families emigrated from countries in the Middle East and North Africa (such as Iraq and Morocco), whose slightly darker skin color and Arabic accent made them look somewhat similar to Palestinians.[1] Nevertheless, blue eyes, which are rare both among Mizrahi Jews and Palestinians, were regarded as an advantage when choosing candidates for suicide missions. Perhaps this is because they are considered beautiful in the Middle East and identified with absolute Israeliness. The Palestinians proudly stated that the suicide terrorist who blew himself up in Café Moment had blue eyes and was appropriately dressed in a fashionable motorcycle jacket, enabling him to penetrate an area full of alert security guards.

Successful disguise depends mainly on the appropriate clothing, but it can stand or fall on the most subtle details, such as current idioms of Hebrew slang and cool, urban body language. We have information about human bombs who went so far in distancing themselves from their Arab look as to bleach their hair blond, wear headphones, carry laptops, and even learn some Jewish prayers.[2] Al-Masri, the human bomb who attacked the Sbarro restaurant in Jerusalem (August 2001) carried a guitar case on his back, which was where he hid the explosives. In the Middle Eastern associative space, a guitar is a decidedly Israeli artifact, as distant as possible from Arab.[3] In a preliminary survey of the area to gather information, his handler and accomplice, Ahlam Tamimi, discovered there was a musical instrument store near the target, and that many young people walked about with guitars. She also asked him to wear a new, clean shirt. She was not checked on her way to the target, and she had aroused no suspicion in all of her previous scouting trips to Jerusalem, despite the presence of many Israeli security personnel. A central Palestinian operative in this suicide bombing explained that this was because she "looked Jewish" in her costume. Similarly, the attack on the pedestrian mall in Rishon LeZion (May 2002) was committed by two terrorists who looked like a parody of Israeliness: the woman (Arin Shibat) spoke English, wore tights, and had a bare midriff; the man (Isa Badir) dyed his hair with colored streaks.

The infiltration and assimilation of female suicide terrorists was less difficult because women (like elderly people) were regarded as relatively harmless and subjected to somewhat limited body searches. Nevertheless, the Palestinian organizations did not make frequent use of women, mainly for patriarchal and puritanical religious reasons. In some cases, female human bombs (mainly middle-aged women) acted while dressed in a way that easily and unequivocally identified them as Palestinians. They wore long embroidered dresses down to their ankles, like traditional village women, under the assumption that, since they were so obviously Arab, they must be innocuous and have nothing to hide. The male variant of this innocent appearance was to wear a keffiyeh and drive a cart hitched to a donkey, as in more than one attack in the Gaza Strip. However, most often the handlers decided to increase the chances of female human bombs blending into the Israeli target crowd by adopting an Israeli appearance, which is to say, revealing clothing that emphasized their femininity. In Hamas and the Islamic Jihad, which are religious organizations that highlight women's modesty, especially covering the body, this requires overcoming traditional constraints. The instigators of suicide terrorism testified to a need to give the human bombs a "Western look," which, to their mind, meant an immodest appearance. This led to exaggeration in the disguises of suicide terrorists, especially the female ones. Blue jeans were not enough. They had to be tight. Rather than a short-sleeved shirt, they preferred sleeveless T-shirts. Going to these extremes entailed a provocation directed no less toward the Palestinian populace in the rear than toward Israeli society at the front. Ahlam Tamimi, who led her operative to the entrance of the Sbarro restaurant, was disguised as a stylish young Israeli woman,[4] that is, according to local orthodox Muslims, a whore. On the campus of Birzeit University near Ramallah, she used to wear a hijab (a veil that covers the head and neck). A religious ruling by Sheikh Ahmad Yassin was necessary to permit her to wear a tight, sleeveless shirt. In certain cases it was simpler to send a man disguised as a woman, as in the attack at the Park Hotel in Netanya (March 2002), when the male human bomb concealed himself behind a three-quarter-length coat, a wig, and high heels.

The vast majority of Palestinian human bombs had neat haircuts and were closely shaved, both to avoid identifying them with traditionalism and Islamic piety and also not to project the neglect of personal appearance connected with manual labor and poverty—characteristics identified with Palestinians in the region. The haircut and especially the shaving were done just before setting out on the mission. Suicide terrorists who were apprehended began to grow their beards again immediately after being imprisoned. A ceremonial dimension was added to the operational logic of shaving. In some cases human bombs adopted a neat appearance for religious reasons as well: thorough washing was part of the purification ritual required for performance of the suicide attack—a sacrament, a holy commandment. Probably this was also another effort to avoid the orientalist stereotype linking Arabs to dirt. This colonialist perspective, which was attributed to the Israeli conqueror, might have been internalized to a degree by the Palestinians themselves and caused alienation and self-disgust among them.[5] In several instances, human bombs were sent on their missions dressed elegantly, even slightly foppishly, in the style called *faranj* in Middle Eastern slang, a term that originally meant "French," a leftover from the colonial period. The result was somewhat exaggerated and ridiculous because, paradoxically, it was so conspicuous that it actually attracted the attention of Israeli guards. In a local film about suicide terrorism, made with a sympathetic attitude toward the Palestinians, the filmmaker also permitted himself to include satirical criticism of the phenomenon: in the broiling summer heat of Israel, the human bombs are dressed in elegant suits and ties, like a groom at a formal wedding.[6] Though it is absurd, this element echoes a basic truth about Palestinian human bombs: while showing the ceremonial and cultic aspect of suicide terrorism,[7] it also expresses the effort to adopt Israeli manners (and at the same time to parody Israeliness).

The response on the Israeli side of the equation of Middle Eastern terrorism was suspicion. Because Palestinian suicide terrorism was based on imitation, disguise, and infiltration, it gave rise to increasingly effective technology for detecting signs that betray the human bomb. This did not prevent the development of a spontaneous social regime in Israel, marked by mistrust and the nervous examination of the people around one. Nothing confirms this better than a description of travel by public transportation in Jerusalem in the early 2000s. Because of fear, the number of passengers declined significantly, while those who, despite everything, did ride abandoned the indifference and alienation that usually characterize people thrown together in public places in an urban context. Everybody constantly surveyed the other passengers, focusing their gaze on other people's faces, their expressions, the movements of their hands, their clothing, prominent outlines of their profiles, their belongings. They especially looked for the end of a wire peeking out from the hem of a coat. They wondered: Was the person in front of them a Jew or an Arab? They worried and tormented themselves: Should they ask him a simple question ("What time is it, please?")? A question would cause him to betray his accent but was also liable to pressure him, so he would panic and set off the explosives.

Inside the Target Car

Human bombs and their victims are in a face-to-face confrontation. Sometimes it is short, and sometimes prolonged; sometimes banal, casual, with little communication, and sometimes complex, dense, nuanced, and eventful. However, it is never symmetrical: one side is all knowing, in possession of a secret, the truth, whereas his opposite numbers, the many people around him, remain in ignorance, innocence, until the explosion, and perhaps, in certain instances, until a moment before it, when suspicion is aroused among some of them. It could be that certainty prevails then, and everyone present shares acute knowledge of what is about to happen very soon. In any event, when the disguised human bomb comes into immediate contact with his or her target public, some sort of interaction begins— verbal or mute—between him or her and them.

Once the encounter ends in an explosion, one can only imagine what looks, gestures, or sentences were exchanged the moment before. This is the case in most acts of suicide terrorism, as in the following example: a human bomb, disguised as a Haredi Jew, waited for a ride on the road leading to a remote Jewish settlement in an area densely populated by Palestinians. A car stopped for him, and in it were four Israelis from the same settlement, whose religious residents all knew each other well. Naturally we are curious about the dynamic that developed among the people riding in that car, all but one still unknowingly imprisoned in a mobile trap, four of whom belonged to the same homogeneous and cohesive primary group. They probably were interested in the identity of the fifth man, who looked like one of them and tried to behave similarly. It is hard to imagine they didn't include him in their conversation or ask him whom he was going to see, and about what. Whether or not he answered them, at a certain stage their confidence was surely shaken, and then most likely they tried to make him respond in a way that would confirm or deny the possibility they feared. Then, perhaps, they might have tried to persuade him to abandon his vicious scheme. They might also have struggled with him. It is also possible that all the Jewish passengers were seized by panic and froze in mute paralysis. At the gate of the settlement, after a ride of at least ten minutes, the doubts were resolved: the explosion took place, and they were all killed (March 2006).[8]

In some cases, retrospectively, a full and reliable picture of the interaction between the human bomb and his intended victims emerges. As an example of faulty communication and an only partially successful effort at disguise and blending in, consider the following excerpts from an interview with an Israeli driver from Eilat.[9] "I stopped for a hitchhiker, but I immediately sensed there was something wrong. He was wearing a coat closed up to the neck, and he didn't take off his big knapsack. He kept his hand in his pocket, his eyes rolled, and he looked strange and tense. I asked him where he wanted to go, but he didn't answer. He just made a sign with his hand for me to keep driving. Finally he spat out something with a heavy Arab accent. I was 99 percent sure he was a terrorist. But I thought better of it, because he might have been an innocent eccentric. I let him out of the car in an isolated place and immediately called the police." The efforts to find the suspect were futile. In a short time he set off the explosives at a bakery in a shopping center, and three Israelis were killed with him. The driver was called in to identify the human bomb's body and make it possible to separate him from his victims. Three different Palestinian organizations took credit for that act of suicide terrorism.

This fraught situation, which is characterized by one-sidedness regarding knowledge of the identity and intentions of everyone present, and their imminent end, also preoccupies the ZAKA volunteers. They try to enter the skin of the human bomb, who is disguised as one of the crowd into which he has blended, while concealing his true, evil nature, and who keeps his secret as his assignment requires. When they discussed this situation, they used an analogy taken from the world of believers known to them. They compared the human bomb to a member of the pious community who has sinned, and no one except him ("and God") knows it. They couldn't deny that all of them had encountered that kind of unsettling situation, so they were speaking on the basis of personal experience. They assumed that the human bomb who approached his target felt exactly like a religious Jew who had violated the Sabbath when he was alone in his house or eaten food that wasn't kosher when he was out of the country. Then, when he was again with a congregation, he was very tense and feared that the truth and his inner feelings would be visible on his face. They repeatedly said he would be sure that everyone was looking at him, because, to quote the Hebrew proverb, "the thief's hat burns on his head." In this discussion, which included confessions, they went on to present the other side of the experience of sinning in secret. Because the offender is not suspected of his shameful act and reprimanded by the others, he sees this as a sign that God is with him. This makes him feel tranquil, even happy. According to ZAKA volunteers, the human bomb derives confidence, even pleasure, from his success in persevering on his mission without having his secret revealed. The Palestinian, with his evil intention, manages to answer the question asked by the Israeli guards at the checkpoint—"How's it going?"—without betraying his Arab identity because he is high, and he is high because he managed to deceive everyone without being caught.

Figure 3. ZAKA squad caring for the mutilated remains of the seventeen Jewish victims of a suicide attack on a bus in Megiddo Junction, carried out by the Palestinian Islamic Jihad, June 5, 2002. (Photo: Courtesy of Ziv Koren, Tel Aviv)

The effectiveness of suicide terrorism derives not only from the lack of any means to deter the human bomb from carrying out his heinous act but also from the difficult problem of spotting and uncovering the human bomb once he is on his way, committed to accomplishing his mission. Does knowing this really put an end to our interest in the relationship between the human bomb's outward appearance and the truth behind it? As shown by our previous arguments, the effect of the human bomb's imitation, disguise, and blending in is not a minor, obvious parameter of suicide terrorism that can be explained solely in operational terms. Rather it is an essential part of suicide terrorism, of great importance to our understanding of its uniqueness. The literature on suicide terrorism tends to underestimate the value of this characteristic, to deflate its significance as if it were a technical matter, with the result that it hardly appears in descriptions and analyses of the phenomenon, and never in its definition.[10] The present book argues, among other things, for detrivialization and deconstruction of the theme of creating a deceptive impression regarding the intention and identity of the human bomb and of his effort to pass as one of the others against whom he is acting and with whom he seeks to die.

Let us return to Maxim's restaurant. The twenty minutes before the explosion are an infinite expanse of time for the human bomb. So are the ten minutes after another human bomb has been let out of his handlers' car on the outskirts of a city, while he walks through the alleys of a neighborhood, past vegetable stalls, until reaching the concentration of shoppers in the heart of the market, where he blows himself up. So are the five minutes while the human bomb who has boarded a crowded bus travels to the next stop before exploding. Likewise, the single minute while the human bomb pushes in among young people who are drinking and having a good time in a bar, before he sets off the explosion in the center of the dance floor, is a moment crammed with vast tensions and enigmas. Sixty seconds can last a long time, as we all know when trying to hold our breath. The two human bombs who attacked Mike's Place, a pub in Tel Aviv, lingered in the crowd at the entrance for ninety minutes (April 2003).[11]

Sometimes lingering in the target area, among the people who will be victims, makes communication with Israelis possible for the suicide terrorist, even providing an opportunity to display degrees of humanity, concern, and some weird solidarity. The testimony of survivors of suicide terrorist attacks indicates that in some cases the attacker warned one of his intended victims by hinting at what was about to happen and thus saving their lives. In the attack on a bus on the Acre-Safed highway, quite some time after boarding the bus at the stop and joining the passengers, the suicide terrorist spoke to a woman sitting next to him, after recognizing that she was a Palestinian citizen of Israel, and told her: "Get off as soon as you can, because something terrible is going to happen here." A few minutes later the suicide terrorist blew himself up along with nine Jewish passengers (August 2002).

Mahmud Maramash, the human bomb who committed the attack at a shopping center in Netanya in which five Israelis were killed and eighty-six injured, stood at the entrance to the shopping center for a long time, observing the target area and waiting for more people to gather while he smoked a cigarette. Before that, on his way there, he had bargained with taxi drivers, rejecting the ones who asked for two or three hundred shekels, until he found a taxi that asked only for a hundred shekels, which he boarded along with three other passengers (May 2001).

This stage, which the literature on suicide terrorism tends to ignore, is critical for the success of the operation and fascinating in its study. From the human bomb's point of view, this is the most complex and precarious part of the mission. After it, there remains only activation of the explosives: standing at the right angle and pressing the on-off button, a rather simple matter that doesn't demand talent, experience, or preparation.

Micro-Sociology of Suicide Terrorism

In his remarkable work on violence, Collins relates to a moment similar to the one discussed here.[12] He argues that the situation of face-to-face confrontation between attacker and victim is especially demanding, and reminds us that it is not easy to kill other people (and, one might add, it is not easy to kill yourself). Hence, we may assume that the assailant is prone to experience unbearable tension. There are two ways to cope with this difficulty. One is to seek to minimize the situation of confrontation, mainly by decreasing the time that it lasts. The second is to select and train an attacker so that he can control his emotions and overcome fear and excitement in order to assure effective performance. The type of violence that Collins focuses on to prove his thesis is professional contract killing, familiar from the folklore of big-time organized crime. The carefully chosen and methodically prepared hit man restricts the confrontation with his victim to a fraction of a second by sneaking up on his target in secret, lurking in hiding, suddenly emerging, and then clearing out in the wink of an eye. The process of natural selection and the accumulation of experience make the contract killer a master of cold-blooded violence. Incidentally, Collins briefly suggests an analogy between the hit man and the human bomb. According to him, the arena of suicide terrorism is also characterized both by a situation of minimal confrontation and by an attacker with superb control over his emotions. The following effort to show that Collins's latter thesis is based on two false premises will enable me better to present the uniqueness of suicide terrorism, especially the Palestinian version.

First, analysis of dozens of cases of Palestinian suicide terrorism shows that just a few of them were characterized by a face-to-face confrontation between attacker and victim that lasted only a minimum amount of time. In fact, the attacks that lasted only a second or two were generally failures. One sometimes has the impression that, due to deliberate initiative on the part of the perpetrators, or to some other reason, the time of confrontation is extended beyond the absolutely required minimum as if it had intrinsic meaning as a source of gratification. It seems that extending the time in which the attacker lingers at point-blank range from his victims, when he is naturally exposed to their suspicious gaze, is a goal in itself. One could view the confrontation in suicide terrorism as if it began only with the human bomb's shout of "Allahu Akbar" and ended immediately after with the explosion. In such a case, as in criminal murder, the duration of the act would approach zero. But this conception ignores a vital component of suicide terrorism, which is characterized by the extended presence of the attacker among his victims in a way that makes possible a kind of interaction between them. Moreover, the disguising and mingling bound up with suicide terrorism definitely softens the confrontation, but also charges it with additional tension with which the attacker must cope. A professional hit man who leaps out of a car with darkened windows with his gun pointed at the victim does not have to pretend to be someone else, to lie, to communicate, or to violate trust, as does the human bomb.

As for the exceptional abilities demanded of the attacker, one may say that the human bomb is anything but a virtuoso in the manner of Igor the Assassin, Mad Dog, or other avatars of the hit man as heroes of popular culture in Mafia films. It would be hard to describe him as relaxed or, alternatively, as having a powerful personality indicating mastery of his environment and behavior. Collins bases his arguments on a few pictures of Tamil and Palestinian human bombs before setting out on their missions. According to him, they demonstrate composure. Other photographs show human bombs on their way to the attack, taken by security cameras on trains, where they display what Collins interprets as indifference (London, 2005). Was he surprised to see that their eyes were not glowing and their mouths were not foaming with saliva? His first example is an official photograph taken by the terrorist movement and very carefully staged. In his second case, it is also possible to interpret the facial expressions and body language of the terrorists as showing lack of concentration because of tension and rather forced efforts to appear innocent. There is various evidence of the distress felt by attackers as they approached their targeted victims, such as a telephone conversation in which the human bomb begs to be relieved of his obligation. Indirect evidence can also be found in the considerable number of efforts at suicide terrorism that failed because of complications arising in proximity to the target. Interviews held in prison confirm the impression that even in failures explained in technical terms, fear, nervousness, and excitement definitely play a role.

Collins advances counterintuitive arguments: that suicide terrorism is a type of violence suitable to members of the respectable middle class, and indeed those who come from its nonboisterous, well-behaved sector, whose subculture typically values and promotes lack of spontaneity and concealment of emotion.[13] This is a thought-provoking idea but clearly not applicable to the empirical circumstances of suicide terrorism. Palestinian culture, and Arab and Muslim culture in general, from which the recruits for suicide terrorism are drawn, is unlike restrained Western culture, which emphasizes self-consciousness and self-control. On the contrary, it has an ethos of externalizing and exaggerating emotions. Moreover, the recruitment of candidates for the mission of suicide terrorism is unconcerned with "bourgeois" personality traits of people trained to look and act properly or normal. The human bomb is not equipped with techniques for managing emotions that enable him to avoid betraying his murderous intentions. Nevertheless, Collins's thinking does contain a fertile suggestion. Systematic observation of the behavior of human bombs shows that they are indeed relatively restrained, not to say expressionless. Unlike their handlers, they radiate no charisma or any conspicuous features that could make them stand out and therefore fail. Spokesmen for suicide terrorism organizations, especially the spiritual leaders of Islamic movements, emphasize that a major criterion for choosing human bombs is "humility." They are referring mainly to puritanical values but also to a sort of self-effacement or unpretentiousness, which are required of an attacker for effective functioning in confrontation with his apprehensive would-be victims. This alternative reading of what appears to be lack of feeling in the pictures should be related to the findings of psychological tests, which show that perpetrators of suicide terrorism are characterized by a tendency toward acquiescence and that they are somewhat submissive. The latter characteristic can help the human bomb in his effort to disguise himself and blend in, which precedes and conditions the explosion.

Suicide terrorists are required to look and behave in a way that would not attract attention, so that the security forces won't detect and arrest them on the way to the target. From statements of handlers of human bombs it emerges that this demands not only the physical appearance of an Israeli but also the ability to conceal what distinguishes one, to suppress one's presence so that it won't stand out as different from others. Suicide terrorism requires a personality type that knows how to give up what is its own; self-denial is required of the human bomb so he can pass through barriers and give up his life.

Suicide terrorism is built on anonymity. While penetrating Israeli space and especially while approaching the target, the human bomb must be faceless.[14] He must appear to be part of the multitude, invisible within it, until the explosion. Then, for a fraction of a second, his true, individual identity emerges and imposes itself. The explosion redeems him from anonymity. Immediately afterward, in the pile of burned, disfigured bodies, he loses his face once again. However, apparently from the start, before he was conscripted, before setting out on the mission, while still within the community from which he came, even there he was rather anonymous. Middle Eastern suicide terrorism is the story of a faceless Palestinian who disguises himself as a faceless Israeli.

The disguised human bomb is not only a hybrid creature—walking dead, Arab and Israeli, a conspiring enemy and an innocent fellow citizen—but also a fluid creature, formless and invisible. These characteristics add to the subversive potential of the human bomb. Thus he becomes a sort of ghost, elusive and evading capture, whose uncanny presence is both frightening and repugnant, abominable. The human bomb, like a demon, is seen as illusory and deceptive. As such, he is said to control mysteriously mighty forces, inaccessible to ordinary mortals.

Dressing Up

It is difficult to assume that the moments of imitation, disguise, and blending in, as short as they may be, could pass without making a strong impression on the human bomb. The part played by an actor in the theater is also supposed to influence his mind, even if it is not connected with life and death. Disguise, like performance in general, leaves its mark on the body and the soul. Most likely this also applies to the disguise of the human bomb.

It is hard not to be astonished by the costumes of anti-Zionist, ultra-Orthodox Jewish children in their ghetto community in Jerusalem at the annual masquerade carnival of Purim. Many of them dress as policemen, paratroopers, pilots, firemen, and other icons of Zionist masculinity— naturally secular—which is so alien and contrary to them and, in fact, expresses everything their ideology condemns. First, they are led to this by their fantasies, underlying which there is always deficit, denial, inferiority, envy, hidden or forbidden desires. One day a year they are given permission to accomplish that which both threatens and tempts them, that which is prohibited according to the values that obligate them throughout the year. They take pleasure in fulfilling a dream, and ever so much more pleasure in the freedom to be someone entirely different, who has what they don't have and deprives them of it. Second, the masquerade has a dynamic of its own, bound up with total identification with the new image. A transformation takes place on its own in the nature of the person in disguise. When a Haredi boy dresses up like an Israeli combat officer, imperceptibly his gait begins to sway from side to side, changes his body language and his speech, emitting signs of arrogance and belligerence. Thus, the masquerader frees himself from a problematic identity with which he is in conflict and in fact denies himself for a while. With the adoption of the alternative identity, he gains temporary empowerment. Even if the Israeli symbolizes the anathema of the Palestinian and the embodiment of evil, to imitate him and to disguise oneself as him is more natural than to dress up as Martian.

Our children dress up as Spiderman, and when they put on his cape, they are convinced they can fly and are omnipotent. In tribal societies men used to wear a tiger skin and thus draw on the power of the beast of prey to protect themselves against it and overcome it. Following a similar logic, they also disguised themselves as members of the rival, militant tribe that was attacking them. Israeli commandos who penetrate the casbah in the cities of the West Bank disguised as Arabs report that they are endowed with the sharp senses that, in the region, are regarded as characteristic of rural Palestinians. Perhaps the Palestinian human bomb disguised as an Israeli believes that he is equipped with the capacities of Jews, and by means of the Israeli costume and identification with the Israeli he is protected against him and capable of defeating him.[15]

During the intifada, in Palestinian towns, there was a popular roleplaying game: a wrestling match between children who called themselves freedom fighters and others who played the part of thuggish occupation

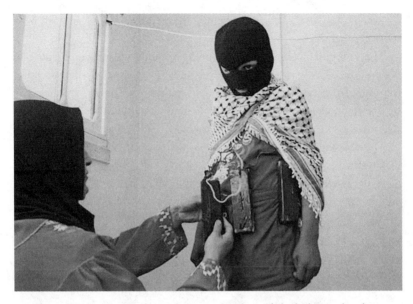

Figure 4. A Palestinian mother and son. During the intifada the human bomb was a popular children's costume in the West Bank and Gaza. (Photo: Unknown)

soldiers. Unexpectedly, among the Palestinian children there was no clear preference for the role of the self-sacrificing patriot. The ones playing Israelis were regarded as villains, but in the end they were the winners.[16]

It is reasonable to assume that something of the two characteristics of carnivalesque masquerading that were described above is also expressed in the Palestinian human bomb who disguises himself as an Israeli. The criticism and hatred that he feels toward Israelis does not diminish the desire to resemble them. On the contrary, perhaps we have here a subtle expression of the well-known phenomenon of identification with the aggressor.[17] Perhaps in suicide terrorism, as in the carnival, the disguise provides an opportunity to get rid of a contemptible identity and adopt a splendid one, and at the same time to defy the owner of that other, desired identity and mock it.[18]

The slave who disguises himself as a king expresses his inferiority to him and his yearning to resemble him, but he also criticizes him and makes fun of him. An IDF soldier or an Orthodox Jewish settler—disguises common among Palestinian human bombs—are objects of both hatred and admiration or envy. Palestinians feel tense ambivalence toward these types of Israelis, and a sure way of dispelling that tension, at least in part, is by mocking them.[19]

The Palestinian human bomb's preferred identity for the purpose of passing on his way to the target in Israel is always one of the two polar opposite, stereotypical images of Israelis: either a religious Orthodox Jew or a secular, casually dressed student—and sometimes the image of the IDF fighter, in the sense of going all the way.

The costumes used by human bombs also sting the Israelis, being a flirtation with Israeliness with an implicit mockery of Israeliness. The handlers of women human bombs made sure that they dressed like Israeli women, that is, according to their conception, not just as modern Western

Figure 5. A mural depicting the Sbarro pizzeria suicide attack (Jerusalem, August 2001, seventeen dead, including seven children) was presented in a special exhibition at An-Najah University in the West Bank on the occasion of the first anniversary of the intifada. Inside the walk-through diorama two Palestinian students step over a representation of corpses in plastic bags sunk in pools of blood and look at the image of screaming Israelis in skullcaps being blown apart by the blast, complete with dismembered limbs hanging from the ceiling along with slices of pizza flying in the air. A sign for kosher pizza was prominently displayed outside the Palestinian student artistic re-creation of the Hamas operation, and in a reference to the Izz ad-din al-Qassam Brigades—the military arm of the organization—the painter wrote: "Qassami Pizza is more delicious." (Photo: Reuters)

women, but also pretty and sexy, and somewhat "cheap," making them simultaneously attractive and repulsive. In disguising themselves as Israelis they both idealized them and expressed their disgust. The human bomb who imitates an Israeli and disguises himself as one—so that when he is standing among a crowd of Israelis he looks and behaves like them—not only shows tactical sophistication but also sarcasm. Al-Masri, the Palestinian human bomb who murdered nineteen Israelis in the Sbarro pizzeria in Jerusalem, passed through the restaurant, stepped up to the counter, looked at the menu, asked one of the workers how long it would take until he was served a portion of spaghetti, received an answer, and then activated the explosive device (August 2001).

The human bomb probably savors being with his enemy before killing him. This is in addition to the pleasure of the human bomb who appears to be a soldier and thus passes through the checkpoints where he had always been stopped and humiliated.

The Palestinian human bomb who disguises himself and blends in with Israelis is released from the experience that has marked his life: the poverty and remoteness of a small village, patriarchal tyranny, suppression of freedom of speech and freedom of relations between the sexes, corruption of the authorities, and other characteristics of the Palestinian regime. Mainly, of course, he is freed of the restrictions imposed on him by Israeli military occupation and the harm it does both to his body and to his morale. Instead he experiences the illusion of privileges offered by Israeliness: free movement, abundance, advanced technology, relative tolerance. What does a young Palestinian from a dusty, crowded refugee camp experience when he is disguised as an IDF soldier, like those who confront him with threatening rifles in their hands, blocking his way, degrading him and his peers, and who may have killed his friend? And what does a young Palestinian woman feel like after shedding her pious costume and putting on tight jeans, letting her hair down to her shoulders, free of her family, of herself, free to be different? To be Israeli is to be exhilarated and liberated. To be the enemy, the oppressor, is an intoxicating and redeeming experience. In the Palestinian human bombs' penultimate stage in Israel there is doubtless horrible dread, and maybe also a trip—the momentary illusion of an Israeli paradise, ending with the illusion of a Muslim paradise.

It has already been stated that blowing oneself up amid the target crowd requires dehumanization of the enemy. The stage of disguise and blending in that precede the explosion does, however, contain a kernel of humanizing the enemy. In moving toward his target, the Palestinian human bomb shows obsessive interest in the Israeli enemy: desire to kill him but also to mingle with him.

Secrets and Lies

A significant part of the project of suicide terrorism is bound up with a social practice known in the United States as "passing," meaning concealing one's original racial or ethnic identity and presenting an alternative identity, that of the majority culture—at least on the visible level, such as by means of adopted mannerisms—in order to advance a personal interest. In passing, one presents oneself as what one is not.[20] Passing is a transgression not only of formal or legal boundaries but necessarily of cultural boundaries too. It is a rather familiar technique for moving between various statuses, mainly climbing from a lower class to a higher one, but also the opposite. The human bomb depends on passing too.

The project of suicide terrorism is bound up with double passing. Before the Palestinian human bomb hides his original identity from the Israelis and disguises himself as one of them, he hides his operational goal from his Palestinian brethren, mainly from his family, disguising himself as one continuing the routine of a normal life. Once he crosses the border between the two societies, the human bomb transitions from one kind of passing to another.

The human bomb's passing is not just a fiction of identity. It usually has a greater dimension of authenticity, which is hidden or denied. The human bomb's passing has depth. As in many instances of passing that are not cynical, it is nourished by a genuine expression of self-identity and ambivalence containing sincere attraction to both rival identities, which in extreme cases are mutually exclusive. Like other manifestations of passing, suicide terrorism entails not only self-denial and imitation but also something of deceit, fooling those around him. The human bomb has a secret, and keeping it is the key to success in delivering a blow against the enemy.

The secret in the heart of the human bomb has an inner logic typical of any secret. On the one hand, keeping the secret offers gratification independent of its content and purpose. That which others are forbidden to know has extra value. Secrecy enriches human experience by creating a parallel experience, another world to live in. A secret gives a sense of uniqueness and superiority to the person who keeps it. On the other hand, the longer a secret is kept, the greater is the pressure to reveal it. Revealing the secret promises particularly great pleasure. Thus the secret contains an inner tension between the advantage of keeping it and the satisfaction of revealing it, between the urge to hide and urge to divulge. Revelation of the secret destroys its value but it has value of its own. The value of revelation derives to a great degree from relief of the increasing effort invested in keeping it. Therefore, revealing a secret has a tempting charm that may run counter to achieving the goal for which the secret was originally kept. However, sometimes the prospect of revealing a secret can be the goal of keeping it. This inherent dialectic of the secret characterizes the final stages of suicide terrorism.

The human bomb shares characteristics of the spy (or confidence man)—a secret agent whose mission necessitates concealing the truth about his alarming identity and the adoption of a counterfeit but comforting identity. Ostensibly, the human bomb is like an ordinary terrorist, like the one who secretly plants a time bomb and removes himself inconspicuously. Yet in contrast, he reveals his secret in the end. Indeed, the revelation of his original identity, and of course his true intention, is the climax of his operation, bringing to an end his entire effort of disguise and infiltration. Only revelation of the truth constitutes the fulfillment of the potential stored up in its concealment. Revelation of the human bomb's secret is the climax and the central feature of the entire project of suicide terrorism. Revelation of the human bomb's identity is synonymous with the explosion in the midst of the targeted crowd.

The moment of the explosion—perhaps it is more accurate to say a second before it, when the human bomb stands up, puts his hand in his pocket, and shouts, "Allahu Akbar"—is the moment of truth, in every sense of the term. This is the moment between life and death, the fateful, critical moment of the mission, and it is the moment of disclosure, and also of confession. Revelation of the secret makes the explosion a cathartic moment. Unlike the human bomb, the spy who keeps his secret forever remains frustrated. The intrinsic pleasure of secrecy and strangeness are insufficient. His ultimate satisfaction is forever deferred. He cannot even celebrate a victory. By contrast, the human bomb enjoys both the secret and its revelation, in which his redemption is inherent.

Pressing the button that activates the explosive is like coming out of the closet, an act of defiance and pride. The human bomb overcomes his distress as a conquered and humiliated Palestinian and the misery of someone who flees from his truth or is forced to hide it. Only with the explosion do the people around him learn the truth, which was hitherto hidden. Revealing a hidden truth about oneself is gratifying, and the truth that is revealed receives added value and doubled potential.

One might point to an analogy between the human bomb's stage of imitation, disguise, and infiltration and the celebrated Harun al-Rashid syndrome.[21] In the collection of Arab folktales known as *One Thousand and One Nights*, stories are told about the wise and generous Harun al-Rashid, the caliph of Baghdad, who used to disguise himself as an ordinary person and wander about the markets incognito. Under the cover of anonymity he would approach people, observe their actions, and encourage them to speak out. When he had enough information, he would suddenly emerge from his anonymity and proudly display his identity as the omnipotent and judicious ruler, correcting injustice and restoring order to the world. He rewarded those who behaved lawfully and mercifully, and he punished those who acted illicitly and cruelly.[22] Some of the lessons of this story can be seen as further commentary on suicide terrorism. First, the story of Harun al-Rashid reminds us that the center of gravity in the stage of disguise is at its end, its dissolution, when the truth is revealed about the nature of the masquerader and his objective. A complex and prolonged process is tested by a short, sharp act. We have also learned that an important aspect of being in disguise is the knowledge that constantly accompanies it that soon the imposter—the human bomb—will present his origin and his calling in the world to the people around him. He can then relax, for the inconsistency between his inner self and his outward appearance has been resolved. Then he will be honored by moving from the margins to the center of the arena, to the heart of the great drama. It is especially important to note that the medieval caliph and the human bomb both aspire to restore justice and order, which have been violated, to the world. This is the purpose of the disguise and the entire process tends toward that purpose. The moment of revelation is a moment of reversal and of reforming the world. The human bomb provides victory and fame for the Palestinians, and he brings pain and sorrow to the Israelis.

Concealment of identity and its revelation at the critical moment is a classic mythological motive, and it lives again in the popular literature of our day thanks to superheroes.[23] Everyone knows that Superman walks among ordinary people, looking like them, gray, without distinction or charisma. At a specific point in the plot, when things get complicated, he does exactly what the human bomb does: he puts his hand on his chest and reveals what had been hidden beneath his standard clothing. Superman shows the red "S" on his chest, and the human bomb shows the switch, the fuse, and the explosive at the end of it. This moment of revelation is their moment of truth. Both of them are then filled with an extraordinary potential, with courage and a sense of mission, and they perform an act that will change people's fate. The human bomb and Superman cross borders, and nothing can stop them. They are entirely free, intoxicated with the feeling of power and justice. It may also be said that they are both variations on the theme of vigilantism: because the system does not work as expected in preserving law and order and restoring justice, they act outside of the normative patterns and, if necessary, with violence, in order to establish a more congenial system of intergroup relations. Revelation of the truth gives Superman greater vitality, whereas to the human bomb it brings death.

Middle Eastern Twist

Abomination and Purification

Confrontation with the human bomb takes place in two stages. The first, preceding the explosion, is the effort to prevent the attack. This begins when the bombing is first planned, continues as the terrorist is chosen and trained, and concludes when the terrorist crosses the Green Line and arrives at his target site. It ends if he manages to yank the fuse. The security forces are responsible for confronting the suicide terrorist during this stage. In the second stage, beginning with the explosion and ending after the evacuation of the site, the identification of the bodies, and their preparation for burial, the responsibility lies with the Haredi volunteers (along with the National Institute for Forensic Medicine). The work of the ISA before the attack and that of ZAKA thereafter are parallel and continuous. In the preattack stage, the ISA agents seek to locate the human bomb in order to thwart the attack. In the postattack stage, ZAKA volunteers seek to locate the human bomb in order to minimize the symbolic impact of the attack. In both stages the goal is to reveal the attacker's identity, to counteract mixing and assimilation.

Before his death the human bomb's opposite is the ISA agent; afterward it is the ZAKA volunteer. Both reestablish boundaries. By mixing blood, the attacker erases or denies identities. ZAKA works to restore the identities of the dead. Giving the victims back their identities as Jews and as individuals makes it possible to honor and bury them in accordance with Jewish tradition. Restoring an identity to the Palestinian attacker makes it possible to separate him from the rest of the dead. By establishing his identity, ZAKA ends the state of ambiguity and assimilation that is the subversive foundation of suicide terrorism.

Uncovering a hidden identity, or distilling a single identity from a mixed one—deconstructing hybrids—is an act of purification.[1] ZAKA is an extension of the purification system implemented by the State of Israel in a number of areas. Along with security forces, governmental agencies, and informal, cultural mechanisms, ZAKA stands in the forefront of the Israeli battle to preserve boundaries. Reestablishment of boundaries—purification—is the response to the subversive impact of suicide terrorism.

The Israeli effort to retain and settle the disputed territories beyond the Green Line is based on the principle of identification and purification. ZAKA's practice of sorting and separating belongs to the sorting and separating practices used by the governmental authorities, primarily the military, who administer the Arab-populated areas under Israeli control. Just as these agencies seek to keep Israelis and Palestinians apart through space management (e.g., separate roads and separate lines at roadblocks), time management (e.g,. a different schedule for prayer services for Jews and Muslims at the Tomb of the Patriarchs), and population management (e.g., separate legal and transportation systems), so ZAKA does it through managing death at the site of suicide attacks.

The Haredi volunteers themselves use the term "purification" to describe their acts of location, classification, and separation of flesh and blood at a site of terrorism. ZAKA's mission at Israel's religious and national front line, its assignment to a project of Jewish purification, is based on identification. Indeed, the name "ZAKA" is an acronym for the Hebrew words *Zihui Korbanot Ason*, meaning "identification of disaster victims."

ZAKA's mission can be defined essentially as the detection and elimination of impurity and ensuring the purity of Israel. According to Mary Douglas's classical model of *Purity and Danger*, the defiled are things and beings that are not in their proper places and lie outside accepted categories.[2] This pollution is regarded by Jewish tradition as abomination (*shikutz*). The impure upsets the classification basic to the social order. It threatens the boundaries and identity of the collective. The defenses against this danger are taboos that forbid mixtures and indeterminate states. Correspondingly, the Palestinian human bomb undermines Israeli order by obliterating binary divisions and blurring the principles of classification at the site. The Jewish response is to return everything to its proper place and to reestablish the lines of separation.

In time, when ZAKA improved its methods, the volunteers would be supplied with two types of plastic bags. White bags with blue writing were used for Jewish victims, and simple black bags were used for the body of the human bomb. The rabbis of the organization ruled that placing the abominable body of the suicide terrorist in a white bag was a sacrilege. In a terror attack in Jerusalem, in which a Jew was killed by police fire, he was mistakenly identified as a terrorist and his body was placed in a black bag. As soon as the error was discovered, the Jew was wrapped again in a pure and purifying bag.

Since Palestinian suicide terrorism has emerged in a situation of an asymmetrical conflict between East and West, traditional and modern, subject and occupier, the application of the postcolonial model is also appropriate. The latter directs attention to the dynamism and generativity of the frontier and to the phenomenon of hybridism. In the following pages I therefore employ some insights offered by postcolonial thinkers (specifically, Fannon, Memmi, Said, and Bhabha) to describe and analyze ZAKA's project and the Palestinian suicide terrorism's project as well. In light of their theorizing, it is possible to see not only the Israeli establishment, but also the Palestinians and their Jewish victims as active subjects. Further, the relations between Israeli citizens and Arabs of the West Bank can be seen no longer as linear and binary, but rather as reciprocal and notable for their ambivalence. Each side not only rejects and resists but also is fascinated and attracted by the other. The Palestinian criticizes and hates Israelis, but he also yearns to be attached to them. From this perspective, we may also see the attempt to resemble and belong to the other, just like armed resistance to the other, as active participation in the conflict.

Suicide terrorism differs fundamentally from other types of terrorism in that it is built on the premise of fusion, of hybridity. Its subversive power to shatter categories, in addition to its murderousness, makes it doubly effective. The suicide terrorist is mixed in at least four ways. His identity is hyphenated, first, in that he is both aggressor and victim. Second, he is alive-dead. Third, he is human and bomb, operator and weapon, subject and object. And fourth, as discussed later, he is an Arab-Jew. Because of this fourfold hybridity, suicide terrorism dissolves a number of binary categories. By disguising himself as an Israeli before his death, and by the fusing of his body with Israeli bodies after his death, the suicide terrorist transforms himself from an other who confirms and reifies a separate Israeli identity into a hybrid who challenges the very foundation of the Israeli claim to be a distinct, self-evident collective.

The absolute otherness of the Palestinian human bomb is not what threatens Israelis but rather the blurring of this otherness as a result of the human bomb's effort to appear very much like his victims and blend in with them. The mingling of the occupied with the occupiers and the former's imitation of the latter erode the binary opposition between them.[3]

Some Israelis see the very existence of the 1.8 million Palestinian citizens of the state of Israel (21%) as a similar threat of hostile Arab otherness that intrudes upon, mimics, and appropriates Israeliness, and they feel similarly threatened by the possibility of intermarriage between Jews and Arabs.[4] In the occupied territories, Jews address these challenges with acts of purification that adopt one of two alternative, parallel strategies. The first is purification by means of physical or political elimination (military action, economic sanctions, the shutting down of universities, disbanding civil associations, etc.). The second is purification by relegating the threat to the other side of a border (the disengagement strategy of Israeli withdrawal from the Gaza Strip, the siege and closure of cities and villages, population transfer, as well as the two-state solution—an envisaged peace treaty between Jewish and Palestinian independent entities—are all ways, actual and potential, of effecting this). The human bomb frustrates these efforts at purification with the challenge of an otherness that turns into hybridism, and the effort to meet this challenge takes the form of purification by means of a primarily ritual act.

The Challenge of Enforcing Boundaries

There are indications of a certain desire on the part of Palestinians on both sides of the Green Line to resemble Israeli Jews, get close to them, and assimilate among them. This is not by any means to say that the Palestinians are abandoning their criticism and animosity toward their neighbors The outcome of this desire on the part of the Palestinians is an inner conflict of rejection-attraction regarding Israel. The common and largely convincing explanation of Israel's appeal relates to its higher quality of life compared to Middle Eastern standards. Naturally the Palestinians wish to enjoy preferred status, which confers many privileges, from advanced health and educational services to freedom of speech and rewarding employment. The efforts of residents of the Palestinian village of Isawiya, in East Jerusalem, to move westward and buy an apartment in the Jewish neighborhood of French Hill, is just one of many illustrations. At the same time, it has been argued that the Palestinians' drive for Israelization is not solely a desire to upgrade their standard of living. Rather, the dilemma is deeper. The attraction of Israeliness also has an antagonistic aspect. Clarification of the multilayered Palestinian ambivalence regarding Israel, including attraction to Israeliness with the aim of combating it, will contribute to our discussion of suicide terrorism.

At least among the Palestinian elites, there is awareness of the complexity of their attitudes toward tendencies to adopt Israeli values and behavioral norms. In a certain Palestinian discourse there is a subtext of doubt regarding the benefit and legitimacy of the desire to resemble Israelis and assimilate. See, for example, the debate among Palestinians about resistance to Israeli dominance by means of various strategies of encouraging or limiting the birth rate.[5]

In parallel, sensitivity has developed among Israelis toward what is interpreted as the danger inherent in the inclination among various Palestinians to imitate and assimilate. The campaign to eliminate this danger begins with obsessive efforts at detecting the other. The Israeli establishment and informal bodies have cooperated in developing a regime of suspicion focused on Palestinian efforts to cross the borders by blurring the differences between the populations. It is expressed just as much in enhanced gathering of intelligence in the Palestinian territories and tightening of military supervision of the border between them and the State of Israel as it is in the behavior of civilians in the public realm within Israel—the street, the market, restaurants, and buses. Ordinary citizens have become identification agents, utilizing a set of indicative signs. Over the decades of the Middle East conflict, and especially since 1967, the Israeli Jewish population has become expert in locating the Arabs among them.

During the intifada, in response to waves of suicide terrorism committed by Palestinians disguised as innocent passersby, the ethic of alienation, indifference, and avoiding, which is regarded as typical of interpersonal relations in a modern city,[6] was replaced by an ethic of concentrated, nervous, and intrusive attentiveness. Strangers began to examine one another closely. There was no longer a superficial and rapid relation to the appearance of others, ignoring their identity, which remained unknown, but a categorical classification, which did not allow others to be experienced apathetically as unknown but imposed an identity on them that left no room for doubt. The need arose to determine the degree to which people's appearance and observable communicative gestures were appropriate to their inner self, which is to say, their intentions. Dress and verbal and facial expressions were considered merely symptoms of a hidden, true essence. Thus one actively penetrated the space of strangers' identities, dealing with their otherness. This was done by means of basic discursive categories imposed on strangers and making it possible to take them in.[7]

Israel makes great efforts to separate and distinguish itself from the Palestinians, especially in response to the offensive of the human bombs. To defend against them a concrete wall was built, electronic fences, and moats. The number of suicide terrorism attacks has decreased, but thousands of Palestinians without work permits cut the fence, climb over the wall, or walk around it to earn a crust of bread for their children.[8] They manage to do so because, among other reasons, many Jews break the law and take a risk in order to get cheap labor. Proximity and interdependence make gaps in the border and blur it. Not only human enterprise overcomes the efforts to enforce a boundary, but also natural forces. The bacteria that go from one side to the other, borne by wind and water, bringing diseases to animals and humans, demonstrate that defensive walls are useless. The geomorphology of the region makes the sewage of the West Bank flow into Israel without stopping at the Green Line.[9] Lack of goodwill on both sides exacerbates the problem. Neither brainstorming on the Israeli side nor partial efforts at Israeli-Palestinian cooperation manage to provide solutions to the problem of the penetrable or effaced border. Efforts at separation and differentiation seem hopeless, and this is precisely the message of suicide terrorism, as if the human bombs were saying: we shall die together with you, Israelis, in embrace.[10]

Jewrabs and Arajews

No, these are not misprints, they are neologisms. I propose "Jewrabs" as a translation for the modern Hebrew coinage *Mista'arvim*, which literally means "people who turn themselves into Arabs."[11] *Mista'arvim* is habitually used in Israeli vernacular, denoting Jews who disguise themselves as Arabs for various purposes, mostly instrumental. They may also be charmed by the Arab mystique in the manner of Lawrence of Arabia. Fortuitously, the same Hebrew root also bears the meaning "to mix or mingle" and may imply "infiltration" and "assault."[12]

Now "Arajews" is proposed here as a translation for my invented Hebrew title *Mista'avrim*, a word I made up by switching two letters of the word *mista'arvim*. It is coined to mean those who turn themselves into (Hebrew speaking) Israeli Jews.[13]

The two words—*Mista'arvim* and *Mista'avrim*, that is, Jewrabs and Arajews[14]—are phonetically and etymologically similar and quite naturally carry the almost identical connotation of a systematic transformation of appearance and a conscious adoption of the identity of the politically or culturally other in the context of the Middle East. However, *Mista'arvim* and *Mista'avrim* point in diametrically opposed directions. Each is oriented toward its regional nemesis. They are very much alike, and yet they turn each other inside out and consequently may be analyzed as deconstructing each other.

The Hebrew word *Mista'arvim*[15] originated in the early days of Zionist immigration to pre-World War I Ottoman Palestine, when it referred to (orientalist) Westerners, particularly Jews, who lived among local Arabs, spoke their language, and dressed and behaved like them.[16] The word was later adopted by the Palmach, the elite military force of the pre-state Jewish community in Mandatory Palestine. There the *Mista'arvim* were small detachments of Arabic-speaking soldiers, usually made up of Jews born in neighboring Muslim countries who had "Levantine" features. These men disguised themselves as Arabs to carry out covert missions in Arab population centers. Today, the word is used to denote IDF Special Forces units that operate in the Palestinian territories and Middle Eastern countries disguised as Arabs.

I propose the neologism *Mista'avrim* to refer to Palestinian Arabs who conceal their ethnonational identity by taking advantage of ostensibly Jewish physical features, such as light skin, to which they add further Jewish markers, such as a *kippah*, to pass as Israelis. They use this disguise to enter Israel and mingle with Israelis. The term *Mista'avrim* also preserves the other sense of the word, "to mix or mingle," inasmuch as one common interpretation of the term *'ivri* is a gloss on its root, which signifies crossing (a border).[17] "Arajew" conveys something of the nature of the word *Mista'avrim*, though it misses a lot.

The Jewrab/Arajew phenomena are not restricted to intelligence and combat missions. For example, novelists and poets belonging to one group who write as if they were members of the opposite group also publicize a fabricated or hyphenated identity, one that is often perceived by members of both groups as intriguing, though also infuriating or even threatening.[18] This is a subcategory of the phenomenon known as social and cultural hybridity, which, in turn is connected both to the issue of "passing" and to the phenomena expressed in the Latin preposition and prefix "trans" (from which the word "trance" is also derived). Both indicate crossing and going beyond. Some label it ethnic or tribal transvestism. On some occasions this impersonation or doubling has subversive intent, while on others it is simply a means of personal advancement. It is common in the context of crossovers between sexes, classes, races, and national groups, to name a few. Such is the case of light-skinned blacks who present themselves as whites and those who switch between the genders, such as transgendered individuals. All these undermine fundamental dichotomous distinctions, as do the Arab and Israeli hybrids discussed here.

The Middle East is haunted by the idea of the Jewrab/Arajew. These optional identities have seized the imaginations of many of the region's unsettled inhabitants, playing on local wild fantasies and anxious suspicions.[19] In a certain sense—rather unwitting—all Israelis and Palestinians are, at least potentially, Jewrabs (*Mista'arvim*) and Arajews (*Mista'avrim*).

We all possess something of the other, and in every other there is at least a little of ourselves. In today's world, there is hardly any absolute otherness, and this applies also to the crowded space inhabited by Israeli and Palestinian neighbors and rivals. Take the two dominant vernaculars in the region. For the past century, the local Hebrew speech has adopted a multitude of Arabic expressions (along with "oriental" foods), and Palestinian Arabic can no longer function without Hebrew idioms (and syntax).[20]

Despite mutual antagonism, the boundaries between Israelis and Palestinians are porous. Israeliness—both detested and craved—reaches into every corner of the occupied territories and permeates the Palestinian soul, while Palestinianness—laden with the anguish of the occupation on the one hand and the horrors of terrorism on the other—imbues Jewish Israel.

At the vanguard of the border crossers strides the human bomb, an extreme manifestation of the Arajew. Suicide terrorism is the endpoint of a complex act of assimilation, the final stages of which are impersonation and incorporation into the crowd of passengers on a bus or diners in restaurant, ending, with the explosion, in total integration into the surrounding Jews. The other from the east of the separation wall may seek to enter the public and private lives of those to the west of the separation wall in various ways. If a Palestinian young man fails to penetrate Israeli life and participate in it by nonviolent means, such as marrying a person holding Israeli citizenship or joining the Israeli workforce, he is left with the option of dying with Israelis.

Ibrahim or Abi

A stimulating book depicts the *Mista'arvim* as one of the hybrid types that Zionism created in order to deal with the problem of boundaries between it and the local Arab population.[21] It proposes a distinction between two types, or stages, of *Mista'arvim*. Prior to the establishment of the State of Israel, these Jewrabs did not conceal their Jewish origins, and even highlighted their hybrid nature. They were careful to preserve a small but noticeable separation between their original and adopted identities. This gained them authoritative status among both peoples, and indeed they worked toward bridging the gap and moderating the conflict between the two camps, pointing the way to possible coexistence. They were perceived as emissaries of the Zionist public who, by assuming an Arab habitus, became a source of inspiration for their society. In contrast, from Israel's independence to the present, *Mista'arvim* have exploited their dark complexion and native familiarity with Arabic to be taken as Arabs, infiltrating Arab society for espionage and sabotage. Their success depends on concealing their original affiliation and hybrid nature. The two components of their identities remain intact, and no interchange takes place between them. They are totally Arab on the outside and totally Jewish on the inside. To put it another way, they are Arabs and only Arabs at the front lines, and Jews and only Jews in the rear. Unlike their predecessors, their activity sharpened distinctions and exacerbated the conflict between Jews and Arabs.

Conversely, the human bomb embodies the phenomenon of *Mista'avrim* (the Arajews). As such, he shares the traits of the *Mista'arvim*, in mirror image. The human bomb is also a hybrid who is both there and here and neither there nor here, but rather on the boundary. Ostensibly, the human bomb is more like the post-1948 kind of Jewrab, the one whose intentions are hostile, whose inner being remains distinct from and opposed to his outer appearance, a truth he hides from those around him. But like the pre-1948 Jewrab he has a profound interest in the other side and is preoccupied with fantasies about it. The imitation and assimilation involved in the Palestinian human bomb's project cannot be dismissed as simply a tactical device. Behind the operational need for the disguise lies a need for self-actualization and an expression of revolutionary identity. In the assumption of Israeliness lies an aspiration for a realization of the essence of Palestinianhood.

Both Jewrabs, the Israeli Jews who take on Arab identity, and Arajews, the Palestinians who take on Jewish identity, are boundary workers who cross the lines between sides and thus blur the distinctions between them. At the same time, by doing so they mark the lines and highlight the distinctions. The hybrids both undermine and reinforce the dichotomy. One way they do the latter is through impelling the other side to react by performing distinguishing acts—that is, acts of purification. The Israeli response to the threat of border crossing and hybridity began with the refusal to allow Palestinian refugees to return after the 1948 war and continued through imposition of a military regime on the Arab citizens of Israel, which was dismantled in Israel (1966) and imposed on the Palestinian Arabs after conquest of the West Bank and Gaza Strip. The effort to separate Jews from Arabs also includes the physical separation barrier between Israel and Palestine, the ideal of "Hebrew labor" (the demand that Jews must hire only Jews and not Arabs), the bringing of the Jews of the Arab lands to Israel, and municipal division of mixed cities, like that between Arab Nazareth and Jewish Nazareth Illit. The response to Palestinian suicide terrorism is similar—both in ISA's and ZAKA's work of identification. Suicide terrorism, comparable to the Jewrab syndrome, looks like a protest against the orientalism that has created binary distinctions such as East versus West and Arab versus Jew, but both the terrorists and the Jewrabs have adopted and deepened these distinctions. Assimilation via self-immolation among Israelis is also an act full of inner tension that unites two contrary attitudes toward the boundaries between Jews and Arabs.

Naturally, there are similarities between Israeli Jewrabs and Palestinian Arajews. For example, the Arajew (*Mista'avrim*) assumes the false identity of an Israeli of a certain type, but that Israeli type is itself a hybrid in many respects. For obvious reasons—the color of his skin and his accent—the human bomb tends to disguise himself as a Mizra'hi Jew, occasionally considered to be Arab Jews. In other words, his manifestation as a human bomb contains two strata of ethnic hybridity implanted within him and supporting one another. This parallels the hybridity "squared" of the Israeli Jewrab, who is also usually of Mizra'hi origin, so that beneath his adopted Jewish/Arab identity lies an authentic Jewish-Arab identity. Several of the physical and cultural similarities between Palestinians and the Mizra'hi Jews call attention to the arbitrariness of drawing a boundary between them.[22]

However, we cannot ignore the differences between Jewrabs and Arajews. Among other things, the Jewrabs, especially the later version, "dress down." They adopt a religious and national identity that, in their view, is inferior to their own in terms of power and prestige. But the human bomb belongs to a conquered people and thus, as an Arajew, climbs up and adheres to the identity of the conqueror. Unlike most Jewrabs (*Mista'arvim*), the Arajew (*Mista'avrim*) aspires to an Israeliness that is not merely external and momentary. The success of the impersonation and assimilation on which suicide terrorism is based is an assurance of liberation and empowerment, of fulfilling a dream, and not only the dream of destroying the enemy.

The Arajew appears in a number of avatars, most of them unconnected to terrorism. Some members of the Palestinian elite are obsessed with Israeliness, swinging from hatred to admiration and envy of their oppressive neighbors.[23] Arajews of this benign sort can be found among middle-class Palestinians as well. The Palestinian suicide terrorist has a sort of twin brother, a parallel and complementary figure, one who is also a master of passing, a quasi-"terrorist" in disguise, another underground agent who specializes in mimicry and short-term assimilation that undermines Israeli confidence. He is a good-looking, intelligent, resourceful—and typically manipulative—young man who works hard and takes risks to stick to the Israeli side of the border. After a few years his Hebrew skills are polished, nuanced with updated "cool" idioms and with no trace of an Arabic accent. By day he washes dishes in the back of a Tel Aviv restaurant. At night he changes into fashionable clothing and frequents popular bars. His aim is to date nice Jewish girls.[24]

The young man's name is Ibrahim, or Isma'il. At night, however, he introduces himself as Abi or Sami, standard equivalent Hebrew nicknames. The epitome—or climax—of his success is having sex with a local young woman. He labels it "doubly screwing the Jewess"—"doing it" to them in both senses of the word. Frantz Fanon tells us about the African man who sleeps with a blonde who belongs to the European colonists' outpost, and at the moment of orgasm he yells and cheers the abolition of slavery and conquest.[25]

Suicide terrorism, somewhat like interracial, or interclass, sex is an instance of subversive linkage, a peculiar physical bond, a truly corporeal (or should I say, fleshly) project. The Palestinian human bomb who assimilates among his target crowd in a bus or pizzeria maintains, in the few minutes before the explosion and immediately after, a sort of embodied closeness with his victims. In another chapter I call it "macabre intimacy."

A triumph cum physical union is particularly strong. Of all the hypothetically possible hybrid combinations in the Middle East—such as Jewish self-consciousness with an Arab accent or Arab self-consciousness with Jewish dress—the most radical is the hybridity of the Jewish body with the Arab body, when the bodies are fused with one another indistinguishably. "And they become one flesh"—the Bible speaks thus of the union between Adam and Eve, man and wife (Genesis 2:24). This can also be actualized in suicide terrorism.

The question is often raised as to what causes people to be willing to die for their fellows, as, for example, in the case of soldiers who storm the enemy's bastion shoulder to shoulder and die together. One enlightening answer is connected to the fact that a shared death creates equality and closeness between people who are distant from one another in background and class, race and education. Thus comradeship is taken to its ultimate height and harmony is achieved.[26] The fallen marines in the heroic, bloody battle of Iwo Jima built a utopia of comradeship peculiarly similar to the comradeship the human bombs build with their victims.

Whenever Palestinians disguise themselves as Jews, they challenge a critical binary classification and are viewed by the Jews as a threat. But the human bomb's hybridity goes further than the hybridity of a manual laborer from Gaza who is known in Tel Aviv only by his Hebrew alias. By dying along with Jewish victims, the human bomb succeeds where many Palestinians have failed. Few Palestinians have succeeded in fulfilling either of these contradictory elements of their dreams: killing Jews or becoming one flesh with them. In his special way, on his final trip, the human bomb both executes and amalgamates. Assimilation contains an extermination plot.

In May 2002 Fatah sent two human bombs to an attack in Rishon LeZion. The woman terrorist changed her mind and returned to the West Bank without carrying out her mission. After her arrest she said that before she separated from her partner in the mission, he told her that he "wanted to stay in Israel for two or three days, . . . to be around different kinds of people."[27] He blew himself up a few hours later, killing two and wounding forty.

This appears to express a certain component in the experience of the Palestinian human bomb, or perhaps one should say in the experience of those who operate suicide terrorism. The ones who are imbued with hatred of Israel and at the same time are fascinated by Israel and addicted to it are those who dispatch the human bombs, terrorists who are merely their agents, on behalf of their organization. In blowing himself up, the human bomb fulfills the fantasies of many Palestinians, for whom he is their proxy.

Second Person Singular

Recent scholarship views Palestinian suicide terrorism as an act of defiance against the Israeli who has assumed control not only over the lives of the inhabitants of the occupied territories but also over their deaths. The management of death is a political matter par excellence (thanatopolitics), and depriving a group of this power is a radical form of denying their independence.[28] The terrorist's suicide is thus an assertive display of autonomy in a place in which autonomy hardly exists. The suicide act reclaims control over Palestinian death. Suicide terrorism is thus seen by the Palestinians as a means of national liberation. However, the exterminating and assimilating human bomb points the Palestinians along a path toward liberation from themselves as well, toward being others.

People often fancy being someone else. Many people in the developing world imagine what it is like to be American. It is said that Israelis are preoccupied by imagining being Arabs. In a widely read novel by the famous Israeli author A. B. Yehoshua, a Jewish professor who visits a Palestinian village cannot resist an invitation to stay there overnight as he is charmed by the idea that sleeping in the bed of his Arab host will allow him to dream (sweet) Arab dreams.[29] Various phenomena reinforce the claim that a fundamental element of the Palestinian experience on both sides of the Green Line (including the occupied territories) is a kernel of desire, perhaps envy, in relation to Israel. We find this, for example, in literature. In the works of two prominent Palestinian authors who write fiction in Hebrew, and whose novels became best sellers, the main protagonists of the revelatory narrative—local Arabs—show a primal, uncontrollable urge to look and feel like Israelis, to be swallowed up among them until they are unrecognizable. Sayed Kashua's novel *Second Person Singular* tells a life story based on the author's biography.[30] Two figures are central to the plot. The first is a rather stereotypical young man from Jerusalem who represents the Zionist-Jewish elite. Just before being conscripted into the army he tries to commit suicide, fails, and remains a vegetable. As his situation deteriorates, a Muslim Arab from the village of Jaljulia enters his home as a caretaker. He has come to Jerusalem to study and supports himself with part-time work, taking care of the invalid, who can neither move nor communicate. They are similar in age and appearance. Gradually the Palestinian's presence in the company of the Israeli, a kind of intimate but asymmetrical coexistence, takes over the caretaker's identity, until he borrows the patient's identity. He uses his personal belongings, listens to the music he liked, adopts his hobby of photography, and even registers at the art academy in his name. In the end, when the Israeli dies, an exchange of their identity papers is arranged, and the Palestinian has his double buried under his name. The theft of the new identity is described by the metonymy of the exchange of clothing, a familiar motif in folk literature:

> I got into the pants easily, and they fit me, then stuffed the shirt into my pants and put on the jacket. . . . "This isn't me," I said. My movements felt stiff in that disguise. "It is you, and how," [said the mother of the Jew who has just died]. "You look very good in those clothes." It was nice to hear that I looked good. It planted hope in me, and for a moment I really felt like a totally different person, the way I'd always wanted to be.[31]

For Kashua, the national conflict is sharp and intense, and the solution proposed is to have the Arab reborn as a Jew. The Palestinian's rebirth is conditional on his close physical connection with the Israeli Jew. This Palestinian redemption is bound up with the final death of the Jew, but maybe also in the symbolic death of the Arab identity.

Mimicking the Israeli occupiers as a means of assimilation among them enables the conquered Palestinians to rid themselves of a partly unbearable identity. Suicide terrorism embraces a promise to get rid of (metaphoric) blackness.[32] When the dark and the oppressed feel that they have shed their skins, they feel great joy. Crossing the lines (without being uncovered) and attaching themselves (to patrons of a coffee shop or the passengers of a bus) is a heady experience of freedom (from otherness).

Curiously, this is an inverted echo of the Zionist delusion that the Jews could be emancipated from their own disconcerting (diasporic) nature by assimilation into the Middle East—as if being absorbed by the indigenous culture would miraculously correct inborn inadequacies. The dream of merging into a diametrically opposed collectivity, of vanishing in one's antagonist's embrace—a peculiarly orientalist or occidentalist fantasy[33]—is liable to be neutralized by inner tensions or end up in violence.

The more or less naive Israeli craving for assimilation in the local Arab scenery is obliquely manifested in provocative Jewish settlement located in an area heavily populated by hostile Arabs. The not necessarily romantic Palestinian craving for assimilation in the nearby Jewish scenery also has aggressive implications.

After a visit to a Jewish settlement in the Palestinian territories inhabited by radical advocates of a "Greater Israel," Amos Oz, a leading Israeli novelist who often speaks out publicly in favor of territorial compromise and accommodation with the Palestinians, reflected on

> the elusive cunning of the biblical charm of the [West Bank] landscape: Isn't all of this charm Arab, through and through? The shade of the fig tree and the pale silver of the olive. . . . The hypnotic shepherds and the tinkle of the goats' bells which entwined, like magic webs, the hearts of Zionist settlers who came from Europe thirsty to don Arab garb and to speed their horses toward Arab Biblicality. . . . Yearning for merger into the bosom of these gentle, sleepy settings so very far removed from the [exilic] ghetto and the [urbanite] alienated Western culture right into the heart of Oriental rock-strewn tenderness. But does not a curse prey within this ancient wish: are these not the environments of the life-and-death enemy? . . . The penetration will not be one of harmonious integration but of occupation and capitulation and destruction. Where shall we turn our longing? . . . Unto devastation? Unto death?[34]

Palestinian IDF Soldiers

The ambivalent relations between conquered and conqueror might diminish the disparities between one's selfhood and one's borrowed appearance. Suicide terrorism makes possible a switch in identity, at least potentially. The human bomb's outer appearance—his dress and speech—embodies the option of a true crossing of the border, gaining an entirely new inner self. Resources build up in any Arajew's body that can, under certain circumstances, express him in a new way, fit him out with a different image, and thus turn him from an impersonator to a person with an opposite sense of self. The Arajew thus not only disrupts the homogeneity of the Israeli occupier with his successful impersonation, but he also effects a change in the nature of the conquered Palestinian and blurs the boundary between them even more. The act of suicide terrorism implies the ultimate impersonation of the other, as well as a certain transformation of the self, canceling the differences between the sides.[35]

Jewish mytho-history is filled with obsessive attempts to preserve the boundaries of religion and nation. From the struggle against intermarriage in the biblical book of Nehemiah, through the Maccabees' fight against Hellenizing Jews in the second century BC and the struggle against the Christians and Samaritans in the first centuries of the Common Era, Jews have grappled with hybrids who have sought to usurp their identity. The expertise of ZAKA's Haredi volunteers in locating Ara-jews stands on the foundation of an ancient sacred legacy of uncovering proto-*Mista'avrim*, Gentiles who have masqueraded as Jews and adhered to the Jewish community for any number of purposes.[36] The Talmud (fourth to seventh century) tells of a Gentile who plotted to gain access to the Temple so that he could experience what it was like to offer a sacrifice. How could he be identified? The canonical solution is identical to that proposed by rabbis in our own day who seek a way to identify human bombs. In the Talmudic story, the counterfeit Jew is asked which cut of the sacrificial animal he wishes to offer to God. Innocently, he says the fat tail of the sheep, which seems to him the choicest part, most worthy of heaven. In doing so, he reveals his ignorance, for Jews know that the sheep's tail is not acceptable as a sacrifice.[37]

In the early 2000s, at the height of Palestinian suicide terrorism in Israel, a poster was tacked to the bulletin boards of police stations around the country. Its title was "Identifying Features of the Haredi (Jewish ultra-Orthodox) Male." Underneath was the figure of a man surrounded by legends such as "Brimmed hat or black *kippah* (skullcap)," with an arrow pointing to the appropriate spot on the figure's head. Some of the features were easily identifiable markers of Haredi dress and grooming such as "usually a white shirt, never a colorful shirt or T-shirt," but others were less familiar. When an expert guest speaker presented a PowerPoint briefing for patrol officers, he called the audience's attention in particular to those items that "only a Jew can tell—Gentiles wouldn't notice." For example, "no rings on the fingers." The lecturer zoomed in on small details that betrayed their wearer as a counterfeit Haredi, like blue jeans. Of course the real purpose of the poster was not to identify genuine *haredim* but to expose Palestinian human bombs disguised as *haredim*. That intention was obvious from the recommendation at the bottom of the poster. If a police officer suspected someone who looked like a Haredi man of being a suicide terrorist in disguise, he should ask him something about Jewish tradition, like, "What is the weekly Torah portion?" An officer familiar with Jewish religious mannerisms added, "If we spy a Haredi man who doesn't sway while praying or reading, he should be shot on the spot."

The ancient Gentile's effort to gain access to the Temple is parallel to the Palestinian human bomb's endeavor to penetrate the Jerusalem pedestrian mall, the heart of Israeliness. They both do it in the same way: by mimicry that enables total assimilation, which itself contains the kernel of subversion. Bonding with otherness, in life and in death, cancels out otherness and defeats it. Fanon wrote of the difficulty the native encounters in seeking to liberate himself by suppressing the urge to identify with his conquering master and resemble him.[38] It is difficult for the oppressed to free himself of his envy of the oppressor and his desire to touch him. Homi Bhabha emphasized the element of mimicry on both sides of the colonial system, adding the parallel desire of the oppressor himself, who imitates the oppressed and is attracted to him. This mutual mimicry strengthens the relations of colonizer to colonized. The former utilized mimicry of the latter to make the conquest more effective, but the mimicry and assimilation weaken the occupation and threaten the occupier. An element of resistance is inherent in the connection between the sides, including physical connection. A policy of opposition is located here by means of blurring differences and mingling instead of a confrontational struggle. The human bomb is both an expression of the confrontational struggle and also an effective substitute for that struggle.

The ZAKA volunteers feel that the choice of the Palestinian human bomb to disguise himself as a Haredi Jew is extremely threatening because it targets the standard bearers of the ultimate Judaism. In contrast, agents of the security forces say that it is most disturbing when the human bomb is disguised as an IDF soldier because it touches on the embodiment of the ultimate Zionism in the trickiest way. Infiltrating Israel disguised as Jewish soldiers is regarded as most challenging to security, and not only because of its operative aspects. The Israeli attitude toward human bombs who disguise themselves in IDF uniforms shows sensitivity bordering on insult.

This Israeli attitude implies vague awareness of the Palestinian aspiration to "truly" resemble IDF fighters, which is as dangerous as terrorism itself. An indication of this is found in the ambivalent response of Jewish Israelis to the initiative among some Palestinian Christian citizens of Israel to encourage volunteering for service in the IDF as a basis for the demand for full citizenship in the Jewish state. Along with the satisfaction expressed by Jewish Israelis, there was also a feeling of discomfort and suspicion. Research into the hidden phenomenon of Arabs who serve in the IDF shows, among other things, that at home, among their Palestinian brethren, they behave like Palestinians in every respect, whereas when they are among Israelis, they do not stand out at all.[39] According to a Palestinian scholar's thesis, they are not to be seen as victims of a situation packed with inner contradictions but as active agents who, by enlisting counter to the national ethos of their community, they express a deep drive to join up with the Israelis. It has been claimed in Israel that the desire of some Palestinians to be Israeli soldiers is an extension of the well-known logic of colonialism.[40]

One Israeli journalist related that in a recent visit to a Palestinian village on the West Bank, he was hosted by a typical family, and when he asked one of the boys what he wanted to be when he grew up, the boy answered, "An IDF soldier." The Israeli journalist provoked his Hebrew readers by suggesting, "Take Palestinian boys into the army—and make their dream come true."[41] There is further testimony to what has been described as the "powerful desire" of Palestinian youth, even in Hebron, known for its religious and nationalist extremism, to be like IDF soldiers and connect with them.[42] This surprising fact may be explained in several ways that do not contradict each other. Mainly we have here an expression of a need, entirely independent of any strategic logic, to release the physical urges of adolescents who are naturally prone to violence.[43] This is also a desire to take part in the institutional celebration of regional violence, which only the Jewish population enjoys. Another explanation goes beyond the tendency to identify with the active, strong, aggressive, victorious side. Joining the army would make possible total assimilation into Israeli society and thus its subversion and undermining from within. Since the gate to enlisting and serving as an IDF fighter is closed to young Palestinians from the territories, they found an alternative during the intifada: disguising themselves as IDF soldiers, standing together with other soldiers at a bus station like one of them, boarding the bus with them, and then blowing themselves up and dying with them—like comrades in arms.

The Palestinian director of the film *Paradise Now*, which deals with suicide terrorism, told me that when he cast Palestinian actors from the West Bank in the parts of the enemy Israeli soldiers—border guards and intended victims of suicide terrorism—costuming them in IDF uniforms and placing rifles in their hands, at first they were embarrassed, shy, and frozen in their acting. But they quickly got into the role, and even fell in love with it, and in the end they refused to part from it. He described how, without noticing it, they adopted the body language of Israeli soldiers ("macho and lordly") and began to act with exaggerated violence toward their colleagues, who were playing Palestinians, far beyond the demands of the role and the director's instructions.[44]

Ritual Coproduction

Victimizer, Victim, and Sacrifice

Allahu Akbar

When Israelis hear the loud cry of "Allahu Akbar" ("God is great" in Arabic),[1] they are terrified. This traditional profession of faith in Islam has become automatically identified with suicide terrorism in the past few decades in the Middle East. With this cry, after which the human bomb will set off his deadly explosive, he reveals his true identity, declares his creed, and proclaims his mission. Perhaps he also encourages and arouses himself, and surely he paralyzes the people around him, who will immediately become his victims.

The command given to the terrorists who crashed into the twin towers (2001) was "When the confrontation begins, . . . shout 'Allahu Akbar,' [the phrase that] . . . strikes fear in the heart of nonbelievers." Among the belongings of Muhammad Atta, the leader of the 9/11 attack, was an instruction booklet laying out the religious aspect that reinforces the operative aspect of the suicide mission. Copies of it were also found in the luggage of the apparent leaders of the teams in the other planes, and these instructions probably were recited and observed by all nineteen of the suicide terrorists. Later that text was published on the Internet and became available to Sunni suicide terrorist organizations in the Middle East, which adopted it as a source of inspiration. Here are selected quotations from the document, which I take to be a formative model of the rite that preceded and accompanied the acts of suicide terrorism also committed by Hamas and the Palestinian Islamic Jihad:[2]

   3. [On the last night before the operation] make an oath to die. Shave excess hair from the body, shower and wear fragrance.
   7. Pray during the night and be persistent in asking God to guarantee victory.
   9. Purify your soul from all unclean things. Forget something called "this life." The time for play is over and the serious time is upon us.
   10. You should feel complete tranquility because the time between you and your marriage [in heaven] is very short.
   14. Bless your body with some verses of the Koran [by reading the lines into one's hands and then rubbing the hands over parts of the body or articles, such as a weapon, that are to be blessed].
   16. Tighten your clothes [to avoid the exposure of the groin] since this is the way of the pious generation after the Prophet used to do before battle.
   24. Do not seem confused or show signs of nervous tension. Be happy because you are heading for a deed that God loves.
   30. When the confrontation begins strike like a champion. God said: strike above the neck, and strike at all of their extremities.
   31. Dedicate the slaughter to your fathers because you have obligations toward them. Do not cause the discomfort of those you are killing because this is one of the practices of the Prophet. However, do not become distracted and do not pay attention to the enemy because that would do more damage than good.
   35. When the hour of reality approaches, the zero hour, either end your life with praying, seconds before the target, or make your last words: "There is no God but Allah, Muhammad is his messenger."

The act of suicide terrorism is highly structured; with prescribed, precise, and repetitive patterns of behavior. The logic of this act is not only operational but also symbolic. It is largely ritualized. What precedes the attack and leads up to it—such as the human bomb's videotaped testament—and also that which comes in its wake—such as the construction of a mourners' tent in the home of human bomb's family—are regulated by rigid norms and laden with symbolic significance. Predetermined ritual elements are also present in the conduct of the human bomb during the attack itself. For example, the human bomb's parting with the agent of the organization who accompanies him to the target has a ceremonial dimension: they kiss, and one recites the phrase "There is no God but Allah," and his comrade responds, "And Muhammad is his Prophet."

A great deal has been published in the press and in academic literature about the videotaped testament of suicide terrorists, recorded on the eve of their mission and broadcast by Palestinian media immediately after the Israeli announcement of the explosion.[3] Of the Palestinian human bombs, 78 percent left a testament or last will (55% left a written one, 42% a videotape, 3% an audio cassette).[4] The testament is organized according to a more or less set procedure: presentation of the shahid, his name, his place of residence, and his membership in the organization; his testimony about the strengthening of his faith; the motives for his volunteering; instructions to his family as to how to take his death; farewell to his mother; condemnation of Israel and the occupation; praise for the Palestinian nation and its struggle; praise to the Prophet and the Koran. Below I point out one motive that was generally overlooked, although it touches on the core of the phenomenon. The ones who did notice it and presented it with sensitivity and talent are the makers of the Palestinian film *Paradise Now*, whose subject is suicide terrorism. One of the impressive scenes presents in detail the recording of the terrorist's testament before setting forth on his mission, with three revealing and pointed comic episodes inserted in it.

In the first, after the prospective human bomb has nearly finished reciting his testament, it turns out that there was a technical hitch in the camera, and the entire dramatic performance was "wasted on nothing." After the camera is fixed, the obedient suicide terrorist is asked to repeat the text from the beginning, and he does it somewhat mechanically—with exactly the same words and intonation. In the second take, the body language and facial expressions are exactly the same, following the instructions of the director. In the next episode, as the suicide terrorist utters farewell words

to his beloved parents, notifying them through the camera of his imminent death, his handlers and the heads of the organization are standing in
a corner of the room, watching heartlessly, while chatting casually with
each other, and one of them bites into a sandwich stuffed with delicacies.
In the third episode, while the prospective human bomb is speaking to the
camera about his joy at the prospect of soon meeting earlier shahids in
the other world, he suddenly remembers that he forgot to tell his mother
something important, so he inserts a personal message in the recorded
text, telling her that he saw the kind of water filter she needs for the
kitchen faucet for sale at a good price in a certain store in town. She will
get the message only after her son's death.

The audience chuckles, but they can't help shifting uncomfortably in
their seats because of the chilling dissonance between this heartbreaking
scene and its actual dull pettiness and manipulated practicality. The first
two sarcastic moments included in the script (the camera that failed and
the sandwich that was gobbled) shatter the veil of pompous rhetoric
that concealed the tragic behind the ridiculous, and the third moment
(the water filter), also a kind of interpretation, implies revolt against
the disciplinary straitjacket that the organization's rituals impose on the
protagonists. Violating the rules shows how rigid they were, and relief of the tension indicates how high it was. Similarly, in a survey of
dozens of recorded testaments of actual suicide terrorists, which were
broadcast by the organizations,[5] the inner contradiction with which the
situation is laden is notable: the typical gap between the forced effort to
show optimism, spontaneity, firmness, and self-confidence and the frozen looks and awkward movements that indicate perplexity, confusion,
and shock, and the effort to control emotions, most likely anxiety, in the
face of death. The nature of the occasion is marked by a chasm between
the eloquent, bombastic text, sometimes even rhyming verse, which is
dictated, and the prosaic, inarticulate manner of the suicide terrorist
when he is interviewed.[6]

The testament is a personal, touching farewell to parents and to the
world, with formalistic propaganda slogans belonging to the organization, directed at both the Palestinian and Israeli public. In a typical testament of a Palestinian human bomb he mechanically rehearses a line about
his "thirst to drink Jewish blood" while his face remains expressionless.
Like a programmed robot, he then addresses his mother, saying, "Wipe

your tears, because with the help of Allah, I am fulfilling all my dreams. Do not let me see you sad on the day of my wedding with the black-eyed virgins and joining my relatives in the Garden of Eden."[7] At that stirring moment when he sentences himself to death with his own words, when he is actually about to kill himself, he tells his father in a rehearsed formula, "Forgive me, I am in a hurry to my wedding, I can't wait even a moment"; and then, "Be joyous, give away sweets"; and also, with opaque pathos, "Come with me, seek death, ask for it, because it is life."[8]

For fear of indirectly disclosing operative secrets about suicide terrorism, several Palestinian activists expressed opposition to the recording of testaments, but other considerations of the organization prevailed, and the tradition that was consolidated during the few years of the intifada won out. There were almost no exceptions to the standard pattern of this largely staged testament: against the background of the golden Dome of the Rock in Jerusalem, pictures of earlier shahids from the same movement, and verses from Muslim scripture, the suicide terrorist stands with his forehead wrapped with a green band, holding a rifle and a Koran, reciting the text. The message of the recorded testament is to spread and solidify the ideal of Palestinian Islamic martyrdom, to advance the political aims of the movement. Specifically, it strives to persuade the listeners that the human bomb goes out on his mission of his own free will and with enthusiasm, and not because of coercion or distress. In addition to the propaganda function of the testament, it serves to create commitment, so that no remorse can deter the suicide terrorist. Along with the testament, other ceremonies are performed to assure completion of the deed, such as paying debts to friends, giving instructions for division of property after death, and writing a detailed list of seventy family members who will gain entry into paradise by virtue of the human bomb's death. Another function of the testament is to ensure that credit for the attack will be given to the organization that dispatched him. The competition between Palestinians for the glory of *shahada* was so intense that on one occasion two organizations claimed responsibility for the same attack.[9]

The characteristic dissonance of the ritual of suicide terrorism is apparent also in the act that parallels the testament and complements it: the mourning rites held after the explosion is made known and revelation of the human bomb's identity. In the mourning tent, immediately erected in the courtyard of the terrorist's parents, the hosts and guests behave as if it were a wedding.[10] Loud music is played, sweet coffee is served, dates and cakes are offered, people smile, and women ululate.[11] At the entrance guests greet the parents of the "groom" with *mabruk* (congratulations) and they kiss. Only after the representatives of the movement and members of the community have left, as time passes after the event, a deeper, more empathetic observation cannot miss the restrained sorrow, especially that of the mother, and the repressed anger, especially that of the father, against the handlers, "who never choose a young man from their families for a suicide mission."[12]

The Middle Eastern post–suicide terrorism rituals begin even before the mourning-wedding banquet in the parents' home.[13] Right after the explosion—but never before news of the attack is announced by Israeli media—one of the Palestinian movements takes credit for it. Sometimes the identity of the human bomb is not known until Israeli security forces arrive at the home of his family to investigate. Then the shahid's mother and sisters go up to the roof of their house and break out in loud warbling to announce their pain and joy. The name and fame of the shahid are announced on the loudspeakers in the minarets of the mosques throughout the West Bank and the Gaza Strip. The shahid is blessed, for he is already in paradise.[14] Verses of the Koran are also recited, as well as hymns (*anshid*). In some cases mourning music was sounded even before the announcement to the human bomb's parents of their son's death, and thus it became a code announcing a suicide attack. In response, ecstatic crowds gather in the street, flashing "V" for victory, whistling, waving Palestinian flags and movement banners, burning Israeli and US flags, shooting in the air, blowing car horns, giving out candy. Later the movement holds a mass meeting and mourning banquet open to all, demonstrating the movement's strength. At the same time pictures of the shahid are posted on walls in the streets of the cities and villages, cassettes of the testament are distributed, and the television broadcasts facts about his modest and saintly life and his heroic action. There are also popular film clips that vividly portray the human bomb's meeting with the virgins in paradise.

The funerals of all the shahids who were killed in the Palestinian-Israeli conflict were events orchestrated by the movements with the participation of thousands. The funeral of a suicide terrorist requires a special ritual procedure, because there is no body to bury. In such cases an empty coffin or stretcher is carried in a procession that leaves from the central mosque and ends at the entrance of the cemetery. A symbolic funeral of this kind is an opportunity for emotions to break out, with enthusiastic shouts of sorrow, hatred, and thirst for revenge.

There is not much reliable information about the rituals preceding attacks and preparation for them, since they take place in secret, sometimes hurriedly, for operational reasons. It is difficult to determine to what degree the rites I describe below were actually observed. Perhaps as a result of Israeli pressure and tight schedules, as in the second wave of suicide terrorism, the procedures were practiced partially or not at all. Nevertheless, the Palestinian movements, particularly Hamas, proudly insisted that they kept observing these rites.[15]

An ideal suicide attack should adhere to the following procedure developed during the intifada: before the mission, the human bomb fasts, concentrates on religious lessons for four hours a day or more, and makes sure to pray, especially throughout the final night.[16] He participates in at least one public prayer in the mosque, the prayer before going into battle, in which he also asks forgiveness for his sins. He then places a Koran in his left pocket, over his heart, to accompany him on his mission, but not before reciting especially the verses of the Koran that deal specifically with jihad, war, the birth of Islam, and the importance of faith. During the five daily prayers, which involve several repetitions (*reka'at*), the human bomb adds an extra bow of submission for his (temporary) departure from life. Before this he has performed a special act of purification—scrubbing his whole body. This is because (beyond the ordinary ablutions, before all prayer, in which one washes only one's hands and feet) he is on his way to his wedding, to his death, and to "the killing of heretics." This description was given to me by a religious functionary connected with Hamas. The ZAKA volunteers added that some of the suicide terrorists had shaved their whole bodies, including their pubic hair, and an ISA investigator claimed that some of the human bombs took pains to erase tattoos from their bodies before setting out on their missions. This was all done so they would enter the gates of paradise pure and whole.

In the same vein, the prospective suicide terrorist should leave no debts behind.[17] Many also had themselves photographed in videos and stills, in striking warlike poses to be circulated after their deaths on memorial pages on the Internet. With a somewhat boastful tone, the movement propagandists mention another macabre preliminary stage, both ceremonial and part of the terrorist's physical and mental training: the human bomb is required to get used to death by wearing a shroud or by spending several hours of a dark night alone in a grave.[18]

Violent Rites, Rites of Violence

The procedure preliminary to suicide terrorism has elements of rites of passage, such as wearing new (Israeli-style) clothes, having a close shave and a haircut, and putting on the explosive vest. Then comes the fateful transition—crossing the border fence, infiltrating toward the target with a different identity.

The arena of the suicide attack is a stage. The drama of suicide terrorism takes place in a public space in the heart of a city, in daylight, in the presence of many witnesses, in the eyes of the mass media and the whole world.[19] On this stage a ritual act is performed. The rationale for the attack is also sacramental. A religious and national ceremony is acted out in which the human bomb displays courage and faith in relation to the community he represents, and hatred, revenge, and moral superiority toward the enemy. It is a violent rite and a rite of violence of the type, for example, that characterized the religious wars between Catholics and Protestants in sixteenth-century France.[20] Mainly it is a cult of death.

The attacks were dramatized in the Palestinian street theater that flourished during the intifada. Crowds gathered in the squares of Palestinian population centers in the territories to celebrate the reenactments: wooden models of buses with logos written in Hebrew were burned and cries of pain were imitated while entering a precise cardboard replica of a restaurant with puddles of red liquid on the floor and walls plastered with human limbs that had been thrown in the air. The spectators and participants laughed and cheered, waved Palestinian and Hamas flags, fired shots, and shouted, "Allahu Akbar."[21]

The human bomb sends signals backward, to the Palestinians who sent him, and forward, to the Israelis against whom he fights. The Palestinian suicide terrorism ceremony is projected far beyond the borders of the Palestinian community; it implants itself deeply in the center of the Israeli community. The ceremony, which embodies Palestinian nationalism and religiosity, is performed in the streets of Jerusalem and Tel Aviv. To achieve a daunting effect the Palestinian suicide terrorists aimed at the Mahane Yehuda market in Jerusalem and a café in north Tel Aviv, temples of Israeliness.[22]

Similar to and combined with the ritual dimension of Palestinian suicide terrorism there is also the ritual dimension of the treatment of suicide terrorism on the Israeli side. Both to the offense and the defense against suicide terrorism there is a logic that is not only political and operational but also symbolic and ceremonial. Standing against the Islamic suicide terrorist is the Jewish ZAKA volunteer, the other martyr: the former penetrates and blends, and then shatters and scatters, while the latter gathers and assembles, and then separates and distances. One erases boundaries, and the other reestablishes and sharpens them. The ceremony on both sides struggles with the challenge from the other side and testifies to it. In the arena of suicide terrorism two symbolically structured systems appear, intermingling and complementing one another; each is attentive to the other and speaks to it, borrowing and providing typical elements. Ritual killing and ritual healing meet.

One example among many is the title "engineer" (*al-muhandes*), a central concept in the rhetoric of both sides, a magic word in the regional cult of suicide terrorism. Originally the term referred to Yehiya Ayash, a terrorist who specialized in making explosive belts and dispatching human bombs, until he became a senior commander in the military arm of Hamas. The engineer was regarded as the founding father of Palestinian suicide terrorism. Among the Palestinians his epithet was a synonym for national hero, and among the Israelis it was a synonym for the most frightening and detested enemy of all. The epithet was born in a confidential chat between the assistant director of the ISA, Gideon Ezra, and Prime Minister Rabin. It was leaked to the Israeli press and immediately adopted by the Islamic resistance movement. After Ayash was eliminated by Israel (1996), successors arose among the leaders of suicide terrorism. Both in the Palestinian territories and in Israel they were called the second engineer, third engineer, and so on. Thus, in the encounter between suicide terrorism and those who try to overcome it, there emerged a tight symbolic snarl whose components were difficult to untangle and whose sources and transformations were hard to trace. In Palestinian suicide terrorism in Israel two rival national cults become a common, Middle Eastern cult. The symbol of this common cult are the twisted, burned remains of a bus. It is central both to Israeli memorial ceremonies for the victims of suicide terrorism and to Palestinian memorials for suicide terrorists.

The human bomb and ZAKA volunteers meet at the terror site as the emissaries of two battling nations and two rival religions. They represent two distinct cultures of death, each with its abundance of rituals. At the site, two dormant but precedent-rich martyr traditions become vibrant and aggressive. They interpret themselves to themselves and to the world in the context of this encounter, and in so doing they gain momentum and take the form of two full-fledged death cults. The struggle at the site between the different kinds of martyrs develops into a grand scene of sacrifice. The Palestinian-Muslim and Haredi-Israeli death cults clash and compete, but at the same time engage in a tacit dialogue. Their complexities and the fullness of their meanings can be appreciated only in the context of their encounter.

History sometimes creates circumstances in which the rituals of two antagonistic religions are acted out next to each other, on the same thematic axis. Such ceremonial situations are generally notable for their provocative and disconcerting nature and their tendency to degenerate into violence.[23] One classic example is the outbreak of violence between Hindus and Muslims at the Ayodhya shrine in 1992–93, in which thousands were killed.[24] The conflict over this site, claimed as holy by both religions, resembles that over the Tomb of the Patriarchs in Hebron, an important site of prayer for both Jews and Muslims. Worshippers of both faiths go there to pray at the tombs of the same saintly forefathers. When Baruch Goldstein, a Jewish settler, opened fire in a Muslim prayer room at the site on the Jewish festival of Purim in 1994, which, in that year, fell on a Friday, the Muslim holy day, in the holy month of Ramadan, the attack brought home the explosive potential of such ritual contacts for exacerbating conflicts in mixed communities.

Another analogy is the relations between Jews and Christians in medieval Europe, and especially the Crusades and the Jewish legacy of the sanctification of the name of God in the eleventh and twelfth centuries. The latter refers to Jews murdered by papal armies and local mobs; in some cases Jews killed their families and themselves rather than accept Christianity at sword's point. Jewish self-immolation thus mirrored Catholic ritual murder.[25] This deadly Jewish practice cannot be understood without understanding its deadly Christian counterpart, and vice versa. A subtle dynamic of influences and counterinfluences developed between the faiths involved in this bloody conflict, so that it is difficult to distinguish between cause and effect, between active and passive. It engendered a ritual complex in which both sides grip each other so tightly that they cannot easily be separated. The two lethal cults are not only contiguous but intertwined—though their adherents neither intend this nor are aware of it—and each is construed through the mirror it holds up before the other. The victims of this violence became sacrificial, atoning and redeeming for the two neighboring communities, who worshipped two different gods but shared core symbols and values. Thus the consciousness of Jewish suffering in the Diaspora is grasped very well in the Christian consciousness of the suffering of the Passion.[26] The Middle Eastern suicide terrorism site, with its mutually embracing rituals, has a similar ironic-tragic fabric.

Middle Eastern suicide terrorism offers abundant testimony for the mythical and ritual similarity in the way the rival sides treat killing at the arena. From the early stages of the conflict, certain cultural and political motives shifted sides, and to this day they both correspond with one another. For example: Haredi rabbis devote themselves to campaigns to win secular Jews "back" into the bosom of religious orthodoxy, and, like many missionaries in Christianity and in Islam as well, they frighten their listeners with rhetoric of hell, fire and brimstone, the divine response to lives of sin and heresy. During the intifada they often rebuked the Israeli public and presented Palestinian suicide attacks as a punishment from Providence for abandoning the Jewish religion. Strangely, the opposite view found its way into this evangelizing rhetoric, according to which the suicide attacks were a unique opportunity for repentance and redemption. One famous preacher in Jerusalem told an audience of women about a Jewish lady who was very fearful of a "beating in the grave" (according to a medieval mystical tradition, rooted in the Talmud, the angel of death stands next to the body of the deceased before his soul rises to heaven; he interrogates the deceased about his actions in life and beats him and torments his flesh, unless the deceased was meticulous in his observance of the commandments). The rabbi's argument was that out of consideration for the woman's apprehensions, God made sure that she would be at the Sbarro pizzeria in Jerusalem just when the suicide terrorist struck. Led by a mysterious power, the suicide terrorist drew near the woman and killed her, and she became a martyr, a saint whose soul ascends directly to paradise, free of any torments in the grave.[27] At the very same time, Muslim clerics in the Gaza Strip repeated that the holy suicide terrorists, whose place in paradise was assured, were also exempt from "beating in the grave," which figures in the parallel Muslim tradition (the dead person is interrogated strenuously by the angels Munqar and Niqar—the ugly and the repulsive—and after answering them he is made unconscious, until he awakens once again on Judgment Day).

The cross dialogue between the two death cults, their mutual influence, and their intermingling are reflected in the folklore of both sides. During the intifada, the costume of the human bomb was popular not only in the streets of the Gaza Strip and the West Bank but also, ironically, among Jews in Israel, mainly in the settlements of the radical religious right. In the Haredi neighborhoods of Jerusalem, children were also seen with their faces masked with an Arab keffiyeh, wearing a white garment, and a make-believe explosive belt. According to an urban legend that I was unable to confirm, one Jew who was dressed up as a Palestinian suicide terrorist shouted, "Allahu Akbar" in the street, causing panic and even shooting, in which he was wounded.

The regional representatives of suicide terrorism, the Palestinian human bombs and the Israeli ZAKA volunteers who resemble each other, have become model figures in their communities, inspiring the costumes of children who dress in gleaming white from head to foot on their holidays, the white of pure angels. On the Palestinian side, the white costume represents the holy spirits of the dead who have gone to heaven. It symbolizes both the shrouds in which corpses are wrapped and union with the white-clad virgins who await the shahid in paradise.[28] On the Israeli side, the white costume alludes to the sterile overalls of those who deal with bodies after an attack. Both the human bomb and the ZAKA volunteer wear a kind of sleeveless garment, one to carry the explosive, the other for protection and identification.[29]

More on Blood

The high priest at the ancient temple in Jerusalem presided over the ritual sacrifice, a central element of which was collecting the blood of the slaughtered animal on the altar, dipping the priest's hand in the blood, and sprinkling the blood in front of the entire people. After the flesh was cut up, the priests would pour the blood on the altar and around it, marking their earlobes and big toes with blood, and sprinkling blood on their garments (Exodus 29). Direct contact with the blood would sanctify the priest and heighten his capacities. By offering sacrifices, believers attained atonement and salvation. After all, blood symbolizes life, and spilling it is the equivalent of giving up the most precious thing of all (Leviticus 17; think also of the ritual of the blood of Christ). Touching blood is an exalted yet dangerous act, between life and death, a virtuosic unmediated connection with the most impure that is at the same time the purest.

Shamans in the Abrahamic religion, as in others, touch blood and thus augment their magic potency. Like the priests in the ancient Israelite temple, and like sacred death specialists in aboriginal Siberia and in India,[30] the ZAKA volunteers touch blood frequently as an essential part of their death cult. For example, in a manner reminiscent of the Aghori priests, an ascetic Hindi cult in Varanasi, the Haredi Jews who tend to the victims' bodies of terrorism are not deterred from dipping their hands in blood. On the contrary, they appear to touch the blood intentionally and emphatically, beyond what is required, in order to bring the victims to burial and clean the scene of the attack. In interviews, they admitted that they smear their hands and clothes with blood in a way that seeks to create the impression that it was done inadvertently and out of necessity in the bustle of activity at the scene. They made sure that the blood on them would be seen by their colleagues and observers, including millions of television viewers. The ZAKA volunteers flaunt their connection with blood, the blood of the Israeli victims and the Palestinian suicide terrorist. Thus ultra-Orthodox Jews share the cult of holy death with Muslims. Haredi ZAKA volunteers, like Palestinian terrorists and their admirers, show the blood on their hands to the world. The blood on their hands is a demonstration of their identification with the victims, their self-victimization, as well as a demonstration of the extermination of death and victory over the enemy.

During the wave of suicide terrorism the ZAKA volunteers, like most residents of the region, saw on television the final stages in the career of Palestinian shahids: in the morgues of the Gaza Strip and the West Bank, and afterward in the mass funeral processions, comrades in arms and admirers crowd up to the stretcher to touch the dead terrorist's wounds, wave their blood-smeared hands, and spread the saint's blood on their clothes or foreheads.[31] Contact with the blood of shahids is not only a sign of solidarity but also an entry ticket into paradise. The blood gives power and promises regeneration. Apparently, under Jewish but mainly Christian influence, touching blood atones and redeems in Islam as well.

The waves of suicide terrorism made the theme of Middle Eastern blood central and endowed it with almost biblical qualities. Elsewhere I note the symbolism of blood and its uses for ZAKA.[32] On the Palestinian side, the association of terror with blood also received great importance. Speakers for the resistance movements have declaimed on countless occasions that the blood of shahids slakes the thirst of the Palestinian warriors and nourishes the intifada. Like the Jewish victims of suicide terrorism, the Palestinian martyrs are also buried in blood-soaked garments. Immediately after the flow of the first drop of their blood, they are promised a place alongside the Prophet in heaven. Note the equivalent Jewish belief in the magic impact of the first drop of blood of Israeli martyrs and the victims of suicide terrorism in particular.

The intifada brought the element of blood to new heights among the Palestinians, and this has found rhetorical, poetical, and especially visual expression.[33] There are the slogans chanted again and again: "With blood we will liberate Palestine"; "Only with blood will we redeem the shahids"; and "Blood removes blood." In a popular patriotic song, the singer repeatedly chants the word "blood," dozens of times in a row. In another song, the chorus is "We are in love with the color of blood." Posters hung in Palestinian towns and villages, on murals that decorate many walls, are replete with rivers, lakes, and waterfalls of blood. Torches of the revolution are fueled by blood rather than oil; blood becomes stones in the hands of the youth of rebellion; blood flows from the bodies of warriors and forms the letters of the slogan "The intifada will bring victory;" those loyal to the struggle cross a bridge over gushing streams of blood. The Palestinian media is full of photographs and drawings of bleeding wounds. Even on television they are not reluctant to broadcast pictures of spilled blood.[34]

The sense of smell is also enlisted in the attack of the senses revolving around the blood of saints. According to their belief, the spilled blood becomes perfume. It is apparently so suggestive that there were cases when masses of villagers in the Hebron Hills, in the southern part of the West Bank, streamed to the graves of shahids to be enthralled by the marvelous fragrance.

In this rich repository of linguistic and graphic imagery, it is sometimes hard to distinguish between Jewish and Arab or Muslim blood. The blood mixes not only on the site after the explosion, but also in Palestinian fantasies. At assemblies of Islamic resistance movements they sing: "O Muhammad, we shall restore your religion and we shall drink the blood of those who make of themselves our enemies."[35] When someone drinks someone else's blood, their blood mingles. During the intifada, in the Gaza Strip, people chanted, "I am an Arab, and when I am hungry, I eat the flesh of my prey." The meaning of such cannibalistic metaphors is total bodily union between attacker and victim. In a popular drawing of a severed Palestinian hand plunging into a Zionist heart, one cannot determine the source of the drops of blood dripping onto the earth. There are also cases in which the Palestinians speak explicitly of dipping their hands in the blood of saints as well as in that of their victims.[36] During the intifada Palestinian youth used to paint their hands red and press them against light-colored walls to ornament the entire urban and village landscape in the occupied territories with handprints dripping with blood. Some claimed it was real blood. Whose blood? Usually the answer was categorical: "the blood of shahids." But here and there I heard that it was the blood of Jews slaughtered in the intifada.

"Blood on their hands" is a familiar expression in the local political discourse—on both sides of the Israeli-Palestinian conflict. It is used to describe direct responsibility for initiating and perpetrating murderous terrorist acts. In the Israeli judicial system and in public opinion a sharp distinction is made between a prisoner from the Palestinian organizations with blood on his hands and the others. The guilt of the former is regarded as infinitely more serious. The expression "blood on his hand" received a dramatic demonstration in relation to the Ramallah lynching (2000): early in the intifada two IDF reserve soldiers drove into the center of the Palestinian city by mistake. They were dragged from their car and taken to the local police station. In response to the demands of a shouting mob, they were handed over to hundreds of worked-up people who had gathered around and begun to break into the building in order to wreak their fury on the Jews. An Italian television team documented the torture, murder, and mutilation of their bodies, which included tearing off limbs, thrusting objects into orifices, and pouring out the internal organs. Before that they were thrown headfirst from an upper story, and afterward the bodies were burned. At the end of the event one of the leaders of the violent actions appeared at the window and, to the cheering of masses crowded into the square, with a huge smile he displayed his hands, smeared with the victims' blood.[37]

When the attacker smears himself with his victim's blood and proudly displays the enemy's blood on his hands, he is symbolizing a great victory over the other, his defeat and humiliation. As suggested, there might also be an element known from classical mythology and the anthropological literature, when the attacker is smeared with the blood of his victim in order to assimilate the powers of his enemy, a kind of identification and self-display. As we have already seen, the tendency of the ZAKA volunteers to touch the blood of those who died in suicide attacks, to be smeared with blood and to show it publicly, does not only relate to the blood of the Jewish victims. They are drawn by magical attraction to touch the Palestinian suicide terrorist's blood as well. On both sides of the conflict, people ritually dip their hands in the blood of the dead, both "ours" and "theirs."

Sacred Murder

The connection of the blood of the slaughtered to the sacred and the ceremonial brings us to consider the arena of suicide terrorism in terms of sacrifice. Both the Palestinian act of suicide terrorism and the Israeli act of caring for its victims can be seen as a sacrificial rite. Sacrificial rites connect murderous violence to that which is most exalted.[38]

The classical sacrificial ceremony comprises four interconnected elements. First, the destruction and extinction of a living thing, such as killing by means of slaughter and/or burning, drowning, throwing off a cliff. Second, subjection of the killing to strict rules of conduct and its regulation according to a procedure scripted by tradition. Departure from the precise ceremonial norms is forbidden and incurs punishment (since it is liable to express the dangerous core of the violence and reveal the uncontrolled impulse to kill). Third, from something plain, normal, profane, lacking particular value and meaning, the killed creature is made into something laden with symbolism, great potency, and supreme religious value. Thus the object becomes sacred and ipso facto taboo as well. Fourth, the creature is killed for the sake of life. Its function is to reconcile a higher power, to restore order, to secure atonement and redemption, mainly in situations of distress.

"To sacrifice" in Latin means to make holy, and the Hebrew word for sacrifice, *qorban*, is connected etymologically to the root for closeness, as in prayer, effective communication with God. The connection between killing and sanctifying can be understood in two ways: one kills in order to sanctify, or one sanctifies in order to kill. The goal is sanctification, and the means is killing, though perhaps killing is the goal, and sanctification is what makes it possible.

The paradigmatic, ultimate sacrifice is human sacrifice, known in both history and mythology.[39] Ritual slaughter of an animal on an altar or the offering of something precious, like chosen fruit of the soil, to the temple, are substitutes for the real thing. Suicide terrorism is human sacrifice. Neither human sacrifice nor suicide terrorism can be summed up simply in the act of killing. Rather, it requires a modus operandi according to an elaborate formula.[40]

To be effective, the living sacrificial object must be flawless, healthy, good-looking, and wholesome, with all its parts in place. In various traditional cultures, for example, a pretty child is an ideal sacrificial victim.[41] At the same time, the act of sacrifice entails spoiling the victim's body, tearing its limbs, splitting its flesh, and burning it. Dismembering the body sanctifies it. But later, the parts of the sacrificed object are rearranged and placed in proper order.[42] The sacrificial act thus has a violent, deconstructive element, and also a restorative, creative, beneficial element of reparation. The sacrifice enacted in Middle Eastern suicide terrorism is the product of collaboration between the Palestinian human bomb, who is responsible for rending the flesh, and the Jewish ZAKA men, who are responsible for putting the flesh back together.

The sacrificial ceremony consists of several stages.[43] First, obtaining who or what is to be sacrificed. It must represent the sacrificers, those for whom it is a substitute. That is, it must resemble the original figure. However, usually one is careful not to choose a candidate who holds a vital position or prestigious status, so that his expected loss will not be unbearably painful to the community. Usually sacrificial victims are relatively peripheral or socially weak, such as children, slaves, prisoners, or nomads. There have hardly been any Palestinian suicide terrorists who are privileged according to their family origins or personal stature. At this stage the sacrificial victim is customarily presented to the community. In the case of the Palestinian suicide terrorist, the community is informed about the chosen person by means of still photographs and videos, which state his name, his family, his place of residence, his organizational affiliation, and also his faith and the meaning of his sacrifice. This vital move is made before the sacrificial act, and, in an exception to the normal way sacrifices are made, the sacrificial victim is displayed publicly only after the performance of the act. To make certain that the presentation follows the rules, it is dictated by those responsible for the sacrifice.

After being chosen, the sacrificial victim must undergo a transformation in his nature and image: he is deprived of his past and his social ties and rights, he is separated from the community and isolated, and he becomes alien to his original identity. Then he is anointed and initiated, and finally he adopts a new identity. Thus he is purified bodily and renewed spiritually. The case of Palestinian suicide terrorism exemplifies this stage very well, as detailed earlier (removal to a secluded hideout, prayer, fasting, shaving, and change in appearance, the kiss of departure, etc.). Only afterward comes the stage of shedding blood. What brings this chain of classic sacrificial ceremony to a close is the banquet and celebration. In the case of suicide terrorism, this takes place in the mourning tent, in the mass rallies and street processions, and also on television screens. On these occasions of catharsis, the community receives a reward for the sacrifice.

Some of the ZAKA volunteers who come into frequent contact with the bodies of the victims of suicide terrorism, including the body of the human bomb, imagine themselves as priests in the biblical temple that "placed their hands on the sacrificial animal." According to the common interpretation, the touching of the sacrificial object (*karev*) by the sacrificer (*makriv*) symbolizes the connection between them, their identification. In terrorism attacks where most of the victims were Haredi, the identification of the ZAKA volunteers with them was apparent.[44] Of the attack on bus number 2, the volunteers said, "*We* were the victims. We collected our limbs there, we scraped the fragments of our bones, and we soaked up our own blood" (August 2003). In that event, some of the volunteers wanted to remove their rubber gloves "so they wouldn't separate" them from themselves, the sacrificer from the sacrificial victims. The suicide terrorist and the ZAKA volunteers are representatives of their respective communities, who preside over the sacrificial ceremony. All the victims of the attack—from both camps, the target community and also the attacker—are sacrificial victims who rise up to heaven in flames, sanctified, serving the collective who remain behind, for purgation and to boost unity and morale. As we have shown, before the explosion the attacker mingles with his future victims at the site. Here we add that, after the explosion, too, the Palestinian victim of self-sacrifice mingles with his Israeli sacrificial victims. One of the macabre manifestations of the difficulty in distinguishing between them is the confusion regarding the number of victims of a suicide attack. Often there is a difference of one among the various reports. Some include the suicide terrorist in the count, and others count only the Israeli victims. The ZAKA volunteers are also in doubt as to whether the attacker is (also another) victim.

A distinction is made between two meanings of sacrifice.[45] The first appears in the Bible and in ancient Greece and Rome. It refers to a gift that people give to their gods in order to appease them, to atone for their actions, to be purified, and to be redeemed.[46] This is a phenomenon of *giving to*. However, sacrifice can have the slightly different meaning of *giving up* something of value. This refers to what human beings forgo for the sake of their gods or for the sake of an idea such as freedom, equality, and democracy, or some entity like the homeland, the nation, the family, or a friend. The first meaning is connected to religion, particularly to ritual. The second meaning is connected to ethics and politics. In both cases, the rationale for the sacrifice demands that what one donates or what one forgoes is something precious. Of course, nothing is more valuable than the life of a person's loved ones or his own life.

Sacrifice in the sense of giving is connected to the ritual killing of the other, usually an enemy. The sacrifice in the sense of giving up something is connected to self-sacrifice, and the latter amounts to ritual suicide. In studies of suicide terrorism no distinction was made between the two aspects of sacrifice, nor, of course, has the connection between them been noticed. The prisoners of war whom the Aztecs slaughtered on the altar were sacrifices of the first kind, gifts in the form of the life of others.[47] The Buddhist monk who immolated himself in protest against the war in Vietnam sought his own death, and thus he was a sacrificer of the second type: he forwent his own life.[48] Suicide terrorism combines both meanings of sacrifice. The suicide terrorist sacrifices the lives of his enemies at the same time as he sacrifices his own life.

It has been pointed out that, in contrast to the conception of redemptive sacrifice in the Western tradition, in traditional Islam the sacrifice (an animal slaughtered according to certain rituals) serves only as a mark of obedience to the commandment of God (like the hajj), as an expression of gratitude to God (for rescue, for example), or as repentance for a sin. Hence, commentators conclude, the interpretation of Palestinian suicide terrorism as a sacrifice and redemptive martyrdom is invalid.[49] Implicit in this argument is the view of Islam as a single, consistent, pure, and self-contained body, isolated from its environment and immune to influence. This, of course, is an unrealistic conception of Islam, which in fact is no different from other religious cultures in which signs of exchange with neighboring cultures are evident, and which absorb ostensibly alien cultural elements. Thus, the Muslim Arabs of Palestine, who maintained daily interaction over generations with their brethren, the Christian Arabs, and with their enemies, the Jewish Israelis, consciously and unconsciously took bits of political and religious ideas from them, which were integrated in the weave and gradually authenticated. Just as Palestinian Arabic abounds with embedded Hebrew words organically integrated,[50] so too Palestinian Sunni Islam—even in its radical versions—was permeated for a generation or two with idioms of messianic theology originating in Shiite Islam, on the one hand, and with the Judeo-Christian tradition, on the other.[51] If the Hamas ideology of the waqf reverberates with the settlers' ideology of the Whole Land of Israel, it is no wonder that the Palestinian idea of sacrifice would be tinged with both Catholic and Zionist martyrology.[52]

The Palestinian suicide terrorist views himself as a sacrifice, and he is also seen as such by the community that sent him and received him back as its hero. As we know from the testimonies of suicide terrorists, the Palestinian organizations miss no opportunity to emphasize that the human bomb does not commit suicide, which would be condemned by traditional Islam, but that he is a shahid, of exalted value in that tradition. He gives up his life and delivers it to Allah and to Palestine as a gift. Sacrifice, as it is known to us from history, is fundamental to religion and to the building of a nation and a state. Like any sacrifice, religious or national, it is justified and effective only if the life that is willingly lost is precious. If it is not of high value, both in body and soul, its sacrifice is unworthy, and if the life had no meaning, then neither has the death. For that reason, the effort to explain the motives of the suicide terrorist as an expression of despair because of his bitter fate, although it is prevalent among sympathizers with the Palestinian cause, is not acceptable to the leaders of the suicide terrorist movements themselves. Like the sacrifice demanded in the Bible, so the Palestinian sacrifice is meant to be someone whose fate is blessed, with no blemish.

The suicide terrorist Ayat al-Akhras, a girl of seventeen, blew herself up in a supermarket in Jerusalem with an explosive charge she was carrying in a black pocketbook, leaving two dead and twenty wounded (March 2002). The next day her picture was hung on the gates of the Daheisheh refugee camp from which she came, and her testament, filmed in advance, was circulated on the Internet. According to gossip that was circulating in the area at that time, she volunteered to go on a suicide mission with a friend, who was rejected by the organization because "she was too ugly." The reliability of this information is unconvincing, but the fact is that the story was circulated widely, and that those who heard it passed it on without challenging its veracity. For many people in the West Bank it was common knowledge, as it were, that female suicide terrorists were beautiful and were chosen because of that. Behind this view lay the assumption that people sent on a holy mission against the Israelis represent the most exalted qualities of the Palestinian people. The organizations tried to convince the Palestinian public, and public opinion in Israel and elsewhere, that they did not recruit miserable people, but people outstanding in their virtues and achievements.[53] The appearance of the suicide terrorist, just like his piety, was important because as a sacrifice, he must be perfect.[54] This applied especially to female suicide terrorists. Highlighting their strengths was also intended to counter the stubborn rumors that attributed moral and other flaws to them, which would provoke severe criticism on the part of their communities and thus impel them to commit suicide in a manner that would restore some of their honor.

The female Palestinian suicide terrorist Hanadi Jaradat was the ideal Palestinian sacrifice (Maxim restaurant).[55] Not only was she an

outstanding operative, and not only did she act both from motives of
sonal revenge and also for religious reasons, but before her heroic de
she was regarded as possessing social assets and cultural capital.[56]
stood out above all the suicide terrorists before and after her in her edu
tion and professional status as an attorney. Jaradat was also conside
a good-looking woman. The Jihad presented her as modest and pious
the same time as they emphasized her beauty in all the Palestinian publi
tions after the attack. Thus on the movement's website, a photograph
the site of the attack was given a central place, with the victims' blood a
body tissues still covering the floor and clinging to the shattered furnitu
Under one of the tables in the corner of the dining room lay Jarada
severed head. In the original, uncensored photograph, taken by the Isra
police, her hair was disheveled and her face was twisted and bleeding.
the public Palestinian version of the photograph, her head was wrapped
a headscarf, her face was intact and clean, her eyes were made up, and he
lips were covered with red lipstick. The image had to honor the religious
national cause. After all, Jaradat had taken center stage and appeared a
a representative of the Palestinians before the whole world. Perish th
thought that the Israelis and others might believe the Palestinians had
sent a miserable, ugly woman, whose life was worth nothing in any event,
on a mission of suicide terrorism. Presenting the female suicide terrorist
as a success story and allusions to her beauty were meant to enhance the
impact of her sacrifice.

In the literature about suicide terrorism the Palestinian human bomb
has been discussed in terms of a sacrifice offered on the altar of liberating the land and the people from Israeli occupation.[57] But until now the
subject was not documented empirically, nor was it developed theoretically. Pointing out the sacrificial nature of suicide terrorism was not sufficient to produce new insights to explain this phenomenon. Subtle but
vital distinctions were not drawn regarding the peculiar nature of the
sacrificed object and the sacrificer, or regarding the relations between
them, and that is where an important key to the mystery of suicide terrorism is hidden.

First, it must be stated that the suicide terrorist is both his own sacrificial victim and that of his community: he sacrifices himself, and the
community also sacrifices him. And the same suicide terrorist is also
the sacrificer, both of himself and also of his enemy. In terms of ancient

sacrificial cult, the suicide terrorist is the priest who slaughters on the altar and also the offering that is slaughtered on the altar. The slaughterer is both the suicide terrorist and also the Palestinian organization that takes credit for the slaughter, and, according to a certain Palestinian argument, Israel, too, for it occupies the homeland. The suicide terrorist is the offering, but so are the Israelis whom he slaughters.

In suicide terrorism the sacrificed sacrifices, and the sacrificer is sacrificed. There are two sacrificers here: the suicide terrorist and the Palestinian collective. There are also two sacrificial victims: the suicide terrorist and the Israeli casualties of the explosion. Not only that, the two sacrificial victims—the Palestinian suicide terrorist and his target, the Israeli enemies—rise to heaven as an offering intermingled. Jesus, too, the ultimate offering, is sacrificed and sacrificer, which enables the violence that is found in his case as in all cases of sacrifice to be contained in a closed circle, thus making peace and tranquility possible. In contrast, in the sacrificial act of the suicide terrorist, the circle is burst open, because the sacrificer is not the only victim, for there are other victims, and consequently it devolves into belligerency and vengefulness.

We have already seen that the suicide terrorist's self-immolation is ritually structured, and now we see that the killing of Israelis is also ritualized. The sacrificial logic of suicide terrorism regulates its suicidal component as well as its murderousness. Palestinian terrorism is laden with associations of the duality of the sacrifice, meaning that it explicitly acknowledges the Israeli target as a sacrificial victim as well. Uda and Bashir Kharuv, the Palestinian Hebronite terrorists who murdered an Israeli farmer in the Jordan Valley, told their ISA interrogators that they intended to give the murdered man "as a present to the Palestinian nation and to Hamas for Eid al-Adha," also called the Feast of the Sacrifice.[58] As noted, the sacrificer must purify and renew himself in preparation for the ritual act, and indeed, during the days before the mission, the Kharuvs intensified their religiosity and prayed often. When they learned, during preparations for the action, that the target chosen was not only a settler but also a former senior IDF officer, they knew he was the perfect sacrificial victim. A reminder of the ritual dimension in the murders committed by the suicide terrorist organizations can be found in the instructions for action that were circulated among the four units who committed the 9/11 attack.[59] Muhammad Atta, their leader, describes the murder of the flight crew while taking over the plane as if they were sacrificial beasts whose throats would be slit in ritual fashion. It says: "Make your knife sharp (not to discomfort) your animal during the slaughter." The analogy to Jewish sacrificial rites is clear, beginning with the binding of Isaac in Genesis, through the offering of sacrifices in the Temple, as detailed in the Talmud, through the acts of murder-suicide for the sanctification of the name of God during the Middle Ages. Hence, in ritual slaughter, according to religious law, the knife must be extra sharp.[60]

In sacrificial rites, the act of slaughter sanctifies both the slaughterer and the slaughtered victim. In Middle Eastern suicide terrorism, the Palestinian killer is killed and sanctified, and at the same time the Israeli dead are also sanctified. Suicide terrorism makes the human bomb into a sacrificial victim along with those whom he kills, his sacrificial offerings. As expected, on the Israeli side the Jewish victims of Palestinian suicide terrorism are regarded as sacrificial. This is how they are presented in the official announcements of the government, in reports in the media, and especially in ZAKA discourse. Although their death is random, and of course they neither sought nor planned it, by virtue of their having been the chosen target of terrorism as Jews and Israelis they become sacrificial offerings retroactively—sacrifices to consecrate the name of God on the altar of the nation and the state. In the Islamic terrorist attack on the Jewish school in Toulouse, France, the rabbi, two of his children, and the pupil Myriam Monsonégo were murdered (March 2012). All four were buried in Israel as martyrs.[61] At the funeral, Myriam's mother said to the Haredi volunteers who took care of her body, "You are holy priests, report it in the Temple that I have brought an offering to Jerusalem, I have brought the best of my children as a sacrifice to God." This is almost a literal parallel to the evocation of sacrifice on the Palestinian side. In a ceremony in memory of the martyrs at An-Najah University in Nablus, the mother of the human bomb Imad Zubeidi (Kfar Saba, April 2001) lamented, "I gave my son as an offering to Jerusalem."

A sheikh identified with the Hamas leadership in the northern West Bank described the entry of the suicide terrorist into the area designed for the attack as "a moment of holiness."[62] The rabbis of ZAKA share this perspective. The replication of the shattered and charred Israeli bus, the iconic location of suicide terrorism, appears in Palestinian media with traits of a holy place, as it is experienced, for example, by those

who visit the intifada exhibition at An-Najah University in the West
Bank. Similarly, the discourse of the Haredi volunteers abounds with
references to the terrorism site as a holy place. More specifically, they
describe it as the heart of the holiest place for Jews—the altar where
sacrifices were offered to God. The arena of suicide terrorism is the altar,
the axis that links heaven and earth. Like any altar, this is a holy and
dangerous place, purifying and defiling. In a sermon given by the spiritual leader of ZAKA, he said, "We must approach the scene of the attack
with fear, awe, and compassion [de'khilu u'rekhimu], the way the priests
entered the Temple, because treatment of the victims of the attack is
comparable to offering a sacrifice." ZAKA activists compared the "holy
service" at the arena of suicide terrorism to a supreme test of faith, and
some of them added, "like the binding of Isaac." The restaurant, the bus
stop, or the supermarket, destroyed after an attack, are temples, which
require entry "with fear and trembling" (khil ve'ra'ada). Therefore, in
the arena, a place of extreme chaos, absolute order prevails, which, even
if it is not evident, is clear to the believers and organizes their activity
at the event. After crossing the police barriers to the area where the
victims are concentrated, the ZAKA volunteers encourage one another
by shouting, "Inside! To the Holy!" The arena is ordered in concentric
circles, and as one approaches, their focus on the sanctity increases. In
several instances one had the impression that the focus of holiness was
the suicide terrorist's head.

The market, which stands for the material and vulgar, and the restaurant, which represents abundance and leisure, are sanctified at the moment
of the explosion. The volunteers are aware of the dissonance between this
sanctity and the previously profane nature of the site. Furthermore, they
point out that many suicide attacks occurred in places contaminated by
sin and heresy, and often places of actual "lewdness," as in the attacks on
pubs and cafés, and especially at the Dolphinarium club in Tel Aviv, where
men and women danced together, consumed alcohol, and wore revealing
dress (June 2001). The Hamas movement, which began in the Gaza Strip
as puritan squads of enforcers that struck at Palestinian women in immodest dress and at parties where there was loud Western music,[63] and which
presents Israel in general as a country of sexual permissiveness, also refers
to the immorality and wantonness in the targets chosen for suicide attacks. Behind the similarity between the religious views of the Islamic and

Jewish organizations is concealed, as it were, a tacit belief that the attack is punishment from heaven for abandoning traditional values.

Ethic of Victimhood and Aggression

Palestinian suicide terrorism in Israel is somewhat reminiscent of Aztec sacrificial rites.[64] There, too, intertribal confrontation receives a ritual dimension. There, too, the killing involved stripping the body and chopping it into pieces. More important, there, too, closeness between the attacker and the victim was achieved, between the sacrificer and the sacrificed. The Aztec was connected in the most physical way to his victim, his sacrifice, by the eating of his flesh, which made them into a single body, as at the arena of suicide terrorism after the explosion. The Aztec also removed his victim's skin and wore it on his own body, to identify with him and make himself invulnerable to him. Similarly, the Palestinian human bomb wears Israeli clothing on his way to the site of the explosion. The attacker wears his victim's skin, substitutes for him and connects to him. Like the Palestinian human bomb in Israel, the attacker and the victim, or the sacrificer and the sacrifice, become one.

The Hebrew word for religious sacrifice, *qorban*, appears in the Bible. In modern Hebrew it has received additional meanings: someone who is the object of violence or of another kind of harm (such as crime, accident, war) is also a *qorban*—that is, a victim. At the scene of a suicide terrorist attack, there is of course a great deal of victimhood, and some of it is viewed as sacrificial. A person or animal that is sacrificed is always a victim, but not every victim is sacrificial. The Palestinians view the Muslim victim of suicide terrorism as a sacrifice. ZAKA regards the Jewish victims of suicide terrorism as a sacrifice. Contrary to expectations, they sometimes also attribute sacrificial qualities to the Palestinian victim.

Victimhood is occasionally highlighted as the defining politics of the twenty-first century. The Middle East conflict, like quite a few other ethnonational or religious conflicts, is characterized by discourse centered on the question of victimhood.[65] Each side emphasizes that it is the victim of the other's violence, and that it is *more* of a victim than the other. Within the conflict, victimhood becomes an asset, even a virtue, and each side is interested in having the other side and the world acknowledge that.

The regional conflict is not just over opposing strategic interests, but it concerns alleged virtue, justice, uprightness. And righteousness, in the politics of the Middle East, is equated with victimhood.[66] The result is a competition over victimhood (e.g., August 2014 Gaza War). The arena of Palestinian suicide terrorism in Israel is a microcosm of this competition. The victor, as it were, is given a pretext for claiming ethical superiority.[67] The human bomb has a claim to be the ultimate victim, and as such he bids for the moral high ground.[68] He is regarded by his supporters as more righteous than his victims, and this in turn legitimizes the act that generates further victimhood.[69]

The suicide terrorist in the Middle East is a victim on three levels: first, he is the victim of the aggression he committed against himself, his suicide. Indeed, the suicide terrorist is an aggressor against himself and is his own victim. He is also the victim of the Palestinian community and the organization, which sent him on his mission, as emphasized in Israeli propaganda. Likewise, he is the victim of Israeli policy, which occupies and humiliates him. Naturally Palestinian propaganda focuses its rhetoric only on the latter aspect of his victimhood, and this is what is useful to it in the effort to obtain a monopoly on victimhood, as opposed to letting the Israelis claim it for themselves.

Some regard the suicide terrorist as representing the fate of the Palestinian people, whose victimhood at the hands of Israel is its main characteristic. Others see the suicide terrorist as protesting against the national Palestinian fate in that he deprives Israel of the role of the victimizer and takes it upon himself. There is a certain tension in Palestinian rhetoric between presentation of the suicide terrorist as a victim, whose death is caused as a result of Israeli violence, and his presentation as someone who chose his death and in fact is not dead at all but has won eternal life.[70] This touches on the difference between victim and sacrifice. The former is passive and casts the responsibility on the other, whereas the second is active and connotes agency. The Palestinians adopt simultaneously both the identity of the object of Israeli aggression and that of the subject who seeks his death in confrontation with the Israelis, and they vacillate from one to the other.[71] Suicide terrorism partakes of them both.

Spokesmen for the Palestinian terrorist organizations have described themselves on several occasions as "victims of the victims," relating to the fact that Israel has appropriated the victimhood of the Jews throughout

history and bases its right to exist on the foundation of the monopoliza-
tion of the trauma of the Holocaust, so that, as it were, Zionist aggression
against the Palestinians is justified. The Palestinian suicide terrorist works
to inflict maximum suffering on the Israelis and at the same time to outdo
them in the suffering index. The claim to excel in suffering in itself gives it
the right to cause suffering to the other.

In the tangle of implicit competition at the arena of suicide terrorism
between the Palestinians and the Israelis one can distinguish between the
question of who wins in victimhood and who sacrifices himself more. In
fact the sides challenge each other around the issue of who is the ultimate
martyr. The ZAKA volunteers join this tacit discourse, too, by positioning
themselves up against the suicide terrorist as moral rivals.

The ZAKA volunteers enter their own victimhood and self-sacrifice in
the competition between the two sides: on one side, the Haredi community and the Jewish population of Israel, and on the other, the suicide terrorists and the community they represent. This is the background for the
frequent mention of the psychological price the volunteers pay. Exposure
to horror causes them to suffer from apathy, anxiety, and even nervous
breakdown. Some are broken and quit, and even the veterans, who have
functioned for a long time, are in need of professional therapy. Many of
them confess boastfully that they have gone crazy. When Haredi rabbis
rebuke ZAKA volunteers for abandoning the ideal of yeshiva study, they
feel the need to apologize. In a paraphrase of a well-known saying in the
Haredi community, according to which yeshiva students "die every day in
the tabernacle of the Torah,"[72] volunteers say of themselves that they "die
again and again in the arena of suicide terrorism."

Martyrdom always contains an element of provocation. The victimhood of the martyr is accompanied more or less conspicuously by aggression toward himself as well as toward those who victimize him. The
suicide terrorist strikes at the Israelis not only by killing them but also in
that he kills himself.[73] This is yet another mark of the mix-up and linkage
between attacker and victim at the scene of suicide terrorism.

Three kinds of martyrs play a role in the arena of suicide terrorism:
the human bomb, those whom he kills on the Israeli side, and the ZAKA
volunteers. All three have the qualities of Christian saints, the paradigmatic martyrs. In the course of history there has been a close connection
and mutual influence between Jewish and Christian martyrdom. See the

concurrence of the "ten killed by the empire" (prominent rabbis in ancient Palestine, who, legend has it, were tortured and killed by the Romans) and the early Christian believers, tortured and killed by the Romans, (on whose legacy the church was built), or those who "sanctified the name of God" in 1096 and the Crusaders. Inspiration from both these sources penetrated Islam as well. On the other hand, the martyrdom that developed on the Israeli side during the waves of suicide terrorism in the intifada was probably influenced by the groundswell of martyrdom (*shuhada*) among Palestinians. ZAKA especially presents the Israeli victims of suicide terrorism as martyrs—people who sanctify the name of God—and this is to create a kind of balance or canceling out of the Palestinian martyr, the shahid. In an attack that left eight Israelis dead, they described the arena as the altar on which Hannah and her seven sons consecrated themselves in death as told in the epic of heroism and martyrdom, the book of Maccabees, which was written in the Second Temple period, achieving a degree of canonization in the Apocrypha. ZAKA volunteers create symmetry between the suicide terrorist and the people he killed, as if the latter actively and consciously had sought their own death for a goal more exalted than life.

In Palestinian suicide terrorism in Israel, as in the history of relations between European Jews and Christians, one side appropriates the mythic-ritual language of the other and acts in its terms. In the martyrological thought of the three Abrahamic religions, there is a hierarchical order that places those killed by their enemies in a confrontation in the name of heaven beneath those who killed themselves in such confrontation. The ancient Christian martyrs were killed by the Romans because of their faith. Among the Jewish martyrs of two thousand and one thousand years ago, some killed themselves because of their fate, as if they were saying to their Christian rivals, "Our sacrifice is greater than yours." Now the Muslims have come and said to the Jews that their sacrifice is more exalted.

In the internal rhetoric used by ZAKA, suicide terrorism is described as a wrestling ring in which Islam and Allah, the God of deceit and murder—according to the volunteers—grapple with Judaism and the God of Israel, whose moral supremacy is, of course, unchallenged. But there are moments at the site in which a hint of insecurity about which side is stronger steals into the speech of the ZAKA volunteers. Despite everything, they find themselves dumbfounded by the terrorist's willingness to sacrifice himself and are unsettled and challenged by his act of self-immolation. They are compelled to think about the human bomb using terms such as *mesirut nefesh*, a term that in Jewish tradition means absolute devotion, and which is often used in contexts involving Jews who give up their own lives or well-being in order to save others or for the sake of heaven. ZAKA volunteers ascribe this quality to themselves as well. Despite their obvious condemnation of human sacrifice, and precisely because they take pride in their own willingness to sacrifice so much without hope of reward— what they call *hesed shel emet*,[74] true kindness, true compassion—the volunteers find themselves in doubt and feeling somewhat inferior when faced with the mutilated body of a Palestinian who volunteered to die. The arena of terrorism imposes a comparison of who went further in his ascetic piety—who performed a more sublime act of religious dedication, one that demonstrates willingness to give all, including one's life, for God or for the nation. One ZAKA activist confessed to me that, faced with the acts of suicide committed by Hamas terrorists, he found himself increasingly critical of his own Haredi society, where idealism was waning and which was unwilling to make necessary sacrifices, not even to go out to the streets to protest against the secular Zionists.

The phenomenon of contention between two groups of believers, both of which have a tradition of martyrdom, is familiar from the annals of religion, and especially of interfaith relations. When such groups encounter and contend with one another, each tries to impress and gain a symbolic victory over its rival by claiming more ardent willingness for self-sacrifice. Such was the case with the largely tacit competition between Judaism and Christianity during the Middle Ages. While medieval Christianity proclaimed that it had replaced sacrifice of flesh with spiritual sacrifice, the church also implied that Jews practiced animal sacrifice as a ritual substitute for the true sacrifice at the basis of Christianity—the sacrifice of a flesh-and-blood man on the cross. Jews responded by sanctifying the name of God, accepting death rather than forced conversion. The current macabre round of this contest is between Jews and Muslims. ZAKA volunteers go to great lengths to convince themselves of the moral superiority of preferring life to death. But they cannot help but be fascinated and impressed by death, and their encounter with the radicalism of the human bomb makes them, as it were, irresolute. The body of the human bomb seems to taunt the volunteers with the charge that they are less religious and patriotic than he was.

In the arena of suicide terrorism two opponents contend for the championship in martyrdom and for top ranking in religious virtuosity. The attack site is a stage on which to display ardent devotion, measured by a willingness to kill and to be killed. ZAKA volunteers acknowledge, grudgingly, that the man whose shredded body they see before them, for all his loathsomeness, beat them in the game of ultimate religiosity. One ZAKA rabbi admitted to me that a Muslim human bomb is measured not only by the extent of the destruction he wreaks and his effectiveness in forcing Israel to change its policies but also, and principally, by his ambition to exalt the value of self-sacrifice. According to a certain Haredi Jewish outlook, which resonates with the Islamicist attitude, the human bomb's action is less one of aggression than of sacrifice. According to this rabbi, the act of suicide terrorism is largely a matter of religious braggadocio—it seeks not only to annihilate Jews but also to humiliate them by setting a higher religious standard than they can meet.

The object of aggression, the victim, can be slaughtered ritually and provide atonement and redemption, that is to say, he can be sacrificial. The victims of suicide terrorism on both sides are set up as sacrificial by their brethren, offered on the collective national and/or religious altar. The Israelis regard the victims of terrorism, retroactively, as sanctifying the name of God, slaughtered on behalf of the ideal of Jewish existence. On the Palestinian side of suicide terrorism, death is very good from the start—justified and yearned for. Their sacrificial victim, the shahid, sought only the exalted goal of the Palestinians. Their national-religious culture is permeated by the rhetoric of active martyrology (*istishhad*). An outstanding example of Palestinian martyrdom in its double meaning—victim cum sacrifice—is found in the testament of one suicide terrorist, filmed on the eve of his mission and broadcast only after the fragments of his body had been located by ZAKA. Against the background of the Dome of the Rock the young man is seen holding a tray, and on it, in photomontage, his severed head, with Photoshopped blood flowing from the neck. He offers his head, living or dead, as a gift to Allah and the nation.[75]

Mainly in their own eyes, those responsible for Palestinian suicide terrorism appear to be the victims of their Israeli rivals, and therefore they have the privilege of victimizing (and sacrificing) them. The human bomb himself is a victim of his own aggression, and thus, paradoxically, the duality in his identity, the combination of his victimhood and his aggression, is what gives him a special moral status. The suicide terrorist is not only a victim, but also, as said above, a sacrificial offering, that is, someone who consciously and voluntarily elevates himself above his egotistical instincts for the sake of a cause more exalted than his personal, physical needs. Thus he immunizes himself against the possibility of being accused of inhuman murderousness. Someone who kills himself while killing others is ostensibly not a villain but a saint. Self-sacrifice is an excuse or retroactive legitimation even of a massacre. Because the killer has proven his ability to overcome his egotism, the relatives of the slaughtered people are denied the option of accusing him of lack of humanity.

Clarification of the relation between the two original meanings of the word "sacrifice" (offering something valuable to a god and giving up something precious) and the current, additional meaning, victim, points to a kind of ethics of deadly aggression—that is, a deep connection between self-transcendence and extreme murderousness. The desire to transcend self-centeredness can lose its way and become a conscientious mandate to eliminate the other.[76]

The human bomb's self-sacrifice, of which the Palestinian ideologists of suicide terrorism are so proud, binds the attacker to the victim and mingles them in yet another way. The aggressor (the suicide terrorist and particularly his handlers) presents himself as someone who has been forced by his enemies to commit acts against them that imply denial of his humanity, and this renders him, again, in an especially subtle way, a victim of his Israeli adversaries. This logic makes him the victim who is bursting with self-righteousness. Golda Meir, Israel's prime minister (1969–74), said, "I can forgive the Arabs for killing our children; but I can never forgive them for forcing our children to kill them." A similar sanctimonious rationale characterizes the Palestinian suicide terrorist: the aggressor feels guilty toward his victims and accuses them of forcing him to act violently against them. Then his violence increases.

The suicide terrorist creates a vital connection between murder and self-sacrifice, meaning that he links deadly violence to the exalted value of absolute self-denial and giving himself to the community. Someone who kills himself makes it easier for him to kill others. This logic relates the suicide terrorist to other cases of slaughter that appear in entirely different cultural contexts and historical circumstances. Take the People's Temple in Jonestown, for instance.[77] There nine hundred people died in an act whose ritual characteristics are hard to mistake. For most of the dead, who were both victims and sacrificial offerings, it is hard to tell whether they committed suicide or were murdered. In one sense, the "revolutionary (and vengeful) suicide" of the leader and his followers for a sacred goal were meant to weigh on the consciences of the enemies of the cause.[78] To wit, making oneself the victim of one's own violent deed is intended to disgrace and humiliate one's adversaries. In another sense, it is likely that this suicide made the massive murder possible. Similarly, the suicide of the Palestinian human bomb is also a morally presumptuous gesture, designed to provoke shame among the Israelis, and at the same time it grants the Palestinians license to slaughter Israelis.

Atonement

In the arena of suicide terrorism two parallel sacrificial rites take place: one is Palestinian-Muslim, and the other is Israeli-Jewish. The two rites allude to each other. There is mute dialogue between them and tacit cooperation. The arena is a ritual coproduction, neither intended nor, in general, conscious. It has been pointed out that both sides sacrifice themselves, at least in retrospect. It may be assumed that both sides also sacrifice the other. We have adduced some evidence regarding the Palestinian conception of the suicide terrorist as offering the Israeli casualties on the altar of the Middle East conflict. Below is evidence of a different sort, complementary and entirely unexpected: the conception of the arena of suicide terrorism as a Jewish sacrificial ceremony in which the ZAKA volunteers are the priests, while the offering, whose blood has been shed, is the suicide terrorist or the parts of his body. Thus the attacker is not only a victim but also a sacrifice from the view of the Palestinians and possibly also from that of the Jews. ZAKA men reminded me that in the Jewish canon there are precedents for offering the enemies of Israel as a sacrifice. One rabbi called my attention to a chapter of the Bible that appears to describe the work of the volunteers in the arena of terrorism: purifying the holy earth from the bodies of the enemies of the Jews who died in their territory, the location and burial of their body parts, and offering them as a sacrifice to God (*zevakh*). At the end of the passage an almost Bacchic orgy is described of drinking the blood of the victim.

> Son of man, prophesy against Gog.[79] Give him this message from the sovereign Lord: I am your enemy, O Gog. . . . I will leave you helpless. You and your army and your allies will all die on the mountains. . . . That day of judgment will come. Everything will happen just as I have declared it. . . . I will make a vast graveyard for Gog and his hordes. . . . [Then] teams of men will be appointed to search the land for skeletons to bury, so the land will be made clean again. Whenever bones are found, a marker will be set up so the burial crews will take them to be buried . . . so the land will finally be cleansed. And now, son of man . . . call all the birds and wild animals. Say to them: Gather together for my great sacrificial feast. . . . Eat the flesh of mighty men and drink the blood of princes. . . . Gorge yourselves with flesh until you are glutted; drink blood until you are drunk. This is the sacrificial feast I have prepared for you. (Ezekiel 39)[80]

The conception of the Palestinian human bomb as a sacrifice of the Jews in Israel is demonstrated by the following observation, taken from my field notebook. The event under discussion is depicted in a photograph in my possession and confirmed by several interviews.[81] For ethical and aesthetic reasons, and so as not to embarrass the people who were involved, I abbreviate and disguise details.

During the al-Aqsa Intifada, toward the end of ZAKA's "holy service" at the site of a suicide attack, some of the Haredi volunteers headed for the depths of the arena, far from the public eye, and took the severed limb of a body (which they determined categorically was that) of the human bomb. They picked up the limb, which was relatively large, raised it above their heads, and swung it around three times. While doing so they recited the following verses, which, like every Haredi, they know by heart: "This is my substitute, this is my contribution, this is my atonement, this . . . will go to death, and I will go to a good long life and peace."

No mistake can be made in identifying this text: it is a precise recitation of the ceremony known in Jewish tradition as "kaparot" (atonements), which to this day is performed on the eve of Yom Kippur by the Orthodox and ultra-Orthodox. It is assumed that this is an attenuated version of biblical sacrifice, or of the scapegoat ceremony, another way of asking forgiveness for sins by placing the guilt on another body, from the time of the Temple. In recent generations the offering that is swung in the air for atonement is a live chicken, which is then slaughtered.[82]

Most likely in the scene described above there was a certain degree of gallows humor to relieve the tension that had accumulated during ZAKA's work, and, of course, this is an expression of the volunteers' contempt for the Palestinians and anger in response to the slaughter. Perhaps there is another, deeper level, an authentic sign that points to repressed remnants of the desire to deal (legitimately) with blood and flesh, perhaps also attraction to human sacrifice. While hostile critics described this as a manifestation of mental pathology, someone close to the participants in the event suggested that it shows a true need for expiation.[83]

The ZAKA volunteers report that while they are still in the arena of terrorism, and especially when some of the casualties are children, they are very disturbed by the matter of blame: Who is responsible for the terrible killing? When the head and body parts of the suicide terrorist are found, they place the blame on him.[84] Despite a certain consolation they find in this, they are unable to free themselves from the feeling that their own sins also have a part in causing the tragedy. Hence, they attribute the power of atonement to their holy service. Still, in the presence of the killing, the question of guilt and its connection to the complex of sin and atonement continue to trouble them.

Indeed, the exegetical space is open, and several strata of interpretation are available for this rite, some charged with internal tension.[85] Often a ritual, like a dream, may have unconscious and other interpretations, which evolve into being different from the conscious and apparently reasonable interpretations. The power of a ritual can be attributable to its contradictory meanings.[86] Here I propose an interpretation shared with me by a well-read religious Jew distinguished by a consistent Haredi mentality and espousing ZAKA's outlook. He is convinced that what happens in our world has a metaphysical cause and purpose, and a religious moral. He says of himself that he is used to thinking in terms of sin and atonement, and he always tends to link them to bloodshed (murder? sacrifice?), while he automatically associates any bloodshed with sin and expiation. In the early 2000s, he disagreed with the many liberal Orthodox Jews who argued that a terrorist attack is "just an attack." In the wake of the suicide attack on bus no. 2 in Jerusalem (August 2003, twenty-three dead, almost all of them Haredi, many of them children, on their way to the Western

Wall), he joined a small number of rabbis who called for declaring a day of fasting and for a campaign of penitence, and he was contemptuous of those religious people who did not understand that they must examine their deeds and repent.[87]

In trying to explain the aforementioned kaparot ceremony performed by ZAKA, the man said this was like a "usurpation of the expiation potential" inherent in the body of the suicide terrorist. He claimed that, assuming the ZAKA volunteers are true believers, they certainly think that the blood of the rooster assures atonement, so that human blood would be even more effective, because it is closer to the thing itself. If a corpse lies before us, why should someone have died in vain? It is better to exploit the privilege that he confers for the sake of the atonement we need so badly because of our sins. The suicide terrorist is an "available sacrifice." Compare the case of Jesus, the ultimate sacrifice. Christians believe that the Messiah is so pure that his death was not needed to atone for his sins; hence he could be used as a sacrifice to atone for the multitudes who believe in him. The suicide terrorist, by contrast, is a champion sinner, and it is clear that we cannot regard his death as atoning for his sins. But his spilled blood still has the ability to atone for sins, so it is better for it to atone for our sins rather than his. The death of the Israeli victims of the human bomb, his sacrifice, will atone for their sins, and the atonement that can come from the death of the suicide terrorist can be directed away from the enemies of the Jews for the benefit of the Jews. This in fact is the logic behind the slaughter of an animal as an offering. Because of its bestiality, the sacrifice cannot atone for its sins, but for ours. It is doubtful that the suicide terrorist was a man with a pure conscience. In any event, those who recruited and dispatched him imbued him with the tormented feeling that he was a sinner in need of atonement. The mission of the suicide terrorist was meant to assure his own purification from sins, as well as purifying the sins of all the Palestinians who stood behind him. Now the Jews have come and deprived him of this atonement and appropriate the catharsis intended for the opposing community. Seizure of the suicide terrorist's expiatory power and that of the community that sent him, and its preemption and enlistment in the service of the ZAKA volunteers, punishes the Palestinians, as it were, and restores justice to the world. Blood that has been shed always has a core of atonement, and in retribution against the murderers their blood serves the atonement of their victims.

The position presented above receives an additional dimension if we take into account the possibility that the human bomb regards himself as a sinner in need of forgiveness, so that his mission to Israel would be self-cleansing for him. In any event, his Palestinian recruiters and handlers made him believe that his life was religiously and morally deficient, and that in his death he would be purified of these deficiencies. That is, suicide terrorism is a holy mission of sacrifice, which brings atonement for the terrorist and for the community from which and in whose name he set out. Now the ZAKA volunteers came and diverted the religious expiatory energy that was in the severed members of the human bomb's body in the Jewish direction. The Jews got vengeance against Islam by usurping the magical power inherent in the dismembered limbs of the suicide terrorist and directing it for the benefit of Israel.

In the arena of suicide terrorism, both sides in the bloody Middle East conflict are sacrificed by themselves or by those who dispatch them, and both sides sacrifice themselves and their enemies. The suicide terrorist sacrifices himself and, with him, those whom he kills, and thus he unintentionally sanctifies them. The Haredi volunteer sanctifies the dead Israelis and makes them into sacrificial offerings, and perhaps he sacrifices—unconsciously sanctifying—the Palestinian suicide terrorist as well.

RESEARCH STRATEGY

Sources and Methods

Informants and Collaborators

One of my most vital sources of information and insight into suicide terrorism is Salah Afifi, a Palestinian from the northern part of the West Bank. He is fifty years old, the head of a family, and he is punctilious in praying and fasting according to the tradition of Islam, though he is not deeply religious. When he was young, he was a member of the patriotic Palestinian youth movement, the Shabiba, and the head of Fatah student cell at the college where he studied. Later he became a central figure in the military wing of the organization. He was arrested by the ISA for "incitement" against the Israeli occupation. During the first intifada he was tried and sentenced to five years in prison for what was then defined as "hostile activity." While in prison he completed his BA in Israeli studies, and after his release he remained close to Fatah leadership and assumed administrative and military functions. He is a man of status and influence in the area of his residence, which has produced quite a few figures involved in suicide terrorism, including human bombs. I was in contact with him over a long period, meeting with him numerous times in conversations that lasted for hours. Our meetings usually took place in locations that can be thought of as between the lines—in a cafeteria in a shopping center that both Jewish settlers and local Arabs patronize. In calm periods, this place is a symbol of tense and fragile coexistence. While I was writing this book, a number of terrorism attacks took place there—kidnappings, shootings, and knifings. I maintain a friendly relationship with Salah.

Salah is a pseudonym. In order to guarantee his safety and avoid discomfiture for him, I concealed and blurred several details that could identify him. I was also forced to screen and disguise several identifying details about the following important source who also contributed greatly to my research. For the sake of confidentiality I will call him Uzi Banai, an Israeli, a little older than Salah, a retired ISA agent who is now a businessman. After military service in an elite unit, studies of Arabic and the Middle East at the university, and extended professional training, he served as an intelligence operative in the West Bank. In that capacity he recruited and handled Palestinian collaborators with the aim of preventing terrorist attacks or capturing the terrorists after the fact. He was a senior member of the team that solved some of the more deadly suicide terrorism cases discussed in this book, and he actively participated in interrogating several of the figures who star in various chapters. At a certain stage in his graduate studies, he attended my courses. He lives near me, and we have acquaintances in common.

The above two sources are quick thinking and knowledgeable, imaginative and courageous. They know the Middle East conflict well, including terrorism, from both sides of the barrier. Both of them were in close contact with the Palestinian community during the intifada, with suicide terrorism organizations, and with the handlers of suicide terrorists. Both of them have had occasion to know human bombs, and I do not rule out the possibility that Salah and Uzi know quite a bit about each other, and perhaps they ran into each other on one level of friction or another. Neither of them is now involved in terrorism or counterterrorism, and they are no longer part of a rigorous organizational framework, and thus they allowed themselves to speak with me with some freedom, and even with more than a hint of criticism, perhaps remorse, though I assume they hid no less than they revealed. Naturally they had personal agendas that lay behind their willingness to expose and be exposed and to take a certain risk. I had relations of mutual trust and reciprocity with both of them—relations that extended to helping them in attaining their academic aspirations.

Salah and Uzi were not just standard interviewees. In the terminology of classical anthropology, they were key informants, that is, smart and inquisitive respondents, who were authentic representatives of the phenomenon under investigation, located in a strategic position within it, giving them the ability to observe themselves and their surroundings from a certain distance.[1] They showed sincere interest in adopting the point of view of the researcher regarding the phenomenon; thus they became informal research assistants or, one might say, sophisticated collaborators. As such they provided me with reliable data from primary sources and documents of restricted circulation that I probably could not have obtained without them, and they also suggested fertile conjectures about suicide terrorism and interesting interpretations of it. They even returned to the field to ask questions, to verify information, and to provide further facts and ideas. In the end, they were torn between two loyalties: to their patriotic project and to the academic projects they were sharing with me.

I had a number of other priceless informants of various kinds, including a sheikh claiming to be familiar with Hamas functionaries and an Israeli intelligence officer with an advanced degree in political psychology. Ironically, in the course of his work, the latter may have gathered information about the former. Needless to say, neither of the two heard a word from me about the other nor could either one have known that I was in contact with the other. In addition, I had a variety of informants who were not as useful as the former, but they provided me with relevant information and insightful observations. All the interviews with them were in-depth and open-ended and took place in two series: the first was during the years of Palestinian suicide terrorism, mainly toward the end of the al-Aqsa Intifada, and the second was about ten years later, with a retrospective view. As expected, there is a difference between the findings that emerge from the two periods. The main difference was that the enthusiastic support of the Palestinian community and organizations for suicide terrorism gave way to a far more nuanced position. With the passage of years, Israeli defense people also revised the positions they had expressed while they were still in active service or shortly thereafter.[2]

The number of Palestinian interviewees was smaller than the number from the Israeli side, and the former were much harder to locate and get to speak than the latter. Intermediaries and sponsors helped me make contact with them and gain their consent to speak with me. In a number of instances I was forced to make do only with telephone contact or brief indirect exchange. The sampling of interviewees was somewhat random and based on snowballing, which began with a few well-connected people who agreed to my request and directed me to others. The representation of the Palestinian side is skewed toward areas of the West Bank close to Jerusalem, mainly the Ramallah and Hebron districts, while the Gaza Strip is not so well represented. Usually I did not need a translator, because communication with the Palestinians took place in a mixture of the three languages spoken in the region: Hebrew, Arabic, and a little English, making for a rich and fluent conversation.

Among the battery of Palestinian interviewees only two were activists in organizations involved in suicide terrorism. Many of those whom I tried to interview evaded me or flatly refused. The few who agreed to be interviewed did not do so only with the intention of transmitting a message that was important to them through me. Indeed, they tried to induce me to divulge my conclusions. In addition, I interviewed a small selection of clan members, neighbors, and acquaintances of suicide terrorists. Similarly, I interviewed an unsystematic sample of young Palestinian men whose profile was similar to that of the suicide terrorists, many of whom could have been candidates for enlistment and committing suicide terrorist attacks, and some of them seriously considered that possibility. I held multiple conversations in the street and over coffee on the subject of suicide terrorism with Palestinian opinion makers, with residents of the West Bank and East Jerusalem, and with some representatives of the Palestinian Authority, businessmen, professionals, and academics, such as sociologists, teachers, and physicians.

On the Israeli side of the barricade, in addition to ZAKA volunteers, witnesses to suicide attacks were interviewed, such as workers in restaurants where the attacks occurred, as well as survivors. Second, I interviewed senior ISA agents, including two former chiefs of the organization, the assistant head, the director of the research division, and various investigators and operators of agents. Third, I interviewed police officers and rescue workers who arrived first at the scene of attacks, including sappers, experts in criminal identification, and paramedics. I also interviewed psychologists and experts in trauma who treated survivors, and a prosecutor, pathologist, and physical anthropologist from the Israel Forensic Medicine Institute who examined the bodies of the human bombs and their victims. Fourth, people from the news media who specialized in covering suicide attacks closely throughout the intifada were interviewed. Prominent among them were Arabic-speaking journalists who were responsible for covering and commenting on events in the West Bank and Gaza Strip; and a photographer whose career took off because of his uncensored pictures of the arena of the first suicide attack in the intifada and his exclusive photographs of a series of many attacks in the center of Israel. These images brought him international publicity, making him a famous photographer of suicide terrorism and a kind of expert on the phenomenon. He made his archive available to me for this research.[3] Fifth, I interviewed a number of Israelis who happened to have long-term acquaintanceship with suicide terrorists who failed and were arrested, and with their handlers. Mainly these were jail wardens, senior and junior, in the prison service who observed the terrorists closely on a day-to-day basis and even developed intense mutual relationships with them. I also received information and insights on suicide terrorism from the directors and producers of documentary films made on the basis of mutual trust and a certain intimacy with suicide terrorists. Sixth, I learned from talented artists with penetrating and imaginative perception, who placed the suicide terrorists and their handlers at the center of their work. This includes a Palestinian who directed an interesting prize-winning feature film about suicide terrorism,[4] an acclaimed author who wrote fiction on the subject,[5] and an eminent artist whose work deals with suicide terrorism.[6] Seventh, I spoke with rabbis, educators, social workers, civil servants, and municipal workers who dealt with the results of suicide terrorism. Eighth, I benefited from the work of scholars of Islam, the Arab world, and Palestinian society in the social sciences and humanities.

Interviewing Demons

Three categories of interviewees whose importance cannot be doubted are missing from the list presented above: (1) suicide terrorists whose attacks were thwarted, and who were captured and imprisoned; (2) the parents of suicide terrorists; and (3) candidates for suicide terrorism.[7] The results of interviews with all the above have already been extensively reported in the literature.[8] Furthermore, these three substitutes for an interview with suicide terrorists who completed their missions and blew themselves up is not free of methodological problems. The validity of the interviews with failed terrorists is dubious for two reasons. First, they might share certain traits, because of which they failed and which distinguish them from real suicide terrorists. That is to say, there is no assurance that they are a representative sample. Moreover, they are in an apologetic situation, which impels them to present themselves in a way that provides them with an alibi with regard to their fellow prisoners, the organization, and the community, lest they be regarded as cowards and traitors. This leads to the second problem, which is connected to their being in prison, where they are subject to obedience to the official party line of the organization, or to the desire to please the Israeli authorities.

In the testimony of the suicide terrorists who failed and were interviewed in prison, one notes two opposing tendencies. A minority of them report they were solicited by the organizations' assistants, so as to deflect some of the blame from themselves and arouse sympathy among the Israelis. This tendency stood out mainly in the first stage after their capture. However, once they were imprisoned, most of them tended to exaggerate the motive of volunteering, in order to enhance their image in the eyes of the Palestinians, so their failure would be forgiven.

It is also hard to ignore the unreliability of interviewing the imprisoned entrepreneurs of suicide terrorism. When asked about the way they made contact with the human bombs they dispatched they tend to respond that the suicide terrorists "volunteered" for the mission and sought to reach the functionary of their own free will and on their own initiative. Among researchers there is a difference of opinion as to the relative proportion of suicide terrorists who actually volunteered as opposed to those who were conscripted after a systematic process of solicitation, though there is no doubt that a large number belong to the latter category. The entrepreneurs of suicide terrorism deny this fact, mainly in order to exonerate themselves from moral responsibility for what could be regarded as cruelly exploitative behavior, and to support the purity of the image of the Palestinian suicide terrorism project.

Several studies based on such interviews suggest that the bias of both the suicide terrorists and their handlers would probably be toward diminishing their responsibility and appeasing the Israeli side—the prison guard and the interviewer—and thus perhaps to lighten their punishment and improve that attitude toward them. Consequently, failed terrorists might report that at some stage on their way toward the target a feeling of remorse arose within them, causing them to be captured. I would like to point out the possibility for bias in the opposite direction. Rather than using the interviews to address their enemies, in whose hands lay their fate as prisoners, they were speaking to their brothers, on whom their image as manly patriots depended. The suicide terrorist and his handlers direct their words toward their colleagues and superiors in prison and outside it, to their organization, and to the community from which they came and to which they hope to return. As their verdicts have already been issued, and they can expect to be in prison for many years, they have nothing to lose with regard to the Israelis. On the contrary, extremist expressions will be useful to them if they are released early, as they wish, following a prisoner exchange agreement.[9] Therefore, they could well exaggerate their commitment to suicide terrorism and to the Palestinian cause, attributing their failure and capture to a technical foul-up. I tend to agree with ISA investigators who doubt the value of making people involved in suicide terrorism talk in prison. They argue that anything that failed to emerge in the interrogation immediately after their arrest is no longer authentic, and the longer the time of imprisonment, the smaller the value of their testimony. The prisoner constructs a new and improved story about the circumstances of his involvement in suicide terrorism and his motivations. In the end, the difference between the testimony of the suicide terrorist and the propaganda of the organization becomes minimal.

As prison officers report, during their many years of imprisonment, the Palestinian terrorists talk and think just politics. With time, their testimony is recomposed and transmuted from a personal story to an ideological manifesto.[10] At the height of the wave of suicide terrorism, the Israeli minister of defense asked permission from the ISA to interview imprisoned suicide terrorists with the aim of understanding what lay behind their dream to be shahids. Although in the past he had been an experienced interrogator of prisoners, spoke Arabic, and was a good conversationalist, he emerged in frustration, because he learned nothing that he could not have known from reading the prejudiced Palestinian press.[11] There is a huge difference between the words of suicide terrorists who are interviewed by Israeli or Western scholars and their words in the interrogation rooms or in free conversation with other prisoners. Only in the latter case can an open confession emerge, such as that of the suicide terrorist who reports in a matter-of-fact way what preceded his departure on the suicide mission: "Life is a headache. . . . I just once thought before the action, I thought to myself, what would happen if I went on a mission like that? As a joke. And by chance, after a short time, my cousin came to me, and suggested that I should do the deed."[12]

There is quite a bit of sound research based on interviews with the parents of suicide terrorists or on their answers to questionnaires. These research methods are naturally prevalent among Palestinian scholars. Because of the relatively small and well-defined dimensions of the phenomenon of suicide terrorism, there is no need for a sampling, and the entire population of suicide terrorists can be included. The problem with this method is that the credibility of the interviewees is doubtful, given their tendency to present their dear one in a favorable light and make the human bomb's motivations appear honorable.[13] In the literature, the voice of families testifying to their son's personal weaknesses or any kind of failure is rarely heard. Similarly, no family describes itself as underprivileged or dysfunctional. The families on whose testimony about themselves the research is based seldom express criticism of suicide terrorism or of dispatching their sons. Emphasis of the commitment of the suicide terrorists and their families is intended to ensure their upgraded social status and the material benefits extended to them by the organizations.

Interviews with the families of human bombs, like interviews with imprisoned suicide terrorists and with spokesmen for the organizations, hardly penetrate beyond the nationalistic and religious clichés, repeated ad nauseam. The interviews drown in a sea of set formulations and familiar slogans. The hardest task is to extricate oneself from the prevailing narrative, which is dictated, almost like the recorded testament.[14] Tellingly, two suicide terrorists, a teenager and a sixty-four-year-old grandma, use the exact same words to express their motivation.[15]

A third category of interviewees that could contribute to research into suicide terrorism includes those who might be called would-be human bombs, that is, youngsters from the Palestinian community who declare that they yearn to embark on a suicide mission, and even some who claim that they were already chosen to go on such missions. They gather in typical situations, such as among the enthusiastic people in the crowd at the movement's victory celebrations or the funerals of shahids. They are sometimes sent to be interviewed by the organization, giving reason to suspect their authenticity. Most likely they were not really on the path toward enlistment as suicide terrorists or serious candidates. If they were, they would not be so easy to locate or so willing to reveal themselves. Those who are eager to tell any and all about the wonders of suicide terrorism, who speak at length about the details of the actions, and who boast to strangers that they have been promised all the good things that suicide terrorism supplies do not represent human bombs, and researchers should lend little credence to their testimony.

This survey of the aforementioned flaws is not meant to deny the value of research into suicide terrorism based on the above prevalent methods, but rather to call for a cautious and critical reading of their conclusions. In the present study of suicide terrorism, I made no effort to carry out such research again, mainly because in the previous decade several studies had already been done based on these methods, and their conclusions are widely available. In any event, by now most of the intercepted suicide terrorists have been freed from prison and sent to the Gaza Strip or to other countries where it is difficult to locate them.[16]

There have been innumerable studies of the demographic, biographical, and personality characteristics of the typical Palestinian suicide terrorist during the fifteen years of suicide terrorism in Israel, but very few are based on reliable empirical research. In my work I chose to rely mainly on two studies that stand out over the others in the solidity and methodicalness with which their authors relate their argumentation to firsthand research that draws on data from primary sources.

The first important work that I considered to be worthy of use for scholarship of suicide terrorism is the unpublished doctoral dissertation by Bassam Banat, entitled "Palestinian Suicide Martyrs: Facts and Figures from the Point of View of Their Families."[17] It is poorly written, its scholarly apparatus is careless, and its conceptual, analytical, and comparative level barely exists. In addition to its theoretical shallowness, it also lacks objectivity. The PhD candidate did not even pretend to conceal his identification with the Palestinian cause and his admiration for the suicide terrorists. Nevertheless, this study contains an assemblage of data that is rare in its authenticity and comprehensiveness. Appended to the dissertation are the results of a field study that presents almost verbatim the testimony of the families of two hundred suicide terrorists who spoke with Palestinian research assistants in their homes, in addition to background information about the suicide terrorists that was supplied by the social service department of the Palestinian Authority, as well as other Palestinian sources to which the researcher had direct access. This is a resource from which, with more skillful and critical treatment, pure gold could have been mined.

The second study that provided me with a rich reservoir of particularly trustworthy primary data about Palestinian suicide terrorists, as well as a source of inspiration for thinking about suicide terrorism, was *Driven to Death: Psychological and Social Aspects of Suicide Terrorism*.[18] The author, Ariel Merari, a well-trained experienced psychologist with a refined research agenda, is cautious and fair in his conclusions. His research focuses on a considerable number of suicide terrorists who failed, were imprisoned in Israel, and were interviewed by a team of qualified psychologists, assisted by specialists in Palestinian affairs.[19] The results achieve soundness and an interesting twist in comparison to a sample of imprisoned terrorists who were not involved in suicide missions and young men with similar demographic characteristics in the general Palestinian population. In addition, the book presents the results of professional personality testing administered to the two imprisoned samples. Though I differ from Merari's theses on some matters, I find his results and discussions valuable.

Another significant contribution to my work was a third research project on Palestinian suicide terrorism the results of which, for reasons that I was unable to ascertain, are classified to this day. Indeed, its very existence remains a secret. I was told about the findings of this project by one of its directors, who included Israeli police officers, psychologists, criminologists, and Arabists. They took a sampling of about thirty suicide terrorists in prisons and held partially structured interviews with them, in addition to the administration of a series of projective personality tests (TAT, etc.). This research was conducted in circumstances and with methods that differed from Merari's, but its conclusions are very similar and corroborate his findings. The trustworthiness of this research is quite high, seeing that it was the first of its kind and took place when the suicide terrorists had only been imprisoned for a short time and were still fresh and relatively unguarded.

I obtained demographic characteristics of the suicide terrorists from additional sources. Their findings differ slightly from each other, and in light of their flaws and advantages, it is possible to take a rough average among them. Prominent are the findings of the US political scientist Robert Pape and his Suicide Attack Database (CPOST), based mostly on a survey of press reports.[20] Pape's study suffers from lack of familiarity with the details of specific cases, their operational circumstances, and their cultural context, but it is comprehensive, its perspective is comparative, and it is statistically sophisticated. Also valuable are the publications of the International Institute for Counter-Terrorism at the IDC Herzliya.[21] Another worthy source is the research conducted by Israeli security forces, mainly the ISA, as well as that of institutes connected with the defense and governmental establishment.[22] They are based on covert and overt intelligence, and their results are only partially accessible.

Contending with the Difficulties of Investigating Suicide Terrorism

All forms of terrorism are difficult to research. This is mainly because terrorism is characterized both by physical risk and by secrecy, as well as by irregularity in time and place. Since it is unpredictable and inaccessible, it cannot be directly observed, and it is hardly possible to interview a few of the activists involved in it. Even if in some cases the researcher manages to gain access to the areas of armed conflict, making direct contact with people connected with terrorism, chances are they will impose censorship on the truly significant substance, and it will be difficult to estimate the reliability of the information. The classification of authentic materials applies both to the terrorists and to the counterterrorism agents. Because information about terrorism is liable to endanger the lives of people and impair the achievement of critical political and organizational aims, willingness to be interviewed, on both sides of the barricade, arouses the researcher's suspicion that people are trying to exploit him and achieve goals of which he is not cognizant or which he is not interested in advancing. Moreover, the researcher's respect for the secrecy of his informants prevents him from indicating his sources in his publications with their real names and identifying details, so readers are unable to evaluate the credibility of the research.

It is also difficult to research terrorism because the subject is particularly charged and controversial. The fact that the phenomenon is the focus of a dramatic and violent conflict in which the stakes are high can send the research down the slippery slope toward romanticism and sensationalism or cause the researcher to take sides, at least to express implicit judgment. One result of this methodological obstacle, especially against the background of the lack of precise, hard facts, is the abundance of mythical elements in the literature and reliance on unconfirmed data, such as speculations presented as if they were reflections of reality.[23]

Research into the unique case of suicide terrorism is far more difficult. Students of suicide terrorism must overcome the fact that the central figures in this phenomenon cannot be located or contacted before their death, and then they simply disappear. The difficulties of researching suicide terrorism explain the disproportion between the abundance of publications on the subject and those that are based on responsible, empirical research. Most of the bibliographical items on suicide terrorism are not based on field research but instead process secondary data, unverified and imprecise data. Recently a few pioneering books on terrorism field-research methods have appeared.[24] Although these are useful, they tend to ignore the special case of suicide terrorism, with one or two exceptions.[25]

To gather data beyond that which had been collected through interviewing and to validate it, I used further research methods, some of them unique to my project. One method was observation. First of all, I went to see many places where suicide attacks had occurred, shortly after the event. I examined almost all the restaurants and cafés in Jerusalem that had been chosen as targets by suicide terrorists. On some occasions I was able to speak with the owners of the places, as well as workers and neighbors, some of whom had witnessed the explosion. I also went to some of the villages, camps, and cities from which the suicide terrorists came, such as Hebron and its vicinity, and sites where they were conscripted and dispatched. I also observed the routines at the checkpoints where the suicide terrorists had crossed, and I followed the route of their movement toward the target and their penetration of it. Naturally I rode many

Figure 6. Handkerchief secretly illustrated by an activist in the al-Aqsa Martyrs' Brigade from Gaza, who was caught by the ISA and imprisoned for taking part in a terrorist campaign against Israel. The image depicts the sacred Islamic shrines in Jerusalem, Fatah's flag and insignia, lines from the Koran, a map of the Whole Land of Palestine, and a dagger symbolizing revenge and armed resistance to Israeli occupation. It was given to me by the prisoner who painted it, clandestinely, over the prison bars, following extensive conversations. (Photo: Gideon Aran private collection)

times on buses that had been targeted by suicide terrorists, making sure to conduct my observations on the exact route and schedule of the earlier attacks. My experience in riding buses 14 and 18 in Jerusalem, where several human bombs had blown themselves up during the intifada, contributed to the feeling of closeness to suicide attacks. The same stops, same hour, repeatedly.

Another research method was content analysis of written and electronic documents, mainly the websites of the Palestinian organizations, such as the martyrs' section of the al-Qassam website, published by the information office of the military arm of Hamas in Gaza. Dozens of testaments recorded by suicide terrorists as well as pamphlets in their memory were an important source. Official Palestinian publications were interesting, despite the distinct element of propaganda they contained.[26] The annual reports on Palestinian terrorism issued by the ISA research branch were also surveyed. Rich material was found in the indictments and verdicts of military courts in the trial of suicide terrorists, their dispatchers, and their accomplices. I found of special interest rare material that I reached in an indirect way: a number of authentic transcriptions of ISA interrogations of Palestinians who played key roles in suicide missions.

I also analyzed the stills and videos of press photographers, directors of documentaries, and security cameras. They provide rich information about the arena of suicide terrorism in real time. Mainly I was given access

Figure 7. Image posted at the entrance to Daheisheh refugee camp, depicting Ayat al-Akhras, shahida (female martyr), the perpetrator of the Jerusalem supermarket suicide attack, launched by the Fatah military arm, two dead, March 31, 2002. She was eighteen years old, a senior at Bethlehem High School, sister to eight siblings, from a poor refugee family. Her father was suspected of collaboration with the ISA. (Photo: Courtesy of Ronni Shaked)

to an exceptional trove of sixty-seven uncensored and unedited close-up video clips documenting the immediate aftermath of suicide attacks. I also possess copies of dozens of items from the private visual archives of a leading photographer who documented eight suicide attacks, as well as items from members of the rescue forces and artifacts connected to suicide terrorism.[27]

Of course, I also made use of secondary sources. In addition to scholarly literature, I referred to printed and electronic press reports from 2000–10. I surveyed material touching on suicide terrorism on both sides of the barricade, mainly the Hebrew daily newspapers *Haaretz* and *Yedioth Ahronoth*, as well as the IDF website in Israel, and the popular *Al-Quds* and the publications of *Wafa*, the news agency of the Palestinian Authority. I also watched countless broadcasts dealing with suicide terrorism on Israeli and Arabic television networks. After all, the media is an integral part of terrorism. I found useful information in resources collected by the International Institute for Counter-Terrorism in Herzliya and the Chicago Project on Security and Terrorism. I was not the first to gain insight on suicide terrorism from the hundreds of posters, murals, museum exhibits, video art, and theater performances dealing with suicide terrorism on the Palestinian side.[28] I was especially interested in three documentary films about Palestinian suicide terrorists,[29] as well as works of fiction that focused on suicide terrorism.[30]

A significant part of research on suicide terrorism, including Palestinian terrorism in Israel, was done by US and European scholars. The present research has been done by a native, for better or worse. As an Israeli citizen who was born in Palestine/Israel and who has lived ever since in Jerusalem, I have followed the Middle East conflict closely for many years and have been involved in it in many ways.[31] I speak the local language, am familiar with the local mentality, am connected socially and institutionally with the local people, and I enjoy access to local sources and insiders. Hence I have privileged knowledge and sensitivity to the delicate nuances of the phenomenon under investigation. True, certain obstacles stand in the way of a local person. Whether they want to be or not, locals are a party in the conflict, and this can impair their objectivity. I hope that my identification with the role of scientist and my fidelity to professional codes overcame all the sympathies and antipathies that naturally clung to me, and that the research is fair.

Despite the problems it entails, being part of the phenomenon under investigation, if only as an object of it, can also be a source of insight. During the intifada and the rise of suicide terrorism, I underwent moments of distress and anger, pain and confusion. I was afraid for the fate of my children, who attended schools in town. I seldom frequented central places of entertainment. I was even tense in the corridors of the university campus where I work. Finding myself in the eye of a violent storm, I could draw material for research into suicide terrorism from my personal experience, which would add to interviews and observations. Fieldwork sometimes placed me in threatening and baffling situations such as meetings with strangers at night, alone, among a hostile population. In these situations I learned something about terrorism beyond what I heard from informants and read in my office. One might say that, among my research methods, I also used what is called participant observation. That was true, too, of my work with ZAKA at the arena of suicide terrorism toward the end of the intifada.

ZAKA volunteers played a key role in the research into suicide terrorism presented in this book. First, it was because of them that I was able to reach the scene immediately after the explosion. Thus I could observe the results of suicide terrorism without intermediaries, in order to form conjectures about the circumstances and causes of suicide terrorism. Second, from my observations at the arena, I learned that ZAKA is an organic part of the scene of Palestinian suicide terrorism in Israel and an active element in it. The study of ZAKA and its activity at the scene of the attack proved to be vital for understanding suicide terrorism in its full extent and complexity. Third, ZAKA volunteers offered interesting interpretations of the phenomenon of suicide terrorism from their unique and surprising perspective, which proved to be a fertile source of other insights into suicide terrorism. Fourth, I discovered that ZAKA had a complex relationship with the suicide terrorist, the present-absent person at the arena. Observation of the subtle interaction between ZAKA and the suicide terrorist provided me with hints about the latter.

I had a particularly intense connection with two central ZAKA field activists in Jerusalem.[32] There was not a single suicide terrorist attack in Jerusalem where one of the two was not profoundly involved. I also had close contact with heads of the organization and their associates,[33] and with the rabbis who gave them spiritual and Halachic authorization.[34]

Figure 8. Rabbi Bentzi Oiring, the chief of operations and leader of Jerusalem ZAKA squads (standing at center), at his daughter's wedding, surrounded by his young, ultra-Orthodox followers, 2005 (the author of this book is on the left).
(Photo: Gideon Aran private collection)

Similarly, I accompanied the activities of about fifteen other permanent rank-and-file members, and I interviewed them.

Though I did not conceal my identity as a social scientist from the ZAKA volunteers, and I shared with them my research objectives, and although I was unusual among them, particularly as a secular, liberal Jew, they accepted me with cordial openness. I mingled with them, gained their trust, and received their cooperation. I came to be on excellent terms with some of them. They invited me to attend lectures, consultations, briefings, sermons, and prayers in the organization headquarters, as well as to join them in their family's meals and weddings. They made the archive of the organization and their private collections available to me.[35] I held conversations with them for hour after hour, especially at night, in their homes, in the yeshivas where they studied the Torah, in their places of work, and on long trips. Some of them told me that they found therapeutic value in their open exchanges with me, helping them to cope with the horror they experienced. On one occasion they went out of their way to call me in especially so that I could observe an event they thought would interest me. On another occasion, when the police prevented me from entering the scene, they showed resourcefulness, placing a blood-soaked roll of paper in my hand and shoving me in. Once I arrived on the scene before ZAKA volunteers and helped them find their way.

More on ZAKA and Suicide Terrorism

This book adopts a somewhat Foucauldian approach: to follow the *resistance* in order to get a practical analysis of power mechanisms. It traces two rival strategies of action that confront each other and precondition each other, conflicting practices, each of which shapes the field of possible behavioral patterns open to the other side.

To enhance our understanding of suicide terrorism we divert the focus from only the terrorists and their act to examining their complementary activity, mainly that of ZAKA. Inferences about suicide terrorism can be drawn by observing the work of those who deal with the consequences of suicide terrorism and who labor to undo the havoc wrought by the attack and restore the status quo.

ZAKA's operations constitute a mirror image of the operation of the human bomb. Researching ZAKA's activity is like a reconstruction in negative, so to speak, a retroactive observation of the suicide terrorism act. ZAKA's implicit understanding of the lethal arena, expressed in its ritual behavior on site as it cares for the victims, is a reservoir of insightful comments on the human bomb project.

I observed ZAKA volunteers at the arena of Palestinian suicide terrorism as they repeated, over and over again, with slight variations, the same pattern of behavior that can only be interpreted as a sorting process, one of division, separation, and distancing. Then I gained the impression that these actions are analogues, extensions, and complements of the actions of the Israeli security agencies. At a more advanced stage I considered the possibility that the actions of the suicide terrorist were truly the opposite of those of ZAKA and the Israeli security agents. Hence it was likely that the patterns of behavior on both sides of the blood-soaked conflict correspond with one another and react to each other.

Several insights emerge from observing the conduct of ZAKA. First, the Israeli response to Palestinian suicide terrorism is not wholly pragmatic but also symbolic or ritualistic. Second, at the level of practice, the pragmatic and symbolic responses—represented by the Israeli defense establishment and Haredi ZAKA, respectively—coincide. ZAKA—as well as the IDF and ISA—identifies, separates, and removes. This is done in reaction to the strategy of the human bomb and his dispatchers, which is clearly to disguise, infiltrate, and blend, a strategy that in itself can be seen as a counterstrategy to the general Jewish-Zionist strategy of demarcating borders and erecting walls—in other words, insulating and disengaging.

The barrier that the suicide terrorist must cross separates the occupied territories from the occupying state, and it is truly a wall between Palestinian distress and frustration and the yearned-for fulfillment of a dream. A suicide terrorist who was mortally wounded, sent back to his home, and, in time, against all expectations, recovered, reported his feeling when he was chosen to set out on a suicide terrorist mission: "It is as if a very high impenetrable wall separated you from paradise. . . . So by pressing the detonator you can immediately open the door to heaven." Now, heaven is represented by the imagined reality of the afterlife, as described in the Muslim religious tradition (seventy-two virgins, rivers, birds, a place of honor next to the throne of the Prophet, etc.), and it can also be represented as the earthly reality on the other side of the Green Line, within the boundaries of the State of Israel, as seen on the television screen (material abundance, a lively urban atmosphere, liberated women in revealing clothing, advanced technology). These two fantasized images mix and substitute for one another.

By portraying the human bomb as acted on, not just acting, and ZAKA as an active agent in the fabric of suicide terrorism, we arrive at a vision of the arena where various actors indirectly cooperate. It is not a rigid, one-dimensional, hierarchical dichotomy of aggressor and his target. Victimizer and victim, Palestinian and Israeli—the conquered and the conqueror in postcolonial terms, like Nietzsche's master and slave—grip each other. Terrorism and counterterrorism are an organic unit, and ZAKA not only copes with the results of terrorism, but it is also an essential component of the cycle of violence, an integral part of the regional reality of bloodshed.

9

CONCLUDING COMPARATIVE AND ANALYTICAL NOTES

Five Levels of Explanation

It is possible to describe and analyze suicide terrorism on five different levels. First is the individual level, which addresses the personality of the human bomb and his dispatcher, their biographical data, their interaction with each other and with their surroundings, and their activities as terrorists. Second, there is the level of the organization that initiates and carries out suicide attacks, including the structure and functioning of the organization, the ideological, strategic, and operational aspects of the organization, its leadership, the composition of its personnel, finances, logistics. Third, the level of the community, meaning the local milieu and its typical attitudes toward suicide terrorism, the family, the village, or the refugee camp, educational institutions, means of communication, and other components of the environment in which suicide terrorists and their organizations function. Fourth comes the cultural level of ethos and mythos, which refers to ideas and ideals that guide the overall collective to which the individual and community belong. Discussion on this level touches on worldviews, moral principles, ceremonies and customs that typify the nation, the region, and the imagined community of the suicide terrorist, and especially the religious background of suicide terrorism. Beyond the Palestinian community that has adopted the suicide terrorist, he also acts within a broader framework of two circles: the Arab and the Muslim. Common to both of them is a broad range of values and norms in the context of which suicide terrorism is to be understood, such as patriarchalism and tribalism. Common to these is the global jihad movement, of which Palestinian suicide terrorism is a radical offshoot. The fifth level is that of the particular historical circumstances or the international, political, social, and economic situation under whose sway suicide terrorism grows, by which it is influenced, and to which it responds. A full explanation of suicide terrorism should refer to factors such as poverty and density in the Palestinian territories, the schisms among the organizations, and other characteristics of the situation. Among these, primary significance is given to the hundred years of violent conflict between Israelis and Palestinians, the tribulations of the occupation since 1967, and, of course, the behavior of the opposite side—that is, the State of Israel in general and its counterterrorism agencies in particular.

All five of these levels of discussion are important, but none is sufficient for a comprehensive and exhaustive explanation of suicide terrorism. Among the various levels there is partial overlap, influence, and mutual dependence. Certain data and arguments can be examined in terms of several levels, and the decision as to what category to place them in depends on the theoretical context, or may be arbitrary. The connection among the levels can be understood by means of a theoretical paradigm such as the "value added model," originally proposed as an explanation for the emergence of social movements and then applied to suicide terrorism.[1] The literature on suicide terrorism acknowledges the limitations of reduction to a mono-causal explanation, and several researchers have presented useful proposals for discussing suicide terrorism on its various levels.[2]

Observations that can be placed in the framework of the discussion of the five levels of explanation appear in earlier chapters of this book. I will add a few comments on this below, in selective fashion. Let us begin with the level of the organization. In fact, there are no exclusively suicide terrorism organizations in the full sense of the term. Palestinian suicide terrorism, like suicide terrorism elsewhere, is only one of a variety of practices employed by religious and national resistance organizations like Hamas. These may be large bodies with many branches, sophisticated and charismatic leaders, and a broad popular base. They specialize in several areas of terrorism and guerrilla warfare along with suicide terrorism. To ensure public support, some of the organizations develop social projects, from free health services to the provision of welfare benefits. They might open schools, pave roads, and install sewers. In certain cases, for the benefit of their military and civilian initiatives, a complex organizational machine is established, including effective financial and indoctrination divisions. However, those of the organization's activists who focus on suicide terrorism are not necessarily an organic part of it. The latter maintain strict compartmentalization, and this is not only in order to ensure information security.

Nevertheless, the conclusion that emerges from the data presented in the book is that the common claim that for suicide terrorism to be effective it must possess a centralized and hierarchical organizational structure, an efficient division of labor, an orderly decision-making process, and an authoritative leadership should be qualified. Here is a sample of the relevant findings of my research: the connection between the suicide terrorist and the suicide terrorism organization is sometimes superficial, short, and random. A local suicide terrorism cell mediates between the organization and the suicide terrorist. The cell is semi-independent in its operational functioning and sometimes in its strategic conception as well. Often such a unit is ephemeral, established for launching one or two suicide terrorist attacks, after which it disappears with no continuity. As a result of the effective pressure on the suicide terrorism organizations exerted by the ISA and the IDF, they were forced to adopt a flexible and decentralized structure, in which the secondary units are rather autonomous and organized on a local ad hoc basis. This move was made possible by the improvement in means of communication, mainly the Internet and cellular phones. Because of the separation between the suicide terrorism cells and the chiefs of the organization and their organic connection with elements in their nearby surroundings—student unions, for example—in a number of suicide attacks there was cooperation between organizations known to be competitors, such as Hamas and the Jihad, and even Hamas and Fatah. At the same time, there were a number of suicide attacks in which the identity of the responsible organization was a matter of bitter dispute and remained a mystery. Moreover, inner tensions appeared more than once in Palestinian suicide terrorist organizations. The press has reported the conflicts between the political and military leadership, while conflicts between the local cells and the head leadership have yet to be reported. In some cases local activists initiated and committed suicide attacks without the approval of their superiors, and even in violation of explicit orders. At the same time, the suicide terrorism cells remained in close contact with local entities outside the organization, such as clans and the village notables. These factors did not always promote suicide terrorism. In some cases locals confronted the suicide terrorism entrepreneurs, preventing them from enlisting suicide terrorists and launching attacks.

When the decision to commit suicide attacks is made and the act is carried out spontaneously by mid-level people who are dispersed on the ground, this can be seen as something more authentic, a bit rebellious, making the organization slightly superfluous and diminishing the importance of the role of the organizational elite.[3] This is the background for the suggestion made by prominent scholars of suicide terrorism to shift the discussion from formal organizational terms to discussion in terms of social networks. The work of Ami Pedahzur and Arie Perliger made a seminal contribution on this matter.[4] Based on the Palestinian case in the intifada, they developed a model that presented suicide terrorism as conditioned by social frameworks, which are only loosely organized. The theoretical emphasis in the conception of local suicide terrorism networks, which are diffuse and tentative, is on the transition from a hierarchical, authoritative structure to a formation that is "under-structured, horizontal, and democratic." The leaders of the organization do not play a central role in suicide terrorism networks but rather hubs—local, not necessarily well known—that stand out in their large number of social connections and their familiarity with nearby surroundings. Empirical research points to a correlation between the functioning of these hubs and the number of effective suicide attacks. Despite the prominence of Nablus in militant resistance to the Israeli occupation and its deep involvement in terrorism, fewer suicide attacks were launched from Nablus than from Jenin and Tulkarm. In Nablus, the resistance organizations acted in a centralized, hierarchical organizational manner, whereas in Jenin and Tulkarm, suicide terrorism was initiated by dense networks and a number of talented hubs. The recruitment of suicide terrorists is also presented in terms of networks. The recruits have few, weak connections with other members of the network, and their contribution to the functioning of the network is minimal. Thus their disappearance will not prevent the continued existence of the network.

Let us now address the community level, which refers to the Palestinian population in the West Bank and the Gaza Strip, as well as secondary communities and social networks in the cities, villages, and refugee camps, including university students, worshippers in the mosques, sports club members, coffee shop regulars, childhood buddies, colleagues at work, and neighbors. During the intifada, public opinion, influenced by the press and television, and the political and religious leadership encouraged suicide terrorism. In the Palestinian community, with its emphatic collectivist ethos, public support for the policy of suicide terrorism gave the organizations legitimacy, prestige in comparison to competing organizations, and also financial resources and logistical and tactical help (like offering hiding places, carrying messages, keeping lookouts, informing). Above all, in the Palestinian community social pressures emerged that made possible the formation of a reservoir of potential suicide terrorists who were relatively easy to recruit. The Palestinian community gave suicide terrorism such an intense and total network of socialization and moral, organizational, and material support that counterterrorism ISA agents agreed that in the context of the Palestinian-Israeli conflict, the term "lone wolf terrorism" had become meaningless. Between 2000 and 2007 almost no Palestinians were indifferent to suicide terrorism, and there were only a very few open opponents. There is no other instance of suicide terrorism in the world that enjoyed such favorable public opinion. Unlike the absolute majority of Palestinians who supported suicide terrorism at the time and adopted it as a focus of inspiration and pride, such that it became a unifying force and a definer of identity, in all the other Muslim societies where suicide terrorism was a conspicuous presence it aroused the opposition of a solid majority and became a bone of contention that divided the community.

The popularity of Palestinian suicide terrorism is reflected in public opinion polls. The results are repeated in various studies that indicate that the support reached a fantastic peak of 70–75 percent popularity.[5] Even after Palestinian suicide terrorism ceased and Palestinian public support for it declined, there was still a majority of 62 percent of Muslim Palestinians who responded positively to the question of whether suicide terrorism is "often or sometimes" justified to defend Islam from its opponents.[6] Even as late as 2013 the proportion of those supporting suicide terrorism was the highest by far in the Muslim world[7] (about half, compared to 3% in Pakistan, 8% in Nigeria, and about 33% in Lebanon).[8] Of course, the support for suicide terrorism in the Palestinian population fluctuated. After spectacular success in suicide attacks, support rose (Park Hotel, March 2002, 72%; Maxim Restaurant, October 2003, 74.5%), whereas after severe Israeli retaliation, support declined (Defensive Shield Operation, May 2003, 55%).

Palestinian support for suicide terrorism changes not only on the time axis but also according to various populations. Young people favor suicide terrorism more than adults, students and graduates of universities more than the less well educated, and, surprisingly, women more than men.[9] Similarly, as expected, supporters of Hamas are more in favor of suicide terrorism than supporters of Fatah, the Gazans more than residents of the West Bank, residents of refugee camps more than those living in large cities.[10] Palestinian support for suicide terrorism has local characteristics, with even higher resolution. Of course in areas where there is a Christian presence there is less support than in purely Muslim concentrations of population, and especially if they are known to be more religious. This emerges in the comparison of (largely Muslim) Bethlehem to the neighboring (largely Christian) Beit Sahur. For this and other reasons, among the cities of the West Bank, there is more support for suicide terrorism in Hebron than in Nablus, although the latter is no less militant and involved in general terrorism. Jenin, which is not the largest Palestinian city, is regarded as the capital of suicide terrorism. This is seen both in documents of the Palestinian organizations (*a'atzamat al-istishhdiyn*) and in those of Israeli intelligence.[11] Twenty-eight suicide attacks were launched from there, most sponsored by the Jihad organization, and a large number of them succeeded. Certain refugee camps are identified with suicide terrorism, notably Balata and Jenin. The strength of local support for suicide terrorism may be inferred, first of all, from the number of suicide terrorists who are enlisted from there. This is also expressed in the multitude of posters with photographs of shahids, the demonstrations of support, and other signs of the *istishhad* culture that appear in public, mainly funerals.

The high rate of Palestinian community support for suicide terrorism is especially impressive if one takes into account that this phenomenon is entirely new and unprecedented. No less astonishing than the massive level of Palestinian support for suicide terrorism is the speed with which that popularity grew from zero. Contrary to the rhetoric of suicide terrorism organizations and unlike the version presented in a considerable part of the research literature, there is no tradition of suicide terrorism in its present sense in Islam in general or in the Middle East in particular. The *istishhad* is an original creation of the late twentieth and early twenty-first centuries. Only retroactively were efforts made to tie *istishhad* to traditional elements as if they were a model, and thus to give it legitimacy.

Until the early 1980s the concept of suicide terrorism was entirely unknown, and its Muslim-Arab, *istishhad* version did not exist. It first appeared on the margins of Palestinian interest on the Lebanese front. Ten years would pass before the concept began to be absorbed in Palestinian consciousness, but even then it was still far from the popularity and dominance that it attained only ten years later. Even after the first wave of Palestinian suicide terrorism, on the eve of the second intifada, public support for suicide terrorism was only 26 percent (March 1999).[12] Within two years the level of support doubled, and in another year it tripled. Only a decade before Palestinian suicide terrorism reached its peak, there is no mention of it in the sermons of sheikhs at Friday prayers in the mosques of the Gaza Strip and the West Bank. Nor is it mentioned in the Palestinian press or the propaganda of the resistance organizations. In 1996 it took weeks to enlist a volunteer to be a human bomb in Hebron or Ramallah.[13] In 1997 the bookshops in the West Bank were already flooded with masses of pamphlets and leaflets and audiocassettes that disseminated a popularized version of the fatwa of Sheikh Tantawi in praise of suicide terrorism. Overnight a public climate was created in support of suicide terrorism and facilitating the recruitment of volunteers. In 2007, after suicide terrorism had conquered the Palestinian public imagination for a decade, it disappeared. The rapidity with which suicide terrorism left the stage of the Israeli-Palestinian conflict is no less striking than the rapidity with which it took over the regional stage.

The behavior of the Palestinian public regarding suicide terrorism from 2000 to 2005 has characteristics that bring to mind a phenomenon called "collective behavior," the explanation of which is located in the space shared by sociology and psychology.[14] Some social scientists describe collective behavior as when a large group of individuals act in a way that violates the conventional rules of behavior, those which ordinarily regulate the life of the community. Others claim that it occurs when individuals act in a manner contrary to that in which they would act were they by themselves and exercising the judgment they ordinarily use in their lives. In this situation there is regression in the group, as if it were freed from the laws that restrict it, and it acts against its own interests, as well as regression of the individual, as if he lost his reason and submitted to forces of which he was unaware. This is a social state that is only loosely structured, and the laws that govern it are at the opposite pole from highly structured social situations such as formal organizations, where there is stability over time, a clear hierarchy, and well-defined division of labor. Collective behavior is a fluid social situation, spontaneous, dramatic, unpredictable, and short term, appearing and disappearing suddenly. Collective behavior is manifest in a broad spectrum of phenomena, from fads and rumors to moral panic and mass hysteria (e.g., the 1965 Watts riots, the Hula-Hoop craze of the 1950s, and seventeenth-century Dutch tulip mania).

Collective behavior is regarded as primitive, activated by the logic of an epidemic, and subject to the effects of suggestion, possession, and imitation. There are essentially three classic explanations of collective behavior. First, the contagion theory argues that the crowd exerts almost hypnotic pressure on its members, causing them to act in an uncontrolled, even violent manner. The individual submits to the contagious emotions of the crowd. Second, the convergence theory maintains that the presence of a large group causes people to show a side of their personality that existed but was hidden from others, and even perhaps from themselves. The group magnifies such sentiments by creating a critical mass of like-minded individuals. Three, the emergent norm theory argues that when individuals are in a vague, tense, and confused situation, new rules of behavior emerge, which may contradict the old, familiar norms of behavior, and in the framework of a specific time and place, individuals tend to adopt the emergent norms.

Perhaps it is possible to analyze the curious behavior of the Palestinian community, which encouraged—one might say, compelled—its members to support suicide terrorism and even to volunteer to be suicide terrorists by means of the principles of collective behavior. I have met Palestinians who swore to me that at night they smell the fragrance of the rose water rising from the holy bodies of the saints from their village who sacrificed their lives to blow up a bus full of Jews.

Suicide terrorism was absorbed and flourished in the Palestinian public despite its novelty because, among other things, it was connected to traditional motives and echoed familiar and influential elements of the local culture. A prominent example of this is the Islamic motive of martyrdom, about which much has been written. We shall add only two short comments: first, it is paradoxical that while the Palestinian community that brought support for suicide terrorism to a peak is Sunni, the motive of martyrdom is far more developed and emphasized in the heritage and history of Shiism; and second, let us recall that the motive of religious martyrdom suits the conception of victimhood, which occupies an important place in Palestinian nation building.

Another motive that has hardly been discussed in research into the Palestinian case is the congruence of the cult of death typical of suicide terrorism and the relatively natural conception of death that is still prevalent in the Gaza Strip and the West Bank. Unlike people in the urban, bureaucratic, and technological West, many members of the Palestinian community experience close and palpable contact with death in their daily experience. The slaughter of a sheep in the courtyard of a family household is not a rare event. Against this background, it is easier to understand the way people touch the body of shahids at their funerals and spread the martyr's blood on their faces as an expression of solidarity and veneration for the holy ones. The custom of physical contact with flesh and blood offers a partial explanation of the eroticization of death that is reflected in Palestinian suicide terrorism. Suicide terrorism is nourished by the fascination with death. The lack of repulsion by death, which is reflected in the routine of life, plays a role in the behavior of those involved in suicide terrorism. The propaganda of Palestinian suicide terrorist organizations contrasts their love of death with the Israelis' "fear of death." It is maintained that the positive attitude toward death is a source of power, and the negative attitude to death is contemptible. Spokesmen for Hamas claimed that the Zionists' yearning for life makes them ideal targets, and the spiritual leader of Hamas, Sheikh Yassin, said that the Zionists' preference for life indicates moral inferiority.[15]

Another theme current in the Palestinian public that contributed to the popularity of suicide terrorism is the vehement hatred of Judaism and Zionism. Opposition to the occupation has been reinforced by rooted anti-Semitism. The Palestinian education system, news media, sermons in mosques, and political discourse were laden with demonization of the Israelis, going far beyond seeing them as a threat to individual and collective life. They are presented as monkeys and pigs, adding impetus to the efforts to recruit suicide terrorists. The research literature has scant discussion of the kernel of hatred in suicide terrorism. In the rhetorical and visual imagery of the Palestinians, intended to motivate and legitimize suicide terrorism, their target is depicted as Satan, with a tail, or as a serpent with a rifle for a head. Typical descriptions specifically associated with suicide terrorism rather than terrorism in general include Israel as the source of corruption all over the world, and especially of the children of the Arab world, by means of drugs; Israel as a cancerous growth on the body of the nations of the world; and Israel as a wicked dwarf or as dogs, rats, and vampires.[16]

The support of the Palestinian community for suicide terrorism is assisted by an intense attack on all the individual's senses, creating a total experience.[17] In the West Bank and the Gaza Strip in 2000–5, it was impossible to escape the dominance of suicide terrorism in the public space. Suicide terrorism ruled the street, the kindergartens, the universities, the ether, poetry, and fiction. Pictures of suicide terrorists were also hung on the walls of living rooms, and verses from the Koran glorified their deeds. Palestinian suicide terrorism also acquired iconographical expressions. Unlike the Catholic world, which celebrates martyrs by means of artistic imagery—sculptures and paintings—in the Muslim tradition visual representations of martyrs is lacking. Against this background the rich culture of relics and the abundance of iconic images that developed in the Palestinian territories during the intifada constitute a revolution in the tradition. Take the colorful murals and retouched video testaments preserving the memory of the suicide terrorist depicted as a celestial being. In the foreground are drops of blood, the first one of which alone is sufficient to atone for all the sins in the suicide terrorist's past, while in the background green birds appear, which, according to a verse in the Koran, will bear the soul of the shahid to paradise.

A measure of the power of Palestinian public opinion can be found in the central role played by children and mothers in the culture of suicide terrorism. The Palestinian children and mothers are the bearers of suicide terrorism on behalf of the community, partners with the human bombs in bringing the message of suicide terrorism to Israel, the world, and the Palestinians themselves. The indoctrination of children was particularly effective during the intifada.[18] Their identification with the project of Palestinian suicide terrorism was obtained by means of all the tools at the disposal of the community, from textbooks and rhymes for small children to animated cartoons. The children's culture hero was a masked Palestinian wearing a shroud, with an explosive vest on his chest. Vast quantities of little dolls in this image were sold, and this was a popular costume to dress children in on festive occasions. In research conducted by educational psychologists in Gaza at the height of the intifada, it was found that nearly 70 percent of children expressed the desire to be suicide terrorists when they grew up. When they were shown a picture of a sad girl and were asked what could be done to solve her problems and the distress of Palestinian society, 67.8 percent responded that suicide terrorism was the answer.[19]

On the streets of Gaza and the West Bank during the intifada, people used to say that the mothers of suicide terrorists belonged to the highest level of Palestinian heroine, leading the struggle of opposition to the occupation. The most famous of these was "the mother of Shahids" Um Nidal (Farahat), who lost three of her sons in confrontation with Israel, the last of whom blew himself up as a human bomb. According to rumors spread by Hamas, she herself addressed Salah Sh'chada, the leader of the military arm of Hamas, and obtained his permission for her son, who was not yet seventeen, to volunteer. The mothers' expressions of joy on receiving news of the death of their loved ones as suicide terrorists are meant to testify to their infinite devotion to the Palestinian cause and the policy of suicide terrorism in particular. As pointed out earlier, there is dissonance between their public demonstrations of joy, which are emphasized in the organization's propaganda, and the signs of deep sorrow expressed privately, which are also accompanied by criticism of the organizations that seduced their sons to their deaths. In addition to grief, concern for the welfare of the family also emerged with the absence of one of the breadwinners, as well as fear of retaliation by the IDF, which might destroy the family house. This dissonance reflects the impact of social pressure exerted on the family by the Palestinian community. One must not deduce from this that the families necessarily surrender to the expectations of their neighbors and the dictates of the organizations, and pretend with cynicism. It is certainly possible that these two apparently contrary responses are both genuine and express the duality that exists in their personality and in the culture of the community.

In the period of the intifada the Palestinian community was entirely captivated by the charms of suicide terrorism. Concluding this point, I will list several more illustrations of the suicide terrorism fever that gripped most of the Palestinians for several years. The folklore of the community is laden with stories about suicide terrorism, conflating reality with fantasy. One urban legend, for example, deals with a human bomb who reached his target in the heart of Israel and pressed the button to activate the charge. It did not explode, however, and he was forced to retrace his steps. In a debriefing done by his handlers, it turned out that at the critical moment he stopped thinking about the paradise promised to him, and therefore the supreme power caused a break in the electric circuitry, which was supposed to cause the attack. There were also newspaper reports about a large number of young men who rushed to be photographed in the poses that were the trademark of suicide terrorists, with a rifle and a Koran in their hands. They did this in case they might be asked to volunteer and die, and thus they would be remembered as martyrs.[20] In parallel, throughout the Palestinian territories, young men wrote testaments as if they were about to commit a suicide attack.[21] Early in the intifada the official daily of the Palestinian Authority published an item about a twelve-year-old Palestinian boy who wrote graffiti on the walls of houses in his neighborhood announcing his death as a suicide terrorist.[22]

The Palestinian Case in Global Context

With the exception of books and articles written about 9/11, most academic publications on suicide terrorism are based mainly on the study of the Palestinian case. This is still true today, in 2018, although Palestinian suicide terrorism ceased a decade ago, and despite the appearance of other types of suicide terrorism on a horrific scale in more and more places around the world. Instances of suicide terrorism in various places during the period of research that is the focus of this book, 2000–8, numbered 2,490.[23] During that time the number of Palestinian suicide attacks in Israel was roughly 150.[24] In all, until mid-2015 there were 4,600 instances of suicide terrorism in more than forty countries. That is to say, since 2008 the number of instances in the world was about 2,100,[25] while during that time only another instance or two of Palestinian suicide terrorism was added to the list. Hence, before 2008 Palestinian suicide terrorism consisted of 6 percent of all the attacks in the world, and in the interim it has fallen to only 3.25 percent. The disproportion between the extent of Palestinian suicide terrorism and its centrality in research is conspicuous.[26] This disproportion is also notable with respect to the number of victims: to date, about 45,000 people have been killed in suicide terrorism, of whom about eight hundred were victims of Palestinian suicide terrorism (1.8%). Nevertheless, a far greater number of articles and books have been published on Palestinian suicide terrorism than on suicide terrorism in Iraq, Afghanistan, or Nigeria, where suicide terrorism is flourishing, overshadowing Palestinian suicide terrorism both in the number of events and in their murderousness.

There are several reasons for the dominance of the Palestinian case as a source of empirical data and theoretical arguments about suicide terrorism. First, this suicide terrorism occupies a significant place in the Middle Eastern conflict, which is a focus of international attention both because it concerns control over the Holy Land for hundreds of millions of believers of the three monotheistic religions, and also because one of the sides in this territorial rivalry—the Israeli (and, to a lesser degree, the Palestinian side as well)—is an integral part of the West, which is the center of gravity of cosmopolitan concern and academic research. In addition, this conflict is prominent in world consciousness as a result of the great investment and expertise in worldwide propaganda, which both sides view as an important component of their strategy.

The second reason is the abundance of material about Palestinian suicide terrorism, which is relatively accessible, reliable, and detailed. The Palestinian territories and, even more so, the State of Israel, offer optimal conditions for gathering this material: a limited geographical scope and proximity to the arena of events; stability and physical security even at the height of the intifada; advanced technological infrastructure; freedom of information and a tradition of independent, activist, and investigative journalism; effective and energetic cooperation on the part of the authorities and organizations on both sides, for they are sensitive to public relations, though they do not always show full openness and tolerance; accessibility of officeholders, activists, and those involved in the vicinity of the terrorist organizations and of the establishment combating terrorism; social density, which makes it difficult to keep secrets; and an informal and outgoing atmosphere that facilitates interpersonal communications even with foreigners and people in power, encouraging candid exchanges on matters calling for confidentiality as well. To this must be added the sophisticated intelligence that the Israeli security agencies reveal with some liberality, even though these disclosures are occasionally manipulated. The experts at Israeli universities are also of great importance. Scholars have devoted effort and proven research talent to the study of Palestinian suicide terrorism, exploiting their natural advantages, such as long familiarity with the region, knowledge of the language, and personal connections. Not surprisingly, there are several prestigious research institutes in Israel that specialize in the study of terrorism, and Israeli academics are among the eminent experts on terrorism in the world. Palestinian academics also play a role in the study of suicide terrorism, contributing a complementary and balanced perspective to making the Palestinian case one of special value in the study of suicide terrorism.[27]

A third reason for the prominence of Palestinian suicide terrorism is that it was one of the first manifestations of the phenomenon (preceded only by the cases of Lebanon and Sri Lanka). Palestinian suicide terrorism was also special because of its popularity, whereas in other places it aroused vehement dispute or substantial opposition. More important is the fact that the Palestinian case is one of suicide terrorism par excellence in the sense that almost 100 percent of its targets were civilian. In contrast, the Hezbollah and Tamil Tigers hit mainly security forces or symbols of government.

The ability to obtain rich and solid research materials concerning Palestinian suicide terrorism stands out in comparison to the paucity of information in other places, where the scope of the murder of innocent civilians may be infinitely greater. The concentration of severe incidents of suicide terrorism has passed from Israel-Palestine to places where Muslims murder other Muslims, and people in the developing world kill other developing-world people. Perhaps this, too, is a reason why research into these cases is partial and superficial. Very few researchers collect primary material in the field there because of the rough and dangerous conditions, while information published in the local and foreign media is general and unverified.[28] For illustration, I analyzed approximately fifty scraps of information about three severe suicide terrorist attacks in Iraq and Afghanistan. Only scarce and inadequate information was given about the personal, social, or organizational background of these events.[29] In such deadly attacks, which no longer shock us, both the perpetrators and the victims are anonymous, at least to newspaper readers and most academic researchers. In contrast, we possess basic biographies of each of the Palestinian suicide terrorists and quite accurate information about his family and locality, the structure, functioning, and ideology of the organization that dispatched him, and the attitude of the public in whose name he acted.[30]

The core of my research is on Palestinian suicide terrorism. It is a case study that serves as a basis for comparison with other instances of suicide terrorism, and which can then be used to develop elements of a theory of suicide terrorism. An incomplete model of suicide terrorism is implicit in this book. Is it universal? Can the conclusions of my research be generalized and applied to other cases of suicide terrorism? To what degree is the paradigm proposed in earlier chapters still relevant, and does its explanatory value persist in the light of later developments? In any event, even if the arguments I present in this book, in the context of Palestinian suicide terrorism, are not a categorically convincing explanation of several prominent instances of suicide terrorism, it does not mean that these arguments are not valid.

Normative practices or institutional setups (e.g., rituals, technologies, policies) can reverberate and gain diffusion that brings them into a social environment with traditions and geopolitical contexts that are entirely different from their original setting. There they can prove to be more or less fitting, and be adopted with slight adaptations, while receiving entirely new meaning. This process, which has been widely studied in the social sciences, is called institutional translation.[31] Just as it is possible for a particular symbolic value to be related to a variety of behavioral patterns, so, too, the transposition from culture to culture of a particular behavioral pattern is possible, and while many of its characteristic features are essentially preserved, it undergoes a radical change in its symbolic value.[32] Thus the specific configuration of suicide terrorism can appear in various regions of the world, in differing historical circumstances, and in each case it can be given distinct meaning, and perhaps also serve slightly changing objectives.

For now this specific form of Palestinian suicide terrorism at the center of the book has abated, but suicide terrorism itself appears in other places, and who knows whether it will once again vex Israel in the future. About a decade after the last suicide terror attack by Hamas, the leadership of the organization is issuing vehement exhortations to resume the splendid tradition of *istishhad*.[33] Ever since the end of the second intifada, suicide terrorism has lost its sensational value. It is no longer new and surprising, and it has become—most tragically—part of the routine. Public and academic interest in it also decreased because it wandered to distant places far from the eyes and hearts of people in the West.

Meanwhile, suicide terrorism has roamed from generation to generation and place to place, among nations and religious factions, proving its attractiveness and ability to adjust to particular situations. The adaptability of suicide terrorism appears in all its dimensions, including the techniques it uses and the values attributed to it.[34] Suicide terrorism has appeared in dozens of countries, mostly after its association with the Israeli-Palestinian confrontation.[35] Suicide terrorism became a generic type, a phenomenon that has a diffusion dynamic of its own, and its attributes no longer depend on its distinct sources, connected to defined circumstances or to any set ideology. The course of its propagation or translation may be convoluted and unpredictable. It was surprising to discover that immediately after the explosion of several suicide terrorists in Chechnya, their prerecorded video testaments were published.[36] But then it was difficult not to identify the inspiring model in the West Bank, thousands of miles away.

Suicide terrorism is yet another *glocal* phenomenon. First it appeared in the Middle East, and within a short time it proliferated as far as China, India, Kenya, Chad, Argentina, Kashmir, Sudan, Spain, Indonesia, Turkey, Algeria, Russia, and the United States, constantly adapting its meaning to different circumstances. If it eventually returns to the Middle East, most likely foreign contents will be concealed beneath its familiar guise. The largely Muslim religious identity of suicide terrorism is a global and local factor at the same time. Islam, or belonging to the Islamic *ummah* (nation), leads and joins suicide terrorism from Lebanon to the Philippines, to Uganda, Kosovo, and Uzbekistan. Recently Mali, Syria, Niger, and Dagestan, as well as France and Belgium, joined the list of countries where suicide terrorism has occurred. In every one of the manifestations of the universal Islamic suicide terrorism mentioned here there are ethnic and territorial characteristics suited to the particular surroundings.

The very idea of suicide terrorism and its operational aspects migrate by means of electronic communications, mainly the Internet and television, and by means of interpersonal encounters, when the experienced representatives of various organizations travel from front to front as advisors or volunteer fighters. The appearance of suicide terrorism in the LTTE (Liberation Tigers of Tamil Eelam) cannot be separated from the visit of emissaries of the Tamil underground to Hezbollah activists in the Beka Valley in southern Lebanon (1980s),[37] and the suicide terrorism of Hamas cannot be separated from the meeting of 415 activists of the Palestinian resistance organizations with representatives of Hezbollah at Nur A-Shams in southern Lebanon, whence they had been deported by Israel (1992). Explosive vests were not used in Middle Eastern suicide terrorism until the method was learned from the LTTE, which developed it first. With the proliferation of suicide terrorism, the purposes for which it is employed change. In the 1980s it was used by Hezbollah to drive an invader out of their country. In the 2000s the organizations that adopted suicide terrorism to drive a foreign army from their land were only a minority of 3 percent.[38] From observation of suicide attacks today, a bit more than thirty years after it first appeared, one gains the impression that in some cases it would have been possible to achieve the same strategic goals by means of nonsuicidal terrorism, but nevertheless they used suicide terrorism, from inertia and perhaps because the medium is the message.

History is replete with examples of "cultural packages"[39] that pass from community to community, with variation and even reversal of meaning (e.g., the *afikoman* of the Jewish Passover seder became the holy wafer of the Christian Mass).[40] Suicide terrorism can develop as the result of the proximity of segregated communities, between which, although they are inimical to each other, processes of reciprocal learning and subtle exchanges still take place. Suicide terrorism can pass from one side to another, even if there is an armed confrontation between them. In this context, an interesting argument has been advanced, that Palestinian suicide terrorism did not appear at first as a reaction against the Israeli-Palestinian peace agreements (Oslo, 1993)[41] in an effort to overturn them, but that it began as a vengeful but imitative reaction to the massacre of Arabs in the Cave of the Patriarchs in Hebron (February 1994) committed by the settler Baruch Goldstein, which was mistakenly but understandably taken to be an act of Jewish suicide terrorism.[42] A better-known example are the Palestinian Sunni shahids who adopted some rituals typical of Shiite shahids in Iran.[43] Between the two cases there is a gap of twenty years, and one of intra-Islamic rivalry between hostile factions with different histories and opposing mythologies. It is no coincidence that Fat'hi Shkaki, the leader of the Palestinian Jihad, which is subject to Iranian influence, played a role in introducing suicide terrorism into the Palestinian repertoire.

The patterns of behavior typical of suicide terrorism can also cross the border between the religious and secular spheres, in both directions. Classical suicide terrorism, which embodies Muslim radicalism, can be replaced by suicide terrorism embodying national or tribal radicalism that does not proclaim its Muslim roots. Much has been written denying that the line dividing the world of believers from that of nonbelievers is sharp, hermetic, and unchanging, especially in the Middle East. In addition, sometimes the migration of institutions and social values from one context to another can bear an invisible seed within it and plant it in an ostensibly alien land. Then, over time, it can sprout, stand out, exert influence, and even seek to impose its original hidden logic on its new environment.[44] Although Saad Hanani, an eighteen-year-old from Beit Furiq in the West Bank, who blew himself up at a central crossroads near Tel Aviv (December 2003) was originally from the Popular Front for the Liberation of Palestine (established by George Habash, a Christian social-democrat), he was assimilated by tradition, the *istishhad* for the glory of Allah, and became an organic part of it. There is not a single recorded testament by suicide terrorists sent by ostensibly secular Palestinian organizations that is not replete with decidedly religious Islamic expressions.

A decade after the decline of the wave of Palestinian suicide terrorism, which inspired the theoretical model inherent in this book, an incident of suicide terrorism occurred in another area of conflict, changing the "lethal embrace," which is central to my argumentation, from a metaphor to reality. An important Iraqi politician held a reception for the moderate notables of his Sunni community. A local radical, later identified as a partisan of al-Qaeda, infiltrated the area, passing himself off as a supporter of one of the highly placed politicians. He stood in line like the invited guests, shook his host's hand, hugged him warmly, and then activated the explosive vest that was attached to his body (June 19, 2013).[45] Something similar happened in Mogadishu, Somalia: a suicide terrorist from the al-Shabab organization approached a senior official, who was thought to be backed by the West, placed his arms on him, hugged him warmly, and then activated the explosive.[46] Meanwhile, the plot of a radical Islamic group to assassinate the pope during his visit to Manila (1995) has also been reported. The chosen suicide terrorist was supposed to disguise himself as a Catholic priest, advance toward the stage where a large public Mass was to be held, kiss the pope's ring, and then activate the charge under his cassock.

The uniqueness of Palestinian suicide terrorism is to be seen in the context of the circumstances of the conflict between the Palestinians and Israel, which are different from the circumstances of other conflicts in which the late phase of suicide terrorism has arisen. The relations between Palestinians and Israelis can be characterized as armed political antagonism between two national-religious entities that are almost entirely segregated. They dwell on either side of a boundary, the crossing of which is restricted and supervised. Between the two collectives there is not only a clash of interest and an ecological separation, but also sharp differences in the systems of justice, the economy, the society, and the culture. However, since 1967 this border has been breached in two directions, not only by clandestine or violent activity but in a massive, institutional, and orderly manner. On the one hand, the Jewish settlement project in Judea and Samaria invades deeply into Palestinian territory and, with the protection of the IDF, seizes ground in close proximity to the locals. On the other hand, thousands of Palestinians enter Israel every day, mainly to make a living and to make use of a variety of services. Thus common spaces are created, shared by the two populations. In the streets of certain neighborhoods and mainly in blue-collar workplaces, there is interaction between Palestinians and Israelis that, while usually not on an equal basis, is not necessarily belligerent.

The area between the Mediterranean and the Jordan River can be divided into three subareas: the exclusive area of the homogeneous Palestinian population, to the east of the Green Line; the exclusive area of the homogeneous Israeli (largely Jewish) population to the west of the Green Line;[47] and an area where the two populations meet each other. As expected, there was a high level of violence against Israelis, including intense terrorism, in the third area, mainly the parts adjacent to the Palestinian population centers. However, contrary to expectations, in this area only an insignificant minority of Palestinian suicide terrorism took place. About 95 percent of the suicide attacks took place in the area where there is a pure, decided, and more or less agreed-upon Israeli presence, and only 5 percent of the attacks were committed in places where control over them arouses resistance and is a matter of contention.[48] Most of the suicide attacks were in West Jerusalem and, after that, in Tel Aviv and its vicinity. The third-greatest concentration was in the Netanya-Hadera-Afula region. The few suicide attacks near West Bank Jewish settlements (and, earlier, on the roadways in the Gaza Strip) were rather minor. These middle (third category) areas are the natural habitat of terrorism. However, almost no suicide terrorists have appeared there.

The late model of suicide terrorism—Iraqi, Syrian, Pakistani, and Nigerian style—is concentrated in the heart of these countries, in places where boundaries are blurred and the rival populations mix with one another, and it is difficult to distinguish between them, where there is chaotic coexistence. In contrast, most of the Palestinian suicide terrorism was directed elsewhere, far from its place of origin, over the border, at a place where there was no coexistence, and there was a regime of separation. Iraqi suicide terrorism and its ilk takes place on the home ground, and its target population lives on the next street over, in the terrorists' own city, whereas Palestinian suicide terrorism occurs far away, in foreign territory, in an alien atmosphere. The Iraqi suicide terrorist acts in regions of certain doubt regarding people's identity, where otherness is common and accepted. The Palestinian suicide terrorist had to assimilate in an area where identity—the identity other than his own—was self-evident, and otherness was suspicious and alarming. His mission was to undermine the security of the residents of the area with respect to the identity of those who share their public space. The Israelis defined this area as "sterile," and there they were usually free from the need to be concerned with the true identity and hidden intentions of other people. This in particular was the area to which the Palestinian suicide terrorist was drawn, and this was the area where his subversive effect was the greatest. The Palestinian suicide terrorist crossed the border into Israel, to seek an area where there was no tolerance for doubt, so that there was limited ability to absorb a Palestinian who clearly demonstrated his "Palestinianity," but not any ability to absorb someone with a vague and deceptive figure.

The Iraqi suicide terrorist is exempt from the complex effort to conceal his identity, and he can remain who he is, as long as he hides the explosive vest and his intention to activate it. The Palestinian suicide terrorist is required to make a greater effort at concealment—he has to control more variables of disguise: accent, dress, manners, body language, and so on. The Iraqi suicide terrorist hides only his malicious intent, whereas the Palestinian suicide terrorist conceals his entire identity. The former only keeps a secret; the latter actively lies, and in addition to the secret he must keep, he also has to broadcast a deceptive image of himself. The mission of the Palestinian suicide terrorist is more demanding than that of the suicide terrorists active today in Asia and Africa. The Palestinian must evade and deceive the inquisitive gaze of the Israeli, which creates his otherness. The concern of any suicide terrorist is the dialectic between blending in versus differentiation and separation, thus various suicide terrorists make the boundaries into an issue. The Iraqi wants to erect barriers where they only partially exist, and the Palestinian tries to destroy walls where they are high and fortified.

Ten Years Later: Current Trends

During the past decade, suicide terrorism has become part of dreadful daily life in numerous regions of the world. In 2014 there were 592 suicide attacks (an increase of 94% compared to the previous year), which inflicted 4,400 deaths (compared to 3,200 in the previous year).[49] The increase in the scale of suicide terrorism may have ironic aspects, as when the victim of a suicide attack responds to the attacker by means of suicide terrorism. Iraqi organizations specializing in suicide terrorism use it to combat other organizations that specialize in suicide terrorism.[50] The sad absurdity of suicide terrorism today is also expressed in Syria, where in some cases there is doubt about the identity of the organization responsible for the suicide terrorism, and it is not clear what purpose it sought to achieve by means of the attack.

Starting around 2016, suicide terrorism once again has seized the attention of the West with the appearance of a new type of suicide terrorism. I refer to the suicide attacks at a Parisian nightclub and in the Brussels airport, both attributed to ISIS (2016). The third decade in the age of suicide terrorism was characterized by several other trends. First, suicide terrorism fits into the process of globalization that includes the Islamic world. It moves from place to place and develops with the help of television and online social networks, which are used for indoctrination, conscription, and instruction; with the help of the cheap and free mobility of experts and fighters; and with the help of fundraising and bank transfers. The entrepreneurs of suicide terrorism also now have universal ambitions. Suicide terrorism has been harnessed to the Salafi Sunni movement, which seeks to unite the entire *ummah* and establish a supernational, even transcontinental, caliphate. African suicide terrorism is connected to the suicide terrorism of ISIS in Iraq and Syria. While ISIS lately suffers from considerable setbacks, other fundamentalist Islamic organizations, mainly al-Qaeda, are still pushing for the decontextualization of suicide terrorism. Second, a significant majority of suicide attacks are not aimed at civilians but rather at governmental bodies and army and police forces (71% of the attacks in Iraq).[51] The rest of the suicide attacks are aimed at civilian and religious targets, and contrary to the claim that is still voiced out loud, only a negligible fraction of them are aimed at liberating territory occupied by a foreign power.[52] The withdrawal of a foreign army is neither the goal nor the result of suicide terrorism, but rather part of the circumstances that contribute to the emergence of suicide terrorism.

There are other recent trends, such as the change in the profile of the suicide terrorists. Many of them are volunteers who come to the battlefront from far away—a kind of international brigade. Some of them are Muslims whose families migrated to the West, and some are Westerners who converted to Islam. Among the local suicide terrorists there are more and more women and children. Not unconnected to this, suicide terrorists are increasingly hostages who have been reeducated or who have the mission forced on them. Similarly, in recent years a reserve of suicide terrorists has been organized as members of suicide terrorism orders, who were especially recruited for the mission of suicide terrorism, some against their will, and they are waiting to be sent on attacks after being indoctrinated and trained. The trends of change described above, and others, reflect the distancing of worldwide suicide terrorism from the Palestinian model on which my research focused. The Palestinian human bomb from the period of the intifada, unlike today's human bombs, had a local, national emphasis, solely invested in a specific territorial conflict, and was not interested in worldwide jihad.[53]

No incident of suicide terrorism has taken place where other kinds of terrorism are not prevalent. At the same time, there are very few, if any, cases of a conflict involving high levels of violence, including types of terrorism, where suicide terrorism does not appear as well, if not at an early stage, then later. In Asia and Africa, it is hard to find regions where there was no presence at all of suicide terrorism. Indeed, today there are places where suicide terrorism is predominant, as reflected both in the absolute number of suicide attacks and in their share in the total number of terrorist attacks. These places may be defined as suicide terrorism lands. At the end of the past millennium these were southern Lebanon, Sri Lanka, and Israel-Palestine. At the start of the new millennium, they are Iraq, Syria (with overflows into Lebanon), Afghanistan, Pakistan, and Nigeria. To the countries associated with suicide terrorism can be added, to a lesser degree, Yemen, Libya, Somalia, and others. In 2014 there were 271 suicide attacks in Iraq, 124 in Afghanistan, 54 in Syria and Lebanon, 36 in Pakistan, 32 in Nigeria, 29 in Yemen, and 19 in Somalia.[54]

What are the characteristics of these countries, which can be seen as the conditions for absorbing suicide terrorism or for its emergence and growth? First, these are countries with a Muslim majority and hegemony (like Pakistan), or a significant Muslim minority concentrated in a certain area, which feels that its rights and autonomy are impaired (as in China and the Philippines). Some are Arab (like Iraq and Syria), and some are not (like Afghanistan and Nigeria), but there is Muslim fundamentalism in them all, mainly Sunni Jihadist, and some revolutionary Shiites. Frequently in the Islamic revivalist bloc there are concentrations of other religions, as in Iraq and Syria, where the Sunni confront Shiites and Alawites, Christians, and members of small, deprived groups such as the Yazidis. Second, there is political chaos in these countries, along with social upheavals, which are expressed in civil or regional wars, revolutions, putsches, and the intervention of foreign forces or their departure. As a result of a crisis of legitimacy, lack of stability, and schisms, these countries are characterized by a high level of violence: violence of the government against the citizens, including the violation of human rights, and violence of the opposition and nonstate or subnational bodies against the government. This is accompanied by violence in politically neutralized areas, such as crime, and lack of trust in interpersonal relations. Third, the process of modernization has not been completed in areas of suicide terrorism. It takes root in postcolonial states whose independence is young, whose political establishment is ineffective, corrupt, and brutal, and whose society is relatively poor and backward in various respects such as hygiene, technology, and the status of women. Nevertheless, those who are directly involved in initiating suicide terrorism are usually not from the weakest strata. Fourth, suicide terrorism appears in the context of lack of unity among "primordial" groups. There is disintegration among various ethnic and religious communities, and sometimes there is a long-standing tradition of competition and antagonism among tribes and nationalities. The inner tension is exacerbated when the political, cultural, and socioeconomic cleavages overlap.

Paradigm Shift

Clarification of the essential link between mass murder and self-murder is the key to understanding suicide terrorism. In suicide terrorism there is a close, multidimensional connection between aggression and victimhood, and the aggressive component has only partial meaning separate from the victimhood component.

For an action to be considered suicide terrorism, first of all it must have the general characteristics of terrorism.[55] For example, it must entail violence directed intentionally against citizens chosen randomly as a target. This characteristic of suicide terrorism is necessary but definitely not sufficient. To be regarded as suicide terrorism, the action must have further characteristics distinct from other kinds of terrorism. Essentially, the terrorist must kill himself in order to kill his target population. Thus, arguments that are valid to explain terrorism are valid to explain suicide terrorism as well, but they are not enough. The test for an explanation of suicide terrorism is that it must provide convincing explanations *only* of suicide terrorism as opposed to other types of terrorism.

Many researchers of suicide terrorism fail this test. When they present the causes or functions of the phenomenon, they list motives that are indeed applicable to it but that apply also to various kinds of terrorism, of which suicide terrorism is just one. For example, take prominent scholars in the field such as Robert Pape, who argues that suicide terrorism is used to compel foreign occupation forces to make concessions or withdraw from territories to liberate them, or Bader Araj and Robert Brym, who claim that the effort to deter or take vengeance for harsh state repression is the cause of suicide terrorism. I do not claim that these factors, or various combinations of them are not relevant for explaining suicide terrorism. However, they relate to terrorism in general, without relating to the particularity of suicide terrorism. Analysis of suicide terrorism, which is almost entirely in the hands of political scientists, sees it just as it sees other types of nonsuicidal terrorism. Therefore its contribution is unsatisfactory.

Whatever the goals of suicide terrorism may be, it usually does not appear by itself, but as part of a comprehensive strategy, as another component in an assortment of methods of violent political struggle, along with ordinary terrorism, guerrilla warfare, and even nonviolent political struggle. There are various forms of terrorism: booby traps, sharpshooters, knives, mortars, and so on. All of these differ from one another mainly tactically and technically, and it is possible that, as a result, they also differ in their degree of strategic effectiveness. Suicide terrorism is another kind of terrorism that also has tactical and technical characteristics influencing its effectiveness. This, however, is not the end of its uniqueness. Suicide terrorism, as a kind of terrorism, shares various common characteristics with other kinds of terrorism. However, it is different from them in several salient characteristics that belong to it alone. As noted, the most important characteristic of suicide terrorism is that it necessarily entails the death of the attacker along with his victims. Is this difference equal in importance to the differences between, say, terrorism by means of shooting from a speeding car and terrorism by means of mines? A basic argument of this book is that the answer to that question is negative.

Suicide terrorism is a sui generis phenomenon, a category of its own. The technical and tactical difference between suicide terrorism and other kinds of terrorism have a sociological and psychological significance, which also has crucial ethical consequences.

To suggest a possible analogy, there are various kinds of warfare, including armored warfare, infantry, artillery, and sea warfare. Is it possible to add atomic warfare, which has appropriately been called unconventional warfare, to this list? While it, too, is warfare, and it has much in common with the other kinds of warfare, at the same time to analyze it in terms unique to it is justified, and not only because it is more destructive. It has vital uniqueness that acts on the human imagination differently from conventional types of warfare. This is true, too, of suicide terrorism, constituting a class alone, which, when it first appeared, caused an entirely different experience among its actual and potential victims, and for the assailant, requiring a conceptual change among observers of the phenomenon as well. Like the atom bomb in Hiroshima, the appearance of suicide terrorism was a quantum leap.

It is often claimed that suicide terrorism is distinguished by its operational advantages, meaning that it is much more likely to claim a relatively large number of victims. In 2000–8 there were 30,600 instances of Palestinian terrorism against Israel, claiming 1,065 casualties. In 147 Palestinian suicide terrorist attacks during that period, 525 Israelis were killed.[56] That is to say, 0.5 percent of Palestinian terrorism attacks in Israel caused about half of the deaths.[57] Taking a broader view, while only 4 percent of all terrorist attacks around the globe during the years 1981–2006 were suicide attacks, they caused 32 percent of the casualties.

These figures demonstrate the operational logic of the suicide attack, which, according to authoritative observers, explains terrorism initiators' preference for this method. However, if that heightened effectiveness refers to the success of suicide terrorist organizations in bringing about a change in policy on the part of the side that is attacked, the record does not look impressive. The widespread use of suicide terrorism in the Tamil-Sinhalese conflict in Sri Lanka or in the Israeli-Palestinian conflict during the second intifada testifies to dubious effectiveness, to put it mildly. Nevertheless, in both cases and in others, it was a game changer. Suicide terrorism is a unique phenomenon, regardless of its effectiveness, or, perhaps, its effectiveness must be grasped in terms that are not necessarily connected to the dimensions of murder or change in policy. I refer mainly to its impact on the level of cultural significance, which is expressed more in terms of subversion than coercion. The power of the suicide terrorist lies in the threat to our understanding of the world more than to our physical safety.

My research is intended to answer the question that is frequently avoided: What does suicide terrorism have that other methods of terrorism or methods of warfare do not have, and how does that make it more appropriate for carrying out the functions mentioned in the literature that describes and explains it? For example, quite a few interesting efforts to understand Palestinian suicide terrorism call our attention to radical interpretations of political Islam and particularly to the concept of jihad.[58] But such factors can be in the background when groups make decisions about a wide variety of terrorism methods, and even in the background of violence that is not terrorism, such as guerrilla warfare. Learned explanations of suicide terrorism, with which the scholarly literature is replete, may be appropriate and persuasive in relation to the use of terrorism by means of camouflaged explosive charges that are operated from a distance or by means of rockets. The idea of jihad and political Islam in itself, as well as the thirst for revenge and the need for deterrence, in themselves explain nothing about the preference for terrorism by means of suicide.

In this book I tried to explain the phenomenon of suicide terrorism in terms that relate to the "extra" distinct characteristics that apply only to it. I focused on the consequences of the fact, first of all, that the attacker is also the victim, and that the attacker mingles with his victims at the scene of the attack. Hence I discussed the implications of victimhood at length, as, for example, the basis for the claim of moral superiority, or the implications of the fusion of the living and dead bodies on both sides in the final moments before the explosion and in the first minutes after it. These and similar factors play no role at all in other types of terrorism. It may be said that my research sets out from the point where the rules of the game of suicide terrorism are substantially different from those of other types of terrorism. I deal with suicide terrorism only to the extent that there is something additional or unique about it. I see the emergence of suicide terrorism and its institutionalization as an epistemological rupture.

The transition from standard terrorism to suicide terrorism is a paradigm shift. The analogy between the structure of scientific revolutions and the appearance of suicide terrorism is limited, and yet Thomas Kuhn's famous model can help us in conceptualizing the phenomenon before us.[59] At the end of the nineteenth and start of the early twentieth centuries young Russian idealists, radical opponents of the czar, surprised the world with a revolutionary kind of political violence: terrorism.

The phenomenon aroused bewilderment and anticipation, but spread to various places and matured. In the ensuing century, what gradually turned out to be "normal" terrorism became prevalent all over the world. In the early 1980s, mainly in the Middle East, this routine terrorism generated dissatisfaction among those who used it. New political problems arose, and resistance organizations felt that the answers offered by various forms of the old terrorism were no longer adequate. Proposals for solving the problems did not deviate from the customary but rather adjusted to the common way of thinking. At this stage an entirely different form of terrorism shone on the horizon, perhaps the product of genius, perhaps a chance mutation, and it was immediately seen as pathbreaking. After suspicions, hesitations, trial, and error, it was adopted. A new form of terrorism was created: suicide terrorism. Systems of political violence that had become institutionalized over time were shaken up until they adapted themselves to the new rules of the game, which changed substantially in one fell swoop.

The revolutionary paradigm of suicide terrorism did not develop linearly within the bounds of the traditional paradigm of terrorism. Suicide terrorism is not an improvement on normal terrorism, but rather something else that cannot be understood in terms of its predecessor. Not only do the answers change, but so do the related questions that are raised. The new model, like the earlier one, was accompanied by a world of concepts and characteristic discourse that captivated the imagination of the community within which the resistance organizations operated. The old tradition and the one that supplanted it spoke different languages. To an extent, normal terrorism and suicide terrorism became incommensurable. Once the new paradigm was established, the earlier ways of thinking were of limited relevance, and options for thought developed that had previously been inconceivable and were not even considered hypothetically. Manifestations of the old paradigm that remained on the scene were overshadowed by manifestations of the new paradigm. Within a short time routines were molded and a consensus emerged around the new paradigm. Suicide terrorism was established and took on characteristics of normalcy. After a decade of dominance, this paradigm, too, encountered a crisis. Not only did the circumstances creating reality on the ground change; the pattern of thought also underwent a revision. It became increasingly difficult to understand and justify suicide terrorism, and expressions of discomfort with it increased. When suicide terrorism lost its self-evident unsullied status, new ideas arose, and the search for a new paradigm became more intense.

Whereas the prevailing wisdom in the scholarly literature on suicide terrorism sees the act of suicide as no more than a modus operandi, I would like to point out the metaphoric value of suicide terrorism. As in literature, in politics, too, metaphors have immense potency. We live by metaphors.[60] Metaphors organize the world for us: they are the axis enabling us to arrange—and then rearrange—our experiences, emotions, and ideas. The use of a new metaphor gives a group a sense of power and optimism, as if one overcomes the problems of the world by a new understanding. Suicide terrorism is a new metaphor. Between 1993 and 2005, suicide terrorism—*amaliyat istish'hadiya*—was the central metaphor in the world of the Palestinians. This metaphor opened revolutionary consciousness for them and promised to create a different reality. Suicide terrorism focused the collective attention of the occupied collective and touched deep strata in its identity, including its internal tensions.

The metaphor is accompanied by a figurative expression, the icon, and the iconic figure of suicide terrorism is, of course, the human bomb. Just as an alternative world arose in Russia at the end of the nineteenth century, the icon of which was the fragile intellectual wielding a pistol and shooting his victim—the symbol of autocratic dictatorship—at point-blank range, so, too, at the end of the twentieth century an alternative world was born in the Middle East, the icon of which was the refugee who donned an explosive vest and mingled with his Israeli victims, the humiliating occupiers, exciting and stirring the imagination.

At a certain historical moment, usually in dramatic circumstances, the effect of a specific event is taken as laden with significance. It is absorbed and becomes dominant, gaining the status of a potent, popular metaphor. In 1881, in Saint Petersburg, it was the bomb thrown by the Narodnaya Volya anarchist that killed Alexander II. After this, for a generation terrorism was the metaphor that created the new Russian world. In the Middle East, in 1994, it was the Hamas attack in Tel Aviv that killed twenty-two civilians in bus no. 5, after which for a decade suicide terrorism was the metaphor that created a new Middle Eastern world.

The metaphor of suicide terrorism was woven into political language, becoming hegemonic and playing a central role in the organization of reality for some time, until it exhausted itself and lost its magic. The charisma of the *istishhad* eroded, and its potential was dissipated with it. This does not mean that the *istishhad* disappeared. It may appear in other places and also return to the Palestinian arena. Meanwhile, this metaphor is regarded as irrelevant, and use of it is seen as anachronistic, even pathetically retro.

The decline of a metaphor is often parallel to the rise of another one, with its own iconic figure. The validity of the suicide terrorism metaphor is temporary. The *istishhad* took the Israeli-Palestinian conflict by a storm, became the bon ton for a decade, and then faded away silently.[61] Perhaps the knife-wielding teenagers have replaced it. Every generation in the Middle East has its own violent icon.

Before the mid-1990s and after the mid-2000s there was no Palestinian suicide terrorism. The entire episode lasted ten to fifteen years. The phenomenon has a fairly clear starting point, and a sharp endpoint. Until the first Hamas attack that was recognized as suicide terrorism, there was no indication that Palestinian suicide terrorism would emerge. Even in retrospect it is difficult to locate earlier Palestinian rhetoric or practice in which the potential for suicide terrorism might be actualized. Until the early 1980s the concepts of jihad and *shuhada* were a notable presence in the air of Palestine, but there was not even a hint of *istishhad*.

It is unsound to attribute the beginning of Palestinian suicide terrorism to a specific decision, thought out and agreed on, the result of the methodical deliberations and rational considerations of a resistance organization (Hamas). In contrast, the end of this suicide terrorism was the fruit of a strategic choice made by the resistance organizations, though the end of the phenomenon also had a degree of spontaneity and was influenced by unpremeditated factors. Palestinian suicide terrorism ceased rather dramatically after the death of Arafat and the rise of Abu Mazen (Mahmoud Abbas), who imposed a change in policy on the Palestinian Authority, and in the end Hamas accepted the verdict. The new orientation was expressed in supervision of imams in mosques, who stopped calling for *istishhad*, and restrictions on the number of television broadcasts glorifying the act. Graffiti praising suicide terrorism began to fade.

Palestinian and Israeli analysts agree on the list of reasons that led to the cessation of suicide terrorism. First, there is recognition of the effectiveness of initiatives by the ISA and the IDF intended to deter suicide terrorism and increasing success at preventing it. These initiatives include building the separation wall between the State of Israel and the territories; blocking roads between centers of the Palestinian population and preventing Palestinian workers with permits from entering Israel; uncovering the secrets of the organizations by introducing agents and tapping Palestinian telephones and monitoring computerized networks; eliminating leaders and central activists; halting the flow of money to the organizations; and inflicting collective punishment such as the destruction of houses. Counterterrorism efforts peaked in the Defensive Shield campaign, which ended with a huge number of Palestinian deaths and the dismantling of the organizational infrastructure in the West Bank (March 2002). Second, as a result of the foregoing, there was a decline in support for suicide terrorism among the Palestinian public. Internal criticism increased because of the heavy price that ordinary citizens were forced to pay while noting that Israeli policy had not changed. Critics added that the victims of suicide terrorism on the Israeli side were not settlers and military personnel, who were worthy targets, but ordinary citizens, and the Israeli public was becoming more united and determined against suicide terrorism. It was further observed that, in response to suicide terrorism the Israeli Right had grown stronger, while the Left was weakened and leaned consistently to the right. Parallel to this political disillusion, reservations regarding the morality of suicide terrorism also began to be heard among the Palestinians. Third, the organizations became more sensitive to condemnations voiced by governments and world public opinion. Despite the Israeli separation and withdrawal of settlers and military forces from the Gaza Strip (summer 2005), the organizations came to the conclusion that suicide terrorism was counterproductive. A fourth reason was that the main instigator of suicide terrorism, Hamas, was no longer a clandestine organization but became a government that had to take care of running the administration of an independent proto-state in the Gaza Strip. Suicide terrorism is a luxury that an establishment that has to administer responsible domestic and foreign policy can no longer afford. Therefore, not only does Hamas refrain from initiating suicide terrorism itself, but it also suppresses such initiatives on the parts of nonestablishment organizations, beginning with the Palestinian Islamic Jihad.

In fact, with the ostensible normalization of Palestinian suicide terrorism, the feeling grew that it had played itself out. Its splendor died away, while other options for combating the occupation arose, such as the firing of mortars and rockets and kidnappings by units emerging from tunnels deep in Israeli territory.

Suicide terrorism is not extinct. It has migrated to other places. In some of them it is flourishing, and it is certainly possible that it will return to the arena of the Israeli-Palestinian conflict. From time to time the Palestinian organizations threaten to return to the path of *istishhad*. In some instances over the decade following the ebbing of the second wave, the ISA has reported discovery of Hamas organizations that are plotting to renew the tradition of suicide terrorism.[62]

It is hard to assume that the era of suicide terrorism has passed without leaving a residue in the collective memory of the resistance organizations and among the Palestinians in general. Most likely the idea of suicide terrorism, along with the normative and emotional complex that is attached to it, has been relegated to the subterranean reservoir of the local Muslim and Arab culture, where they are buried until the time when they will be resurrected and return to the margins of the stage and then, perhaps, to its center. Suicide terrorism is now part of the cultural and political repertoire of the Palestinians, ready and waiting for the proper circumstances to reveal the potential preserved in it. When the need for it is felt, it will be possible to adopt it as a model, a source of inspiration, and a precedent, to breathe life into it again, in accordance with changing conditions. One cannot completely dismiss the possibility of the resurrection of Palestinian suicide terrorism, especially while it is flourishing elsewhere.

AFTERWORD

Two Attacks on Our Moral Order

Excursus

I am the child of Holocaust survivors. My mother was a young Polish Jew who underwent the most horrendous tribulations in WWII, during which her entire family was murdered. From the little that I know, her stamina, her presence of mind, and mainly her unusual beauty played a role in rescuing her from that hell, as well as—of course—no small amount of luck. In retrospect it is clear to me that she hid more than she revealed about that time. But over the years, because of what I remember from my early childhood, it has been difficult to free myself from the oppressive sense that my mother suffered from a feeling of guilt and shame for having survived. Before her death, at a ripe old age, she repeated the claim I had heard many times in the past, that the Nazis' success in their ghastly anti-Jewish program had to be measured not only by the 6 million people they murdered but also by how they deprived survivors of the feeling of innocence for having remained alive despite everything. The horrifying nature of the Holocaust was embodied by the way in which it placed survivors in an apologetic position. My mother remembered Emma G, Bella Y, and few more of her close girlfriends—Holocaust survivors who committed suicide during the postwar years—as Nazi victims.[1]

Robbing the victims of their innocence, and staining them with even a hint of guilt, in the context of the Holocaust reminds one of the particularly tragic case of the Jewish *Sonderkommando*, the "special squads" that were used in Auschwitz and other death camps. These consisted of hundreds of prisoners who were responsible for the "six stations" on the way to death: the *Sonderkommando* received the transports of Jews from the trains and sent them to the supposed showers, where they made sure they stripped and piled up their clothing, and after the poison gas was dropped into the sealed chambers (a job reserved solely for the Nazi guards), they removed the bodies, took their valuables, pulled out their gold teeth, cut the women's hair, and carted the bodies to the crematoriums. They cremated them and took care of body parts that were not completely consumed by the fire, and in the end they dumped the ashes into the river or collected it for use as fertilizer. Thus, at the height of the extermination, from May through September 1944, the Jews of the *Sonderkommando* helped eliminate between ten and twenty thousand of their fellow Jews every day, seven days a week. Usually Jews with strong bodies were chosen to serve in the *Sonderkommando*, but in some cases their conscription was a form of punishment.

Very few members of the *Sonderkommando* survived. After the war they were regarded with suspicion as collaborators in the crimes of the Nazis, and they were therefore treated with contempt, anger, and hatred, while they themselves could not overcome the tormenting feeling of shared responsibility for the horrors committed against their Jewish brethren. The negative self-image and public image of the *Sonderkommando* is an integral part of their tragedy. After all, the cruel fate of cooperating in the murder of their relatives, their fellow townspeople, and the members of their people, was forced on them. The meaning of refusal was immediate death. Instead, their fate was prolonged death. They knew very well that in a few months, once their work was done, they would be executed, like those who had come before them, and those who would come after them. The Germans would not let them live because they knew too much. The veteran prisoners told the new ones as soon as they arrived. Indeed, they were all killed, except for some members of the last group, who remained alive when the camps were evacuated because of negligence or some flaw in the German operation. Twelve squads succeeded each other in Auschwitz. As its initiation, each squad burned its predecessor. They not only witnessed the death of their brethren and were active in causing it, but they themselves were condemned to the death to which they went with clear awareness. In this sense, they were living-dead.

There are several noteworthy historical and philosophical publications on the *Sonderkommando*.[2] Just recently, after finishing the present book, I read a newspaper interview[3] that led me to reread *The Drowned and the Saved* by Primo Levi, an Italian Jew who survived the Auschwitz concentration camp (and who committed suicide about thirty years ago).[4] Levi's last book presents memories and reflections about the Nazi death machine and deadly violence in general. This prominent author very appropriately chose to call the chapter devoted to the *Sonderkommando* the "Gray Zone." In the concentration camps, the Nazis systematically created a gray zone in which there was a blurring of areas, a partial overlap and inadvertent collaboration between the aggressor and the victim.

As I emphasized in the preface, calling attention to the linkage between aggressor and victim and their "paradoxical parallelism" must not conceal the fact that they do not bear equal responsibility, nor are they ethically equivalent. As Levi was careful to point out:

> Both [aggressor and victim] are in the same trap, but it is the aggressor who has prepared it and activated it. We do not want to abet confusion, or small change Freudianism. . . . The aggressor remains what he is, and so does the victim. They are not interchangeable. The former is to be punished and execrated (but, if possible, understood), the latter to be pitied and helped. . . . To confuse the murderers with their victims is a moral disease or an aesthetic affectation or sinister sign of complicity, above all, it is a precious service rendered (intentionally or not) to the deniers of truth.[5]

To understand the world by means of dichotomous division into binary couples, with Manichaean contrast and opposition between them— we and them, and, in parallel, sons of light versus sons of darkness—is a basic and powerful human inclination. Nevertheless, even in the extreme circumstances of a concentration camp, despite the natural tendency and false conceptions (both of those who were there and of the observers and readers of history), it is impossible to speak simply about a world of victims and victimizers, and in any event about harmless people versus evildoers. A dramatic example of this is provided by the privileged Jewish prisoners, who were usually functionaries whom the Nazis used in the intermediate levels of rule and as assistants, in order to make their control and action more efficient, to humiliate, and perhaps to confuse as well. Because this broke down the basic dichotomy between black and white, a gray area was created, and questions arose: Are they on our side or theirs? Are they governors or governed? Are they guilty or innocent? The answer is: both. They were of a third kind, hybrids. They exemplify the tragedy of the situation in the camps. In these violent planets, in a way that slightly recalls the Middle East conflict between Israelis and Palestinians, enormous pressures and temptations are exerted on the weak to become various types of collaborators. Such is the *Kapo*, a prisoner placed in charge of a group of prisoners, commanding them and imposing discipline on them. On the one hand, he is one of them, sometimes acting openly or secretly on their behalf. On the other hand, under Nazi coercion, because of the desire to gain certain benefits, and sometimes because of an egotistical and even sadistic personality, he or she also persecutes them. There were *Kapos* who risked their status and lives to save one of "their" prisoners, while others beat "their" prisoners to death.

The *Sonderkommando* is a more extreme case. Almost all the *Sonderkommando* were Jews. This is to be expected, seeing that most of the prisoners were Jews, but on the other hand, there were enough non-Jewish prisoners in Auschwitz from whom it would have been possible to choose those suitable for the work of running the crematoriums. Gentile prisoners were natural candidates, since some of them were anti-Semitic, and they may have felt no solidarity with those going to their death. Thus they would have been exempted from the need to cope with the inner conflict that arose among those who helped destroy their brethren, and which might also have detracted from their effectiveness. Gideon Greif, a scholar of the Holocaust, concludes that in this cruel way the Germans wished to humiliate the Jews. Levi offers a different explanation, according to which there was a hidden intention to create a gray area in which the distinction between attacker and victim was blurred and thus to shift the blame from the Nazi guards who tortured and murdered to the Jewish prisoners, both those who were already dead and those about to die. A message was implicit in the use of the Jewish *Sonderkommando*: we Germans are committing mass murder, while you, the actual and potential victims, participate in this deed. Thus you are like us, and you cannot pretend to be better than us. This claim of Levi's regarding the creation of the *Sonderkommando* and its operation contains the essence of the demonic force that drove the Holocaust.

During the few months when they served in the special squads, the *Sonderkommando* were sequestered from the other prisoners, they received medical treatment, food, clothing, and sleeping conditions slightly better than the other prisoners. This assured their willingness to work in the worst possible situation. Levi suggests that in addition to this practical aspect, the limited privileges that the *Sonderkommando* enjoyed were intended to create within them, and within those who observed them (in the camp, in real time, and outside the camp, in historical perspective), a feeling that between them and their Nazi operators there was a degree of equality. This was one way of erasing the sharp line that distances and opposes the ultimate attacker from the ultimate victim.

To support this claim, testimony is adduced regarding a soccer match that was held in Auschwitz between a team of SS guards and a group of *Sonderkommando* prisoners, during a short interruption of the work routine in the crematoriums, before an enthusiastic and encouraging audience. This episode appears to be surreal, and such a seemingly idyllic scene could not have taken place between the Nazis and ordinary prisoners, but only between them and those who were used as something like collaborators, on the basis of an illusory sense of closeness and equal footing between the sides. Behind this playing together, once again the Nazi satanic message is heard: these Jewish victims of ours are like us, sharing a game with us, and sharing in the murder of Jews with us. We defiled them with the blood of their brethren, and they bathe in it like us, in the gas chambers and on the grassy field.

Back to the Here and Now

The gray zone in which the distinction between assailant and victim is blurred also exists in the arena of Palestinian suicide terrorism in Israel.

We have before us two variants of a hybrid creation: victim-attacker, attacker-victim. In one case the attacker is the SS guard, and in the second case it is the Hamas or Islamic Jihad activist. In the case of the Holocaust, the victim was forced to take part in the attack, and in the case of the intifada, the attacker was solicited to be partner in victimhood (by literally sharing the fate of his/her target). In both cases an appearance of equality is created: in one instance both sides inflict violence on other people, and in the second case they share victimhood. As a consequence, in one case they share guilt and shame, and in the other case they share a feeling of integrity and self-righteousness. In WWII, the instigators manipulated the victim to bear some responsibility for the spilling of blood and to take on some of the disgrace of the aggressor, and in the Middle Eastern conflict, the instigators of aggression manipulated the attacker into a situation in which he was able to indulge in the virtues of the victim.

The situations under discussion offer alternative options for encroaching on the exclusive status of the victims and to strike out at and compete with their monopoly on victimhood, that is, to prevent the other side from consoling itself with the sense of innocence that accompanies victimhood in the situation of the Holocaust or from enjoying the advantage of moral uprightness provided by victimhood, as in the situation of the intifada.

Both the Nazi and Palestinian entrepreneurs of aggression would seem to envy their victims, and therefore, in one case they implicate the victim so that he will appear to be an aggressor and feel like one, so that he will resemble them, and in the other case they assume victimhood so as to resemble their victim. The instigators of aggression ease their own conscience either by infecting the other side with components of their own status as aggressors, or by usurping and abusing the other side's status as victim. In both cases they act to attenuate the contrast between attacker and victim, and thus receive license to continue their aggression.

As I noted earlier in the book, the analogy between the case of the Holocaust and that of the intifada is very limited, and any comparison between the Nazi campaign against the Jews and the actions of the terrorist organizations against Israel demands maximum caution. By no means must my words be understood as suggesting that the SS and Hamas are similar phenomena with respect to their ideology, motivation, and practice, or in other respects. Nevertheless, I claim that the arena of Palestinian suicide terrorism in Israel is also a gray area.

The creation of a victim-aggressor and that of the aggressor-victim, of the SS and the Hamas respectively, are two base schemes to justify criminal violence.[6] Beyond that, they are both attacks on the moral order of society, beclouding the aspiration for justice and truth, and thus they both subvert our civilization.

NOTES

Preface

1. Many details concerning this suicide attack are drawn from the interrogation of 'Abed's accomplices and their trial. E.g., Jerusalem Police Department protocol, July 2, 2003; Hebron IDF military court protocol, June 19, 2005.

2. Such as the two terrorists who struck a supermarket in Dimona (February 2008).

3. Ami Pedahzur and Arie Perliger, "The Changing Nature of Suicide Attacks: A Social Network Perspective," *Social Forces* 84, no. 4 (2006): 1987–2008. Apropos of social networks and suicide terrorism, 'Abed came from the large Qawasmeh clan. Some members of this extended family are leaders in the Hamas movement in the area and are involved in terrorism against Israel. Indeed, his cousin was also a human bomb, while years later, two other relatives murdered three young Yeshiva students who had been kidnapped (June 2014). His mother said that "he felt great sadness when he saw scenes of armed conflict with the Israelis, the last of which was the martyrdom of his friend Hamza al-Qawasmeh, who was studying with him in the same school."

4. Bassam Banat, "Palestinian Suicide Martyrs: Facts and Figures" (PhD diss., University of Granada, 2010), 291.

5. Amira Hass, "Interview with a Suicide Bomber," *Haaretz*, April 5, 2003.

6. Reprinted in the daily *Yediot Aharonot*, January 2, 2015.

7. Cf. Juliana Ocks, *Security and Suspicion: Ethnography of Everyday Life in Israel* (Philadelphia: University of Pennsylvania Press, 2011).

8. Vered Lee, "Homeless," *Haaretz* weekly magazine, April 3, 2015.

9. Interview with a member of the Israel Border Police (MaGaV), *Yediot Ahronot* (date could not be retrieved). There are various similar testimonies. For example, "I saw a huge smile on the terrorist's face just before he hit me" (interview with an injured survivor, *Arutz Sheva*, November 17, 2017). Yet an authoritative writer on violence claims that "it is extremely rare that killers are in a laughing good humor. The smiling villain image comes across so well precisely because it is unrealistic." Randall Collins, *Violence: Micro-Sociological Theory* (Princeton, NJ: Princeton University Press, 2011), 19.

10. A policeman, age twenty-four, from al-Arroub refugee camp, sponsored by al-Aqsa Martyrs' Brigade (Fatah).

11. See Adriana Cavavero, *Horrorism: Naming Contemporary Violence* (New York: Columbia University Press, 2009). Medusa's gaze has been discussed mostly by literary scholars, social critics, and psychologists. E.g., Marjorie Garber and Nancy Vickers, eds., *The Medusa Reader* (Abingdon: Routledge, 2003).

12. Jane Harrison, *Prolegomena to the Study of Greek Religion* (Princeton, NJ: Princeton University Press, 1991).

13. "Influenced by Jacques Lacan many recent readers have interpreted Medusa's horror as a kind of mirror stage, in which the gazer and the gazed are locked in a dialectic of mutual reflection." Garber and Vickers, introduction to *Medusa Reader*.

14. Cf. Meir Vigoder, "The Story of the Head: The Suicide Bomber, the Medusa and the Aesthetics of Terror in Photography," *Third Text* 20, no. 3/4 (2006): 449–62.

15. Note the distinction between trauma and secondary trauma.

16. Two outstanding examples: Christoph Reuter, *My Life Is a Weapon: A Modern History of Suicide Bombing* (Princeton, NJ: Princeton University Press, 2004); Anne Marie Oliver and Paul Steinberg, *The Road to Martyrs' Square: A Journey into the World of the Suicide Bomber* (New York: Oxford University Press, 2006).

17. E.g., Chris Cleave, *Incendiary* (New York: Knopf, 2005); John Updike, *Terrorist* (New York: Random House, 2006); Martin Amis, "The Last Days of Muhammad Atta," *New Yorker,* April 24, 2006, 152–63.

18. E.g., Boaz Ganor, *The Counter-Terrorism Puzzle: Guide for Decision Makers* (New Brunswick, NJ: Transaction, 2005); Russell Howard and Sawyer Reid, eds., *Terrorism and Counterterrorism: Understanding the New Security Environment* (Dubuque, IA: McGraw Hill, 2006). See also *The 9/11 Commission Report*, https://www.9-11commission.gov/report/911Report.pdf.

19. E.g., Ted Honderich, "After the Terror," *Journal of Ethics* 7, no. 2 (2003): 161–81.

20. Notably, Talal Asad, *On Suicide Bombing* (New York: Columbia University Press, 2002).

21. E.g., Scott Atran, "Genesis of Suicide Terrorism," *Science* 299 (2003): 1534–39; Mohammed Hafez, "Rationality, Culture and Structure in the Making of Suicide Bombers," *Studies in Conflict and Terrorism* 29, no. 2 (2006): 165–85; Huseyin Cinoglu and Suleyman Ozeren, "Classical Schools of Sociology and Terrorism," *Eskişehir Osmangazi Üniversitesi Sosyal Bilimler Dergisi* 11, no. 2 (2010): 43–59.

22. Cf. Adam Dolnik, ed., *Conducting Terrorism Field Research: A Guide* (Abingdon: Routledge, 2013), esp. 188, 199.

23 E.g., Jerold Post et al., "The Psychology of Suicide Terrorism," *Psychiatry* 72, no. 1 (2009): 13–31.

24. E.g., Efraim Benmelech, Claude Berrebi, and Esteban Klor, "Economic Conditions and the Quality of Suicide Terrorism" (NBER working paper no. 16320, Harvard University, Cambridge, MA, August 2010).

25. E.g., Maria Alvanou, "Criminological Perspectives on Female Suicide Terrorism," in *Female Suicide Bombers: Dying for Equality?* ed. Yoram Schweitzer (Tel Aviv: Jaffe Center for Strategic Studies, 2006), 91–106.

26. E.g., Assaf Moghadam, "Palestinian Suicide Terrorists in the Second Intifada: Motivations and Organizational Aspects," *Studies in Conflict and Terrorism* 26, no. 2 (2003): 65–92.

27. E.g., Matthew Bradley, "Terrorism as an Alternative Form of Political Communication," Political Studies Association (UK) Annual Meeting Proceedings, 2008, http://paper room.ipsa.org/papers/paper_494.pdf.

28. A sample of major contributions to the study of suicide terrorism: Ami Pedahzur, *Suicide Terrorism* (Cambridge, MA: Polity, 2005); Ami Pedahzur, ed., *Root Causes of Suicide Terrorism* (New York: Routledge, 2006); Mia Bloom, *Dying to Kill: The Allure of Suicide Terrorism* (New York: Columbia University Press, 2005); Boaz Ganor, ed., *Countering Suicide Terrorism: International Conference* (Herzliya: IDC 78, 2001); Diego Gambetta, ed., *Making Sense of Suicide Terrorism* (New York: Oxford University Press, 2005); Ariel Merari, *Driven to Death: Psychological and Social Aspects of Suicide Terrorism* (New York: Oxford University Press, 2010); Robert Pape, *Dying to Win: The Strategic Logic of Suicide Terrorism* (New York: Random House, 2005); Bruce Hoffman, *Inside Terrorism* (New York: Columbia University Press, 2005); Riaz Hassan, *Life as a Weapon: The Global Rise of Suicide Terrorism* (New York: Routledge, 2014); Mohammed Hafez, *Manufacturing Human Bombs* (Washington, DC: US Institute of Peace, 2006); Shaul Shay, *Shahids: Islam and Suicide Attacks* (New Brunswick, NJ: Transaction, 2004); Meir Hatina, *Martyrdom in Modern Islam: Piety, Power and Politics* (New York: Cambridge University Press, 2014); Hugh Barlow, *Dead for Good: Martyrdom and the Rise of Suicide Terrorism* (London: Paradigm, 2007); Martha Crenshaw, "Explaining Suicide Terrorism: Review Essay," *Security Studies* 16 (2007): 133–62; Rashmi Singh, *Hamas and Suicide Terrorism: Multi Causal and Multi Level Approach* (New York: Routledge, 2011); Mary Sharpe, *Suicide Bombers: The Psychological and Religious and Other Imperatives* (Washington, DC: IOS Press, 2008); Apdesh Kumar and Manas Mandal, *Understanding Suicide Terrorism: Psycho-Social Dynamics* (Los Angeles: Sage, 2014); Forad Khosrokhovor, *Suicide Bombers: Allah's New Martyrs* (Ann Arbor: Pluro Press, 2005); Jeffrey Lewis, *The Business of Martyrdom: A History of Suicide Bombing* (Annapolis: Naval Institute Press, 2012); Assaf Moghadam, *The Globalization of Martyrdom* (Baltimore: Johns Hopkins University Press, 2008); David Cook and Olivia Allison *Understanding and Addressing Suicide Attacks: The Faith and Politics of Martyr Operations* (Westport, CT: Prager, 2007); Eli Berman, *Radical, Religious and Violent: The New Economics of Terrorism* (Cambridge, MA: MIT Press, 2009).

29. There is a kind of division of labor among the authors. Most publications about the attacking side come from the fields of political science and psychology, whereas most of those who write about the victims are anthropologists.

30. Exceptional to this are the arguments about the connection between aggressor and victim in domestic violence.

31. A remarkable exception is Randall Collins's book *Violence: Micro-Sociological Theory* (above, n. 9), in which he seeks to understand violence in terms of the situation in which the attacker and victim meet. This is parallel to my call to concentrate on the arena, but different in essential ways that will be detailed later.

32. Cf. Andrew Silke, ed., *Research on Terrorism: Trends, Achievements, Failures* (London: Frank Cass, 2004), 10.

33. On the difficulties of fieldwork in terrorism in general, see Adam Dolnik, "Conducting Field Research on Terrorism," *Perspectives on Terrorism* 5, no. 2 (2011): 3–35.

34. For an exception, see Nurit Stadler, Eyal Ben Ari, and Einat Mesterman, "Terror, Aid and Organization: The Haredi Disaster Victim Identification Teams in Israel," *Anthropological Quarterly* 76, no. 3 (2005): 619–51.

35. Note, for example, the recent emergence of terrorism medicine as a specialty.

36. See the afterword of this book for elaboration of this point.

37. Gideon Aran, "The Cult of Dismembered Limbs" (unpublished manuscript).

38. Mohammed al-Hindi, age twenty-one, exploded in bus no. 25 in Jerusalem, July 1993. Oliver and Steinberg, *Road to Martyrs' Square*, 148.

39. This information has been confirmed also by one of my interviewees in Israel Institute of Forensic Medicine. However, another source casts some doubts about it. Note the particular items in Muhammad Atta's will found in the aftermath of 9/11 that indicate his obsession with the treatment of his penis after his death.

40. ISA agents claim that a few would-be human bombs "erased" their old tattoos before embarking on their mission, thus making their body wholly perfect so as to ensure smooth entry to paradise.

41. Aran, "Cult of Dismembered Limbs."

42. Micro-sociology is inspired by phenomenology, and related to ethnomethodology and symbolic interactionism. Its opposite is macro-sociology, which concerns social structure and broader systems.

43. In World War II, half the casualties were civilians. In Vietnam and Afghanistan the proportion was even higher.

44. E.g., the legendary mother Hannah and her seven sons (second century BC), celebrated during the Jewish holiday of Hanukkah.

45. Daniel Dayan and Elihu Katz, *Media Events* (Cambridge, MA: Harvard University Press, 1994).

46. Philip Roth, *Humbling* (New York: Houghton Mifflin Harcourt, 2014).

47. The sociologist David Gibson of Notre Dame University commenting on Collins's, *Violence* in an unpublished handout distributed and used in class (November 2014).

48. Bus no. 26 in 1995; French Hill in 2001 and 2002; and bus no. 19 in 2004.

1. Suicide Terrorism Revisited

1. E.g., Rashmi Singh, *Hamas and Suicide Terrorism* (New York: Routledge, 2011), 2. See also https://aoav.org.uk/2013/a-short-history-of-suicide-bombing.

2. IDF intelligence experts claim that in the 1970s Palestinian resistance organizations already employed a warfare technique that seems in retrospect to resemble suicide terrorism, although the concept was not yet in use at that time. Terrorists attacked northern and coastal Israeli towns in an attempt to take hostages, and when they realized that they could not escape alive, they killed themselves. Such attacks have been called, in Hebrew, "sacrificial."

3. Two or three observers note that a Lebanese Shiite detonated a truck loaded with TNT at the entrance to the Iraqi embassy in Beirut as early as December 1981 (claiming ten victims, including the ambassador). See, for example, Ariel Merari, *Driven to Death* (New York: Oxford University Press, 2010), 61. Was it a precedent for Hezbollah suicide attacks? According to the somewhat dubious information available, chances are good that the terrorist driver escaped before the explosion.

4. Years later, Mughniyah was eliminated in a joint CIA-Mossad counterterrorism operation (Damascus, February 2008).

5. E.g., Robert Pape, *Dying to Win* (New York: Random House, 2005), 11–13; Ami Pedahzur, ed., *Root Causes of Suicide Terrorism* (New York: Routledge, 2006), 12–13. Some observers bring this argument to its extreme. See Nicolo Caldararo, "Suicide Bombers, Terror, History and Religion," *Anthropological Quarterly* 79, no. 1 (2006): 123–31.

6. Richard Horsley, "The Sicarii: Ancient Jewish Terrorists," *Journal of Religion* 59, no. 4 (October 1979): 435–58; Morton Smith, "Zealots and Sicarii, Their Origins and Relation," *Harvard Theological Review* 64, no. 1 (January 1971): 1–19.

7. Bernard Lewis, *The Assassins* (London: Weidenfeld & Nicholson, 1967).

8. See David Rapoport, "Fear and Trembling: Terrorism in Three Religious Traditions," *American Political Science Review* 78, no. 3 (September 1984): 658–77.

9. Josephus was a nobleman, priest, and rebel political leader who later collaborated with the Roman occupiers. Naturally he abhorred the Sicarii, as did the Jewish sages of the Talmud.

10. Derek Offord, *The Russian Revolutionary Movement in the 1880s* (Cambridge: Cambridge University Press, 1986).

11. Albert Axell and Kase Hideaki Kase, *Kamikaze: Japan's Suicide Gods* (New York: Longman, 2002). Note the title of Raphael Israeli's book on Islamic suicide terrorism, *Islamikaze: Manifestations of Islamic Martyrology* (London: Frank Cass, 2004). See also Meir Hatina, *Martyrdom in Modern Islam: Piety, Power and Politics* (New York: Cambridge University Press, 2011), chap. 1.

12. Amir Taheri, *Holy Terror: Inside the World of Islamic Terrorism* (Bethesda, MD: Adler & Adler, 1987), 92.

13. David Whittaker, *Terrorists and Terrorism in the Contemporary World* (London: Routledge, 2004), 25.

14. Walter Laqueur, *New Terrorism* (New York: Oxford University Press, 1999), 141.

15. Among the disadvantages of suicide terrorism are a relatively small-size explosive charge with limited lethal effect; relatively complicated logistics that involve more than one person, time spent planning, and at least rudimentary organization; and, of course, the death of the terrorist, who needs to be replaced, thus calling for further recruitment.

16. For a similar conception of suicide terrorism, see Boaz Ganor, "Suicide Attacks in Israel," and Yoram Schweitzer, "Suicide Terrorism: Development and Main Characteristics," both in *Countering Suicide Terrorism*, ed. Boaz Ganor (Herzliya: IDC 78, 2001). See also the definitions in Shaul Shay, *Shahids: Islam and Suicide Attacks* (New Brunswick, NJ: Transaction, 2004); Mohammed Hafez, *Manufacturing Human Bombs* (Washington, DC: US Institute of Peace, 2006); Martha Crenshaw, "Explaining Suicide Terrorism: Review Essay," *Security Studies* 16 (2007): 133–62; and Mia Bloom, *Dying to Kill: The Allure of Suicide Terrorism* (New York: Columbia University Press, 2005). Some prominent writers on suicide terrorism define it in a way that stops short of requiring the certainty of the perpetrator's death. E.g., Pape, *Dying to Win* ("The attacker does not expect to survive the mission").

17. Daniel Kahneman and Amos Tversky, "Prospect Theory: An Analysis of Decision under Risk," *Econometrica* 47, no. 3 (1979): 263–92.

18. An intriguing relevant phenomenon is the tendency of generals to deploy massive infantry and armored forces in challenging battles rather than much smaller special commando units, which would ensure mission accomplishment with significantly fewer casualties. Although the absolute number of casualties in the first case is higher, the death seems more random and anonymous, thus more "bearable," while in the second case death is more probable and "personal," thus harder to tolerate. See also Steven Pinker, *The Better Angels of Our Nature* (New York: Viking, 2011), 13.

19. See, for example, Christoph Reuter, *My Life Is a Weapon: A Modern History of Suicide Bombing* (Princeton, NJ: Princeton University Press, 2004), 156, 165.

20. Mohammed Hafez, *Manufacturing Human Bombs* (Washington, DC: US Institute of Peace, 2006).

21. Anat Berko, *The Smarter Bombs: Women and Children as Suicide Bombers* (Lanham, MD: Rowman & Littlefield, 2011); Yoram Schweitzer, ed., *Female Suicide Bombers: Dying for Equality* (Tel Aviv: Jaffe Center for Strategic Studies, 2006).

22. A few terrorist attacks combine the two techniques: first the perpetrator sprays the target with automatic gunfire (often with hand grenades too); he then detonates the explosive charge.

23. Shaul Shay, *Shahids: Islam and Suicide Attacks* (New Brunswick, NJ: Transaction, 2004), 156–57.

24. Later, Sheikh Yussuf Kardawai, one of the greatest authorities in Muslim law in this generation, ratified this ruling (March 1996).

25. Afulah, November 2001.

26. Pedahzur, *Root Causes*, 17.

27. The aggressor and victim Natan Zada, August 2005.

28. According to this version, she fled from the arena in a taxi. According to a different version, she was not wounded since she was far away, but she clearly heard the explosion and the ambulance sirens.

29. Cf. Assaf Moghadam's distinction between broad definitions of suicide terrorism and narrow definitions, in "Defining Suicide Terrorism," chap. 1 in Pedahzur, *Root Causes*, 18–21.

30. Very much like the (evidently nonsuicidal) terrorist attack in the northern tower of the World Trade Center (February 1993).

31. See Gideon Aran, "Striking Home: Ideal-Type of Terrorism," *Terrorism and Political Violence* 29 (2017): 1–19.

32. Walter Lacquer, *New Terrorism* (New York: Oxford University Press, 1999), 196.

33. The hunger strikes of the Irish Republican Army (IRA) did not make it a suicide terrorist organization either.

34. According to Moghadam's estimation (personal communication), the number of suicide attacks at a certain point in time was below 1,900, whereas Merari, who uses a broader definition of suicide terrorism, estimates the number of attacks for the same period as 2,500. Both base their estimates on the same databases (Haifa database of Pedahzur and Perliger; US National Counterterrorism Center).

35. Compare professional snipers, who carefully observe the target and only after some time choose to focus on a specific object within it.

36. The late Dr. Reuvan Paz, head of ISA Research Division and academic Islamic terrorism expert (personal communication).

37. Gideon Aran, "Cult of Dismembered Limbs" (unpublished manuscript).

38. Aran, "Striking Home."

39. Pape, *Dying to Win*, 11.

40. Implantation of an explosive device in a human body is not essentially different from the surgical procedure of installing a pacemaker. Explosion and forensic experts suggest the option of swallowing charges the way drug smugglers do contraband.

41. Several media report that the al-Qaeda offshoot in Yemen examined the possibility of exploding airliners with charges injected into women's silicon breast implants (*Haaretz*, August 16, 2013).

42. E.g., Eileen Sullivan, "TSA Vows More Interaction with Passengers," *Investment Watch Blog*, July 6, 2011, http://investmentwatchblog.com/tsa-vows-more-interaction-with-passengers/.

43. There were attempts to explain changes in frequency of suicide attacks in terms of seasonal weather variation that enables or impedes wearing heavy clothing that may hide explosive charge.

44. Translated by Lisa Katz, *American Poetry Review* (March/April 2003).

45. The last three victims were Jews, very recent immigrants from the former Soviet Union, Afghanistan, and Iran respectively.

46. Two Chinese construction workers were killed in this attack too.

47. These suicide terrorists are labeled by Israeli press "walking, ticking bombs."

48. Abdallah Bargouti in his ISA interrogation quoted in his trial.

49. Definitive information regarding the rest is missing. Compare global statistics for the first decade of the twenty-first century: 46% in handbags or backpacks, 37% in belts and vests, and 4% in car bombs.

50. Grey Chris, *Cyborg Citizen Politics in the Postmodern Age* (New York: Routledge, 2001).

51. Gayatri Chakravorty Spivak views suicide terrorism as an extreme case of autoeroticism, in "A Speech after 9/11," *Boundary* 2 (2000): 95. Brought to my attention by Professor Raya Morag.

52. For a notable exception, see Merari's thorough discussion of suicide terrorism in light of the theory and findings of research on suicide (*Driven to Death*, chap. 8).

53. E.g., the case of Wafa Samir Bas described in chap. 2.

54. Simanti Lahiri, "Choosing to Die: Suicide Bombing and Suicide Protest in South Asia," *Terrorism and Political Violence* 27, no. 2 (2015): 268–88.

55. Melissa Dahl, "What Do We Know about People Who Turn Suicide into an Act of Murder?" *New York Times Magazine*, March 27, 2015.

56. The reference was to an interesting thesis suggested by Adam Lankford in his book *The Myth of Martyrdom: What Really Drives Suicide Bombers, Rampage Shooters and Other Self-Destructive Shooters* (New York: St. Martin Press, 2013).

57. Karin Andriolo, "Murder by Suicide: Episode from Muslim History," *American Anthropologist* 104, no. 3 (2002): 736–42.

58. See Dean Conant Worcester, *The Philippine Islands and Their People* (New York, 1898). Also Ewing Franklyn, "Juramentado: Institutionalized Suicide among the Moros of the Philippines," *Anthropological Quarterly* 28, no. 4 (1955): 148–55.

59. See preface, note 39, regarding the obsessive concern of Islamic suicide terrorists (Muhammad Atta included) with the treatment of their sex organs following the explosion.

60. Karin Andriolo ("Murder by Suicide") suggestively comments on the association between this phenomenon and other manifestations of "masked suicide" practiced among Native Americans (and also among some contemporary Americans who challenge policemen in order to make them shoot and kill them, an action often called "suicide by cop"). Military experts claim that there is a somewhat similar behavior among soldiers in regular armies who volunteer for especially dangerous missions.

61. Thomas Kiefer, *The Tausug: Violence and Law in a Philippine Moslim Society* (New York: Holt, Rinehart and Winston, 1972).

2. Accidental Monsters, Unlikely Heroes (A)

1. Amira Haas, "Flying to Heaven," *Haaretz*, April 1, 2003.

2. See the roster of idolizing designations that appear as epigraphs in Bassam Banat, "Palestinian Suicide Martyrs: Facts and Figures" (PhD diss., University of Granada, 2010).

3. This depiction was offered in a moment of absentmindedness. Afterward the speaker regretted using the phrase and maintained that he was actually misunderstood. A few, more critical, of my Palestinian informants called human bombs "fools" and "suckers," but asked not to be identified.

4. For a slightly naive representation of human bombs, see Anne Speckhard, *Talking to Terrorists: Understanding the Psycho-Social Motivations of Militant Jihadi, Terrorists, Mass Hostage Takers, Suicide Bombers and Martyrs* (Mclean, VA: Advances Press, 2012). See also Nasra Hassan's somewhat biased "An Arsenal of Believers: Talking to the Human Bomb," *New Yorker*, November 19, 2001.

5. That is why they tend to overestimate the effectiveness of suicide terrorism, in terms of its lethal impact and its potential to change enemy policy. See in this context the Pape-Abrahms controversy. E.g., Max Abrahms, "Why Terrorism Does Not Work," *International Security*, 31 no. 2 (2006): 42–78.

6. According to another version the charge was detonated from afar by cell phone.

7. The author is Professor Arie Eldad. The human bomb is Wafa Samir Bas, age twenty-one. According to another version she was burned accidentally but raped twice in her childhood. The border guards suspected her and ordered her to undress. She then tried to activate the charge concealed in her underpants but failed.

8. The father of Ayat al-Akhras (Jerusalem supermarket bombing, March 2002) was an ISA collaborator, and she was apparently driven to accept a suicide mission in order to cleanse her family name. See also the pro-Palestinian film *Paradise Now,* where the volunteering of a young West Bank man for a suicide attack is presented in light of rumors about his father's collaboration with Israeli agents.

9. See Anat Berko, *The Path to Paradise: The Inner World of Suicide Bombers and Their Dispatchers* (Westport, CT: Praeger, 2009), 39–40. Sheikh Ahmad Yassin needed his assistant to remind him of basic information about the identity of human bombs in 1996, when there were still very few of them.

10. The identity of several Palestinian human bombs is unknown to this day. They appear with no name in the ISA records and were not acknowledged, let alone glorified, by Hamas or other resistance organizations. E.g., the terrorist who committed a suicide attack at the entrance to a Jewish settlement near Gaza in October 2004, about whom we know only his approximate age.

11. Gideon Aran, "The Cult of Dismembered Limbs" (unpublished manuscript).

12. Cf. Yoram Bilu, *The Saints' Impresarios* (Brighton, MA: Academic Studies Press, 2010).

13. Shortly after the human bomb's death, his mother admonished his dispatchers for being "unscrupulous."

14. Among them were Daud Sueid (attack near the Hilton Mamilah Hotel, Jerusalem) and Imad Zubeidi (attack in a bus station, Kfar Saba).

15. During the intifada the concept of "shahid" was broadened to include not only Palestinians killed by IDF troops but also those whose death may be related to Israel in an indirect, rather hypothetically assumed way, such as the organization functionary who was jailed in Israel for a while and several years later died of cancer, seen as the clear result of his ISA interrogation.

16. A commanding example: Dalal Mugrabi, a Fatah terrorist who participated in a bus hijacking, killing its thirty-seven passengers (March 1978). In retrospect she was crowned chief of the operation. Schools and youth camps in Gaza were named after her, and the Palestinian media label her "the greatest freedom fighter in the history of the Middle Eastern conflict."

17. E.g., a photo of Ayat al-Akhras welcomes visitors to Daheisheh refugee camp.

18. E.g., restaurant in Jenin owned by the father of human bomb Muhammad al-Masri.

19. Ariel Merari, *Driven to Death* (New York: Oxford University Press, 2010), chap. 6.

20. The reference is to the Hamas human bomb Osama Bahar mentioned in chap. 4 (Jerusalem, December 2001).

21. Note the revealing analogy of the typically ambivalent attitude of Jewish Orthodoxy toward born-again Jews (*hozrim be'tshuva*). Leading rabbis as well as ordinary believers speak of them as particularly saintly and yet treat them as inferior. While in theory, based

on the sacred texts, they are regarded as of "extrareligious" value compared to ordinary core-ligionists, in practice veteran members don't mingle with them and never marry them.

22. E.g., there are good reasons to believe that Hassan's "The Arsenal of Believers," which is often quoted and highly regarded as particularly authentic, was based at least partly on interviews that were staged with people pretending to be suicide terrorists. Real human bombs were never that accessible and so eager to talk.

23. My informant, formerly an authoritative Palestinian organization functionary, learned this genuine Hebrew slang while serving a long prison sentence in Israel.

24. Data regarding work, education, and political involvement of female human bombs reflect standards characteristic of the general Palestinian population.

25. Note the high proportion of ISIS human bombs in Iraq and Syria who are loners and foreigners removed from their families and natural environment, thus having practically nobody to support them in resisting the pressures to volunteer for suicide missions.

26. Merari, *Driven to Death*, chap. 3.

27. Banat, "Palestinian Suicide Martyrs," chap 4, particularly 213–14.

28. Merari, *Driven to Death*, 108–12.

29. Ibid.

30. Banat, "Palestinian Suicide Martyrs."

31. It is noteworthy that he was recruited by Ramzi Abu Salim, who committed a suicide attack a few minutes after his friend (Café Hilel, September 2003).

32. It seems that the senior Hamas terrorist knew nothing about his nephew's suicide mission until after the explosion.

33. Members of the Palestinian public voiced criticism and expressed anger at the organizations, blaming them for exploiting children. In response, spokesmen for the organizations claimed that it was all an ISA provocation.

34. See the prevalent issue discussed in the literature of the 1980s: Is there a terrorist personality? E.g., Walter Laqueur, *The Age of Terrorism* (London: Weidenfeld, 1987), 76–93.

35. Eileen Barker, *The Making of a Moonie* (London: Blackwell, 1984).

36. Eric Hoffer, *The True Believer* (New York: Harper, 2002).

37. Theodor Adorno, Else Frenkel-Brunswik, Daniel J. Levinson, and R. Nevitt Sanford, *The Authoritarian Personality* (New York: Harper and Row, 1950). Also, Milton Rokeach, *The Open and Closed Mind* (New York: Basic Books, 1960); Erich Fromm, *Escape from Freedom* (New York: Farrar and Rinehart, 1941).

38. Gideon Aran and Ron Hassner, "Religious Violence in Judaism: Past and Present," *Terrorism and Political Violence* 25, no. 3 (2013): 1–8, 44–56.

39. Merari, *Driven to Death*, 119.

40. Robert Pape, *Dying to Win: The Strategic Logic of Suicide Terrorism* (New York: Random House, 2005), 200.

41. Naturally suicide attacks were planned to be operationally simple so as to minimize chances of failure and to suit the level of poorly trained perpetrators.

42. Merari, *Driven to Death*, particularly chap. 5.

43. E.g., Robert Brym and Bader Araj's biased, methodically unqualified, and empirically unsubstantiated argument against Merari, "Are Suicide Bombers Suicidal?" *Studies in Conflict and Terrorism* 35, no. 6 (2012): 432–43. Note Ariel Merari's response in the same journal's issue.

44. In addition to certain depression, a minority of the imprisoned human bombs suffered from PTSD (post-traumatic stress disorder). This might be related also to their failure as suicide terrorists.

45. Unhappiness was particularly frequent among female suicide bombs.

46. Confirmed by Anat Berko's extensive empirical research findings (personal communication, 2015).

47. A veteran ISA agent maintained that the fact that human bombs typically come from unhappy families, which makes them easier to recruit, reminds him of the recruitment dynamics of Palestinian collaborators with Israeli intelligence services.

48. A partial exception is a couple of human bombs who came from an offshoot of the Hebronite Qauasme clan.

49. Khadra's real name is Muhammed Moulassehoul. The book: *The Attack* (New York: Anchor, 2007).

50. *The Attack*, directed by Ziad Doueiri (3B Production, Scope Pictures, Douri Films, 2012).

3. Accidental Monsters, Unlikely Heroes (B)

1. Polichuck was imprisoned in Israel and recently released.

2. The entrepreneurs of suicide terrorism are at the focus of chap. 4.

3. Unlike the human bombs, their dispatchers didn't show signs of depression, let alone any evidence of PTSD. Ariel Merari, *Driven to Death* (New York: Oxford University Press, 2010), chap. 6.

4. The organization's by no means resolute effort to release the suicide terrorism leaders was naturally silent and denied.

5. Victor Turner, "Betwixt and Between: The Liminal Period in *Rites of Passage*," *Proceedings of the American Ethnological Society* (1964): 4–40.

6. Arnold Van Gennep, *Rites of Passage* (Chicago: University of Chicago Press, 1960).

7. These details are drawn from the ISA interrogation of the terrorist's accomplice and his wife. A vastly distorted version of this case appears in the film *Paradise Now*.

8. According to gossip spread in the West Bank, in one instance an organization functionary ordered the human bomb to cross the border by foot to save taxi fare.

9. In Arabic, *khmar*, donkey.

10. Telephone communication few years after the intifada (2012). An almost identical message was conveyed by senior Hamas leader Salakh Shehadeh (later eliminated by IDF) in an Internet interview (Islam online, July 2002).

11. According to ISA officials, many of them were arrested in Operation Defensive Shield (March–April 2002).

12. Contrary to the case of the Tamil Tigers.

13. E.g., Sheikh Yassin ruling in the case of the female terrorist Rim Riashi from Gaza, who was dispatched on a suicide mission against her will following an extramarital affair (January 2004).

14. Shaul Kimhi and Shmuel Even, *Who Are the Palestinian Suicide Bombers?* (Tel Aviv: Tel Aviv University, INSS, 82, 2004).

15. Bassam Banat, "Palestinian Suicide Martyrs: Facts and Figures" (PhD diss., University of Granada, 2010).

16. Gabriel Weimann, *Terrorism in Cyberspace* (New York: Columbia University Press, 2015).

17. One exception: Dia Tawil, a student of engineering in Birzeit University and the nephew of Jamal Tawil, a senior leader of Hamas. On this and another exception, see chap. 2.

18. Elsewhere I argue that despite Palestinian Christians' extremist anti-Israeli ideology and involvement in active violence, not only has there not been a single Christian human

bomb, but no human bomb has come from West Bank areas that are predominantly Christian. Compare, for example, the high involvement in suicide terrorism of Muslim Beit Lehem with zero involvement of residents of neighboring Beit Jallah and Beit Sahur (Gideon Aran, "How Islamic Are Muslim Suicide Terrorists?" forthcoming).

19. My informer contrasted the human bomb with a "real fighter" who dares to look straight at the "white of his enemy's eye."

20. Merari, *Driven to Death*, 5.

21. Ibid., chap. 5.

22. Cf. Assaf Moghadam, "Palestinian Suicide Terrorists in the Second Intifada: Motivations and Organizational Aspects," *Studies in Conflict and Terrorism* 26, no. 2 (2003): 65–92.

23. For an appraisal of suicide terrorism effects in terms of objectives/achievements, see Max Abrahms, "The Political Effectiveness of Terrorism Revisited," *Comparative Political Studies* 45 (March 2012): 366–93.

24. See Rashmi Singh, *Hamas and Suicide Terrorism* (London: Routledge, 2011), 10–14.

25. See the collection of articles on motivations of human bombs in *Terrorism and Political Violence* 16, no. 4 (2004).

26. See, e.g., Kimhi and Even, *Who Are the Palestinian Suicide Bombers?*

27. E.g., Bader Araj, "Harsh State Repression and Suicide Bombing: The Second Palestinian Intifada, 2000–05" (PhD diss., University of Toronto, 2011); Robert Brym and Bader Araj, "Suicide Bombing as Strategy and Interaction: The Case of the Second Intifada," *Social Forces* 84, no. 4 (2006): 1969–86.

28. E.g., Robert Pape, *Dying to Win* (New York: Random House, 2005).

29. Of course, there could also be unconscious motives whose influence on suicide terrorism is difficult to appraise, such as cumulative despair, as argued by the psychiatrist Eyad el-Sarraj, "Paradise Waiting: Experience in Suicide Bombing" (paper distributed at the NATO Advanced Research Workshop: Ideologies of Terrorism, Brussels, January 2005).

30. On many such occasions, relatives, neighbors, and organization supporters offered their help in rebuilding the family house demolished by IDF.

31. Such images are still published even several years after the end of the intifada in the official newspaper of the Palestinian Authority, *al-Hayat al-Jadidah*.

32. Once available on YouTube, the video was recently taken down.

33. E.g., Andrew Singleton, "Beyond Heaven: Young People and the Afterlife," *Journal of Contemporary Religion* 27, no. 3 (2012): 453–68.

34. Yoram Schweitzer, "Conversing with the Adversary: Interviewing Palestinian Suicide Bombers and Their Dispatchers in Israeli Prisons," in *Conducting Terrorism Field Research: A Guide*, ed. Adam Dolnik (Abingdon: Routledge, 2013), 82–83.

35. Randall Collins, *Violence: Micro-Sociological Theory* (Princeton, NJ: Princeton University Press, 2011), 440–49.

36. Arlie Hochschild, *The Managed Heart* (Berkeley: University of California Press, 1983).

37. Merari, *Driven to Death*, 122, 135–44.

38. Ibid., 137.

39. https://www.huffingtonpost.com/2015/06/18/Dylan-roof-snapchat-church_n_7616990.html.

40. Dissociation can also be an effect of drugs or hypnosis.

41. Amira Haas, "Flying to Heaven," *Haaretz,* April 1, 2003.

42. Merari, *Driven to Death*.

43. See Collins, *Violence,* 69–82.

44. *Osun Defender*, Nigeria, May 27, 2014.

45. Compare the experience of skillful commando fighters in action. Limor Samimian, "Violence, Control and Enjoyment" (Shaine Working Papers 10, Hebrew University, Jerusalem, 2005).

46. Merari, *Driven to Death,* 3.

47. The relatives also said that there were several Israeli victims in the explosion, although in this attack the only person to die was the suicide terrorist.

48. The title of Ariel Merari's book on suicide terrorism.

49. Hannah Arendt, *Eichmann in Jerusalem: A Report on the Banality of Evil* (1963; repr., New York: Penguin, 2006).

50. For comprehensive coverage of the public intellectual debate concerning Arendt's thesis, see Richard Cohen, "Breaking the Code: Hannah Arendt's *Eichmann in Jerusalem* and the Public Polemic; Myth, Memory and Historical Imagination," *Michael* 13 (1993): 29–85; Anson Rabinbach, "Eichmann in New York: The New York Intellectuals and the Hannah Arendt Controversy," *October* 108 (2004): 97–111.

51. For a systematic and persuasively documented exposition of this interpretation of Arendt, see Shmuel Lederman, "History of a Misunderstanding: 'The Banality of Evil' and Holocaust Historiography," *Yad Vashem Studies* 41, no. 2 (2013): 173–209. Lederman's argument relates mostly to Arendt's articles "Thinking and Moral Considerations" and "Personal Responsibility under Dictatorship," both reprinted in *Responsibility and Judgment,* ed. Jerome Kohn (New York: Schocken, 2003).

52. Hannah Arendt, "Answers to Questions Submitted by Samuel Grafton," in *The Jewish Writings,* ed. Jerome Kohn and Ron Feldman (New York: Schocken, 2007), 475.

53. Several branches of the Palestinian resistance movements in the West Bank are made of local families and clans.

54. Don Handelman, *Models and Mirrors* (New York: Berghahn Books, 1998).

4. Anatomy of a Suicide Operation

1. The documents that I examined include the trial of Hasan Salama in Hebron Military Court (Adorayim), file p"a 743/96, August 13, 1996; protocols of ISA interrogation of Abdallah Barghouti, Russian Compound (Jerusalem), March 8, 2003; protocols of ISA interrogation of Ibrahim Hamed, Russian Compound (Jerusalem), May 28, 2006; minutes, *State of Israel v. Abas el-Sayid,* Tel Aviv District Court of Justice, 2002.

2. In prison he graduated from al-Aqsa University with distinction.

3. Sections of it were published in the pro-Islamic weekly *Assabeel,* printed in Amman, Jordan.

4. For illustration, see Ronni Shaked and Shon Bayer's documentary film *For the Sake of Allah* (2006).

5. ISA and some Palestinian intellectuals share the view that Palestinians who do not reside in the West Bank, especially those who recently emigrated from Jordan or Lebanon, are relatively more extreme since they have not had the experience of personal acquaintance with Israelis, which mitigates their hatred and makes their attitude toward their enemies/neighbors more complex.

6. See, for instance, https://www.youtube.com/watch?v=EvCSnwO7-UQ.

7. Carmi Gillon, *ShaBaK Bein Ha'Kra'im* [ISA in tears] (Tel Aviv: Hemed/Yediot Ahronot, 2000).

8. As mentioned earlier (preface, personal note), this attack took place in my university's main cafeteria, which I frequent every week. I knew four of the victims well.

9. In addition to police and court records, the presentation of the al-Sayid case is based on testimonies of the terrorist's accomplices and interviews with survivors and medics published in the press. See also Yoram Schwitzer, "Mass Murder on Passover Eve," *Maariv*, April 7, 2007.

10. The title is obviously a paraphrase of *Apocalypse Now*. The director and screenwriter is the Palestinian (an Israeli citizen who lives in Europe) Hanni Abu-Assad. Palestinian-Dutch-Israeli coproduction, 2005.

11. Another scene from this movie—just as amusing and just as miserable—is discussed in chap. 7.

12. As one writer said: "Suicide terrorism reality is closer to bumbling black comedy than to redemptive tragedy." Robert Worth, "Can We Imagine the Life of a Terrorist?" *New York Times Magazine*, June 14, 2013.

5. Passing

1. The outward resemblance of Mizrahim (Israeli Jews of Middle Eastern origin) and local Arabs make the former feel suspect and susceptible to expressions of Jewish animosity in Western-oriented Israeli society, particularly amid times of tension resulting from Palestinian terrorism. In reaction, many Mizrahim tend to highlight their Jewish identity by adopting typically Jewish emblems and gestures, like wearing a *kippah* or a conspicuous Star of David around their necks, to avoid any embarrassing mistaken impressions. The Palestinian human bombs employed an identical strategy of self-presentation.

2. During the early years of the intifada, students at the Palestinian University, which was dominated by Hamas, secretly practiced mimicking Jewish prayer gesticulations. (Ronni Shaked, *Yediot Ahronot* reporter, personal communication. He also showed me photos supporting this information.)

3. Abdallah Barghouti, al-Masri's dispatcher, disclosed in his interrogation that he got the idea of hiding the explosives in a guitar from a Sylvester Stallone action movie. In a later interview he provided a different account.

4. According to another version, she impersonated an American tourist carrying a camera.

5. The idea that the people of the Middle East internalized elements of the identity they attributed to the Western colonialist ruler, typically including contempt toward the natives, was suggested by Frantz Fanon and later developed by Edward Said in his *Orientalism* (New York: Pantheon, 1978).

6. The film is *Paradise Now,* an Arabic-language, Palestinian-Dutch-Israeli coproduction, directed by Hanni Abu-Assad (2005). It was shot in the West Bank and Israel during the later phase of the intifada and won international prizes.

7. In the rhetoric of Palestinian suicide terrorism, immediately after the explosion, the dead human bombs ascend to heaven, full of joy, to be married to seventy-two virgins.

8. I am well acquainted with the daughter of two of the victims. Conversing with her after an extensive visit to the arena soon after the explosion added some insights to my account of this case.

9. The attack took place on January 29, 2007. See Nir Hasson's report on the following morning in *Haaretz*. The perpetrator was Muhammad Siksik, age twenty-one, from Beit La'hyia (Gaza). The next day his wife expressed her gratification and pride in the terrorist act.

10. For examples of common definitions of suicide terrorism lacking the elements of imitation, disguise, and blending, see Rashmi Singh, *Hamas and Suicide Terrorism* (London: Routledge, 2011), 3; Robert Pape, *Dying to Win* (New York: Random House,

2005), 9–11; Ariel Merari, *Driven to Death* (New York: Oxford University Press, 2010), 9; Diego Gambetta, ed., *Making Sense of Suicide Terrorism* (New York: Oxford University Press, 2005), vi.

11. This attack was a joint venture of Hamas and Fatah. The perpetrators were Seif Muhammad Khanif (Pakistani) and Omar Khan Sharif (Jamaican), both carrying British passports. One died with his victims, the other fled from the scene and later drowned in the Mediterranean.

12. Randall Collins, *Violence: Micro-Sociological Theory* (Princeton, NJ: Princeton University Press, 2011), 440–48.

13. Randall Collins, "Suicide Bombers: Warriors of the Middle Class," *Foreign Policy,* January 8, 2008, http://www.foreignpolicy.com/story/cms.php?story_id=4131.

14. Cf. Raya Morag, "The Living Body and the Corpse: Israeli Cinema and the Intifadah," *Journal of Film and Video* 60, no. 3–4 (2008): 3–24.

15. I recall that in my childhood, on the Jewish holiday of Purim, many of us used to dress up as cowboys or Native Americans. Those were the objects of our imagination and yearning at that time. When we were cowboys, with pistols in our belts and wearing boots and broad-brimmed hats, we identified with the figure and shot at the "redskins" with enthusiasm. But when we wore feathers on our heads and smeared our half-naked bodies with war paint, we took the part seriously and tried to scalp the white men.

16. See, for example, the documentary film *Arna's Children*, shot at the Jenin refugee camp, directed by Guliano Mer (2003). The kids who played the role of the IDF soldiers tend to come on strong and hit their fellow Palestinians especially hard.

17. Anna Freud, *The Ego and the Mechanisms of Defense* (New York: International Universities Press, 1966); Bruno Bettelheim, *The Informed Heart* (New York: Free Press, 1960), chap. 4. See also Stockholm syndrome.

18. See Michael Taussig, *Mimesis and Alterity* (New York: Routledge, 1993). Taussig claims that through imitation one can act out jealousy and a desire to switch identities, and at the same time reinforce one's self identity and sharpen his/her otherness.

19. In Palestinian population centers during the intifada, there were theatrical productions in which acts of suicide terrorism were depicted in an infantile, cartoon-like, and vulgar way. The roles of Israeli bus passengers were played by amateur actors dressed in a coarse caricature of Orthodox Jews. After the explosion the victims whined, "Mama, mama," and the crowd roared with laughter.

20. Elaine Ginsberg, ed., *Passing and the Fictions of Identity* (Durham, NC: Duke University Press, 1996).

21. Cf. Peter Suedfeld, "Harun al-Rashid and the Terrorists: Identity Concealed, Identity Revealed," *Political Psychology* 25, no. 3 (2004): 479–92.

22. See also act 4 of Shakespeare's *Henry V.*

23. The Superman allusion was suggested to me by Dr. Adam Oron-Klin.

6. Middle Eastern Twist

1. Bruno Latour, *We Have Never Been Modern* (Cambridge, MA: Harvard University Press, 1993).

2. Mary Douglas, *Purity and Danger* (1966; repr., New York: Routledge, 1999).

3. Homi Bhabha, "Of Mimicry and Man: The Ambivalence of Colonial Discourse," *October* 28 (Spring 1984): 125–33.

4. The Haredi organization Save Fellow-Jews (Yad L'Achim) has an Anti-Assimilation Department that seeks out Jews (mostly young women) involved in intimate relationships

with Arabs. Using persuasion, deception, threats, and violence, the organization tries to force individuals of double identity—Jewish-Arab—to revert to their original unitary identity. ZAKA works closely with Yad L'Achim in the spheres of double identities, with the purpose of distinguishing between Jews and Arabs.

5. The following conclusions, among others, arise from this discussion. First, the Palestinians understand very well that each of the alternative strategies contains a reflection and internalization of parallel trends in Israel regarding the connection between birth rate and nation building. (On the one hand, the traditional conception of the woman as a womb to supply many freedom fighters—the demographic weapon; and on the other hand, a modernistic conception of the woman who nurtures a nuclear family, providing advanced education for her children—which is to say, the weapon of creating a professional middle class.) Second, the Palestinians are well aware that imitation of Israelis (mainly Western ones) not only is a weapon against Israel but also will help Israel reinforce their control of the Palestinians. Third, the Palestinians understand that the tendency to imitate the Israelis sometimes verges on self-hatred, while at the same time it has very little chance of affording assimilation into Israeli society because not even acculturation can overcome the dynamism of Jewish exclusivity. For a remarkable work on this issue, though focusing on those Palestinians who are citizens of the state of Israel, see Rhoda Kanaaneh, *Birthing the Nation* (Berkeley: University of California Press, 2002).

6. Robert Park, *The City* (Chicago: University of Chicago Press, 1984); Georg Simmel, *The Sociology of Georg Simmel* (New York: Free Press, 1950), 402–24; Erving Goffman, *Relations in Public* (New York: Basic Books, 1971); John Lofland, *World of Strangers: Order and Action in Urban Public Space* (Prospect Heights, IL: Waveland Press, 1985).

7. Ido Yoav, "Digesting Others: Identifying Strangers in the Israeli Street," *Israeli Sociology* 13 (2011): 81–105. An illuminating analogy can be found in the case of taxi drivers, who are subject to attack in large Western cities and rely on a range of techniques for examining passengers and avoiding those who are liable to prove dangerous.

8. Roughly 160,000 Palestinians from the territories cross the border daily, 25% unlicensed.

9. Israel and the West Bank share the same rather limited aquifer. Water pumped on one side of the border drains off the other.

10. In the second Gaza war the double of the human bomb emerged, also blurring the boundary between Palestinians and Israelis. He is the Hamas warrior that digs tunnels from across the border deep into Israeli territory. The nightmare of kibbutz members who live in southwest Israel is a terrorist popping up in their backyard.

11. The reflexive form of the root 'a-r-b[v], meaning "Arab."

12. *Hista'arvut = arviut + hit'arvut + hit'arbevut + histanenut + hista'arut*

13. The root 'a-b[v]-r is the core of the word *'ivri*, "Hebrew."

14. Not to be confused with Jewish-Arabs or Arab-Jews, the self-appellation used by some radical activist Israeli Jews of Mizra'hi (Middle Eastern) descent to define themselves in a provocative way that serves their ethnic identity politics.

15. Originally *mista'arbin*. E.g., Menachem Klein, "Arab Jew in Palestine," *Israel Studies* 19, no. 3 (Fall 2014): 134–53.

16. Their traditional trademarks, in addition to fluent Arabic, were growing a mustache, drinking black coffee, wearing the kaffiyeh, the traditional Arabic headdress, and peppering their (self-consciously bristly but figurative and fancy) speech with Arab folk expressions and proverbs.

17. A midrash about Abraham, the forefather of the Jewish people and the first biblical *'ivri* (Hebrew), states that he received that designation because "the entire world lies on one

side ['ever] and he on the other." Another midrash says Abraham received the title of Ivri because he came to the Promised Land "from beyond [me'ever] the [Euphrates] River."

18. E.g., Joe Lockard, "Somewhere between Arab and Jew: Ethnic Re-Identification in
Modern Hebrew Literature," *Middle Eastern Literature 5*, no. 1 (2002): 49–62.

19. The most incredible Jewrab was the founding father of the PLO and Palestinian Authority Yasser Arafat, who, according to one malicious legend, was descended from a Mo-
roccan Jewish family. At the opposite—Arajew—end of this implausible but telling imaginary
spectrum is Israel's former president Shimon Peres: for decades false but persistent rumors
have claimed that his mother was an Arab.

20. See Abd al-Rakhman Mer'ei, *Wallah Be'Seder* (Jerusalem: Keter, 2012). The Hebrew-
Arabic blends and interchanges that were popular prior to 1948 have progressed immensely
since 1967. The initiators of this cultural creativity were Israeli Palestinians, and from there it
spread to Palestinians in the territories. Among its various language products are the neutral
first names that fit both Arabs and Jews, like Amir.

21. Gil Eyal, *The Disenchantment of the Orient* (Stanford: Stanford University Press,
2006).

22. Raya Morag in reference to *Paradise Now*.

23. Yehoshafat Harkabi, *Arab Attitudes to Israel* (New Brunswick, NJ: Transaction,
1974). Harkabi was the first scholar to write on the Arab's admiration and envy of Israel
after 1967.

24. For a curious extreme case of "double passing," a subtle version of Arajew and Jewrab together, see the project of the Israeli journalist Yoram Binur. He is a Jew who first disguised himself as Palestinian and then, having successfully assimilated among Palestinians,
returned to Israel under the cover of his new borrowed identity in order to document the Palestinian experience amid Jews in Israel. The title of his book betrays the explosive absurdity
of the Middle Eastern scene: *My Enemy, My Self* (New York: Doubleday, 1984).

25. Frantz Fanon, *Black Skin, White Masks* (New York: Grove Press, 1967).

26. Steven Pinker, *The Better Angels of Our Nature* (New York: Viking, 2011), 12–13.

27. Anat Berko, *The Path to Paradise* (Tel Aviv: Yediot Aharonot, 2006), 165. The book
is also available in an English translation (Westport, CT: Praeger, 2007).

28. Huneida Ghanem, "Thanatopolitics: The Case of the Colonial Occupation in Palestine," in *Thinking Palestine*, ed. Ronit Lentin, chap. 3 (London: Zed Books, 2008).

29. Avraham B. Yehoshua, *The Liberated Bride* (New York: Harcourt, 2001). See also
Amos Oz, *My Michael* (New York: Alfred Knopf, 1972).

30. Sayed Kashua, *Second Person Singular* (New York: Grove Books, 2012). The other
writer is Anton Shamas, author of *Arabesques* (Berkeley: University of California Press,
2001).

31. Kashua, *Second Person Singular*, 113–18.

32. Fanon, *Black Skin, White Masks*, chaps. 4 and 5.

33. Cf. Ian Buruma and Avishai Margalit, *Occidentalism: The West in the Eyes of Its
Enemies* (New York: Penguin, 2004).

34. Amos Oz, *In the Land of Israel* (New York: Harcourt, Brace and Jovanovich,
1993), 122.

35. Soaking oneself in one's enemy's blood can be a way of defeating him. Assimilating
Palestinians into Israel is an alternative strategy to swallowing Israel up among the Palestinians. Both strategies aim at vanquishing the Jewish side. These two opposite moves are complementary, "functional equivalents." As early as the 1960s, much before the Six-Day War,
some Arab intellectuals were already calling for eliminating borders with Israel and allowing
it to expand so as to cause Israel to lose its distinct character and determined vitality, to be
diluted and diffused within the huge Arab sea until it disappeared. In contrast, following the

blow of Israel's victory in 1967, Palestinians began to adopt Israeli traits and to bond with the Israelis. Later, in the mid-1990s, against the background of the Oslo Accords and the peace treaty with Jordan, there was growing fear among Arabs that Israel's culture and economy would overwhelm their society. In reaction they once again clung tightly to their traditional policy of closed borders. During the decade since the failure of the intifada, as the Palestinians have awoken from the mirage of head-on confrontation, they have again begun to take an interest in traversable borders. There is a deep current among them that seeks assimilation, to the point of hinting at a certain longing for the occupation, but this time it is harnessed to a largely hostile impulse. Support among Palestinian intellectuals for a binational state can be explained not only by the attractive ideal of a common life but also by their understanding that it offers a chance of eliminating Israel by assimilating it into the Arab world, which would nullify its uniqueness. Suicide terrorism might be another manifestation of a repressed and denied desire to be integrated into Israel.

36. Compare Israel's Orthodoxy alarm in face of "provocative" Roman Catholic Church initiatives embodied in figures like Brother Daniel (Rufeisen) and Cardinal Lustiger (of Paris), both converts from Judaism who served as active Christian clergy while refusing to deny their original Jewish identity. Their insistence on being considered Jews, not renouncing their commitment to Jewish ideals despite their papal allegiance, was interpreted as a conspiratorial attempt to blur the distinction between the two religions, and hence "kill Judaism from within."

37. B Talmud, *Pesahim* 3b.

38. The attraction and repulsion felt by the native toward the colonialist is represented by Fanon's biography: he switched his allegiance and identification from black to white and back several times.

39. About three thousand Israeli Palestinians serve in IDF. On the complexity of this phenomenon, see Rhoda Kanaaneh, "Embattled Identities: Palestinian Soldiers in the Israeli Military," *Journal of Palestine Studies* 32, no. 3 (2003): 5–20.

40. It has been also argued that those native recruits to the colonialist army will eventually become the leaders of the liberation struggle of their nations, and then be the progressive elite of their decolonized societies.

41. Benny Ziffer, "Enlist Them in the Military," *Haaretz,* November 14, 2014.

42. The French writer François Bon, who visited the West Bank on assignment from the Marseille Museum of European and Mediterranean Civilizations, confirms Ziffer's impressions.

43. The recent trend of Israeli ultra-Orthodox to join the IDF emanates from similar motivations.

44. Hanni Abu-Assad, personal communication, Nazareth, August 2015.

7. Ritual Coproduction

1. This is the *takbir*, an expression of great reverence rehearsed loudly at the opening of Islamic prayer and in the call to prayer five times a day. It is also uttered to convey greetings, gratitude, awe, amazement, and self-encouragement, especially in situations that involve high risk.

2. For the full text, see, for instance, Bruce Lincoln, *Holy Terrors: Thinking about Religion after September 11* (Chicago: University of Chicago Press, 2002), appendix A.

3. E.g., Anne Marie Oliver and Paul Steinberg, *The Road to Martyrs' Square: A Journey into the World of the Suicide Bomber* (New York: Oxford University Press, 2006).

4. Bassam Banat, "Palestinian Suicide Martyrs: Facts and Figures" (PhD diss., University of Granada, 2010): 217–18.

5. Ronni Shaked, "The Myth of the Palestinian Shahid" (master's seminar paper, Sociology Department, Hebrew University, September 2009).

6. Examples of a rhyming last will and testament are Ali Jara (bus no. 19, January 2004) and Sheikh Ra'ed Misk (bus no. 2, August 2003).

7. Shaked, "Myth of the Palestinian Shahid," 37–39.

8. Ibid.

9. E.g., Hamas and the al-Aqsa Martyrs' Brigade (Fatah) both took responsibility for Ali Jara's attack (bus no. 19, January 2004).

10. The event is financed and organized by the organization that accepted responsibility for the attack.

11. Ululation is a long, wavering, high-pitched vocal sound resembling a howl.

12. Middle East Media Research Institute, "Father of Suicide Terrorist: Why Don't the Leaders of Hamas and Jihad Dispatch Their Offspring?" February 6, 2002. See also MEMRI, November 8, 2004.

13. For more details on such rites, see Shaked, "Myth of the Palestinian Shahid."

14. The Palestinian organizations prohibit use of the word "death." Sheikh Sabri, the Palestinian mufti, decreed that all official announcements about shahids should take up the phrase "ascended to heaven" rather than "killed."

15. E.g., published telephone interviews with Salah Sh'chada (chief of Hamas military arm) before his assassination. (Islam Online) http://www.islam-online.net/arabic/politics/2002/05/article25.shtml 29.5.2002.

16. Observations on intercepted suicide terrorists indicate that many of them have become exhausted as a result of sleep deficit.

17. An ISA agent disclosed that information about debt payment signaled the probability that one is about to go on suicide mission, and therefore collaborators were instructed to forward such information to their Israeli operators.

18. See Shaul Shay, *Shahids: Islam and Suicide Attacks* (New Brunswick, NJ: Transaction, 2004), 20. It is not likely that such rites took place very often during the second intifada.

19. "Martyrdom [in Rome] was solidly anchored in civic life . . . and ran its course in the great urban spaces, . . . the principal setting for public discourse and public spectacle." Glen Bowersock, *Martyrdom and Rome* (Cambridge: Cambridge University Press, 1995). See also Daniel Boyarin, *Dying for God* (Stanford: Stanford University Press, 1999).

20. See Natalie Z. Davis, "Rites of Violence: Riots in 16th-Century France," *Past & Present* 59 (May 1973): 51–91.

21. See Rafael Israeli, "Manual of Islamic Fundamentalist Terrorism," *Terrorism and Political Violence* 14, no. 4 (2002): 29.

22. Samson, the biblical Israelite hero, kills his Philistine enemies by bringing their temple down upon them—and upon himself. This mythological suicide terrorist did not commit his act on the border between the two societies, on the front of the confrontation between them (which is where the duel between David and Goliath took place), but far from there, in the rear of the enemy society, in the shrine of the pagan god Dagon, the sanctified bastion of the eternal nemesis of the Israelites, to whom he was attracted, and with whom he mingled.

23. See Harvey Goldberg, "Rites and Riots: The Tripoli Pogrom of 1945," *Plural Societies* 8, no. 1 (1977): 35–56.

24. On the Ayodhya case and comparison to the situation in Jerusalem and Hebron, see Ron Hassner, *War on Religious Grounds* (Ithaca, NY: Cornell University Press, 2009); Roger Friedlander and Richard Hecht, *To Rule Jerusalem* (Cambridge: Cambridge University Press, 1996).

25. Israel Yuval, *Two Nations in Your Womb: Perceptions of Jews and Christians in Late Antiquity and the Middle Ages* (Berkeley: University of California Press, 2008), chap 4.

26. Israel Yuval, "The Myth of Exile: Jewish Time, Christian Time," *Alpayim* 29 (2005) (Hebrew): 9–25.

27. I first heard about this from Professor Hagar Salamon.

28. Jewish tradition also relates death to a wedding, and both marriage and death are signaled by white. Thus the groom wears an all-white tunic (*kitel*) that is supposed to resemble a shroud (burial garment) so as to make young men conscious of their certain end.

29. Tellingly, the Hebrew term used for both the human bomb's explosive vest and the ZAKA vest is *ephod*, the biblical term for the upper vestment of the ancient Israelite high priest.

30. Jonathan Perry, *Death in Banaras* (Cambridge: Cambridge University Press, 1994).

31. Compare the Shiite Ashurah rites practiced in Iran and South Lebanon. The faithful strike their backs with chains or punch their foreheads until they bleed, and the bloodier the better.

32. Gideon Aran, "Blood Touches Blood," in "The Cult of Dismembered Limbs" (unpublished manuscript).

33. Oliver and Steinberg, *Road to Martyrs' Square* is the source of these and several other examples.

34. Compare *Al Jazeera* broadcasts in English, which censor bloody scenes in a Western way, with its broadcasts in Arabic, which show a lot of unedited close-ups of bloody scenes.

35. Oliver and Steinberg, *Road to Martyrs' Square,* 91.

36. Ibid., 90.

37. He is Aziz Salha, later captured and imprisoned by Israel.

38. Marcel Mauss and Hubert Henri, *Sacrifice: Its Nature and Function* (Chicago: Chicago University Press, 1981); Walter Burkert, *Homo Necans: The Anthropology of Ancient Greek Sacrificial Ritual and Myth* (Berkeley: University of California Press, 1983); René Girard, *Violence and the Sacred* (New York: Continuum, 2005).

39. For example, the biblical stories of the binding of Isaac (Exodus 22), the daughter of Jephtah, and a few more.

40. The Aztecs, for example, cut off the heads of their sacrificial victims, skinned the bodies, and cut out their hearts following established instructions and traditional methods. See John Ingham, "Human Sacrifice at Tenochtitlan," *Comparative Studies in Society and History* 26, no. 3 (1984): 379–400.

41. "Ancient Greek stories of ritual child sacrifice in Carthage are true," claims Oxford archaeologist Josephine Quinn. See Maev Kennedy, "Carthaginians Sacrificed Own Children, Archaeologists Say," *Guardian*, January 21, 2014; and Paulo Xella, Josephine Quinn, Valentina Melchiorri, Peter van Dommelen, "Cemetery or Sacrifice? Infant Burials at the Carthage Tophet," *Antiquity* 87, no. 338 (2013): 1199–1207.

42. Exodus 29, and Mary Douglas, *Purity and Danger* (New York: Routledge, 1999), 76–77.

43. See Georges Bataille on sacrifice in *The Bataille Reader*, ed. Fred Botly and Scott Wilson (Oxford: Blackwell, 1997), chaps. 18 and 28.

44. "The Odd Couple," in Aran, "Cult of Dismembered Limbs."

45. Moshe Halbertal, *On Sacrifice* (Princeton, NJ: Princeton University Press, 2012), part 1.

46. The study of the sociology and anthropology of religion has concentrated on sacrifice in this sense ever since Emile Durkheim, *The Elementary Forms of the Religious Life* (New York: Free Press, 1965).

47. Inge Clendinen, *The Aztecs: An Interpretation* (Cambridge: Cambridge University Press, 1995); David Carrasco, *City of Sacrifice: The Aztec Empire and the Role of Violence in Civilization* (Boston: Beacon Press, 1999).

48. See also the case of Jan Falach, Prague 1968.

49. This is the way Talal Asad presents it in his argument that Western scholars wrongly interpret suicide terrorism because of their uninformed and biased understanding of Islam. *On Suicide Bombing* (New York: Columbia University Press, 2002).

50. "Slowly but surely a new language emerges in the Middle East, a mixed language, Arabic in which Hebrew is a significant component." Abd el Rahkhman Mar'ei, *Wallah Be'Seder* (Jerusalem: Keter, 2012).

51. Note that writers on Middle Eastern affairs employ the word "sacrifice" as a translation of "redemption" (ransoming), related to the Arabic root *nafdik*, which Palestinians often use in the context of their national struggle. Compare the call at human bombs' funerals: "In spirit and blood, we shall *redeem* you, ya shahid."

52. Sacrifice rituals occasionally correspond with each other. For example, on the day of Eid al-Adha, the Islamic Feast of the Sacrifice, Libyan Jews used to wake up very early so as to slaughter their sacrifice before their Muslim neighbors slaughtered theirs. Harvey Goldberg, *Jewish Life in Muslim Libya* (Chicago: University of Chicago Press, 1990), 93–94.

53. A Palestinian villager told me that ugly female candidates were probably rejected since they might be easily identified: ". . . after all, Israeli girls are good-looking."

54. Note the frozen children's corpses found at a Peruvian archeological site. Their preservation allows appreciation of their beauty, which suggests the likelihood that they were chosen by virtue of their perfect appearance.

55. See "Twenty Minutes" in chap. 5.

56. The depiction of Jaradat as an ideal sacrifice should be qualified by reference to malicious rumors that she was pregnant by her assassinated fiancé.

57. A seminal essay on suicide terrorism as sacrifice is Ivan Strenski, "Sacrifice, Gift and the Social Logic of Muslim Human Bombers," *Terrorism and Political Violence* 15, no. 3 (Fall 2003): 1–34. See also Adam Lankford, "On Sacrificial Heroism," *Critical Review of Social and Political Philosophy* 16, no. 5 (2013): 634–54.

58. Gili Kohen, "The Murderers of Sraya Ofer," *Haaretz,* November 14, 2013.

59. Bruce Lincoln, *Holy Terrors* (Chicago: University of Chicago Press, 2002), appendix A, 15, 31.

60. Exodus 22; B Talmud, *Kholin* 3b. Also Itamar Grunwald, "Did Jews Eat Human Flesh?" *Haaretz,* July 24, 2015.

61. *NewsZAKA,* April 2012.

62. The chief of ISA during the first intifada says he perfectly understands what the sheikh is talking about.

63. Compare the Modesty Guards in the Haredi neighborhoods of Jerusalem to their equivalents in sixteenth-century Calvin's Geneva and in revolutionary Khomeini's Teheran.

64. Carrasco, *City of Sacrifice*, esp. 203.

65. For example, Laura Jeffery and Matei Cadea, "The Politics of Victimhood," *History and Anthropology* 17, no. 4 (2006): 287–96.

66. See Benny Morris, *Righteous Victims: A History of the Zionist-Arab Conflict* (New York: Vintage, 2001).

67. Compare to the folklore of Jewish Holocaust survivors who compete among themselves as to "who suffered more." Thus, for example, those who were imprisoned in Auschwitz are regarded as superior to those who were imprisoned in Theresienstadt.

68. Avishai Margalit, "The Suicide Bombers," *The New York Review of Books,* January 16, 2003. This insightful essay is one of my main sources of inspiration regarding suicide terrorism.

69. See Hadas Yaron, "Victims and Perpetrators, Past and Present in Post-Holocaust and Post-Colonial Israel"; and Julian Ochs, "The Politics of Victimhood and Its Internal Exegetes: Terror Victims in Israel"; both in *History and Anthropology* 17, no. 4 (2006): 355–68 and 385–95, respectively.

70. See Anat Berko and Edna Erez, "Ordinary People and Death Work: Palestinian Suicide Terrorists as Victimizers and Victims," *Violence and Victims* 20, no. 6 (2005): 603–23.

71. Some characterize the controversy over Israeli collective identity in exactly the same terms. E.g., Alon Gal, "Their Victimhood, Their Calling: From Victimhood Narrative to Sovereign Narrative" (paper distributed, in Hebrew, at the Israel Democracy Institute, Jerusalem, 2014).

72. Haredim use this idea to justify their exemption from compulsory military service.

73. See Naomi Janowitz, *Fatal Obedience: The Family Romance of Maccabean Martyrdom* (New York: Routledge, 2017).

74. This is ZAKA's former name.

75. Ariel Merari claims that the photo had been reworked by the family of the martyr in the wake of his act of suicide terrorism *Driven to Death* (New York: Oxford University Press, 2010), 95.

76. This argument is impressively advocated by Moshe Halbertal, *On Sacrifice* (Princeton, NJ: Princeton University Press, 2012), chap. 2.

77. John Hall, *Gone from the Promised Land: Jonestown in American Cultural History* (New Brunswick, NJ: Transaction, 2004).

78. Jonathan Smith, "The Devil in Mr. Jones," in his *Imagining Religion* (Chicago: University of Chicago Press, 1982), 102–20, 126–34.

79. A mythic nation regarded as an archenemy of the ancient Israelites. Its defeat in an apocalyptic confrontation will precede, and is a precondition of, the redemption of Israel.

80. New Living Translation (NLT).

81. While some respondents took pride in this event, others doubted its very existence and denied the authenticity of the photo (a copy of which I have seen in the possession of several ZAKA volunteers).

82. Many contemporary Orthodox replace this sacrifice by donating money to charity.

83. Michel Graulich, "Aztec Human Sacrifice as Expiation," *History of Religions* 49, no. 4 (2000): 352–71.

84. ZAKA volunteers argue that caring for the dead in car accidents is more problematic since there is often nobody to blame.

85. Victor Turner, *Forest of Symbols* (Ithaca, NY: Cornell University Press, 1970).

86. Various examples are cited in Harvey Goldberg, *Jewish Passages: Cycles of Jewish Life* (Berkeley: University of California Press, 2003).

87. He added that "in the past this was the standard religious response to catastrophe; whereas since the Holocaust it has become almost impossible."

8. Research Strategy

1. Jon H. Rieger, "Key Informant," in *Blackwell Encyclopedia of Sociology*, ed. George Ritzer (Blackwell, 2007), Blackwell Reference Online, accessed November 29, 2017, http://www.sociologyencyclopedia.com/subscriber/tocnode.html?id=g9781405124331_chunk_g978140512433117_ss1-1.

2. See *The Gatekeepers* (2012), an Israeli documentary film directed by Dror Morea, which contains in-depth retrospective interviews with six former chiefs of ISA.

3. Ziv Koren. See the documentary film *More Than 1000 Words*, directed by Solo Avital (2006).

4. Hanni Abu-Assad, *Paradise Now* (2005).

5. A. B. Yehoshua, *A Woman in Jerusalem* (New York: Houghton, Mifflin and Harcourt, 2006).

6. David Tartakover, an acclaimed Israeli artist and graphic designer. See his series of photos titled *I'm here,* focusing on terrorist scenes (2005), http://www.posterpage.ch/exhib/ex123tar/ex123tar.htm.

7. I also resisted the temptation to interview politicians, high-echelon administrators, and official spokespersons for the government and the defense establishment, since their message already received much publicity in the press and in academic writings, while their contributions to original social scientific research are quite platitudinous.

8. E.g., Jerrold Post, Ehud Sprinzak, and Laurita Denny, "The Terrorists in Their Own Words: Interviews with 35 Incarcerated Middle Eastern Terrorists," *Terrorism and Political Violence* 15, no. 1 (2003): 171–84; Yoram Schweitzer, "Conversing with the Adversary: Interviewing Palestinian Suicide Bombers and Their Dispatchers in Israeli Prisons," in *Conducting Terrorism Field Research: A Guide,* ed. Adam Dolnik (Abingdon: Routledge, 2013): 78–90.

9. After the Shalit prisoner exchange, in which more than a thousand Palestinian terrorists were released, there remained no failed human bombs in Israeli jails (2011).

10. Experienced intelligence interrogators argue that if a person repeats his story exactly verbatim on more than one occasion, he is probably lying. Abdallah Barghouti provided three different versions in response to a question about the origins of his idea to conceal a dynamite charge in a guitar. Ahlam Tamimi provided yet another version.

11. The minister of defense was Binyamin Ben-Eliezer. The text of conversations was published in *Haaretz* on June 21, 2002.

12. Recording of a candid chat between jailed Palestinian terrorists, smuggled from prison. See Amira Hass, "Flying to Heaven," *Haaretz,* April 1, 2003.

13. For criticism of research with deficient methodological basis and biased conclusions, see, for example, Ariel Merari, "Studying Suicide Bombers: Response to Brym and Araj," *Studies in Conflict and Terrorism* 35, no. 6 (2012): 444–55.

14. Another example of semiacademic work on suicide terrorism that uncritically accepts the Palestinian narrative is Nasra Hassan, "The Arsenal of Believers: Talking to the Human Bomb," *New Yorker,* November 19, 2001, https://www.newyorker.com/magazine/2001/11/19/an-arsenal-of-believers.

15. The latter was Fatma Najar, Gaza (November 2006). According to another version, she was just fifty-seven years old.

16. Released female suicide terrorists were permitted to stay in the West Bank.

17. Submitted to the University of Granada, Spain, 2010.

18. New York: Oxford University Press, 2010.

19. Of the sample of fifteen failed suicide terrorists, four were captured very close to the target, while the rest were captured soon after recording their testaments.

20. CPOST-SAD: Chicago Project on Security and Terrorism-Suicide Attack Database.

21. Online database of the International Policy Institute for Counter-Terrorism, Herzliya Institute for Counter-Terrorism, IDC Herzliya.

22. www.terrorism-info.org.il; https://www.shabak.gov.il/Pages/index.html#=1. Publications of the Institute for National Security Studies (INSS) include Nachman Tal, "Israel and Suicide Terrorism," *Adkan Istrategi* 5, no. 1 (2002).

23. Rumors might be of value for research even if their reliability is doubtful, since their persistence reflects norms, popular moods, and so forth. When I refer in this book to rumors of questionable credibility, I explicitly state it.

24. E.g., Adam Dolnik, ed., *Conducting Terrorism Field Research* (Abingdon: Routledge, 2013); Magnus Ranstorp et al., eds., *Mapping Terrorism Research: State of the Art, Gaps and Future Direction* (London: Routledge, 2011).

25. Schweitzer, "Conversing with the Adversary."

26. For example, the telephone interview with the Hamas senior leader and commander Salah Sh'chada in which he "discloses" operative information that is manipulated and only sporadically trustful (Islam Online, May 29, 2005).

27. See Yona Alexander, *In the Camera's Eye: News Coverage of Terrorist Events* (Washington, DC: Brassy's, 1991); Tamar Liebes and Anat First, "Framing the Palestinian-Israeli Conflict," in *Framing Terrorism: The News Media, the Government and the Public*, ed. Pippa Norris, Montague Kern, and Marion Just (New York: Routledge, 2003), 59–74.

28. A fine example is Anne Marie Oliver and Paul Steinberg, *The Road to Martyrs' Square: A Journey into the World of the Suicide Bomber* (New York: Oxford University Press, 2006).

29. Danny Sitton, *Shahid* (2003); Shimon Dotan, *Hot House* (2007); Ronni Shaked and Shon Bayer, *In the Name of Allah* (2006). See also *Suicide Bombers*, PBS, Wide Angle, 2004; and *Inside the Mind of a Suicide Bomber*, History Channel, 2001.

30. E.g., Yasmina Khadra, *The Attack* (New York: Anchor, 2005).

31. For example, I am married to an Arabic-speaking peace activist, am the father of an IDF combat officer, maintain a close relationship with Palestinian neighbors and colleagues, and actively participated in three wars.

32. Bentzi Oiring and Danno Monkatowitch.

33. Yehuda Meshi-Zahav, Haiym Weingarten, and Ozer Zilberschlag.

34. Particularly Rabbi Ruja and Rabbi Nebentzal.

35. Materials from the ZAKA archive included selections from Halachic rulings regarding the treatment of human remains following suicide attacks and protocols of conversations with therapists discussing post-traumatic states. From their private collections volunteers shared with me some of the letters they wrote to their wives and children in which they described their experiences at the arena.

9. Concluding Comparative and Analytical Notes

1. Neil Smelser, *Theory of Collective Behavior* (New York: Free Press, 1965). It was applied to suicide terrorism by Mohammed Hafez, *Manufacturing Human Bombs* (Washington, DC: US Institute of Peace, 2006).

2. For example, Rashmi Singh, *Hamas and Suicide Terrorism: Multi-Causal and Multi-Level Approaches* (New York: Routledge, 2011); Assaf Moghadam, "The Roots of Suicide Terrorism: A Multi-Causal Approach," in *Root Causes of Suicide Terrorism*, ed. Ami Pedahzur (New York: Routledge, 2006), 13–24; Ami Pedahzur, "Toward an Analytical Model of Suicide Terrorism," *Terrorism and Political Violence* 16, no. 4 (2004): 841–44.

3. Cf. Max Abrahms and Philip B. K. Potter, "Explaining Terrorism: Leadership Deficit and Militant Group Tactics," *International Organization* 69, no. 2 (2015): 311–42.

4. Ami Pedahzur and Arie Perliger, "The Changing Nature of Suicide Attacks," *Social Forces* 84, no. 4 (2006): 1987–2008.

5. The Palestinian JMCC (Jerusalem Media and Communication Center), http://www.jmcc.org/polls.aspx; American Pew Research Center, http://www.pewresearch.org/subjects/suicide-bombings/. See also Martha Crenshaw, "Explaining Suicide Terrorism: Review

Essay," *Security Studies* 16 (2007): 149–55; Meir Hatina, *Martyrdom in Modern Islam: Piety, Power and Politics* (New York: Cambridge University Press, 2014), 99, n. 120.

6. Compare to results of a poll conducted in 2007: 64% in the Gaza Strip, ruled by Hamas, felt suicide terrorism was justified, while 60% in the West Bank, ruled by the Palestinian Authority, felt that way.

7. In 2014 the proportion of Palestinians supporting suicide terrorism decreased to 46%, which is still the highest in the Muslim world. Pew Research Center, July 10, 2014, http://www.pewglobal.org/2014/07/01/concerns-about-islamic-extremism-on-the-rise-in-middle-east/pg-2014-07-01-islamic-extremism-10/.

8. The proportion of Lebanese Sunni supporting suicide terrorism is 26%, while it is 39% among Lebanese Shiites. "Muslim Publics Share Concerns about Extremist Groups," Pew Research Center Global Attitudes and Trends, September 10, 2013, http://www.pewglobal.org/2013/09/10/muslim-publics-share-concerns-about-extremist-groups/.

9. Ariel Merari, *Driven to Death* (New York: Oxford University Press, 2010), chap. 7, esp. 179–81.

10. There is a positive correlation among these three demographic variables.

11. Note the report of the Fatah chief in Jenin refugee camp submitted to Marwan Barghouti (September 2001). Archived in the Information Center on Intelligence and Terrorism (Ha'Merkaz Le'Moreshet Ha'Modi'in, Glilot, Israel).

12. Jerusalem Media and Communication Center, JMCC Attitude Poll, 1999 Report, http://www.jmcc.org/Documentsandmaps.aspx?id=460.

13. See chap. 4, section on Hasan Salama.

14. See the classic works on the subject by Gustav Le Bon, Robert Park, Herbert Blumer, Ralph Turner, and Neil Smelser. For a comprehensive summary, see Roger Brown, *Social Psychology* (New York: Free Press, 1965), chap.14.

15. See the "spiderweb" theory of Hezbollah's leader Hassan Nasrallah, according to which Israel's presumed "love of life" is its source of fragility.

16. See even in the Palestinian Authority official organs: www.palwatch.org.il/site/modules/videos/pal/videos.aspx?fld_id=139fdoc_id=4390.

17. See, for example, Ronni Shaked, "The Myth of the Palestinian Shahid" (master's seminar paper, Sociology Department, Hebrew University, September 2009); Anne Marie Oliver and Paul Steinberg, *The Road to Martyrs' Square: A Journey into the World of the Suicide Bomber* (New York: Oxford University Press, 2006).

18. Daphne Burdman, "Education, Indoctrination and Incitement: Palestinian Children on Their Way to Martyrdom," *Terrorism and Political Violence* 15, no. 1 (2003): 96–123; Akiva Eldar, "One of Four Children in Gaza Aspire to Die as a Shahid," *Haaretz,* September 16, 2004.

19. Gaza Community Mental Health Programme. See Samir Qouta and Eyad el-Sarraj, "Community Mental Health as Practiced by the Gaza Community Mental Health Programme," in *Trauma, War, and Violence: Public Mental Health in Socio-Cultural Context,* ed. Joop de Jong, Springer Series in Social/Clinical Psychology (New York: Kluwer Academic, 2002), 317–35.

20. Amira Hass, *Haaretz.*

21. See, e.g., Shaked, *Myth of the Palestinian Shahid,* 15–19, 23.

22. *Al-Hayat al-Jadidah,* November 30, 2000 (quoted in Oliver and Steinberg, *Road to Martyrs' Square,* 75, n. 13).

23. Of all the suicide attacks that occurred in the years 2000–8, 58% were in Iraq, more than 20% in Afghanistan and Israel, and 10% in Sri Lanka and Pakistan. Most suicide attacks

occurred in the years 2005–10, that is, after the end of Palestinian suicide terrorism in Israel. See Merari, *Driven to Death*, graph 2.1 and table 2.1.

24. ISA Report, *Palestinian Terrorism in 2007: Statistics and Trends* (quoted in Merari, *Driven to Death*, 10, n. 2).

25. Chicago Project on Security and Terrorism-Suicide Attack Database, http://cpostdata. uchicago.edu/search_new.php.

26. According to ISA reports, in this period there were 450 planned or attempted suicide attacks that Israeli counterterrorism agencies managed to thwart. Research can learn much from these cases, which make the total number of suicide terrorism cases four times larger.

27. The more important among them live and work abroad, or they at least conducted their research on Palestinian suicide attacks under the sponsorship of US or European academic institutions. Examples include Bassam Banat, Bader Araj, and Eyad el-Sarraj.

28. Here are a few exceptions: Reuven Paz, *Arab Volunteers Killed in Iraq*, Global Research in International Affairs (GLORIA): The Project for the Research of Islamist Movements (PRISM); Occasional Papers 3, no. 1 (March 2005), http://www.imra.org.il/story. php3?id=24396; Stephen Hopgood, "Tamil Tigers, 1987–2002," in *Making Sense of Suicide Missions*, ed. Diego Gambetta (New York: Oxford University Press, 2005), 43–76.

29. For illustration I carefully examined twenty reports in the local and Western press about suicide attacks that took place at the entrance to a provincial headquarters one hundred kilometers north of Kabul (May 20, 2013, fourteen Afghans dead). The only specific reference was to the dignitary killed in the attack.

30. Moreover, while there is almost no instance of Palestinian suicide terrorism from the time of the intifada for which no organization claimed credit, in many cases of suicide terrorism in the past decade, especially in Iraq, Syria, and Pakistan, no one takes responsibility for the attacks, and the press and investigators find it difficult to attribute them to one organization or another.

31. Barbara Czarniawska, "Storytelling: A Managerial Tool and Its Local Translations," in *Global Themes and Local Variations in Organization and Management: Perspectives on Glocalization*, ed. Gili Drori, Markus Höllerer, and Peter Walgenbach (New York: Routledge, 2014), 65–78.

32. Comparative religion studies refer to a certain bodily gesture that plays a significant role in the three Abrahamic traditions: believers strongly pounding their breasts or foreheads. Probably the adoption of this symbolic act in each of these religions is influenced—consciously or not—by the other. In Jewish tradition it is part of Yom Kippur ceremonies related to atonement. From the sixteenth century on, Christianity has borrowed it and used it in connection to confession (*mea culpa*). In Shiite Islam it is practiced on the Ashurah day of remembrance marking the humiliating defeat of Hussein. In the 1970s, after 1,300 years, this rite of self-tormenting interpreted as reliving traumatic experience transforms into an expression of opposition, vengeance, and revival.

33. As recently as 2016 the Hamas television station was broadcasting slogans set to music whose refrain was "Until the roofs of Jewish buses don't fly in the air, this won't be an intifada worthy of its name." The clip shows human bombs disguised as Haredi Jews dancing around burning Israelis (al-Aqsa TV, February 7, 2016). Each year from 2006–16, the ISA claimed to thwart several Palestinian suicide terrorism initiatives.

34. See Pedahzur, *Root Causes of Suicide Terrorism*, introduction.

35. In half the countries there were only one or two cases, in ten countries there were more than ten, and in five countries there were more than one hundred (Iraq, Afghanistan, Israel, Pakistan, and Sri Lanka).

36. At least one of these Chechen videos was aired over al-Jazeera TV.

37. Hezbollah terrorist training manuals were translated from Arabic to Tamil. See Rohan Gunaratna. "Q&A: Suicide Terrorism in Sri Lanka," in *Countering Suicide Terrorism: International Conference*, ed. Boaz Ganor (Herzliya: IDC 78, 2001), 97–104.

38. Yoram Schweitzer, Ariel Levin, and Einav Yogev, "Suicide Attacks in 2014: The Global Picture," Israel National Security Studies, *INSS Insight* 653, January 6, 2015.

39. Compare to "immutable mobiles," in Bruno Latour, *Science in Action* (Cambridge, MA: Harvard University Press, 1987).

40. Israel Yuval, "The Revenge and the Curse, the Blood and the Libel," *Zion* 58, no. 1 (1993): 33–90 (Hebrew).

41. Before the first Oslo Accord there was just one Palestinian suicide attack (Mehula, April 1993).

42. Ehud Sprinzak, "Rational Fanatics," *Foreign Policy* 120 (September 2000): 66–74; Mohammed Hafez, *Manufacturing Human Bombs* (Washington, DC: US Institute of Peace, 2006), 18.

43. Christoph Reuter, *My Life Is a Weapon: A Modern History of Suicide Bombing* (Princeton, NJ: Princeton University Press, 2004), 36.

44. Compare the transformation of Hebrew from a diasporic holy language used mainly for ritual purposes into a national language used in Israel for all daily secular purposes, poetic or prosaic. After a generation or two, however, the Hebrew language might remind its users that they embraced a monster that hides dormant God and Torah in its belly. One day, the latter religious elements may burst into Israeli public life to demand their long gone hegemony. See Gershom Scholem: "Must not this abyss of a sacred language, which is submerged in our children, break out again?" in "A Confession about Our Language," letter to Franz Rosenzweig, 1926, in Scholem Gershom, *Dvarim Ba'go*, vol. 11 (Tel Aviv: AM Oved, 1976) (Hebrew).

45. Reuters, "Suicide Bomber Embraces and Kills Sunni Politician in Iraq," June 19, 2013, http://www.reuters.com/article/2013/06/19/us-iraq-violence-idUSBRE95I0OV20130619.

46. Reuters, "Suicide Bomber Strikes with Hug," *Toronto Sun*, March 31, 2016.

47. In each of these areas there are enclaves in which the others live.

48. Among the rare Palestinian suicide attacks that occurred outside Israel proper, two took place in the Jordan Valley, two at the outskirts of the settlement Ariel, and four near a roadblock in the Gaza Strip.

49. Schweitzer, "Suicide Attacks in 2014: The Global Picture." See also "Report on Annual Suicide Attack Index," Chicago Project on Security and Terrorism, May 14, 2015, cpost. uchicago.edu/news/report_on_annual_suicide_attack_index.

50. For example, a suicide attack was carried out by a Syrian Jihad organization against Abu Khaled al-Soury affiliated with international al-Qaeda (February 2014).

51. Schweitzer, "Suicide Attacks in 2014: The Global Picture."

52. Robert Pape, "It's the Occupation, Stupid," *Foreign Policy,* October 18, 2010. See also Robert Pape, *Dying to Win: The Strategic Logic of Suicide Terrorism* (New York: Anchor Books, 2005). For a criticism of Pape's main thesis, see Assaf Moghadam, "Suicide Terrorism, Occupation and the Globalization of Martyrdom: A Critique of *Dying to Win*," *Studies in Conflict and Terrorism* 29 (2006): 707–29.

53. An exception is the Palestinian Islamic Jihad organization, which, in contrast to Hamas, espouses a supranational orientation. Its frame of reference is the Islamic *ummah*.

54. Schweitzer, "Suicide Attacks in 2014: The Global Picture."

55. Gideon Aran, "Striking Home: Ideal-Type of Terrorism," *Terrorism and Political Violence* 29 (2017): 1–19.

56. Often death counts do not include the suicide terrorist.

57. ISA Report, *Palestinian Terrorism in 2007: Statistics and Trends*.

58. See, e.g., Singh, *Hamas and Suicide Terrorism*.

59. Thomas Kuhn, *The Structure of Scientific Revolutions* (Chicago: University of Chicago Press, 1996).

60. George Lakoff and Mark Johnson, *Metaphors We Live By* (Chicago: University of Chicago Press, 2003).

61. One may also see decapitation à la Daesh (ISIS) as a metaphor, and Jihadi John its fitting iconic figure.

62. Amos Harel, "The ISA Permits Publication," *Haaretz,* January 22, 2014.

Afterword

1. Cf. Nancy Sherman, "The Moral Logic of Survivor Guilt," *Psychology Today,* July 20, 2011.

2. E.g., Gideon Greif, *We Wept without Tears: Testimonies of the Jewish "Sonderkommando" from Auschwitz* (New Haven: Yale University Press, 2005).

3. Ayelet Shani, "Ani Be'sikha," *Haaretz Weekly Magazine,* February 16, 2017.

4. Primo Levi, *The Drowned and the Saved* (New York: Vintage, 1988), particularly chap. 2.

5. Ibid., 48–49.

6. While the two schemes to obfuscate the distinction between victim and aggressor (one by turning some victims into aggressors, the other by turning the aggressor into a victim literally sharing the fate of his/her targets) are partially analogues, there are several important differences between them, like the following formal one: the Nazi practice introduced gradations among the victims so as to create continuity between victim and aggressor, but the suicide bombing practice did not introduce such gradations. On the contrary, it sought to erase gradations (for example, between civilians and soldiers). Here is a substantive difference: the attempt to erase the difference between victim and aggressor was not a conscious ideological goal of the Nazis. It could not be. They were invested in asserting their racial superiority. The erasure was a consequence, perhaps only subconsciously desired. But the erasure is a conscious ideological goal of Hamas entrepreneurs of suicide terrorism. They embark on their deadly mission with a strong belief that they are already victims, that they are the true victims, and that their action will expose that the innocent casualties are really aggressors. (Personal communication with Professor Gil Eyal, 2016.)

Index

Page numbers followed by letter *f* refer to figures.

suicide terrorism *(cont.)*
17–23, 159, 169, 171, 263–64, 269;
vs. suicide, 23–24; transition from
terrorism to, as paradigm shift,
270, 271; unique characteristics
of, xxvii–xxxi, 6–11, 16, 156, 171,
268–70; vs. zero range (no escape)
terrorism, 5–6, 7–9, 11, 16
suicide terrorists. *See* female suicide
terrorist(s); human bomb(s);
Palestinian suicide terrorist(s)
Sunni Muslims: assassinations by Nazari
sect of Shiites, 3; rituals adopted from
Shiite shahids in Iran, 261; Salafi
movement, 265; and suicide terrorism,
266, 306n8
Superman, human bomb's disguise
compared to, 167
survivors: of Holocaust, competition
over victimhood among, 302n67; of
Holocaust, feelings of guilt and shame
among, 276–77; of suicide attacks,
testimonies of, xiii, xiv, xviii, 155
symbolic type, 118
Syria, suicide terrorism in, 260, 264, 266;
educational level of perpetrators, 47;
female suicide terrorists, 44; location
of attacks, 263; recruitment for, 91,
291n25; responsibility for, 307n30; and
training of Palestinian militants, 121

taboo, against suicide, in Islam, 23–24,
29, 40, 207
Takatkah, Andaleeb, 19
Talkahma, Salah, 132
Tamam, Taher, 13, 54
Tamimi, Ahlam, 77, 129–30, 147–48,
149, 150, 304n10
Tantawi, Sheikh, 250
target area, suicide terrorist's:
dissociation in, 107–11; distress in
approaching, 157–58; enjoyment/
lingering in, 146–47, 153, 155, 157,
163–64, 180; illusion of community
in, xiv, 17, 106, 107; immorality

associated with, 212–13; observation/
study of, 236–37; panic/fear in, 10, 11,
15, 84, 87, 104; patterns of behavior
in, 77, 111–14, 146–47, 155–58;
preliminary survey of, 129, 130, 149
Tartakover, David, 304n6
tattoos, on human bombs, xxiv, 286n40
Tawil, Dia, 54, 292n17
Tawil, Jamal, 54, 92, 292n17
Tel Aviv, suicide attacks in, 263; bus
no. 4, 135; bus no. 5, 79, 119, 272;
Carmel Market, 37; central bus
station, 90; Dolphinarium, xiv, 119,
212; Mike's Place, 53, 155
television, Palestinian: broadcasting of
human bombs' testaments on, x, 141,
190; glorification of human bombs on,
193, 273, 290n16; images of blood
on, 201; images of suicide attacks on
Israelis on, 211, 307n33
terrorism: age of perpetrators of,
45; characteristics of, 267; and
counterterrorism, as organic unit,
243; forms of, 268; history of, 63,
270, 272; Jewish, xxx, 13–14, 63–64;
research on, difficulties of, 235–36;
spontaneous, 64; vs. suicide terrorism,
9, 52, 54, 63–65, 67, 80–81; suicide
terrorism alongside of, 246, 268;
transition to suicide terrorism from,
as paradigm shift, 270, 271. *See also*
suicide terrorism
testament(s), of human bombs, x,
190–92; addressing parents in,
191–92; background for, 192, 218;
broadcasting after attack, x, 141, 190;
in Chechnya, 259; content analysis of,
238; and culture of death, 7; depiction
in film, 190–91; dissonance in, 102,
191; ensuring commitment through,
91, 192; photomontage of severed
head in, 218; recording of, 97, 115,
127, 133, 138, 190; references to
dispersed body in, xxii; retouching of,
100, 253